T0322312

The Martyr and the Red Kimono

Also by Naoko Abe

'Cherry' Ingram: The Englishman Who Saved Japan's Blossoms

The Martyr and the Red Kimono

A Fearless Priest's Sacrifice and a New Generation of Hope in Japan

Naoko Abe

Chatto & Windus

LONDON

1 3 5 7 9 10 8 6 4 2

Chatto & Windus, an imprint of Vintage, is part of the Penguin Random House group of companies whose addresses can be found at global.penguinrandomhouse.com

First published by Chatto & Windus in 2024

Copyright © Naoko Abe 2024

Naoko Abe has asserted her right to be identified as the author of this Work in accordance with the Copyright, Designs and Patents Act 1988

penguin.co.uk/vintage

Typeset in 12/14.75pt Dante MT Std by Jouve (UK), Milton Keynes
Printed and bound in Great Britain by Clays Ltd, Elcograf S.p.A.

The authorised representative in the EEA is Penguin Random House Ireland, Morrison Chambers, 32 Nassau Street, Dublin D02 YH68

A CIP catalogue record for this book is available from the British Library

ISBN 9781784744533

Penguin Random House is committed to a sustainable future for our business, our readers and our planet. This book is made from Forest Stewardship Council® certified paper.

For Paul

One would have to have been brought up in the 'spirit of militarism' to understand the difference between Hiroshima and Nagasaki on the one hand, and Auschwitz and Belsen on the other.

The usual reasoning is the following: the former case is one of warfare, the latter of cold-blooded slaughter. But the plain truth is that the people involved are in both instances nonparticipants – defenceless old people, women, and children, whose annihilation is supposed to achieve some political or military objective.

I am certain that the human race is doomed unless its instinctive detestation of atrocities gains the upper hand over the artificially constructed judgment of reason.

Max Born, PhD adviser to J. Robert Oppenheimer
Letter to Albert Einstein, 8 November 1953[1]

Contents

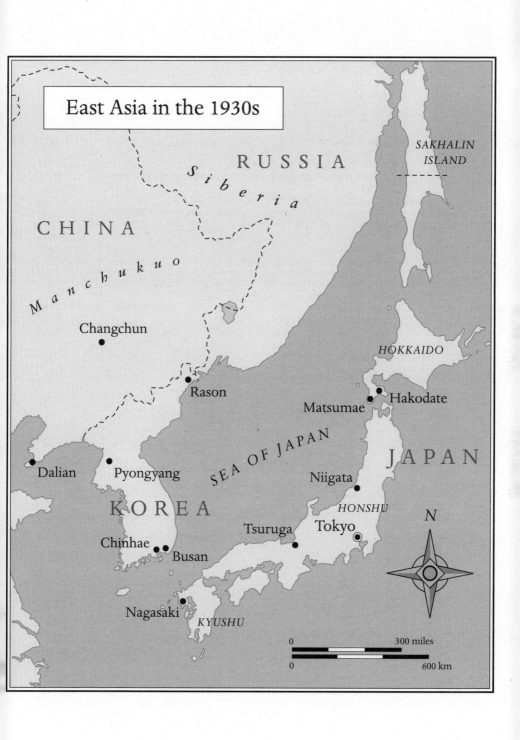

East Asia in the 1930s

RUSSIA

Siberia

SAKHALIN
ISLAND

CHINA

Manchukuo

Changchun

HOKKAIDO

Rason

Matsumae

Hakodate

Dalian

Pyongyang

SEA OF JAPAN

JAPAN

Niigata

KOREA

HONSHU

N

Chinhae

Tsuruga

Tokyo

Busan

Nagasaki

KYUSHU

0   300 miles

0   600 km

Poland Before the 1939
Invasion by Germany

Prologue

Every May, a sixteen-foot cherry tree scatters its large crimson petals on the sacred ground in front of the St Catherine of Alexandria church in the village of Strachocina in southeast Poland, close to the border with Ukraine. Flowering for over thirty years in this depopulated hamlet, the tree was sent here from Japan.

A short distance away, a seven-foot statue stands on a white plinth beneath a wooden shelter. It is an image of the Virgin Mary. Unlike the traditional depictions, this statue has long black hair tied behind her back with white cords. She wears a flowing red Japanese kimono with five pink cherry flowers on her upper chest and traditional white *tabi* socks on her feet.

Strachocina, established in 1369, is best known as the birthplace of St Andrew Bobola in 1591, a saint murdered by the Cossacks. Pilgrims from Europe and the US occasionally visit.

Few give the lonely cherry tree a second glance. Not even the nuns who live quietly in a convent in Strachocina know how or why this Japanese tree ended up in this remote enclave. And although the nuns revere the Oriental sculpture, there are no plaques or other information at the site to explain its origin.

Curious about how flowering Japanese cherries, known in Japan as *sakura*, had spread around the world, I began researching the ties between my homeland and this little-known region of Poland, whose peace had been shattered in 2022 by the Russian invasion of Ukraine. That aggression highlighted to me, as to many others, the horrendous cost of war for every afflicted individual, family and country.

Unexpectedly, the stories that unfolded from my research were also directly connected to war. Both disquieting and inspiring, they were linked by two unlikely witnesses to history.

The first was a survivor of the atomic bomb that exploded over the southwestern Japanese city of Nagasaki in August 1945, instantly killing about 74,000 civilians. The second was the world's most prominent creator of cherry trees, whose flowers blossom each spring in a life-affirming burst of colour, energy and rebirth.

As teenagers, both men had been tormented by the Second World War, and their lives had been for ever changed by their experiences. As adults, I was amazed to discover, both men had been deeply influenced by a Polish priest murdered by the Nazis at the Auschwitz concentration camp.

Prisoner 16670: Father Maximilian Kolbe

14 August 1941 – Auschwitz, Poland

Father Maximilian Maria Kolbe, prisoner 16670, died in a dank concrete cell in the Auschwitz concentration camp following two weeks of starvation. Hans Bock, a morphine addict from the prison infirmary, injected carbolic acid into a vein in the priest's left arm, killing the forty-seven-year-old Kolbe almost instantly.

Just over two weeks earlier, on 29 July 1941, a Polish prisoner had escaped from Auschwitz. In retaliation, the Schutzstaffel, or SS, forced the inmates of Block 14, where the escapee had been living, to stand to attention in the sweltering summer heat as punishment, without food or water.

The prisoners were all Polish, captured following the German invasion of their country in September 1939. Until the Nazis started to send thousands of Jews to Auschwitz in 1942, most inmates there were either resistance fighters or elite Poles such as lawyers, businessmen, religious leaders and newspaper editors.

Next morning, 30 July, Auschwitz's deputy camp commandant, Karl Fritsch, told the prisoners they would remain standing until the runaway was recaptured. Some prisoners had already collapsed and were dragged away. The escapee wasn't found. Fritsch returned in the early evening to announce that ten prisoners would be sent to a starvation cell as retribution, where they would be kept without food or water until they died.

He chose the men randomly, but when one man begged to be saved because he had a wife and children, Father Kolbe volunteered to take his place.

Survival: Kōichi Tagawa, aka Tōmei Ozaki

9 August 1945 – Nagasaki, Japan

'How tragic. My home has disappeared, engulfed in endless fire. I think only of my mother but I could not find her injured body or corpse.'

Seventeen-year-old Kōichi Tagawa survived the Nagasaki atomic bomb blast because he had been assembling parts for torpedoes in a secret factory dug into a nearby mountainside. Hours after the US military dropped the world's most powerful bomb, Kōichi left the armaments tunnel and started writing entries in his pocket diary about the impact of the blast.

Kōichi, who would later change his name to Tōmei Ozaki, witnessed unprecedented destruction as he walked for five hours through the ruins of the city in search of his mother, Wasa. An only child, Kōichi lived with Wasa in the Urakami district of Nagasaki, close to Urakami Cathedral, the largest cathedral in Asia.

The walk usually took him thirty minutes, but the bomb had wiped out most buildings, leaving the teenager disoriented. All around him, orange flames shot into the air. Disfigured bodies lined the streets and floated in the rivers. Some people were frozen in motion, their eyes and tongues hanging out of blackened skulls. Thousands more with severe burns cried out for help.

Along the route, Kōichi tended to some injured victims, but he soon gave up and kept walking. When he finally reached his destination, the home he had left just hours earlier had vanished. Indeed, virtually all of the Urakami district, including the cathedral, was gone. Urakami was the bomb's epicentre. He found no remains of his mother.

He was now an orphan. For eighteen days, Kōichi camped outdoors, burning and burying bodies while scavenging scraps of food to survive.

Shock: Masatoshi Asari

15 August 1945 – Nanae, Hokkaido, Japan

Masatoshi Asari was fourteen when he listened to Emperor Hirohito's statement of surrender on the radio at the agricultural experimental station where he worked for the Japanese war effort.

After a morning bent low in a humid rice paddy, Masatoshi and about twenty colleagues were told to gather in a semi-circle in the yard outside the station's main building. All they knew was that the emperor was set to make 'a very important announcement'. The Hokkaido newspapers had reported that powerful new types of bomb had destroyed Hiroshima and Nagasaki several days earlier. Few other details were given.

Mr Suzuki, the station head, placed the radio on a desk next to an open window. At noon on the dot, the radio fizzed, crackled and faded in and out as the announcer asked all listeners to stand for the national anthem, after which the disembodied emperor spoke for four minutes in a reedy voice. He used archaic Japanese words that were all but incomprehensible.

When the speech ended, nobody appeared to have understood. Then Mr Suzuki said quietly: 'The war is over. We lost.' There was silence. Some adults started crying. Others walked away, deep in thought.

'Defeat' was a forbidden word during the war. Even as American bombing campaigns had destroyed most major cities, the Japanese people were told that victory was in sight. Was it really possible, Masatoshi thought, that Japan had been defeated?

Masatoshi remembered people whispering that if Japan lost, men would be sent to Africa or the Amazon rainforest as slaves, before being murdered. He began shaking, petrified that he'd be taken from his family.

Introduction

On Tuesday, 31 December 2019, just weeks before the coronavirus pandemic brought the world to a virtual standstill, I drove across the rugged southern Japanese island of Kyushu to Nagasaki, a city set on a natural harbour and surrounded by tall hills. After gunning the engine of my rental Toyota up a particularly steep slope, I arrived on a grassy plateau on which sat a two-storey care home for the elderly, overlooking the city. There, in room 220, I met Tōmei Ozaki in person for the first time.

Dressed in his black habit, the ninety-one-year-old Franciscan friar, a tiny man barely five feet tall, greeted me with a deep bow and then settled in an upright rattan chair for an interview. We had talked before at length over the phone from London, and I knew Ozaki was an observant, focused and resolute man. Most times we talked, he was remarkably cheerful and upbeat. Yet on this New Year's Eve, hours before the dawn of a new decade, he told me he was feeling frail and hoped he would survive the winter. The previous year, he had caught pneumonia and ended up in hospital.

He had reason to be concerned about his health. During his life, Ozaki had contracted and conquered catastrophic illnesses that would have killed most people. That he had survived nine decades was striking.

For a start, Ozaki was an atomic bomb survivor. Just seventeen years old when the US dropped an atomic bomb on his home city of Nagasaki on 9 August 1945, three days after annihilating Hiroshima, Ozaki had survived simply because at the moment of the explosion he was working in a tunnel.

Ozaki felt acute guilt that he had not done enough to help the dying people who desperately needed his support on that tragic day. His remorse made him feel worthless and suicidal.

In October 1945, homeless and desperate, Ozaki knocked on the door of a monastery that had been built on a mountainside near Nagasaki by friars from Poland fourteen years earlier. Shielded by the mountains, the buildings had suffered little damage from the atomic bomb's destructive power.

The friars gave Ozaki food and shelter. In return, Ozaki gave them his life. And he later vowed to dedicate himself to the causes of peace and humanity that were embodied by the friary's founder, Father Maximilian Kolbe.

One thousand miles northeast of Nagasaki, on the sparsely populated northern Japanese island of Hokkaido, a cherry-tree breeder named Masatoshi Asari lives in a humble wooden house near the port of Hakodate. I had come to know Asari well during research for a book about Collingwood Ingram, an Englishman who had saved important varieties of Japan's cherry trees from extinction in the 1930s.

Asari, who turned ninety-two in 2023, is a Japanese *sakuramori*, a cherry tree guardian – *the* cherry guardian, in my opinion – famed for having created a group of flowering varieties called Matsumae cherries. There are 116 varieties of these cherries, and they are wonderfully diverse – most are double-petalled and their colours range from white to dark reddish pink.

Thousands of these trees bloom in the world's largest cherry tree park, which Asari created. Matsumae Park and its famous blossoms are the main attraction in Matsumae itself, the southernmost coastal town in Hokkaido. Many Matsumae cherries also grow in Windsor Great Park outside London, as well as in some European countries such as the Netherlands and Germany. A few thrive in Washington DC's National Arboretum.

Like Ozaki, Asari is small – about five feet two inches – and thin, though he is strong-boned with tanned limbs and a weather-hardened face from decades of working outside. He is mentally and physically active and astute. And like Ozaki, Asari belongs to that dying generation of Japanese who survived the destruction of the

Second World War to witness Japan's 'miracle' economic revival in the second half of the twentieth century.

Asari, a former schoolteacher and historian, never stopped questioning how Japan became involved in a worthless war that left millions dead. His deep conviction that innocent people are too often the victims of war led him to dedicate his life to the pursuit of peace and reconciliation.

A lone wolf, Asari collected evidence of events in Hokkaido during the war that the Japanese authorities would have preferred to remain hidden. He yearned to atone for Japan's barbarism and culpability. To do so, he sent thousands of cherry trees to countries that Japan fought or inflicted suffering upon, including China, North Korea, the United Kingdom, Canada and the US.

In November 2018, when I visited him for three days of intensive interviews, Asari mentioned in passing that at one time he had sent several hundred cherry trees to Poland. 'But why Poland?' I asked. 'Japan didn't fight Poland.' He couldn't remember all the details at the time, but he later told me that he'd found his faded diaries from the late 1980s about his 'Polish peace initiative'.

Re-reading his diaries more than thirty years later was a revelation to Asari. 'This is the project of my life, and I must succeed,' he had written on 4 November 1987. It was a venture, he told me, that was directly inspired by one man – Father Maximilian Kolbe.

My original goal was to tell the stories of Ozaki and Asari, two Japanese men born in poverty whose passion for humanity and justice, forged in the crucible of an unforgiving war, remained undimmed and untarnished for more than seven decades. I had been drawn to these dignified and principled men, but the more I talked with them about their lives, the more I understood Father Kolbe's significance to them.

Expanding my research to examine the deep impact that Kolbe had on both men, as well as on the history of humankind in the twentieth century, I found that this fiery friar was the thread that bound everything and everyone together.

His was a remarkable life, defined by his Polish patriotism and his religious convictions. In Rome in 1917, Kolbe had founded a worldwide religious organisation called the Militia Immaculatae or simply MI. In a village west of Warsaw, he established a monastery called Niepokalanów that would become the world's largest. There, he built one of Poland's most influential publishing empires before leaving to live in the Japanese city of Nagasaki in 1930. At the time, he knew virtually nothing about the culture or language of a place he called 'the cherry blossom country'.

To me, this little-known phase of Kolbe's life was an eye-opener, offering unique insights into my own country at a time when it was becoming an authoritarian state. For six years, Kolbe and a handful of Franciscan friars endured extreme poverty and stress as they sought to convert followers of Buddhism and Shintoism to Christianity.

Extraordinarily, the religious community they built on a stark mountainside would be visited years later by the Pope. Kolbe also started an expansive Japanese-language publishing operation that still functions today. After returning to Poland in 1936, Kolbe frequently told his colleagues that he hadn't wanted to leave Japan and had hoped to 'leave my bones' there.

Back in Poland, Kolbe again became the head of the Niepokalanów friary, which had founded one of the nation's largest daily newspapers. In the months before the German invasion in September 1939, the newspaper printed numerous anti-Nazi articles and cartoons. As both a prominent priest and publisher, Kolbe was a threat to the Nazi regime, which arrested him and dispatched him to Auschwitz in 1941.

In death, Kolbe became a globally recognised symbol of humanity. When he was canonised as St Maximilian Maria Kolbe in 1982, Pope John Paul II declared him 'the patron saint of our difficult century'.

Predictably, the circumstances of Kolbe's horrific death have overshadowed all his considerable deeds. His eleven weeks in Auschwitz have been well documented. Less well known are the other chapters in his life – and the characteristics of his life – that ultimately led to his arrest and martyrdom.

Born on 8 January 1894, in a village under Russian rule, Kolbe's patriotism was deeply rooted. His father was a local leader of Polish patriots who secretly sought liberation from the Russian oppressors. As a country, Poland had ceased to exist in 1795. Unexpectedly, Japan's victory over Tsarist Russia in the Russo-Japanese War (1904–05) gave the Kolbe family hope in their fight for independence. Kolbe's patriotism held strong until the very end of his ordeal at Auschwitz.

A prodigious overachiever, Kolbe was a widely read scholar who earned two doctorates and spoke four languages. He was an enthusiastic scientist who designed space rockets and believed in the possibilities of interstellar travel. He was also a media-savvy entrepreneur, always looking to the future and willing to flout tradition if it helped communicate his beliefs to the widest possible audience.

In pursuit of his goals, Kolbe could be uncompromising, obsessive and a zealous disciplinarian, particularly during his time in Japan. He always lived his life with an unrelenting sense of urgency. That was because he was so often seriously ill. Since death was always in sight, he had no time to lose to spread his ideas to the world.

Stricken by tuberculosis, Kolbe spent months in sanatoriums or bedridden in cloistered cells in Poland and Japan. Yet he never allowed his pain and frailties to impede his ambitions. Rather, his persistent sicknesses propelled him to further accomplishments and helped him better understand his fellow man.

Ozaki, Asari and Kolbe never met, but their lives intersected and resonated with one another. Their stories spoke of unprecedented death and suffering. But they also spoke of hope and light, of peace and reconciliation, and of compassion. It was these attributes that ultimately shone through the gloom and emerged triumphant.

Living near London, I found myself one day in early 2023 at Westminster Abbey, the venue for royal coronations and funerals, and the city's most famous religious building. There, above the west porch, sits a statue of Father Kolbe, carved out of French Richemont limestone alongside sculptures of Martin Luther King Jr, Oscar

Romero, Esther John, Dietrich Bonhoeffer and six other twentieth-century martyrs.

Unveiled in 1998 by the Archbishop of Canterbury in the presence of Queen Elizabeth II, the statue encourages visitors to 'remember all innocent victims of oppression, violence and war'. At the time of my visit, these words seemed particularly appropriate for the millions of refugees who had left their homes in Ukraine to escape Russia's belligerence. For the Nagasaki atomic bomb survivor and the Japanese cherry-tree creator, I would learn, there was also no more suitable epitaph.

PART I

The Rulers and the Ruled, 1894–1929

1. The Patriot

September 1905 – Pabianice, Poland

Julius Kolbe was ecstatic. A tall, blond weaver of raw wool, Julius lived with his wife and three boys in a cramped third-floor flat in an undistinguished town called Pabianice close to Łódź in central Poland. It was September 1905, and in an underground Polish-language newspaper Julius read that the exotic island nation of Japan had defeated Tsar Nicholas II's Russia after eighteen months of war. The Treaty of Portsmouth peace settlement, mediated by US President Theodore Roosevelt, signalled both Japan's emergence as a Far East power and Russia's decline.

Russia's humiliation and loss of prestige were a balm to the soul for Julius Kolbe, who hated the tsar and the Russian military forces that occupied and controlled much of Poland, including his home-town, 100 miles southwest of Warsaw. In 1795 – 110 years earlier – the rulers of Austria, Prussia and Russia had divided up Poland and the country had ceased to exist as a sovereign nation.

Julius, aged thirty-four, was one of thousands of Poles who had fought over four generations for the country's restoration. Now, throughout Russia and the lands it controlled, the tsar's influence was weakening, and Polish patriots sensed an opportunity to strike back at their enemy. Julius, a leader of the patriots in Pabianice, and his wife Maria, a small, ebony-haired midwife and shopkeeper, frequently opened their home as a meeting place where neighbours, friends and Catholic clergy could debate how best to revive Poland as an independent state and resist the Russians.[1]

Outside the Kolbes' flat, on Gold Street, excited citizens chanted 'long live Japan' and 'down with the tsar'. The Russian troops who guarded Pabianice did nothing to prevent the celebrations. Inside, the Kolbes' sons – thirteen-year-old Francis, eleven-year-old Raymond (who would later become Father Maximilian Maria Kolbe) and nine-year-old Joseph – shared their parents' euphoria. None of the boys had ever attended school because all classes were taught in Russian, which the Kolbes refused to speak. Instead, Julius and Maria taught the boys themselves in their native Polish, and they learned Latin from a local priest.

Julius was a passionate and romantic man who loved literature and music. Above all, he loved Poland, and Francis, Raymond and Joseph grew up listening to their father and his friends talking about paths to freedom and the celebrated Poles who were promoting this cause. They learned about Madame Marie Curie, for instance, who had won the Nobel Prize in Physics in 1903 for her pioneering work in radio-activity. Curie had studied at a clandestine university in Warsaw before moving to Paris, the centre of European culture at the time. There, she and her French husband discovered a radioactive metal that she named polonium to draw attention to Poland's plight.

The Kolbe family also revered the composer Frédéric Chopin, who had left Poland in 1830 and, like Madame Curie, settled in the French capital. Chopin's dying wish was for his heart to be buried in Poland. His elder sister, Ludwika, carried out that poignant request in 1850 by smuggling it into Warsaw underneath her skirt in a glass urn.[2]

Every Sunday evening the Kolbe family lit oil lamps and Julius, the grandson of a Czech émigré, read aloud to the boys the patri-otic literature of Henryk Sienkiewicz. Sienkiewicz's most revered work was *The Trilogy*, an epic whose second volume climaxed with Poland's heroic resistance in 1655 against Swedish Protestant invad-ers. For forty days, the Swedes had assaulted the sacred Jasna Góra monastery that had been founded three centuries earlier.

The hilltop monastery, Poland's most renowned pilgrimage site, is a shrine to the Virgin Mary. Every summer, Julius walked 140 miles over four days to the monastery in the city of Częstochowa. The pilgrimage culminated on 15 August, or Assumption Day, when the body of the Virgin Mary was 'assumed' into heaven.

Within Jasna Góra is a thirteenth-century Byzantine icon known as the Black Madonna of Częstochowa (so called because a fire had darkened it), which depicts the Virgin Mary holding Jesus on her left hand. The painting was reputed to work miracles that enabled the Poles to thwart the Swedish siege. In 1656, a grateful King John II Casimir Vasa staged an elaborate ceremony at which he crowned the Black Madonna 'the Queen of Poland'.

That title still resonates. Julius and millions of Poles viewed the Virgin Mary as a patriotic and religious symbol of national identity who could always be relied upon to protect the nation and to resist foreign invaders. While reverence towards the Virgin Mary as the mother of Jesus, the Son of God, is normal in predominantly Catholic countries, that reverence in Poland has also been uniquely combined with patriotism.[3]

For the Kolbes' three small boys, Sienkiewicz's words of resistance to Poland's enemies couldn't have been clearer. Sienkiewicz won the Nobel Prize in Literature in December 1905, shortly after Russia's military defeat by Japan, for his novels about Poland's struggles for sovereignty.

Julius also read to his boys the writings of Adam Mickiewicz, a Romantic poet and author who was as esteemed in Poland as Byron in Britain and Goethe in Germany. Mickiewicz had grown up in the early nineteenth century in Russian-partitioned territories in the Lithuanian part of Poland. He was later exiled to central Russia. One of Julius' favourite pieces of literature was Mickiewicz's epic poem *Pan Tadeusz*, first published in 1834, about two feuding noble families brought together by a shared passion to defeat Russia and re-establish Poland.

Gatherings at the Kolbe home usually concluded with Julius playing folk songs on his violin and with the family and its visitors quietly singing a song called 'Poland is Not Yet Lost':

> Poland has not yet died
> So long as we still live
> What the foreign power has seized from us
> We shall recapture with a sabre.

The song had been written by a Polish poet, Józef Wybicki, in 1797, two years after the country had been erased from the map. It would become the national anthem in 1918 after Poland regained its independence.

Since the 1795 dissolution of the Polish–Lithuanian Commonwealth, Poland had followed a tragic path of defeat and disappointment. The emergence of Napoleon, who beat a joint Russian–Prussian force on formerly Polish land, led to the brief creation of the Duchy of Warsaw in 1807. But after Napoleon's failed invasion of Russia in 1812, Russian–Prussian forces regained the land. The Congress of Vienna settlement of 1815 saw Russia occupying more than eighty per cent of the territory and ruling supreme over the Polish people.

Russia crushed two other major insurrections – the first in 1830 and the second in 1863 – with brutal military force. After the first failed uprising, many Polish leaders including clergy were murdered, and tens of thousands were sent to Siberia as forced labourers. Chopin famously wrote a piano opus known as the 'Revolutionary Étude' (Op. 10, No. 12 in C minor) in despair for his fellow countrymen.

Following the second insurrection, the Russians launched 'Russification' policies as a way to consolidate a Russian identity and to combat Polish nationalism. These included a ban on the Polish language in schools and the destruction of Catholic monasteries and convents.

For the Kolbe family and their friends, patriotism and the Catholic religion therefore walked hand in hand.[4] Both Julius and Maria belonged to the Third Order Franciscans, a group of lay men and women committed to living according to the principles of St Francis of Assisi, the thirteenth-century mystic who founded the Franciscan order.[5]

Maria had wanted to become a nun, but gave up this dream because Russia had suppressed the convents in the 1860s. Nonetheless she lived as a devout, strict and pious Catholic and she married Julius, who was a year younger, in October 1891 after meeting him at her parish church. The young couple lived in a poor yarn-weaving town called Zduńska Wola. It was thirty miles southwest of Łódź, the centre

Kolbe was born in a second-floor flat in Zduńska Wola in 1894

of the textile industry known as the 'Manchester of Poland'. The couple lived briefly in Łódź before moving to Pabianice in 1896.

In the Kolbe household, Maria raised the boys with a firm grip to ensure they behaved properly and prayed to the Virgin Mary regularly. In this environment, veneration towards the Virgin Mary was deeply imprinted in her sons from early childhood. For Raymond, the Virgin Mary was an ideal human being – *the* ideal human being – because she was totally pure and free from original sin.[6]

From an early age it was clear that Raymond Kolbe was unusually intelligent, intuitive and independent. From his mother he acquired an unshakeable religious faith. From his father he inherited an intense patriotism and passion. Both parents encouraged their son's pioneering spirit, stoicism and solidarity with the poor and oppressed.

At the age of ten, Raymond experienced a vision, according to testimony given by Maria after his death. Chided by his mother for a misdeed, he prayed alone in front of the Virgin Mary at his local church. The Virgin appeared, he told her, carrying a white crown in one hand and a red crown in the other. White signified purity. Red meant martyrdom. The Virgin asked Raymond which crown he wanted. He said he wanted both.[7]

Many Father Kolbe devotees cite the 'two crowns' as proof of

Kolbe's mother, Maria

Kolbe's readiness to die as a martyr from an early age. Raymond himself, however, interpreted the incident from a patriotic perspective. He told his mother that he thought the Virgin Mary was calling him to fight for his country's liberation. Poland's national flag was red and white, and the youngster believed it was his mission to become Mary's 'knight' in this battle.

Japan's shock victory over Russia in 1905 marked a turning point in the Polish independence movement. When the war had started in February 1904 as a result of the nations' competing imperial ambitions in Manchuria and the Korean peninsula, there was already widespread unrest in Russia. With the economy in crisis since the turn of the century, many workers went on strike, demanding better wages and working conditions. Peasants and university students also demonstrated.

The protests culminated on 22 January 1905 in what became known as 'Bloody Sunday' or 'Red Sunday', when the tsar's troops crushed workers' demonstrations in St Petersburg, the then Russian capital.

More riots followed, including in the Polish part of the Russian

Kolbe (extreme left in the front row), his elder brother Francis (extreme left in the top row) and younger brother Joseph (third from right in the front row)

empire. In the weaving city of Łódź, near to the Kolbes' home, 70,000 workers went on strike, demanding an eight-hour workday, education in Polish and other political freedoms. This insurgence was eventually crushed by the Russian police and army in June, but other strikes and riots continued until 1907.

In a concession made after the disastrous Russo-Japanese War, the tsar permitted children in Russian-occupied Poland to be taught in Polish. Soon after, the Kolbes sent their eldest boy, Francis, to a fee-paying vocational school, but they had no money for Raymond's education. He stayed at home, looking after his younger brother Joseph and entertaining himself by planting trees, playing chess and teaching himself Latin and mathematics by reading Francis' textbooks.[8]

One day, Raymond impressed the owner of a local pharmacy, Mr Kotowski, by ordering *foenum graecum* (fenugreek) medicinal herbs for his mother in perfect Latin. The pharmacist convinced Julius and Maria to send him to school, even though it meant tightening their already stretched budget.

After passing the entrance exams to Francis' school, Raymond was placed in the same year group as his brother. The boys spent little more than a year at the school before another opportunity arose. Maria had always wanted her sons to become priests, and in 1907 a Franciscan provincial priest told the Kolbes that there were openings at a minor seminary for teenage boys in the ancient city of Lviv, known at the time as Lemberg.

About 300 miles southeast of Pabianice, the city was in the section of Poland controlled by Austria. Today, it's part of Ukraine. The Kolbes jumped at the chance, though the journey there was fraught. Lacking the necessary travel documents to cross into Austria-ruled Poland, the boys were smuggled over the border near Kraków in a hay wagon.

At the seminary, Raymond excelled in mathematics and applied physics. He was particularly fascinated by the early twentieth-century powered flights of the Wright brothers in the US and the Voisin brothers in France. As a teenager, Raymond also became obsessed with the idea of space travel and carried with him a notebook of diagrams, sketches and mathematical formulae. These outlined how a spaceship might be built and how the forces of gravity could be overcome to enable it to fly. His passion for space, together with his somewhat dreamy demeanour, led his classmates to give him the nickname 'spaceman'.

Raymond's interest in space was matched by his dedication to the game of chess, which he had learned in Pabianice from his father. Chess tested Raymond's problem-solving abilities and abstract reasoning. It also taught him about patience and calmness under pressure. After learning to recognise patterns on the chessboard, Raymond launched military campaigns with his wooden pawns, rooks and knights and pondered complex defensive moves designed to outflank any opponent.

By moving their boys to Lviv, Julius and Maria had hoped that Francis and Raymond would be able to concentrate on their studies, away from the strikes and riots that had swept through the Russian-ruled towns. What they didn't know was that Lviv was fast becoming a centre of Poland's covert independence activities. And it wasn't long before the revolutionary agitation outside the tranquil seminary would distract both boys from their studies.

2. Doubts and Ambition

September 1908 – Bezdany, Lithuania

At approximately 10.30 p.m. on Saturday, 26 September 1908, a year after the Kolbe brothers had moved to Lviv to study, a steam train bound for St Petersburg trundled to a stop at a remote Lithuanian peasant village called Bezdany.

Within minutes, a well-drilled team of twenty Polish revolutionaries had surrounded the train, disabled telegraph and telephone lines and blasted their way into a postal carriage carrying mail and tax revenues from Warsaw to the capital of the Russian empire. Inside the carriage was a fortune – fifty bags of silver coins valued at 200,812 roubles, or more than $10 million today.

Poland's 'Great Train Robbery' was audacious, spectacular and extremely risky. Had the Cossack troops guarding the train captured the thieves, they would undoubtedly have lost their lives. As it turned out, the heist enabled the conspirators to fund a military force that was essential to creating an independent Polish nation. More important, the robbery catapulted the forty-year-old leader, Józef Piłsudski, into super-stardom. Three other conspirators would become prime ministers of Poland. Piłsudski, the head of the Polish Socialist Party, was lauded by Poles as a combination of Robin Hood and the biblical David taking on the mighty Russian Goliath.

The city of Lviv was at the heart of Piłsudski's activities. Piłsudski's hatred of Russia stemmed in large part from his exile to Siberia for five years in 1887 after being falsely accused of plotting to assassinate the autocratic tsar, Alexander III.

Piłsudski had formed a paramilitary unit in 1904 in the Austrian-ruled city of Kraków and began attacking the Russian police and military officers. That unit evolved into a secret military organisation based in Lviv that eventually became legally recognised by the Austrian authorities: the Polish Riflemen's Association.

Piłsudski believed the path to Polish independence was through a radical overthrow of the Russian empire. His rival, Roman Dmowski, the founder of the National Democracy movement, had a different view, seeing Prussia as the main enemy and favouring non-violent means to achieve independence.

After the outbreak of the Russo-Japanese War, both Piłsudski and Dmowski had travelled separately to Tokyo. Piłsudski had sought Japan's help in driving the Russians from occupied Polish land in exchange for his spying on the Russian military. Although Japan didn't accept the proposal at the time, the idea of Japanese–Polish intelligence-sharing never went away.

In the insulated seminary, devotion was to God rather than to any guerrilla leader, but nevertheless, in the spring of 1910, the patriotic Kolbe brothers were mesmerised by the sight of thousands of riflemen saluting Piłsudski at an emotional nationalistic rally in Lviv. Sixteen-year-old Raymond, concerned that Russia might try to quash the increasingly influential Riflemen's Association, began devising military strategies and fortifications. With Francis and fellow seminarians, Raymond walked the perimeter of the city, pointing out natural barriers that barred access and drawing up plans to resist aggressors.

In the midst of this militaristic atmosphere, Raymond could not resist his urge to participate in the fight to liberate Poland. He made a vow to the Virgin Mary, 'the Queen of Poland', that he would be her 'knight'. 'How I would do this I did not know at the time,' he wrote years later. 'But I visualised fighting with material weapons.'

In the summer of 1910, in a seminary holiday lodge outside Lviv, Francis and Raymond read about a ceremony in Kraków that had reportedly attracted as many as 150,000 Poles. The gathering on 15 July celebrated the 500th anniversary of the Battle of Grunwald, one of the largest clashes in medieval Europe, when a Polish–Lithuanian alliance defeated the German–Prussian Teutonic Knights.

The anniversary ceremony had been organised by a virtuoso

Polish pianist and composer called Jan Paderewski. Wearing a black top hat that covered his long and unkempt red hair, Paderewski delivered a widely reported patriotic speech that would begin his transformation from musician to politician.

After the summer, Francis and Raymond were set to begin their novitiate, the training period for prospective members of a religious order. Two years earlier, their pious mother had visited Lviv to tell them that she and her husband had decided to take vows of perpetual chastity and to live separately as members of different religious orders. Maria became a doorkeeper, or portress, at a Benedictine convent in Lviv while Julius became a handyman at a Franciscan community in Kraków. Their younger brother, Joseph, was also set to enter their own seminary.

The older boys needed to decide about their future – to become priests or soldiers – within days. Raymond agonised, but he chose the Polish army, convinced Francis to follow suit and made an appointment to see the father provincial, Peregryn Haczela, who oversaw friaries and seminaries in Galicia, part of Austrian-ruled Poland. But as he prepared to explain his decision, providence intervened.

As Raymond wrote later, 'the bell in the parlour rang'.[1] At the seminary's front door was his mother, Maria. History doesn't record how her presence changed her sons' minds or what she told them, but the victor was divinity.[2] The boys began as novices in September 1910. The faculty at the seminary gave Raymond the religious name of Maximilianus (Maximilian in Polish), meaning 'he who aspires to the highest goal'. Francis received the name Waleryan, meaning 'strong'.

From that moment, Raymond decided to embrace his future with words not weapons. He told himself that he would save Poland in a different way – as part of an ambitious, though still amorphous, plan to save the entire world.

'Every new generation in its hour of dawn, filled with the dreams of youth, thinks itself called upon to impel humanity towards heights unmeasured, believes itself an appointed path-finder, a doer of deeds greater than any of those which came before.'

Once again, the orator was Jan Paderewski, speaking this time in Lviv on Sunday, 23 October 1910, at the opening of the Chopin Centenary Festival. His speech honoured the memory of Chopin, who 'by a bloodless fight fought on the plains of peace assured the victory of Polish thought'.

Within the seminary walls, students and teachers alike discussed the stirring address. Paderewski's words spoke directly to Maximilian Kolbe, who had begun his novitiate training just a few weeks earlier, and they bolstered his resolve to fight for Poland's freedom through any means other than bloodshed.

In September 1911, after a year of study in Lviv, Kolbe, Francis and other novitiate students made a temporary vow of chastity, poverty and obedience. Kolbe then moved to a major seminary in Kraków for higher studies in philosophy and theology. It was there that he read, in April 1912, about the sinking of RMS *Titanic*. What remained with him after hearing that the 'unsinkable' luxury liner had collided with an iceberg en route to New York City were the actions of two priests.

As the vessel sank, with the loss of 1,500 passengers and crew, Father Thomas Byles from Leeds in England and Father Josef Peruschitz from Bavaria in Germany gave up their seats in a lifeboat and remained on deck. According to newspaper reports, the priests held hands and led the stranded passengers and crew in song and prayer. For Kolbe, it was an indelible image of self-sacrifice.

After two days and nights on a train, an exhausted but exhilarated Maximilian Kolbe arrived in Urbs Aeterna, the 'Eternal City' of Rome on 29 October 1912, a few months after graduating from his major seminary in Kraków. Along with six other Poles, Kolbe had won a prestigious scholarship to study in the Italian capital. It would be his home for almost seven years, a city of relative calm and stability at a time when millions of Europeans were losing their lives.

Europe was at loggerheads in 1912, a continent divided between the Triple Entente countries of Great Britain, France and Russia and the Triple Alliance nations of Germany, Austria-Hungary and Italy. Adding to the tension, several newly aligned Balkan states including Greece and Bulgaria had begun fighting Turkish forces in Macedonia, a territory of the Ottoman empire, that October.

Kolbe arrived in Rome with an impressive pedigree. He was an eighteen-year-old Polish polyglot, who spoke his native tongue along with Latin, Russian and German. His intelligence and mastery of mathematics and astronomy were light years ahead of his fellow freshman students.

In this ancient and multicultural city, however, Kolbe was just another wide-eyed provincial who knew little about the world beyond what he'd read in newspapers and books. His mother had warned her naive second son to beware of Rome's prostitutes and to steer clear of the young hooligans who screamed anti-papal obscenities at the hooded Franciscan friars. Maria herself had moved to a convent in Kraków in 1913, where she remained until her death in 1946.

In Poland, the Church was at the heart of patriotism and nationalism. In Italy, it was the opposite. Between 1870 and 1929, the Pope was a prisoner in the Vatican, refusing to leave his home or to accept the authority of the despised Italian government.[3]

Rome was a revelation. The International Seraphic College where Kolbe studied was at the foot of the Palatine Hill, the epicentre of the Roman empire. His fellow students there and at the nearby Pontifical Gregorian University came from across Europe and the Americas.

Kolbe thrived in this diverse environment and threw himself into the study of theology, philosophy, biology, mathematics, physics, chemistry and astronomy. His interest in astronomy, which had led his classmates in Kraków to call him 'mad Max' and 'the spaceman', prompted him to write a monograph outlining the possibilities of interplanetary and interstellar travel and to design a rudimentary spaceship.

Kolbe's physics professor, Father Gianfranceschi, said the spaceship design was 'feasible, in theory, but not practical at present'. Within the Franciscan community, Kolbe's persistent interest in the future often caused friction with those who were content with the status quo.

On 29 June 1914, Kolbe attended his first audience with Pope Pius X at St Peter's Square in Vatican City. But what should have been a celebratory occasion was marred by the news that on the previous day, Archduke Franz Ferdinand, heir to the Austro-Hungarian throne, had been assassinated in Sarajevo by a Bosnian Serb student, setting in motion events that would lead to the outbreak of the First World War.

Inevitably, Poland's future was at stake. For two years, Józef Piłsudski had been transforming the Polish Riflemen's Association into a potent military force. Piłsudski's strategy was to fight alongside Germany first before switching his allegiance to the British. In this way, he believed, Poland could finally defeat all its enemies and regain its independence.

Even before Austria declared war on Russia on 6 August 1914, Piłsudski's forces had invaded Russian-occupied Poland. Sitting in his tiny religious cell more than 1,000 miles from home, Kolbe felt torn. Years later, he mused that had he not been in Rome, he would have joined the struggle for Poland's liberation like his elder brother, Francis, who was given a leave of absence from the Franciscan order at the outbreak of war and fought alongside the Austrians. Injured badly in the leg, he never returned to his religious studies and his life started to drift out of control.[4]

In numerous letters home, Kolbe asked his mother what had become of his father, Julius. Although his fate is not entirely clear, it's likely that Julius joined Piłsudski's legions and was captured by Russian forces in southern Poland before the end of 1914. He was most likely hanged as a traitor because, having lived in the Russian-ruled part of Poland, he was officially a 'Russian'.

On 1 November 1914, Maximilian Kolbe took his perpetual vows of poverty, chastity and obedience. He also asked his branch of the Franciscan order, the Friars Minor Conventual, to add Maria, the Virgin Mary, to his name. Now known as Friar Maximilian Maria

Kolbe, the young scholar immersed himself in his studies as if to distract himself from the battles that were raging on Polish soil.

In May 1915, Italy abandoned its Triple Alliance with Germany and Austria-Hungary and joined the UK, France and Russia in the war. After Italy declared war on Austria-Hungary, its old enemy, Kolbe's superiors in Rome sent him and another brother to San Marino, a tiny independent republic in central Italy. They feared that the friars' Austrian travel documents would prove problematic. But after a brief stay, Kolbe returned to Rome to finish his studies.[5]

At the tender age of twenty-one, in October 1915, Kolbe obtained his doctorate in philosophy and immediately began studying for a doctorate in theology. 'He had a rare natural genius,' one of his professors, Father Leon Cicchito, told Maria Winowska, a Kolbe biographer.[6] 'This boy asks me questions I cannot answer,' added Father Bondini, the rector of the college.[7]

Exactly 200 years after the first Grand Lodge of the Masonic Order was founded in London, a group of freemasons invaded St Peter's Square in Rome on Saturday, 17 February 1917. They carried black and red flags that read 'The pope will be Satan's slave' and 'Satan must reign in the Vatican'. Under the Vatican's windows, they hung a banner showing the devil trampling on the Archangel Michael.

Maximilian Kolbe was outraged at these anti-clerical demonstrations. He had to be talked out of confronting the Roman freemasons directly, but their actions had lit a spark and his disdain for masonic organisations remained throughout his life.[8] His contempt echoed that of the Catholic Church as a whole, which at the time was battling a wave of secularism in Europe.[9]

Reading the Italian newspapers, Kolbe was appalled and despondent at the massive loss of life and suffering caused by the war, now in its third year. In Poland alone, an estimated 450,000 people had died as two million Polish troops fought both with and against the armies of the three occupying powers.

Further complicating matters was the political and economic

Kolbe in Rome in 1918

chaos in Russia that would eventually lead to civil war between Vladimir Lenin's Red Army supporters and the White Army of monarchists and democratic socialists. But Kolbe's attempts to follow the dramatic events in Europe were soon thwarted. That summer, while playing football with fellow friars, Kolbe began coughing up blood. It was tuberculosis, the contagious and infectious disease often caused by poor ventilation and primitive sanitation. At the time there was no known cure, apart from complete rest, which the impatient and stubborn Kolbe was reluctant to do.

During his forced recuperation, Kolbe's vague plans for a new spiritual movement to save the world from the forces of secularism began to crystallise. Kolbe had long since given up the idea of becoming a soldier to fight for Poland's independence. But he still saw himself as a warrior, a knight for the Virgin Mary, and he used martial metaphors to promote his non-violent vision.

His goal became the launching of an international militia that would resist the Church's enemies, especially the freemasons, and promote Christian unity by using emerging technologies. His dedication to the Virgin Mary echoed that of the Pope at the time, Benedict XV.

Kolbe decided that the most efficient way to spread his ideas to as wide an audience as possible was through the media. He believed that a combination of easy-to-read newspapers and magazines, radio and silent movies, which were in their infancy, would attract the masses to his cause.[10]

Uninterested in society's elite, he sought only to reach the kind of workers and peasants that he'd known as a boy. Despite the opposition of fellow Franciscans, who were steeped in tradition, the restless twenty-three-year-old persuaded six young friars to form a new group within the order to pursue his global goals.

On the evening of Tuesday, 16 October 1917, two Romanians, four Italians and Kolbe gathered secretly in a small room to hear Kolbe explain his intentions for the group. He called the organisation the Militia Immaculatae, or MI. He now poured all his previous patriotic energy into this new spiritual crusade.

3. Cranking the Presses

November 1918 – Warsaw, Poland

After 123 torturous years of foreign occupation and partition by Russia, Germany and Austria, Poland regained its sovereignty in November 1918 at the conclusion of the First World War. The end of Poland's humiliating subjugation came quickly, brought about by a string of events that included Tsar Nicholas II's abdication and the subsequent Russian Revolution, Russia's withdrawal from the war and the Allied defeat of Germany and Austria. All three of the conquered powers renounced their claims over Poland.

Within days of the war's end, Józef Piłsudski, leader of the Polish armed forces, was named Poland's head of state and the charismatic pianist-politician Jan Paderewski became prime minister.[1]

Paderewski had used his star power in the US to gain support for Polish independence from President Woodrow Wilson. After playing Chopin for Wilson at the White House in November 1916, Paderewski had pleaded with America's twenty-eighth president to champion Poland's cause. Wilson agreed. Number thirteen of the 'Fourteen Points' that Wilson followed during peace negotiations, after America's joining of the Triple Entente in April 1917, was that 'there should be a united, independent, autonomous Poland'.

Most of Poland's twenty-seven million people were jubilant at the nation's renewal. But Maximilian Kolbe, sitting in his seminary cell in Rome, had little time to rejoice at Poland's rebirth or the end of the First World War. His own world war against injustice, hate speech and violence was just beginning. Yet no sooner had the global crusade of Militia Immaculatae started than it experienced setbacks. Two of MI's seven founders died in 1918 during the global 'Spanish flu' pandemic.

Kolbe himself suffered what he called 'a grave relapse' that left him spitting blood and coughing uncontrollably. And even though his Franciscan order had officially approved MI's founding, many Franciscans in Rome disapproved of what they perceived as his arrogant moves to create a separate entity within the order. Some also argued that Kolbe's focus on the Virgin Mary was too narrow and neglected broader aspects of Catholic theology.[2]

Kolbe was undeterred. In April 1918 he had been ordained a priest and on 22 July 1919 he was awarded a doctorate in theology. The following day he left Rome to become a professor of theology at the Franciscan seminary in Kraków where he had studied seven years earlier.

Almost seven years in Rome had changed Kolbe immeasurably. He had arrived as an insular student with a potent intellect, but as yet unproven. He left as a confident and cosmopolitan twenty-five-year-old man in a hurry, unafraid of challenging anything he disagreed with, particularly when it came to his beliefs.

Although sickly and weak, Kolbe rarely talked about his illnesses and he settled down to a life of poverty in a tiny cell in Kraków. It contained little more than a straw mattress, a statue of the Immaculata and images of two female mystics, both of whom had died of tuberculosis after years of suffering. One, Gemma Galgani from Lucca in Italy, died at the age of twenty-five in 1903. The other, Thérèse of Lisieux in France, died aged twenty-four in 1897.

Kolbe was delighted to be home, but the contrast with Rome's comparative calm and stability was stark. After years of battle, Poland was an impoverished, barely functional and disunited mess, with nine legal systems and five currencies. On its eastern borders, Poland's army skirmished continually with the expansionist Soviet army.[3]

In Kraków, Kolbe immediately began recruiting 'knights' for his spiritual movement. Although he received little support from fellow Franciscans, he persuaded hundreds of ordinary Polish citizens to join the organisation. By the middle of 1920, Kolbe announced, MI had more than 1,000 members. But the only way to expand that number exponentially and speedily, Kolbe decided, was by publishing a magazine that even the poorly educated could read.

Again, Kolbe's health interfered with his ambitions. That summer, while teaching at the minor seminary in Lviv that he had attended as a teenager, Kolbe vomited blood. His tuberculosis had returned, accompanied by high fevers and splitting headaches. Doctors gave him three months to live. Kolbe was immediately sent to a sanatorium in Zakopane, a spa resort in the Tatras Mountains known as the Polish Alps, and ordered to rest.[4]

After eight months in Zakopane, Kolbe's superiors sent him to a friary in the small town of Nieszawa northwest of Warsaw for further recuperation. Unknown to Kolbe, his father provincial had asked the head of the Nieszawa friary to choose a burial site for the priest because he wasn't expected to survive. Indeed, in June 1921, a requiem Mass was sung for Kolbe in Rome after his death was announced prematurely.

Convalescing in Nieszawa until November 1921, Kolbe immersed himself in the writings of Gemma Galgani and Thérèse of Lisieux. 'The smallest bit of suffering is more valuable than all the treasures of the world,' Thérèse wrote shortly before her death. 'The wind of suffering is a wind of love.'[5] As he fought to overcome the constant pain in his lungs and head, Kolbe clearly felt a kinship with these two young women, both of whom shared his special loyalty to the Virgin Mary.[6]

It was during Kolbe's recuperation that he first read about the rescue by the Japanese of hundreds of orphaned Polish children, mostly under the age of ten, from Siberia. This remarkable event would have unexpected repercussions over the following quarter-century for Japan, for Poland and for Kolbe himself.

Most Poles knew of family members or friends who had been exiled to Siberia for challenging their Russian aggressors. For example, after the Polish–Russian War of 1830, known as the 'November Uprising', as many as 50,000 Poles had been sent to Siberia, where they settled and raised families.

By 1920, at least 200,000 Poles were living in east Siberia, the Far

East and Manchuria. Most were political exiles, economic migrants or refugees.[7] After the Russian Revolution and the subsequent civil war throughout the Soviet Union, tens of thousands were starving, destitute and homeless. They included about 5,000 vulnerable Polish children, whom a schoolteacher called Anna Bielkiewicz was determined to help.

Bielkiewicz set up an organisation in Vladivostok in 1919 to rescue orphans left stranded in Siberia by the deaths of, or separation from, their parents. Because Russia and Poland had been fighting each other, the orphans couldn't go directly to Poland. Bielkiewicz persuaded the Japanese government and the Japanese Red Cross to help repatriate the children to Poland via Japan, which had political ambitions in the region.[8]

In mid-1920, 388 Siberian orphans, many barefoot and clad in filthy rags, sailed from Vladivostok to the port of Tsuruga on the Sea of Japan. There, they took a train to a Buddhist nursery in Tokyo and later sailed to the US before eventually arriving in Poland. Most of the orphans regarded Japan as their second home because of the care they had received.

Bielkiewicz organised a second successful repatriation of 379 orphans to the Japanese city of Osaka in August 1922. Among the children was a thirteen-year-old boy called Innocenty Protalinski. Years later, Protalinski's path would cross with Maximilian Kolbe's amid the Nazi atrocities.[9]

The orphan rescues were widely reported in Polish newspapers. Japan's victory over Russia in 1905 had already created many Japan-loving Poles.[10] In news reports, the Polish media referred to Japan as 'a nation that cherishes children' and as 'the cherry blossom country'. Even today, Poles call the Japanese 'people from cherry blossom country'.

Poland's love affair with Japan was curious because the countries had little in common. One was an island nation. The other was virtually landlocked. Their culture, food, language, religion, philosophy, geography, history, dress and customs were alien to each other. It was also a one-sided romance – few people in Japan knew much about Poland, aside from the names Chopin and Marie Curie.

Japan and Poland shared but one thing. A common enemy: Russia.

On Kolbe's return to Kraków from Zakopane in April 1921, he had met four Japanese students on the train. Impressed with their politeness, he started reading more about 'the cherry blossom country' and about St Francis Xavier, the Spanish-born missionary. Co-founder of the Jesuits, Father Xavier landed in Kyushu, the southernmost of Japan's four main islands, in 1549.

Xavier was the first westerner to bring Catholicism to Japan. Initially, Christianity spread fast, and some 300,000 Japanese were converted in thirty years, mainly in southern Japan. Yet Christianity made little headway over the following centuries, as Kolbe quickly learned.

The ruling shogunate regarded Christianity as a major threat. Fear of Catholicism and other foreign influences led to a ban on Catholicism in 1614 and to the Sakoku era (1639 to 1854) when Japan was closed to most outsiders. Less than one per cent of the fifty-seven million population called themselves Christian in 1920.

Reading about Francis Xavier and the Siberian orphans sowed the seeds in Kolbe that would flourish a decade later. It is easy to imagine him believing that one day he would fulfil Xavier's dream of converting millions of Japanese to Christianity.

Arriving back in Kraków from his recuperation in Nieszawa in late 1921, Kolbe was anxious to publish a Militia Immaculatae magazine as quickly as possible. It was an uphill struggle. Like many nations after the First World War, Poland was virtually bankrupt, jobs were scarce and hyperinflation was rampant.

Kolbe lacked a printing press, paper, support and, above all, money. Most of his fellow Franciscans branded him a naive dreamer. Undaunted, Kolbe and a handful of sympathetic friars started knocking on doors in Kraków's poorest districts to beg for a handful of marka, the new national currency. They also distributed tiny oval-shaped 'miraculous medals', also known as 'spiritual bullets' and 'heavenly weapons', to everyone they met.[11]

Friars preparing the Knight of the Immaculata *magazine for mailing*

By January 1922, Kolbe had gathered enough cash to publish 5,000 copies of the first *Knight of the Immaculata (Rycerz Niepokalanej)* magazine. Kolbe wrote most of the sixteen-page publication himself. The mission, he wrote, was to 'deepen and to confirm faith [and] to work for the conversion of non-Catholics. The journal will remain friendly towards all, no matter what their religion or nationality.'

Kolbe and other friars distributed the magazine around Kraków, giving away copies to those who couldn't afford to pay. But several conservative Franciscans had had enough. They criticised the cheap grade of paper, Kolbe's simplistic approach to profound religious questions and his excess coverage of the mystical experiences of Gemma Galgani.

In October 1922, Kolbe was exiled to a vast dilapidated monastery in Grodno, 350 miles northeast of Kraków. Today, Grodno is part of Belarus. Kolbe was unhappy about the move but was told that Grodno would be better for his health. He was joined there by his younger brother, Joseph, who had joined the Franciscan order and was now known as Father Alfons.

Using a tiny loan from his order and a $100 donation from a friendly Polish-American priest, Kolbe bought a vintage manual printing press. The friars dubbed it 'Old Granny'. To print 5,000 copies of the magazine, the shaven-headed men needed to crank the heavy press 60,000 times. That meant that Maximilian, Alfons and four colleagues had to work in shifts all day and night. Kolbe refused to let his pain and sickness slow down the gruelling operation.[12]

Within months, to everyone's surprise, the magazine's circulation had soared. While other publications lost readership, the *Knight of the Immaculata* prospered because its short articles were written using simple Polish words and expressions that even barely literate peasants could understand.

At a time of acute poverty, readers felt a kinship with the magazine because the journalist friars were even poorer than they were. Kolbe owned one overcoat, which he also used as a blanket. The other friars shared another coat, even in the depths of winter. They also toiled as long and as hard as the peasants, belying the conventional image of hooded men who sang hymns and prayed in relative comfort. From all over Poland, meagre donations arrived in Grodno from the poorest of the poor.

Despite the hardships, Kolbe was convinced his 'military strategy' was working. 'What strategy do we plot?' he wrote in November 1924. 'A war, a real war, but it is not fought with rifles, machine guns, cannon, airplanes or poison gas. The first weapon in the Christian arsenal must be humble, persistent prayer.'[13]

On Sunday, 10 May 1925, a well-dressed, red-haired and blue-eyed man carrying a stuffed suitcase banged on the door of the Grodno monastery. Exhausted by the non-stop printing workload, Father Kolbe had asked his superior in Warsaw to help find him potential new recruits. The man at the door, Władysław Żebrowski, told Kolbe that he hailed from a patriotic farming family in northeast Poland and that he'd belonged to a Polish machine gun corps for three years fighting the Bolsheviks.[14]

Since then, Żebrowski said, he'd been a jack of all trades – a tailor, a shoemaker, a blacksmith and a failed investor in a peat mine. He explained that he was in the midst of a spiritual crisis. He added that he liked Kolbe's Conventual Franciscan congregation compared with some other religious orders because the friars wore 'stylish habits'.

He couldn't have been more wrong. After staying the night, Żebrowski allowed the friars to shave his head, remove his suitcase and show him how to keep the buildings clean. Żebrowski was stunned at the friars' lifestyle.

The friars would get up very early, meditate, pray, attend Mass and eat breakfast. Then they'd rush to the printing room and start typesetting, cranking the printer, folding the magazines and preparing them for mailing. They barely talked to each other, just focused on their work, hour after hour, sometimes all night.

'I'd imagined a quiet monastic life of prayers,' Żebrowski said years later. 'But all I was asked to do was to heat stoves and clean floors all day long, like a maid.'[15]

After a few days, Żebrowski had a showdown with Kolbe. 'I'm not a maid,' he said. 'I'm leaving.' Somehow, Kolbe convinced him to stay and five months after his arrival, Żebrowski donned a black Franciscan habit and became known as Brother Zeno Żebrowski.

By that time, Brother Zeno had become indispensable to Kolbe and his most trusted ally. He was a man capable of mending anything, from the sole of a worn-down shoe to the soul of a worn-out priest. Zeno would later travel to Japan with Kolbe and attain national fame for his actions after the Nagasaki nuclear bomb blast.

By the end of 1926, using a modern typesetting machine and a diesel motor to drive the press, Kolbe was publishing 45,000 copies of each monthly magazine and Militia Immaculatae boasted more than 120,000 members. But MI's success came at the expense of Kolbe's health. In September 1926, he returned once again to Zakopane, the mountain resort. For seven months, Kolbe recuperated from a panoply of illnesses: coughing fits, high fevers, headaches and a painful stooped back. Undaunted, after returning to Grodno, Kolbe began searching for larger offices for the fast-growing publishing operation.

By chance, in June 1927, Kolbe was introduced by a visiting priest to a Polish aristocrat called Prince Jan Maria Drucki-Lubecki. Lubecki owned an estate in Grodno and another at Teresin, twenty-five miles west of Warsaw. The prince donated two-and-a-half hectares of land on his Teresin estate, surrounded by an oak and birch forest, to the penniless friars.[16]

Wasting no time, Kolbe, his brother Alfons, now the magazine's editor, Zeno Żebrowski and a few other friars started constructing a chapel and dormitory, plus a large building for the printing presses, on the site.[17] And in November 1927, the Kolbes and eighteen friars officially moved into the makeshift institution. They called it Niepokalanów, which means 'City of the Immaculate Mother of God'.

The community grew rapidly. By the end of 1929, about 120 men were living there, including friars and seminary pupils. Many worked around the clock to produce the magazine, whose monthly circulation now topped 150,000 copies. Others toiled to produce food, drink and other essentials. When not working, the men prayed or meditated for a minimum of three-and-a-half hours a day.

Most friars supported Kolbe's relentless schedule and the severity of the lifestyle, even though it took its toll on their own health. The growth of MI and its publishing arm left Kolbe elated. 'I want to win souls for the Immaculata,' he wrote to his superior, the father provincial, in December 1928. 'I want to elevate her [the Virgin Mary's] ensign over all media, raise it over the radio antennae, over the centres for art, literature, theatre and film. In short, I want to exalt her standard over the entire world. Lacking this ideal, Niepokalanów has no reason to exist.'[18]

By this time, Europe was suffering from severe economic problems and was witnessing the rise of fascism in Italy and Germany. In Poland, Józef Piłsudski had retired from politics in 1923. But after becoming disillusioned with the country's new leaders, he had seized power in a bloody *coup d'état* in 1926 and became an aloof quasi-dictator of a centrist regime.

It was hardly a time for Kolbe to 'conquer the world' on behalf of 'the Queen of Poland'. But Kolbe, who had turned thirty-five in January 1929, was determined to spread his mission overseas. His ambitions matched the mood within the Catholic Church at the time. More than most of his predecessors, Pope Pius XI encouraged all Catholic orders to send more missionaries to new locales.[19]

Where should Kolbe begin? It was an easy decision. Throughout his life, Kolbe had admired the Japanese from afar. He'd celebrated their victory over Russia as a child and read widely about Francis Xavier and the persecution in Japan of fellow Catholics.

There was no better place, he reasoned, to launch his global plan than in 'the country where cherry blossoms bloom'.

4. A Catholic Boy in Northern Korea

March 1928 – Unggi, northern Korea

On the extreme northeastern tip of Korea, bordered by Siberia to the north and China to the west, sits the ice-free fishing port of Unggi on the Sea of Japan. There, on Thursday, 1 March 1928, a young Japanese nanny called Wasa gave birth on a bitterly cold day to a puny infant whom she and her husband, Matsukichi Tagawa, named Kōichi. The boy would later become known as Tōmei Ozaki.

Wasa had met Matsukichi in Unggi a couple of years earlier, soon after he and two brothers had fled across the narrow Korean border with Siberia to escape anti-Japanese guerrillas. The Tagawas were among 2,300 Japanese who lived in Unggi at the time, along with about 20,000 Koreans.

Matsukichi and three brothers had grown up on a farm west of Nagasaki, the main port on Japan's southern island of Kyushu. But when their parents died, the eldest boy had inherited the farm, leaving the siblings to fend for themselves.

Lacking land or a profession, the three Tagawa brothers moved to the Russian region of Siberia in the late 1910s, where they became relatively wealthy businessmen. But life in Siberia grew difficult for Japanese during the civil war that followed the 1917 Russian Revolution, prompting thousands to head for northern Korea.[1] Korea had become a Japanese protectorate in 1905 following the Russo-Japanese War and was formally annexed in 1910.

In Unggi, the enterprising trio hired Korean men to tend chickens, pigs and cattle on a small farm, and they opened a butcher's shop in which to sell the slaughtered animals to fellow Japanese. The three lived together, along with Wasa, in a draughty Japanese-style wooden house where Kōichi was born. As a toddler, Kōichi

Kōichi Tagawa as a baby

was surrounded by his uncles and parents, who all worked from dawn to late evening in the butcher's shop and on the farm.

Some of Kōichi's earliest memories were of the friendly Koreans on the Unggi farm. 'The men all wore *hanbok* – traditional jackets and baggy pants – and their clothes were always white, which denoted their status as commoners,' he told me in early 2021. 'I sat on their laps and stroked their long beards. But they didn't understand Japanese well and I, of course, being just a young child, didn't understand the hierarchical structure that divided the Korean classes and kept the Japanese and Koreans separated.'

To the majority of Korea's seventeen million citizens, Japan was an aggressive colonial usurper whose land seizures, heavy taxes and discriminatory policies relegated them to second-class status. On 1 March 1919, an estimated two million Koreans had participated in anti-Japanese demonstrations, which Japan violently suppressed. The demonstrations, a catalyst for supporters of Korean independence, were inspired by US President Woodrow Wilson's 'Fourteen Points' declaration a year earlier outlining a country's right to self-determination.

Sometime in 1932, when Kōichi was four years old, Matsukichi and Wasa Tagawa moved 1,000 miles down the Korean peninsula to

Kōichi Tagawa with his mother, Wasa

Chinhae, now known as Jinhae, in the southeast of the Japanese colony. Since 1910, the Imperial Japanese Navy had transformed Chinhae into a major port.

Kōichi had vivid memories of one particular day during his time in Chinhae. It was the spring of 1933, and he was sitting with his parents watching Korean men and women dance under snow-white cherry blossoms at a *hanami* (flower-viewing) party. 'They were all moving in a circle, holding hands and singing loudly in Korean,' he recalled. 'Then, some Japanese sailors came and joined in. There were many, many cherry trees in Chinhae and it seemed such a joyous time.' Today, the Jinhae cherry blossom festival is the largest in South Korea.

Most of the cherry trees under which the dancers caroused had been planted as part of Japan's so-called 'Japanisation' policy, which included forbidding the use of the Korean language. The policy had similarities with Russia's 'Russification' programme in Poland in the nineteenth century. Hanami parties were virtually the only occasions at which Koreans were allowed to sing in their own language and to mix with Japanese.

In 1934, after a couple of years in Chinhae, the family returned to northern Korea so that Kōichi could be educated in a Japanese-only primary school close to his uncles. They moved into a new two-storey concrete house in a recently developed port town called Rason, ten miles southeast of Unggi. Once a tiny fishing village, the community was transformed in the early 1930s into a major Japanese transit and trading town.

Rason's only *raison d'être* was to serve as the gateway to a colossal resource-rich land mass almost twice as large as Texas and three times the size of Japan – Manchuria.

Japan had long held imperial ambitions over Manchuria. After losing the Russo-Japanese War of 1904–05, Russia agreed to evacuate the region, large parts of which it had controlled since the late nineteenth century in a secret pact with China. Japan set up the South Manchurian Railway Company in 1906 to run the railways in the region and to promote Manchuria as a nirvana for frontier settlers. By 1930, more than 230,000 Japanese civilians had moved there.

On 18 September 1931, the Kwangtung Army, a powerful nationalist group within the Imperial Japanese Army, exploded a bomb near a Japanese-owned railway track close to the town of Shenyang in China. The army claimed that Chinese soldiers had detonated the device. In fact, it was a staged event that became known as the Manchurian Incident, or the Mukden Incident.

The Kwangtung Army's staged explosion gave the Japanese a pretext to accuse China of sabotage and to invade Manchuria. The incident prompted an unprecedented show of support within Japan for the military and for the establishment in February 1932 of the puppet state of Manchukuo in present-day northeast China. Japan quickly installed China's last emperor, Puyi, as the chief executive of this new nation.

The invasion of Manchuria was an audacious land-grab. But for many destitute Japanese and their malnourished children it became a place of hope following the depression of the late 1920s. As a means of survival, many families had sold their daughters as maids or prostitutes.

Manchuria had land in abundance for a growing population; in contrast, eighty per cent of Japan was mountainous, and most Japanese lived on a crowded southern strip of land between the Tokyo and Osaka metropolises. While the Japanese government was initially cautious about developing the region, it quickly became clear that a mass emigration of Japanese to Manchuria would serve as a buffer against Russia.

In reality, Manchukuo was a dangerous place to live because anti-Japanese rebels from China and Korea were active there. Among them was Kim Il-Sung, who would create the Democratic People's Republic of Korea (North Korea) years later. Kim's family had fled from Korea to Manchuria in 1920 and he became a member of the Northeast Anti-Japanese United Army, a communist guerrilla group, in 1935.

As Manchukuo's economic and strategic importance grew, one of Japan's priorities was to connect Rason with Changchun, the capital of Manchukuo, by railway. This would give Japan the fastest possible overland route by which coal, steel and agricultural products such as cotton and soybeans could be exported. From Rason, minerals and foodstuffs could be quickly shipped across the Sea of Japan to two Japanese ports: Tsuruga and Niigata.

As a young boy in Rason, Kōichi told me, he watched a ragged army of poorly paid Korean workers pushing soil- and cement-laden trolleys to and from construction sites. Mountains surrounding the town were razed to build homes, hotels, schools, parks, libraries, warehouses and anything else needed to attract pioneers from Japan, like the Tagawa family. Rason's population grew from a few dozen households in 1932 to about 10,000 in 1933 and to more than 50,000 four years later.

'Rason is like a chaotic scene from a gold rush,' a reporter for the Osaka *Asahi* newspaper proclaimed in June 1933 after a visit. 'There's construction everywhere, land prices are soaring, and a lively energy permeates the town.'

Rason itself was a town divided, reflecting Japan's colonial mentality. The Japanese lived around the main road, close to the rail-way station, police headquarters and the best shops. The Koreans lived in smaller homes on narrower streets behind the Japanese district.

Within the Japanese sector, the Tagawas lived a privileged life. After the move from Chinhae, they opened their own butcher's shop, bringing meat and poultry from Matsukichi's brothers' butchery and farm in Unggi to sell.

The family's luxurious house was equipped with a traditional Korean underfloor heating system. And the family all slept in beds rather than on Japanese-style futon mattresses on the floor. 'Even when the temperature would fall to twenty degrees below freezing, I could sleep with only a thin blanket because the house was so warm,' Kōichi told me. 'Because we owned a butcher's shop, mother could make me my favourite food – a beef tempura dish using thinly sliced seasoned and marinated beef that was then battered and deep fried. It was delicious!' Seventy years later, he would ask chefs in Nagasaki restaurants to make this dish especially for him. Beef is not usually used in tempura dishes.

Every morning beginning in April 1934, Kōichi walked to an elementary school reserved exclusively for Japanese children. The atmosphere there reflected the militaristic mood at the time. Kōichi's teacher wore a khaki-coloured uniform. It was similar to that of his counterparts throughout Japan, and to the uniforms worn by the Japanese soldiers who passed through Rason every day en route to the battlefields in Manchukuo.

The textbook that Kōichi was given when he began studying at the school featured striking propaganda slogans. The first page showed a drawing of cherry trees in full blossom. Underneath, in large letters, was written *Saita Saita, Sakura ga Saita* (Bloomed, Bloomed, the Cherry Blossoms Have Bloomed). The second page showed four marching soldiers carrying guns, under which was written *Susume Susume, Heitai Susume* (Advance, Advance, Soldiers Advance). The Japanese government had made cherry blossoms, the country's national flower, a symbol of the nation's glory and power and it promoted this image throughout the 1930s.

In class, Kōichi recalled, the teacher frequently mentioned that

Japan needed to expand its power to neighbouring countries. 'Tell me why we need to advance to China and elsewhere,' the teacher asked the infants. The pupils would all raise their hands. 'Because we don't have any natural resources!' they would cry out in unison. 'That's right,' the teacher said. 'In Japan, all we have is rice and fish. To grow, we need iron, oil and rubber. The British occupy the Malay peninsula, the Americans have taken the Philippines, the Dutch have Indonesia, the French have Indochina. We need to be strong and ready to fight.'

The teacher also taught his tiny students about the greatness of their emperor, Hirohito, the 124th successive emperor in a line that allegedly stretched back more than 2,500 years to 660 BCE. He said that the emperor was a 'living God' who was destined to govern the Asian people. Every day, during morning assembly, the children showed their respect by bowing deeply in the direction of the Imperial Palace in Tokyo. On national holidays, the headmaster would attend school in his best dark tailcoat and open the *hō-anden*, a small wooden shrine set up in the school. Inside it were portraits of the emperor and empress.

The children would then recite the Kyōiku Chokugo, the Imperial Rescript on Education, which stated that every Japanese citizen must be prepared to offer his or her life courageously to the emperor in case of an emergency. Kōichi thought little about the meaning of these rituals. After all, every student in Japan and its satellite states followed the same curriculum and used the same textbooks.

As a small and shy pupil, Kōichi wanted more than anything else for his classmates to accept him. But this meant hiding an embarrassing secret. For while all his school pals and their families followed Buddhist and Shinto traditions and rituals, the Tagawas didn't. Unlike everyone else in the community, Kōichi and his parents were descendants of Japan's most persecuted minority. They were *kakure kirishitan*: 'hidden Christians'.

The story of Japan's hidden Christians spanned a period of more than 230 years and is one of the most unusual and least-known phenomena in the nation's history. In the five decades after the Jesuit Francis Xavier had landed in Kyushu, Christianity had spread widely among the ruling classes and the poor alike. Nagasaki, the centre of Christian activities, became known as the 'Rome of Japan'.

But Catholicism threatened the established order and Japan's samurai leader, Hideyoshi Toyotomi, became determined to snuff out this seditious Western creed. In February 1597, Toyotomi ordered the torture and crucifixion of twenty-six Christians, including six Franciscans, on crosses in Nagasaki. These martyrs were canonised in 1862.

Toyotomi's powerful successor, Ieyasu Tokugawa, went further. In 1614, the Tokugawa shogunate made Buddhism the national religion and forced all commoners to belong to a temple. The shogunate banned Christianity completely and expelled all foreign missionaries. The ban forced religion underground, prompting Catholics in Nagasaki and elsewhere to practise their faith on their own, clandestinely.

Officially, the hidden Christians all belonged to a Buddhist temple network, and the authorities frequently asked suspected Catholics to prove their loyalty by trampling on a crucifix or an image of Jesus or the Virgin Mary. Many who refused were tortured, executed, crucified or thrown into boiling natural hot springs.[2]

At home, the hidden Christians often displayed a Buddhist or Shinto altar, behind which they would hide statues of Jesus or the Virgin Mary that resembled Buddhist statues. Some families simply venerated a statue of Kannon, the Buddhist goddess of mercy, who reminded them of the Virgin Mary.

Most Japanese Christians were uneducated and spoke only their native tongue. But their prayers, which sounded like Buddhist chants, contained Latin and Portuguese words and phrases such as 'Amen', 'Deus' and 'Santa Maria'. During the Christians' 230 years underground, the meaning of these non-Japanese words became increasingly distorted as they passed from one generation to the next.

Kōichi Tagawa's parents hailed from Japan's two main centres of hidden Christianity. Wasa was born in Urakami village in northern

Nagasaki while Matsukichi's family came from Sotome, a coastal village west of the city. Each place boasted a large underground network.[3] During the ban, local authorities occasionally tried to suppress Christian communities, arresting and killing many villagers in brutal crackdowns.[4]

In Urakami village alone, there were four major crackdowns or persecutions during the ban on Christianity – in 1790, 1842, 1856 and 1868. The fourth persecution was the most terrifying. In 1867, the failing shogunate government started to suppress the clandestine network within Urakami. A year later, a new government with the sixteen-year-old Emperor Meiji nominally at its head came to power in a revolution that became known as the Meiji Restoration. That marked the beginning of Japan's modernisation and brought an end to the feudal samurai leadership that had ruled Japan since 1192.

But the new authorities had no sympathy for Christianity. They issued edicts banning the religion and continued to purge the hidden Christians. The government arrested, tortured and exiled 3,394 people, all from Urakami district, to isolated rural villages on Honshu, Japan's main island. At least 662 died. The government eventually relented, legalising Christianity in 1873 after pressure from Western governments and organisations.

Kōichi's maternal great-great-grandparents were part of that fourth persecution, but Kōichi missed the chance to ask his mother for more details because she died in Nagasaki when the atomic bomb exploded.

Even after Christianity was legalised, Catholics were ostracised and shunned in Japan. Most Japanese had been led to believe that Christianity was an 'evil religion' imported by 'European barbarians'.

In Rason, the Tagawas were the only Catholics in the Japanese community so there was no church. The Korean community didn't have a church either. Wasa taught her son that one absolute God had created all human beings, animals, plants and everything else in the universe. Every morning and evening, she made Kōichi clasp his hands together and pray in front of the family altar.

Kōichi said he wondered how Japan's emperor could be a 'living God', but it wasn't a question that anyone else asked. Loyalty to the emperor was paramount. And Kōichi was proud to be part of the expanding Japanese empire after growing up amid the energy and optimism of the fast-growing Rason.

For Kōichi, friends were more important than faith. Fitting in, rather than standing out, was the norm in Japanese society. Anyone who was different or who questioned the status quo would be hammered down and ordered to conform.

It was a lesson that the zealous Polish missionary, Maximilian Kolbe, would quickly learn after he arrived in Nagasaki at the beginning of the 1930s.

PART 2

Men in Black, 1930–1936

5. The Arrival of the Beards

April 1930 – Nagasaki

Father Maximilian Maria Kolbe had a grand – albeit simplistic and naive – pioneering vision of how to spread Christianity around the Far East and the Middle East. First, he would go to Japan and start printing the Militia Immaculatae magazine in Japanese.

Once rooted, MI would expand to India and China, before moving on to Beirut and publishing in Arabic, Persian and Hebrew. If this strategy was successful, he reasoned, it would soon be possible for the MI magazine to reach more than one billion people, almost half the world's population at the time.[1]

Traditional Christian missionaries preached to small groups of non-believers in rural areas of lesser-developed countries. Kolbe wanted to turn that idea on its head. He hoped to reach both the educated and barely educated in the cities of fast-developing nations, such as Japan. Furthermore, he believed that publishing magazines and broadcasting his views on the radio was the best and quickest way to expand the kingdom of 'the Queen of Poland'. His approach had worked in Poland. Why not the rest of the world?

On 14 January 1930, six days after his thirty-sixth birthday, Kolbe left Niepokalanów and travelled by train to Rome to ask permission from his superior, Father Alfons Orlini, to begin his ambitious global plan, starting in Japan. Father Orlini was the minister general of the Conventual Franciscans. Kolbe's direct superior, Father Provincial Kornel Czupryk, had already approved the plan.

The obstacles were enormous. Kolbe knew no one in Japan. He didn't speak Japanese. His health was dire because his tuberculosis could flare up at any moment. He had no money. He knew nothing about Japan's drift towards militarism and authoritarianism. Likewise, he was ignorant of Japanese customs, from bowing and the use of wooden chopsticks to their Japanese religious practices. Perhaps ignorance really was bliss.

And yet, within a couple of days, Kolbe had convinced Father Orlini that it was his mission in life to save the world, beginning in 'the cherry blossom country'. After granting permission, Father Orlini ordered Kolbe to set up one Franciscan branch in China and another in Japan. The father also told Kolbe to 'grow a beard, because men with long beards are venerated as saints in the Orient', and he gave Kolbe $100 (about $1,600 today) to help with the costs.[2] Kolbe himself mocked his own ambition, writing to a fellow priest: 'In considering the new centres which we are to open, I'd like to know how many idiots like us are willing to volunteer.'[3]

Back at Niepokalanów, Kolbe chose three brothers, all in their twenties, to accompany him aboard the SS *Angers* from Marseilles to Shanghai. They were Brothers Hilary Lysakowski, Zygmunt Król and Seweryn Dagis.

He also picked his soulmate from Grodno, Brother Zeno Żebrowski. Kolbe knew that Zeno had talents that he didn't possess – life skills that could transform his ambitions into reality. For while Kolbe was an intellectual, with a razor-sharp and logical mind, Zeno was a can-do pragmatist. Kolbe's younger brother, Alfons, took over as the head of the Niepokalanów community.

Before leaving Europe, Kolbe travelled to Lourdes, the pilgrimage site in the French Pyrenees, and then to Lisieux in northern France where St Thérèse had lived with her parents. In her room, Kolbe noted, was 'her chess set, a comfort for our chess players'.[4]

After thirty-five days, mostly at sea, the five Polish friars arrived in Shanghai on 11 April 1930, armed with Chinese dictionaries and little else.[5] Their experience in the bustling city, the world's fifth largest, was far from positive. A millionaire Chinese businessman and philanthropist, Lu Bohong, also known as Joseph Lo Pa Hong, had offered to be Kolbe's benefactor in the city. But Shanghai was Jesuit territory and the Franciscans were not welcome.

The Jesuit bishop told them bluntly that if they wanted to build a missionary base in China, they would have to travel several hundred

Kolbe and the Polish friars in Port Said, Egypt, en route to the Far East in 1930

miles inland, to Shanxi. Kolbe demurred. Nonetheless, he left two friars in Shanghai – Brothers Zygmunt and Seweryn – to explore the possibilities. The remaining trio – Kolbe and Brothers Zeno and Hilary – sailed for Japan thirteen days later. By then, the men all sported straggly beards, following Father Orlini's instructions.

Kolbe had chosen Nagasaki as the base for his Japanese mission because it was the spiritual centre of Japanese Christianity, past and present. About seventy per cent of all Japanese Catholics lived there in 1930. Kolbe also believed that Nagasaki's location on the southern tip of Japan would be ideal for expanding his mission to other parts of Asia.

Kolbe had read widely about the visit to Kyushu in 1549 of Father Francis Xavier, co-founder of the Jesuits, and about the missionary priests who followed him. Many had succeeded by approaching feudal *daimyō* lords, who were the regional samurai leaders. Portuguese missionaries often accompanied traders who were eager to sell guns and other Western wares to the lords. Cut off from the world, these lords often embraced Christianity to boost their own influence at the expense of rival daimyō.[6]

As Nagasaki grew, so too did its Catholic population, until the shogunate banned Christianity in 1614 and expelled all the

Portuguese. By then, most Christians were practising their faith secretly, as we have seen.

On the afternoon of 24 April 1930, the Polish trio arrived in Naga-saki aboard the SS *Nagasaki* after a twenty-six-hour journey from Shanghai marred by torrential rain and turbulent seas. As the Scottish-built vessel approached Nagasaki Bay, the rain eased, the waters calmed, and the friars admired the lush green leaves on the trees that overlooked the hilly city.

On the left side of the bay, the men glimpsed Kami-no-shima (God's Island) where a large number of Catholics had fled during the persecutions. On the right, the spire of the white Ōura Cath-edral, the oldest Christian church in Japan, shone tall on the hills amid wooden Japanese houses and a handful of European-style homes. 'It is a beautiful place,' Kolbe wrote. 'There are mountains, sea and greenery everywhere.'[7]

More than any other Japanese city, Nagasaki was a meeting place of Eastern and Western cultures. The SS *Nagasaki* docked at Dejima, a tiny man-made island connected to the main port by a forty-foot stone bridge. For more than 200 years, from 1639 to 1854, this artifi-cial island had been Japan's only link with the West.

The Japanese *shōgun* had allowed a handful of Dutch citizens to live on Dejima while the country was closed to foreigners. From this tiny island, Western sciences, medicines and astronomy were introduced to Japan. But the shōgun forbade the Dutch to cross the bridge without permission – upon penalty of death.

After the friars' ship docked, suspicious police probed the Poles about their visit. Japan had become a quasi-police state during the late 1920s and foreigners were immediately suspected of being spies. Brother Zeno later recalled that a Russian-speaking detective asked him why he had brought three cameras – two German and one French – to Japan and whether he'd taken any photos as the ship entered Nagasaki Bay. He hadn't, and eventually the three bearded men, clad in their long Franciscan habits, were allowed into the country.[8]

Unknown to them, the friars had landed at a tumultuous time. Just two days earlier, Japan had signed the London Naval Treaty, limiting the size of the Imperial Japanese Navy's fleet of warships. The treaty had been signed by the five major allies of the First World War – the UK, the US, Japan, France and Italy – in the hope of preventing an arms race by limiting naval construction. But the Japanese military was aghast at the treaty's constraints, and it would soon launch a series of *coups d'état* in a bid to overthrow the elected government.

Surrounded by rickshaw drivers angling for business, the friars threw their battered trunks onto two-wheeled man-powered carriages and asked the men to take them to Ōura Cathedral. But Kolbe didn't like the idea of sitting on a carriage pulled by a human, so the men walked the thirty minutes to the foot of the edifice.

There, a Japanese priest, Father Matsukawa, astonished at the sight of three pasty faces peering out of long black habits, guided them up the steps towards the wooden cathedral. On either side grew bright red azalea flowers. At the top was a ten-foot chalk-white statue of the Virgin Mary.

The friars were already familiar with the statue's history. It had been placed at the entrance of the cathedral in 1867 as a gift from France to commemorate the discovery of hidden Christians after more than two centuries of silence.

The cathedral had been built by a French missionary group called the Paris Foreign Missions Society in 1865. The group had been the first to arrive in Nagasaki after Japan opened its doors to the outside world. Although Christianity was still illegal at the time, the missionaries were allowed to build the cathedral strictly for the city's small community of French-speaking residents and it was dedicated to the twenty-six martyrs who had been crucified in 1597.

Preaching to the Japanese was banned. But on 17 March 1865, a month after its opening, a group of about fifteen Japanese artisans and peasants from the Urakami district of Nagasaki entered the gothic-style church. As the story goes, one of the women, Yuri Isabelina Sugimoto, knelt next to the French priest, Father Bernard

Petitjean, and whispered: 'We have the same feeling in our hearts as you do.'

Stunned, Petitjean reported the incident to the head of the Japanese diocese. After the news reached Rome, Pope Pius IX referred to the event as 'an Oriental miracle'. Until then, the Church had believed that all Japanese Catholics had been wiped out during the persecutions. Soon, hundreds of other hidden Christians from Nagasaki and surrounding towns and islands started visiting the cathedral to announce their faith.[9]

Politically, the timing of the hidden Christians' revelations couldn't have been worse. The samurai-led shogunate was in disarray in the 1860s, and the Meiji government that took over in 1868 continued the ban on Christianity for five more years.

In all, an estimated 60,000 hidden Christians were living in and around Nagasaki in 1873, when Christianity was legalised.[10] Many declared their adherence to the Catholic Church. But a surprising number – perhaps as many as half – kept on practising the quasi-Christian, quasi-Shinto faith they had grown up with. Most underground networks fell apart after the lifting of the ban, but a handful remain in present-day Nagasaki.[11]

The survivors of families who had been exiled from Urakami in 1868 returned home after the ban was lifted, building a small cathedral in 1879 to commemorate their survival. Then, under the supervision of a French priest, they bought a plot of land on a hill in Urakami and began to build a majestic neo-Romanesque brick cathedral with twin bell towers, four miles north of Ōura Cathedral.

Using donations from around the world, including American Catholics, Urakami Cathedral was completed in 1925. Two decades later, this fabled building, the largest Christian structure in the Asia-Pacific region, would be close to the epicentre of the most destructive force ever unleashed by mankind.

Father Kolbe, Zeno and Hilary arrived at their Nagasaki destination two months after leaving Niepokalanów. But to Kolbe's disappoint-

Bishop Hayasaka preaching on the site where twenty-six
Christians were killed; the bespectacled Kolbe is to Hayasaka's right

ment, the head of the Nagasaki diocese, Bishop Kyūnosuke Hayasaka,
was out of town. Bishop Hayasaka had studied in Italy and was the
first Japanese to be ordained a bishop in Rome.

In broken Latin and German, Father Matsukawa and other Japanese priests asked Kolbe: 'Why are you here?' It was as if the Poles
had arrived from another planet. After the bishop returned several
days later, Kolbe immediately asked him for permission to open a
branch of Militia Immaculatae and to publish a magazine. Bishop
Hayasaka was suspicious. He hadn't known that the Poles were
coming, and Kolbe's abrupt requests appeared excessive. But after
learning that Kolbe held doctorates in philosophy and theology, the
bishop changed his mind.

Desperate to find a philosophy teacher for his seminary, Hayasaka allowed the men to stay in Nagasaki in exchange for Kolbe's
lectures. The bishop also agreed that the friars could publish their
magazine in Japanese as a supplement to the Catholic newspaper in
Nagasaki, and he allowed the Poles to remain in his luxurious residence until they could find their own lodgings.

The restless and relentless Kolbe dived straight into his work. Three
times a week, he drilled his Japanese seminary students in Latin
using a philosophy textbook that came directly from Rome. Kolbe

Father Kolbe and his very first philosophy students in Nagasaki in 1930

was an enthusiastic teacher, and his students fondly remembered his words of encouragement –'*bene, bene*' (good, good) – because Japanese professors rarely praised their students. But the pupils found it difficult to understand lectures in Latin, a virtually unknown language in Japan at the time.

After classes, meanwhile, Kolbe began writing articles in Polish, Italian, French and Latin for the proposed Japanese-language *Knight of the Immaculata* magazine, which was called *Seibo-no-Kishi*. In Japanese, *seibo* means Holy Mother and *kishi* means knight. On 24 May, exactly one month after the friars arrived in Nagasaki, 10,000 copies of the first sixteen-page edition rolled off the presses.

The purpose of the magazine, Kolbe wrote, was to lead people towards God through the love and trust of the Virgin Mary. 'She is the path to Christ and the bridge between this world and heaven.'

Later that day, Kolbe sent a telegram to Niepokalanów that said simply: 'Today we published *Seibo-no-Kishi* (*Knight of the Immaculata*) magazine. Glory to the Immaculata!'[12] It was an extraordinary achievement for the Poles. But its publication would have been impossible without help from the highly educated Japanese clerics at Ōura Cathedral. After their initial hesitancy, the Japanese threw themselves into the task of translating Kolbe's articles into simple but beautifully poetic Japanese. And at the clergy's request, a local print shop published the magazine in record time at a discount.

The following day, a Sunday, the friars wandered around the Ōura district after Mass carrying bundles of newspapers with the MI magazine supplements inside. Every time they sold a copy to curious passers-by, or gave one away for free, they asked for a *meishi* or business card. It is customary in Japan for people to carry a card with their name and address on it. The Poles used these to post the next issue to them.

Bearded Polish friars in flowing black habits couldn't help but attract people's curiosity, and the magazine sold quickly. The innately charming Zeno, whose whiskers were a colourful red, was especially skilful in selling the publication. 'Distributed 267 copies by 11 a.m.,' Zeno wrote in his diary on 25 May.[13] A month later, the men published a second magazine.

Kolbe still wasn't satisfied. As in Niepokalanów, he wanted the friars to control the overall printing process. One weekend in May, Kolbe travelled with a French clergyman to Japan's second-largest city, Osaka, and bought an ancient manual printing press and 145,000 metal *kanji*, *hiragana* and *katakana* characters necessary for typesetting the Japanese publication.

Meanwhile, Brothers Zeno and Hilary began studying Japanese with an elderly priest in the hope that they could typeset the magazine, and the resourceful Zeno scoured the neighbourhood for a home for the friars to rent. He found a large two-storey Western-style wooden house near Ōura Cathedral. It was one of four residences built on land originally owned by an Englishman.

Just as in Grodno eight years earlier, publishing the magazine was Kolbe's priority. Inside the house, the men placed the printing press in the middle of the ground floor. They surrounded it with row upon row of the kanji characters so that the typesetters could easily pick them out. The entire ground floor became the office and workspace for the publishing operation.

The friars moved their six trunks of books, religious artefacts and a scant few possessions upstairs and laid charcoal sacks on the floor to sleep on. Zeno made a dinner table and chairs from the wooden boxes that had contained the printing press. There was no kitchen, so the men cooked in the garden, rain or shine, using an enamelled pan on a charcoal brazier to boil vegetables.

The Poles lived, as always, in poverty. The $100 that Father Orlini had given them in Rome had disappeared completely after paying the rent and printing costs. Often, the trio ate small pieces of bread and a banana for dinner, or they made a meagre rice or wheat soup. There was no money for milk or potatoes, still less for meat.

Zeno combed Nagasaki looking for discounts on printing supplies and food. He usually came back with a smile and a few bags of loot. After all, no shop owner could resist helping out a red-bearded, blue-eyed, black-habitted brother whose appalling Japanese accent and limited vocabulary made him such an endearing character.

The friars quickly became famous in the Ōura area. Local Japanese peeped through their open windows at the sweatshop inside. The men always seemed to be working, either writing on a makeshift table or cranking the printer by hand well into the night.

On the streets, little children asked to stroke the friars' whiskers or tugged at the cords around their waists, knotted three times to signify poverty, chastity and obedience.

The Japanese, themselves a stoic and hard-working people, appreciated the Polish men's work ethic, eager attitude and willingness to learn Japanese. And the clergy from Ōura Cathedral continued to guide and assist them. The chief priest, Father Umeki, visited every day to help with typesetting, translation, editing and anything else needed to publish the magazine.[14]

'We were all stunned at what they were trying to do and very sceptical at the beginning because none of them knew any Japanese,' Father Umeki recalled. 'But since their determination [to keep publishing] was clear and unchanging, we offered help. And not just us. They asked everybody – Catholic lay people, Protestants, non-Christians, even Buddhist monks – for help with the translations.'[15]

Kolbe quickly recognised that he would never become fluent in Japanese. 'The Japanese language is difficult for me,' he wrote in one letter. 'When I finally get around to study, my head aches, I'm stressed and fever makes me feel like a washcloth!'[16]

In mid-June 1930, after just two months in Nagasaki, Kolbe's order summoned him back to Poland to attend a provincial chapter meeting in Lviv. He first sailed to Shanghai, where he told the two friars from Niepokalanów to join him in Nagasaki because MI had failed to make any progress in China. The friars arrived in Japan the following month and used their budding knowledge of Chinese kanji characters to help typeset the magazine.

After two more weeks of travel on trains across Siberia and Russia, Kolbe eventually arrived in Lviv for meetings with his fellow Franciscans. But far from congratulating him for his achievements in Japan, Kolbe was harshly criticised. The clerics recognised the success of the Niepokalanów community and of the Polish magazine, whose circulation had topped 300,000 copies a month. But they labelled his operation in Japan 'unrealistic' and a likely drain on their finances.

Kolbe, some critics complained, was a 'Franciscan Don Quixote', like the impractical romantic hero of Miguel de Cervantes' satirical novel.[17] To contain the carping, the father provincial, Kornel Czupryk, decided that any financial help for the Far East mission would come from Niepokalanów, and not from his provincial coffers.

Not all the friars were so disparaging. Realising that converting Japanese to Christianity wouldn't happen as quickly as he had anticipated, Kolbe decided to take two young men back to Japan. He hoped they would commit themselves to the country for several years. One was Mieczysław Mirochna, who would go on to become the head of the friary in Nagasaki and remain in Japan for the rest of his life. The other newcomer, Damian Eberl, had a nervous breakdown in Japan and returned to Poland after a year.

With the additions of the Shanghai and Niepokalanów friars and the arrival of a seventeen-year-old Japanese apprentice friar, eight men lived in the Ōura house by the end of 1930. That was just enough manpower to publish the magazine as long as no one became sick. As time went on, the men also attracted dozens of

Japanese sympathisers to help translate, print and distribute the publication.

The friars had no heat, no beds, and the roof leaked. But the owner of a prestigious family-owned drugstore, Hōjirō Kosone, provided Kolbe with free medicine for his tuberculosis. And a Japanese man called Kōya Takita, who understood German, lived with the men for several months to help them adjust to Japanese customs.[18]

Kosone and Takita weren't Catholic or even Christian. Rather, they were members of a transcendental group called Ittō-en, or 'the Garden of Light'. The movement had been founded by a Japanese philosopher, Tenkō Nishida, in 1904 after he read Leo Tolstoy's *My Religion*. Nishida, who was often referred to as the St Francis or Mahatma Gandhi of Japan, preached that God, Buddha and Nature provided life's necessities and that conflict arose from the competition for survival.[19]

Takashi Nishida, Tenkō's grandson and the present head of Ittō-en, told me that Kōya Takita met many descendants of the hidden Christians while he was distributing the Franciscan magazine in remote areas of Nagasaki prefecture. Takita later became a renowned professor specialising in research of these secretive families.

Ittō-en incorporated 'the essence of various religions', and Nishida's followers included people with different beliefs. All gave up their possessions, like the Franciscans. The group's motto was: 'In having nothing lies inexhaustible wealth.'

In pre-war Japan, Ittō-en became influential among intellectuals as an alternative to the increasingly militaristic state. After Nishida's book, *Zange no Seikatsu* (A Life of Penitence), became a bestseller in the 1920s, the movement gained tens of thousands of followers. The most dedicated lived in a commune in the hills east of the ancient capital city of Kyoto. From there, many followers visited private homes and public sites to clean toilets in a ritual called *takuhatsu* (offering services in repentance).

In July 1930, while Kolbe was in Poland, Nishida visited the Polish men's rented house in Ōura three times. He later wrote for Ittō-en's magazine about the visit.

They [Brothers Zeno and Hilary] both had bare feet and neither spoke Japanese . . . I have rarely seen faces as benevolent . . . They were jubilant for an inexplicable reason . . .

They have come from thousands of miles away to a place where they do not even understand the language. They are just entirely devoted to the Virgin Mary and their expressions do not show any anxieties. They are absolutely untouched by the filth of the world. I thought I would do anything to help them.

After returning from Poland, Kolbe travelled to Kyoto to meet Nishida, who, at fifty-eight, was twenty-two years older than the founder of MI. The men chatted long into the evening about their respective faiths.

'I feel an intimacy with you because we seem to have a lot in common,' Nishida told Kolbe. The encounter was exceptionally polite and friendly and yet a deep gap separated the men. 'Father Kolbe continually repeated that the Catholic faith was the only true faith, and he could not understand Nishida's more inclusive philosophy,' said Saburō Ōba, a German-speaking resident at Ittō-en who acted as a translator at the meeting.[20]

Indeed, for Kolbe, all other religions, philosophies and ways of life apart from Catholicism were built on sand. This was the norm at the time and reflected the dogma of the First Vatican Council of 1869–70, also known as Vatican I. (The Second Vatican Council of 1962–5, or Vatican II, was the Catholic Church's attempt to modernise, adapt and cooperate with other faiths.) 'I was given a very warm welcome,' Kolbe wrote later. 'But we disagreed on one particular issue. I obstinately maintained that there cannot be more than one true religion.'

At that time, in October 1930, Kolbe had spent little more than three months in Japan, and he was still single-mindedly trying to convert everyone he met to 'this one truth'. 'The contrast between Father Kolbe's uncompromising posture and the more relaxed attitude of Tenkō Nishida showed the fundamental difference between the West and East,' Ōba said.

Kolbe, according to Nishida's grandson, tried hard to persuade his grandfather to convert to Catholicism, but Nishida gently rejected the approach, saying: 'I already hold the same God as yours within me.'

Nishida and Kolbe remained friends and exchanged their magazines every month. Indeed, when he left Japan in 1936, Kolbe sent Nishida the statue of the Virgin Mary that he had kept in his room in Nagasaki. Tenkō displayed it in his bedroom and later exhibited it in Ittō-en's museum.[21]

On Sunday, 7 December 1930, Kolbe received a devastating telegram from Poland. His thirty-four-year-old younger brother, Alfons, who headed Niepokalanów and was editor of the magazine, had died unexpectedly on 3 December from a ruptured appendix.

At the time, Kolbe was often so tired, hungry, cold and stricken with violent headaches, fevers and abscesses that he could barely get out of bed. And yet, just two days after learning of his brother's death, Kolbe wrote a detailed eight-page letter to Alfons' successor, Father Florian Koziura, outlining his single-minded goal for MI – 'the conquest of the world for the Immaculata'. He also stressed that Niepokalanów was unique and should always remain separate from other religious institutions in Poland. 'I know that there are priests anxious to see all differentiation eliminated. May God prevent this attempt!'[22]

Concerned that Niepokalanów might fail and that its inhabitants weren't sufficiently dedicated to the cause, Kolbe wrote letter after letter to Father Florian and to his superior, Father Provincial Kornel Czupryk. 'Whoever does not love the Immaculata should leave Niepokalanów,' he wrote. 'I'm convinced that strict leadership is preferred to misguided mildness in forgiveness. Poor discipline may cause the friars . . . to follow their own inclinations.'[23] 'I criticise too much, don't I?' he wrote in another letter. 'But how can I help it? When I die, I'll stop criticising.'[24]

Kolbe desperately needed more help to publish the magazine in Japan, but he didn't want to sugar-coat the challenges that the Polish friars faced. Three days after learning of his brother's death, Kolbe wrote a blunt letter to a priest in Niepokalanów, Father Metody Rejentowicz, who was keen to join him in Japan.

> The task here is quite simple: to work yourself beyond belief only to be regarded by your own as an idiot. Struggle? Yes, [we] struggle to conquer the world, to win the hearts of each individual, beginning with our own. Our strength and power live in the recognition of our own stupidity [and] weakness.
>
> We must strive beyond the limits which nature prescribes. Come here to us and die of hunger, exhaustion, mortification and suffering – for the Immaculata.[25]

Father Metody was far from discouraged. He arrived in Nagasaki with another friar and two seminary students in March 1931 just as Kolbe was beginning the next stage of his global plan. Kolbe ordered his brother's successor in Niepokalanów to 'make an effort to publish the magazine in other languages, especially in English, French and Spanish', as a way to build circulation and obtain hard currency. He also demanded that friaries be built in Arabia, China, India, Syria and Vietnam.[26]

As a first step, Kolbe decided to build a Niepokalanów-like friary in Nagasaki and to expand the publishing operation. His goal was to spread the word about his mission from the south of Japan's Kyushu island to the tip of Hokkaido, its northernmost main island, as well as to its colonies of Korea and Taiwan. It was a project that would prove far more difficult and eventful than anyone could have imagined.

6. Fashioned by Fire

March 1931 – Nanae, Hokkaido

O n Tuesday, 10 March 1931, while Father Maximilian Maria Kolbe was developing his global plan in Nagasaki, a farmer's wife gave birth to her second son in Hokkaido, an island about the size of Austria in the north of the crescent-shaped Japanese archipelago.

Masatoshi Asari's delivery in Nanae, a village in southern Hokkaido, was uneventful. But the circumstances leading up to his birth were anything but. The previous year, Chie Asari and her husband, Asakichi, subsistence farmers who grew rice and vegetables, had lost virtually everything they owned in a fire.

On the evening of the blaze, Chie was alone at home with her three-year-old son, Shōichi, and her mother-in-law. Ironically, Asakichi was drinking sake, a popular rice wine, at a party with the village's firemen on a rare night out. Shortly after going to bed, Chie heard the crackle of burning wood outside their home. She watched helplessly as a driving wind whipped up the flames and devoured the couple's warehouse. It contained a year's rice crop and a barn filled with agricultural equipment and two horses. Both animals perished.

'Everything about that night is still vivid in my memory,' Chie told Masatoshi seven decades later, shortly before she passed away in 2002. 'I'll never forget it, even after I die.'

Chie remembered how Asakichi and the firemen arrived too late to douse the fire and how the couple had to start their lives from scratch. 'We were in debt for a long, long time and had so many mouths to feed,' she recalled. Chie bore four more sons and a daughter after Masatoshi. One son died in infancy.

The hardships that Asakichi and Chie suffered after the fire laid the basis for their attitude towards life, which greatly influenced their offspring. 'The appalling experience of the fire made my mother even more compassionate,' Masatoshi Asari told me. 'As a Buddhist, she repeatedly talked about Buddhist principles to me and my siblings. She'd say: Be content with what you have, even if it's nothing. Appreciate what you're given. Give back to the community. Don't discriminate against anybody. Above all, remember that trust is the most important thing in life. Be honest.' They were words that Asari took to heart.

Japan was in a chaotic state in the years after Masatoshi Asari's birth. The global Great Depression of 1929 had hit the economy hard, wiping out millions of jobs and ramping up political tensions. In Hokkaido, tens of thousands of farmers suffered crop failure in 1931 because the winter was even colder than normal.

The Japanese military was also increasingly influential and was gaining the support of citizens frustrated with the government's inaction. The military top brass were particularly upset at the government for having signed the treaty limiting the size of the naval fleet.

Two attempted military *coups d'état* against the government failed in 1931, but they paved the way for further belligerence.[1] The event that had most bearing on Japan's future and on the public acceptance of militarism was the Manchurian Incident in September 1931. But other occurrences hardened the disdain of the Japanese military and the public towards their colonial subjects in Korea and China. The enmity was mutual.[2]

Japan's militarisation took another step on 15 May 1932, when young naval officers assassinated the prime minister, Tsuyoshi Inukai, in an attempted coup that had originally included killing the film star Charlie Chaplin, who was visiting Tokyo. Chaplin was watching sumo wrestling with the prime minister's son when Inukai was shot. A former naval admiral took over the premiership, putting an end to party-based government. Heavily criticised around the world for its expansion into China, Japan withdrew from the League of Nations in 1933.

Destitute and despondent after the fire, Asakichi Asari needed to find a way to make money quickly. Land-rich but cash-poor, the

Asaris had a twenty-acre garden around their house, brimming with fruit trees, pines and maples and an array of flowers, from primroses and violets to pansies and tiger lilies.[3]

Taking pride of place was an eighteen-foot 'Kanzan' cherry tree, which bore deep-pink double blossoms in late May. The distinctive tree was so rare in Hokkaido at the time that villagers would gather to stare at the somewhat gaudy blossoms. Elsewhere in the garden were about ten other sakura trees, including wild mountain cherries and an ancient cultivar called 'Taizan Fukun'.[4]

Shortly after Masatoshi's birth, Asakichi started growing *hōzuki* fruits, also known as Japanese lantern plants. These had been popular in Japan for hundreds of years, but not for eating. Children played with hōzuki by removing the fruit from inside the bell-shaped sac and then blowing into it like a tiny balloon. The Japanese also placed hōzuki in their family altar during the Buddhist Obon festival each August. They believed that the bright orange colour of the paper-thin sac directed the spirits of their ancestors to return home for a few days.

Asakichi cultivated the tart-tasting hōzuki berries for sale as edible fruits and they soon became extremely popular in Nanae village. A perfectionist, Asakichi sold only the best fruits to the villagers and always added extra hōzuki to every order, his son remembered.

As Japan's militaristic ambitions in Asia grew in the 1930s, the government placed restrictions on fruit production such as apples and pears, ordering farmers to focus on producing staples such as rice and wheat instead. With other fruit in short supply, Asakichi's hōzuki crop became renowned throughout Hokkaido, and merchants would arrive at the family farm day and night in the summer asking for 'Asari's hōzuki'. While Asakichi bartered, Chie cooked rice and corn dishes for the visitors.

Asakichi also sold the fruit at a market in the nearby port of Hakodate. 'We loaded the hōzuki on a horse-drawn cart and I'd help my father select the best fruits,' Masatoshi told me. 'On weekends, we'd be up at 3 a.m. to ride on the cart to the market.'

The hōzuki business saved the Asaris. They sold enough fruit each summer to feed their children and pay off their debts. 'Dad had a

perfectionist work ethic,' Masatoshi recalled. 'For him, winning people's trust was paramount. It was much more important than money.'

It wasn't always easy. Asakichi was a disciplinarian with his children. Masatoshi was stubborn and competitive compared with his
elder brother, Shōichi, and often got into trouble. When Masatoshi
was about six, he refused to wear one of Shōichi's hand-me-down
coats in the dead of winter. His infuriated father threw him into a
freezing river in front of their house and left him to struggle out of
the water.

Asakichi's stoicism and diligence stemmed from his family's history as pioneer farmers in Hokkaido. The Asaris' ancestors had
moved there from the northernmost part of Honshu, Japan's main
island, during the early 1860s. At that time, Hokkaido was, as it had
been for several hundred years, largely an uncultivated island called
Ezo, with numerous active volcanoes and huge primeval forests.

Hokkaido was populated by an indigenous people, the Ainu, who
lived by fishing and hunting. When Japan opened to the outside world
and signed treaties with Western countries in 1858, the windswept
port of Hakodate in the south of Hokkaido became one of five open
ports where the Tokugawa shogunate allowed trade with foreigners.

Around the same time, the shogunate decided to develop the
island. It encouraged immigration from Honshu by offering subsi-
dies to farmers. Among them were the impoverished Asaris, who
settled in the marshy Nanae area, where the family still lives. While
many fellow farmers were unable to cope with the hardships and
returned to Honshu, the Asari family persevered, turning the
marshes into rice paddies and potato fields.

Having settled, the Asaris became leaders in Nanae village and
convinced the government that education was the best way to pull
the area out of poverty. In the late nineteenth century, the family
gave up part of their land to build a village primary school, and they
sent their children to middle and high schools whenever possible.

Asakichi inherited the family's thirst for knowledge. He always
visited the local school on Parents' Day to observe the lessons, no
matter how busy he was on his farm. Three of his sons, including
Masatoshi, would go on to become teachers. Understandably,

Asakichi was particularly strict with his children about lighting fires. None of the children ever smoked and they rarely drank alcohol.

Asari's mother had a different influence on her son. Chie's family had moved to Nanae village to become farmers after the herring trade had declined in the port of Esashi on Hokkaido's western seaboard because of overfishing. After a couple of years of primary school education, Chie helped look after her extended family's young children. She married Asakichi at the age of eighteen after being introduced to him by an acquaintance.

Chie loved flowers and plants. Within the large garden, she allocated each child a plot in which to plant something they liked. 'I don't have any money to take you to fancy places, but I want you to love all living things, like flowers,' Masatoshi remembered her telling him. Masatoshi and his siblings planted the seeds of cornflowers, primroses, daffodils and other flowers, depending on the time of year.

Later in life, Chie was well known in the region for the tulips and other flowers she grew to plant in Hakodate's parks and shrines.

In July 1937, when Masatoshi Asari was six years old, a battle between Japanese and Chinese troops near Beijing, known as the Marco Polo Bridge Incident, escalated into the full invasion of China and the Second Sino-Japanese War. The dispute began after a Japanese soldier failed to return to his post after a military exercise, and China refused to allow his unit to search for him in a town called Wanping. It's unclear exactly what happened next but gunshots were heard and Japan subsequently began shelling the town. Many historians now view this incident as the beginning of the Second World War in the Asia-Pacific region.[5]

One after another, the young men in Nanae village were drafted to join the armed forces. After leaving Hokkaido for training, they were usually sent to Manchukuo or China. The conscripts included Masatoshi Asari's uncles, Takeo and Heizo.

'We went to Hakodate port with my grandma to see off my

Village funeral of a soldier from Nanae killed in China in 1940

uncles,' Asari recalled. 'I waved a Japanese flag, as did most other people, and the adults all sang a popular wartime song together: "How can I return without bringing great success, since I have left home pledging victory". Then everyone shouted, "Long live the emperor!" before we all cried for those who were on the ships.'[6]

After the vessel departed, Asari remembers, an elderly man turned to him and said proudly: 'Finally, we're going to become a powerful nation. You and your friends will all fight for Japan as children of the emperor.'

Asari remembers being startled and scared rather than elated at the old man's comments. 'Others were joyful when Japan was put on a wartime footing,' he reminisced years later. 'But to me, it felt like the country was disappearing into a dark tunnel.'

Twelve hundred miles to the south of Hokkaido, on the overgrown slopes of a mountain overlooking the city of Nagasaki, the Polish friars led by Father Maximilian Kolbe were themselves struggling against this patriotic tide. As Japan strategised and militarised, the men's sole goal was to 'Christianise' the country as quickly as possible.

7. The Struggle

May 1931 – Nagasaki

Ayear after arriving in Japan, an exhausted Father Maximilian Kolbe and six equally weary fellow friars from Poland spent their days and nights churning out Japanese-language magazines inside a stark wooden house near Ōura Cathedral in Nagasaki.

On the surface, Kolbe had succeeded spectacularly. He'd started a magazine in a new country and in a new language to spread the word about the Militia Immaculatae organisation that he had founded in Italy fourteen years earlier. Circulation of the *Seibo-no-Kishi* magazine had grown from 10,000 copies a month in May 1930 to 25,000 copies that December.

But within Japan's small and closely-knit Catholic community, the Polish men were often seen as black-habitted interlopers whose magazine, which was often given away for free, was hurting their own publications. The friars' visibility and popularity rankled.

Brother Zeno was an exceptional salesman. He once travelled by train to Tokyo carrying 10,000 copies of the magazine, which he distributed throughout the Japanese capital. Yet Catholics in Tokyo criticised Zeno for the way he implored strangers to read the magazine, saying that it gave the incorrect impression that Christians were mere beggars.

In Nagasaki itself, some priests complained that the itinerant Polish friars were undesirables who didn't deserve to be helped any more. This jealousy prompted Kolbe to ask Zeno, his go-to man, to search for a permanent headquarters for MI and its publishing operation. Zeno found this in the most inhospitable of places.

At the base of the 1,316-foot-high Mount Hikosan, a six-acre plot, about the size of three football fields, was for sale in a place called Ōkouchi. About two-and-a-half miles east of the city centre, the

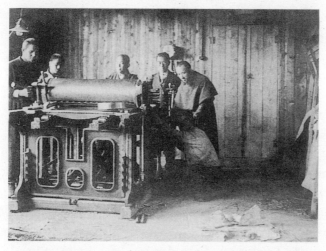

Setting up the press with the help of Japanese clergy in Nagasaki

rock-strewn land, adjacent to a cemetery on a steep hill, was bleak and unwelcoming. The carcasses of rotting cows, horses and dogs lay amid discarded rubbish. Surrounding this fetid dump and stretching up the mountain was a mass of wild bamboo.

The land had two redeeming features – it was dirt cheap, and the sixteen landowners were happy to sell because Japan was in a severe depression. Kolbe agreed to buy the land in five instalments, but he only had cash to pay the first. 'If the Virgin Mary thinks this is a good idea, she will send us money somehow,' Kolbe said.[1] It's unclear how or when the money was raised.

In breaks between publishing the magazine, the friars slashed the bamboo and weeds, flattened part of the land and removed the dead animals. They pulled endless carts of cheap timber and other building materials up the unforgiving slopes.

It was a backbreaking achievement. Working with local carpenters, the Poles built a basic wooden hut. Inside, they fashioned a tiny makeshift chapel, a printing room and a low attic where the men slept on straw mats. Outside, Kolbe placed a statue of the Virgin Mary, made in Poland out of plaster of Paris.

Kolbe slept in a corner of the printing room on the ground floor because he was too weak to climb the stairs. The friars cooked outside under a sheet-metal umbrella. They proudly called their new home Mugenzai no Sono, the Garden of the Immaculate.

It was one of the first Christian monasteries built by foreigners in Japan. Another had been constructed in 1896 by nine Trappist monks from the Cistercians of the Strict Observance on a hill eleven miles west of Hakodate in Hokkaido. It is known today as the Tōbetsu Trappist Monastery. The Trappists in Hokkaido and the Franciscans in Nagasaki both belonged to Catholic religious orders and both venerated the Virgin Mary. But there were stark differences between their lifestyles. The so-called 'Silent Monks of Hokkaido' removed themselves from civilisation to get closer to God, while the Polish friars were city-dwellers used to the cranking of the printing presses and the clangs of the metropolis.[2]

The first night in Mugenzai-no-Sono – 31 May 1931 – was a disaster. The warm and muggy weather attracted a scourge of mosquitoes from the bushes outside, which flew in through the open windows. The friars had no money to buy glass.

The following day, a Catholic butcher, Mr Uraoka, visited the men, their skin swollen with bites. 'You can't sleep without a mosquito net in Nagasaki. Don't you have mosquitoes in Poland?' he asked. 'Yes, but Polish mosquitoes aren't aggressive,' Zeno replied. Mr Uraoka bought nets for the Poles but even these couldn't prevent centipedes, longhorn beetles and other bugs from disturbing their sleep.

In letters to the head of the Niepokalanów community in Poland, Kolbe constantly begged for money and hinted at the men's travails. 'We are cranking the printing presses manually because we don't have any money for electricity,' said one letter. 'We don't have any water pipes and it's a long walk to a communal area to get clean water,' said another. 'The summer in Nagasaki is extremely hot and humid, and some women in the communal area go topless, which embarrasses us.'

Kolbe, meanwhile, pushed the friars ever harder, following some of the draconian principles he had learned as a youth in Lviv from Father Dionysius, the novice master. Father Dionysius had influenced Maximilian in many ways and required that the students under his control obey strict rules. This included having their hair close-clipped to overcome vanity.

Work and prayer came first – there was no time for recreation. Rules were sacrosanct. For example, Kolbe refused to allow the friars to remove their thick Franciscan habits even during the stifling summer. White salt accumulated on the men's ankles when their sweat dried, and their fingers bled from folding thousands of pieces of paper by hand.

That winter, the friars awoke to find their thin blankets covered with snow that had come in through the attic roof. There was no heater. But whenever someone complained, Kolbe would make a cup of hot tea and say: 'Warm yourself from within.'

The austere lifestyle came at a price. Brother Mieczysław Mirochna, the friar whom Kolbe had brought from Poland in 1930, became seriously ill that winter, vomiting and suffering from acute abdominal pains linked to appendicitis. It was a similar illness to that which killed Kolbe's brother, Alfons. After an operation, Mirochna was in so much pain and looking so ill that Kolbe fainted. Only after months in hospital did Mirochna recover.[3]

Kolbe was sympathetic towards anyone who became ill, and he would often stay at a sick friar's bedside overnight. 'The sick are a treasure of the friary,' he would say. 'Suffering is love.' At the same time, those who were suffering often blamed Kolbe's inflexible character for their condition.

Brother Hilary Lysakowski, one of the first four friars to travel with Kolbe to the Far East in 1930, developed night blindness from malnutrition, and Kolbe complained of his 'strange, unpredictable moods'. Brother Zygmunt Król, another of the original four, became disillusioned with Kolbe's intransigence. Kolbe, in turn, complained that Zygmunt disobeyed instructions and greatly annoyed him.[4] Both left for Poland by August 1931.

Kolbe also suffered. He had constant high fevers and headaches from his tuberculosis and often spat blood. He developed boils in his neck, back, belly, arms and legs, which a doctor had to lance.

'When I first saw Father Kolbe, he had had a forty-degree fever the day before, but he was already back working,' one doctor,

Yasurō Fukabori, recalled. 'I told him to do nothing for at least three or four days, preferably a week, but he said he might die at any time and therefore he needed to work while he could.'[5]

New friars from Poland replaced their brethren, eager to experience Japan and unwilling to believe that conditions could be so extreme. They soon became disenchanted. Father Metody, who had arrived with three others in the spring of 1931, was stunned to witness the friars' austere circumstances and Kolbe's refusal to listen to his pleas for more humane working and living conditions.

Metody's patience ran out when Kolbe forbade him from shaving. 'Men with beards are respected in Japan,' Kolbe told him. 'I warned you before you came that you must be prepared to make every sacrifice.'[6]

In a letter to his superior in Poland about Metody's attitude, Kolbe was scathing. '[He] demonstrates no attraction for poverty. He admits he's not happy here, that he feels out of place and that the endless work brings neither joy nor contentment. He doesn't learn well. He has no ambition to learn the language. Hope for improvement is very doubtful.'

It wasn't that Kolbe was unkind or uncaring towards his brethren. Quite the opposite. His high expectations and determination to succeed were simply far beyond those of any other person that his colleagues had met. He was unrealistic, expecting his followers to suffer in the same way that he suffered. And he worried that any easing of discipline could be detrimental to his goal of spreading his form of Christianity globally.

The rules, Kolbe explained to the friars in May 1932, were simple: 'In case of a disagreement, express your reservations. But if the superior doesn't change his mind, accept his judgement. No friary can succeed if it falls into anarchy. Someone must ultimately decide. Obedience confirms faith. Disobedience demonstrates unbelief. The shortest path to Heaven is that of obedience.'[7]

Metody disagreed and departed for Poland after just six months in Japan. A theological student who had arrived with Metody quit the following spring.

Despite the rebellion, Kolbe declined to change his ways, leaving

Brother Zeno to mop up his messes and to keep the publishing operation growing. In December 1931, Zeno bought a more efficient printing machine in Osaka so that the men could publish their biggest magazine so far – 40,000 copies of a thirty-two-page journal.

Yet while readership rose, few non-Christians showed any interest in converting to Kolbe's Militia Immaculatae spirituality. The Ōkouchi district of Nagasaki where Mugenzai-no-Sono was located was a non-Christian area, unlike the central Urakami neighbourhood where most Catholics lived.

The Japanese who lived in this district were curious about the Poles and what they were producing. But this didn't translate into spiritual rebirth to a foreign religion.[8] The eye-catching friars, dubbed *gyōja-san* (Mr Ascetics) by Nagasaki residents, were perceived as odd-bods from another world who didn't understand anything about the Japanese culture. By now, Kolbe recognised that his missionaries wouldn't succeed unless they were fluent in the Japanese language.[9]

'From a distance, the monastery looks like a country elementary school. But up close it resembles a chicken coop,' a reporter from a Nagasaki newspaper wrote in a series of stories in May 1932. One article was headlined: 'A hilltop wonder: Giving up all five human desires.' This referred to the Buddhist belief that humans have five categories of desires – wealth, sex, food, fame and sleep.

The article began:

> In a shabby barracks, twelve friars follow unrelenting rules like the autumn frost. They spend their days in labour, when everyone else in the world is enjoying the pleasures of spring.
>
> Don't the friars ever get tormented because of natural sexual desires? No, the friars say. They say their minds are so filled with God, self-negating prayers and gratitude that they have no time to accommodate secular desires.[10]

Even Kolbe began to question whether he could transform Japan into a nation of believers. For him, non-Christians, whether Japanese or not, were all 'pagans' who needed to be educated about 'the only true' religion – Christianity. 'There are many devils [obstacles] in Japan,' Kolbe wrote. 'If there is one devil in Niepokalanów, there are ten here.'[11]

Kolbe was unable at first to accept that different cultures had their own unique belief systems that reflected the natural wishes and ways of life of the indigenous people. But after months of trying to communicate with Nagasaki residents, he started to understand that it wasn't easy for people to give up the Buddhist and Shinto religious practices that had coexisted in Japan for generations.

On one occasion, while talking to a Buddhist monk, Kolbe was surprised to hear that Buddhists believed in the 'transmigration of souls' or the never-ending cycle of reincarnation. He confessed naively that 'among other things, I came to know that, according to Buddhist belief, the deceased return to the world to help men. Then they die again, and again they return.'[12]

What Kolbe also didn't realise was that Japan's modern leaders had been trying to implant a new ideological 'religion' throughout the nation since the late nineteenth century. The emperor sat at the top of this system as a divine figure and the Japanese people were his 'children'.

Traditionally, the Japanese practice of ancestor worship focused only on one's family. But in the new religion, later known as State Shintoism, people were told to glorify the emperor and the imperial family above their own ancestors, even though they knew little about these shadowy figures. Japan's creation myth held that the first emperor, Jinmu, was descended from the sun goddess Amaterasu and that there had been no break in the bloodline for more than 2,500 years.

This new belief system stemmed from a desire of political leaders to create a modern state as quickly as possible. The government's drive to implant State Shintoism intensified after the Manchurian Incident of 1931 and was the core ideology that promoted Japanese fascism and militarism. During the 1930s, most Japanese children were taught that the nation itself was 'divine' and was destined to rule the Asia-Pacific region.

It wasn't long before Kolbe recognised the power of State

Shintoism and realised why Catholicism was failing to gain ground in Japan. 'Shinto is a national religion and consists in the cult of ancestors and illustrious figures, particularly of the imperial family,' he wrote. 'Every Japanese who refuses to practise this type of cult would be considered unpatriotic and even a citizen suspected of doing harm to the fatherland.'

He concluded: 'The obstacles [to Christianity in Japan] are various prejudices, in particular the false idea that the Catholic religion tends to weaken the patriotic spirit.'[13]

In May 1932, after months cutting down trees on the slopes of Mount Hikosan above the monastery, Kolbe opened a replica of Lourdes, the pilgrimage site in southern France where a statue of the Virgin Mary sits in a cave. Catholics believe that the Virgin Mary appeared there and that the water from a nearby spring cures many illnesses.

The Polish friars carved a grotto into the steep cliffs near a stream and placed a statue of the Virgin there. Local vandals destroyed the figure at least three times in the following three years. But Nagasaki's 'Lourdes' became Kolbe's favourite spot. Steadied by a cane to avoid falling, he visited the serene grotto daily to contemplate the next chapters of his mission.

Alone at night, Kolbe often opened a 1924 world atlas that he had brought from Poland and looked for places where he might continue his task. Most intriguing was India. As we have seen, Kolbe had read widely about Father Francis Xavier, who had arrived in Goa, then the capital of Portuguese India, in 1542 and spent several years as a missionary there before travelling on to the Malay peninsula, Indonesia and Japan.

The obstacles to success in India were enormous. Kolbe was ill. Travel to and around the subcontinent was difficult, and Kolbe knew little about Indian religions, the country's diverse culture, or Gandhi's current civil disobedience campaigns against the British colonial occupiers. But Kolbe told his superior in Poland that he was 'restless' and wanted to set up a new Niepokalanów in India.

Despite – or perhaps because of – his problems in Japan, Kolbe was eager for a new challenge, and the Franciscan order in Poland approved his trip after four new friars arrived in Japan from Poland in mid-May 1932.

The quartet replaced the men who had left because of illness or disillusion. Kolbe placed one of the newcomers, a twenty-seven-year-old priest, Father Konstanty Onoszko, in charge of the institution during his absence. It was a decision he would bitterly regret.[14]

On 31 May 1932, after two years in Japan, Kolbe boarded the SS *Africa Maru* in Kobe for a trans-equatorial voyage via Hong Kong, Singapore and Colombo in Ceylon (now Sri Lanka) to Ernakulum, now known as Kochi, a coastal town in southwest India. 'I am travelling to India to establish a new Niepokalanów,' he wrote to his mother from the ship.[15]

It soon became apparent that establishing an Indian foothold would be as difficult, if not more so, than his earlier bid to spread MI in China. There were no qualified Franciscan missionaries in Poland or Japan to send to India. Furthermore, there was no money because the Polish government had strict export controls on its currency.[16]

Kolbe was also increasingly frail. 'I'm neither strong nor healthy,' he wrote to the father provincial in Poland. 'For brief periods I can't get my breath and am overcome with weakness. My head also gives me trouble after intense intellectual activity.'[17]

After only a few days in India, during which he met the region's Spanish Carmelite archbishop, Kolbe returned to Japan. And although he retained high hopes of setting up a Franciscan outpost there, other events intervened that made his plans impossible.

When Kolbe arrived back in Nagasaki in the summer of 1932, the tension in the friary was palpable. Father Konstanty, whom Kolbe had left in charge, had told the men to pray more to Jesus than to the Virgin Mary. Konstanty, who had attended the same seminary in

Lviv as Kolbe, believed that Kolbe had an excessive fixation on the Virgin Mary, and he told him so.[18]

For example, Kolbe required that the friars in both Niepokalanów and Nagasaki must greet each other with the word 'Maria' to show their dedication.[19] Konstanty also criticised Kolbe for calling the Virgin Mary *mamusia*, which means mummy, and attacked him in a sarcastic article entitled: 'The Virgin Mary – Mumsy? God the Father – Popsy?'[20]

Konstanty thought the magazine was too expensive, that too many articles were about the Virgin Mary, and that it wasn't producing the desired result of converting the Japanese to Catholicism.

Kolbe was apoplectic about Father Konstanty's criticism, telling the father provincial, Kornel Czupryk, in Poland that he 'doesn't love the Immaculata, her Militia or the place of her grace. That which brings joy and edification to the rest of us disquiets, saddens and bores him. In my opinion, this is the reason for his neurasthenia.'[21]

One day in February 1933, Konstanty started shouting at Kolbe about his extreme leadership style, and he told the head of the Conventual Franciscans in Rome that 'a dangerous character in Japan [Kolbe] is now trying to branch off from the Order to create a new order'.[22]

Emboldened, other frustrated friars joined the fray. Brother Seweryn, who had travelled with Kolbe to Japan in 1930, screamed at him that he felt enslaved and 'could no longer follow your leadership'. 'What's the use of printing this darned magazine?' asked nineteen-year-old Brother Bartlomiej Kalucki, who had arrived in Japan with Konstanty. To anyone who questioned Kolbe's publishing methods, he replied: 'The magazines will eventually produce results. Magazines last a long time. People read the articles repeatedly. Have faith!'[23]

Years later, Brother Sergius, who joined the friary in September 1931 and was one of Kolbe's most trusted brothers, told Kōichi Tagawa that Father Konstanty was simply echoing what others were saying. 'All the Polish priests in the order (both in Japan and Poland) were critical of Father Kolbe at the time,' Brother Sergius said. 'Konstanty was only one of them.'[24] Sergius remained in Japan until he died in 2010, aged 103.

Kolbe refused to relent. And as the mutiny dragged on, another serious problem raised its head. The friars were being closely monitored because the Japanese secret police thought they might be Soviet spies.

Established in 1911, the Tokubetsu Kōtō Keisatsu (Tokkō, or Special Higher Police) was a feared and ruthless police force by the early 1930s, tasked with investigating and controlling groups that threatened public order. As Japan's military ambitions grew, the Tokkō started rooting out anybody who did not agree with State Shintoism's thought control or who showed sympathy towards communism or the Soviet Union, the nation's long-time enemy. For example, one well-known socialist novelist, Takiji Kobayashi, was first arrested in 1930 on suspicion of helping finance the Japanese Communist Party. In February 1933, he was rearrested, tortured and died during interrogation by the Tokkō.

Unlike ordinary people in Nagasaki, who treated the Poles politely, the Tokkō were suspicious from the day the friars landed in Japan. From time to time, the police arrived unannounced at the friary to grill the men about their activities. 'They asked us repeatedly when, where and how we were receiving the money to build and run the friary,' Father Mirochna said. 'They suspected that we were being funded by the Russians. They were very rude and arrogant.'[25]

Sometime in 1933, a nondescript man known simply as Mr N showed up at the friary claiming he wanted to assist the men. Mr N ended up living there for three months, helping write addresses on envelopes and cooking meals. The man confessed later that the Tokkō had sent him to snoop, according to Brother Romuald Mroziński and several other brothers.[26]

On another occasion, the Tokkō accused a Polish brother of taking photos without permission. The Tokkō were nervous about foreigners photographing Nagasaki because Mitsubishi Heavy

Industries was building warships and torpedoes there. The man was told to leave Japan immediately to avoid arrest. The charges were eventually dropped after Japanese priests intervened.

These incidents had a chilling effect. Kolbe told the men to avoid doing or saying anything that could be perceived as being critical of the Japanese government. His concern wasn't only to protect the Franciscan community in Japan. He wanted to take advantage of the nation's imperial ambitions, believing that Japan would eventually occupy the whole of Asia.

'This would be good for the MI,' Kolbe told Brother Sergius. 'We can spread the magazine throughout the empire.'[27]

In Poland, the Franciscans who managed the Japanese operation could no longer ignore the numerous complaints about Father Kolbe's uncompromising style as head of the Nagasaki friary. In April 1933, Kolbe was asked to attend a provincial meeting in Kraków to explain how the institution was faring, because senior Franciscans wanted to shut down the Japanese operation.[28] Kolbe's irascible antagonist, Father Konstanty, would be the acting head in Kolbe's absence. En route, he stopped in Rome for the beatification of Gemma Galgani, the young Italian mystic whom he revered.

To avoid closing Mugenzai-no-Sono, Father Provincial Kornel Czupryk came up with a solution. Always supportive of Kolbe, he decided that he himself would become the guardian of the Japanese friary as a way to reinvigorate the institution. He asked Kolbe to focus on the magazine's publication and to cultivate the friars' spiritual life and physical health.

After Kornel and Kolbe arrived in Nagasaki together in October 1933, the impact on the friars' physical and mental health was almost immediate. First on the agenda was meat, including Polish-style pigs' feet and ears, which Kornel himself bought from a local butcher. Every Friday became 'Japanese food day' and the men tried making and eating *miso* soup and sardines with chopsticks rather than forks. Within weeks, Father Konstanty left Japan for Poland.

Father Kornel bought a cooker in which to bake bread. In quick succession, the friars also painted the buildings' floors, varnished the chairs in the dining hall and hung paintings on the walls. Kolbe regarded these improvements as luxuries, but he knew better than to complain to his superior.

Kornel also carved out time for rest, study and recreation. After breakfast every day, the friars learned Japanese. At midday, he instituted siesta time. And in the evenings, the men began playing games, including chess which even Kolbe joined in.

The more relaxed atmosphere paid off in numerous ways. By 1934, just four years after starting publication of the magazine, the men were distributing 65,000 copies a month and the periodical could be found across Japan and its colonies, including Korea, Manchuria, Sakhalin and Taiwan. It had the highest circulation of any Catholic publication in a non-Catholic country.

Increased sales helped the Poles scrape together enough money to build a new three-storey structure, replacing the makeshift building in which the Franciscans had lived since May 1931. The friars still couldn't afford heating, so the monastery was bitterly cold during the winter. But for the first time, Kolbe had a room of his own. There, on a wooden desk made by Brother Zeno, Kolbe placed two artefacts that reflected his passions: a small statue of the Virgin Mary and a globe.

Father Kornel's arrival also gave respite to Kolbe himself. He finally had time to reflect on his beliefs, not least his love for both science and God. Peering at the stars one cool October evening in 1935, Kolbe noted that the Milky Way was thousands of light years away from the Earth and that 'the extent of the heavenly expanses has no limits'.

'I would like to travel in these unknown expanses,' he said wistfully, perhaps recalling the spaceship designs he'd sketched in his youth. 'The grains of dust that are the Earth, the Sun, the stars and the nebula, and also this chair that I'm sitting on, move in an infinite space. To what destination? From what origin? For how much time have they been moving? Until now, science has not found answers to these questions.'

He continued to ponder the role of God in the galaxies: 'Every movement in the universe tends to be transformed in a rectilinear direction, which will lead to its end. A movement having an end must necessarily also have had a beginning at some well-defined moment in the past. It is difficult to say that the cause of the very first movement was matter, for a static body cannot set another body moving. Therefore, it is clear that a non-existent thing cannot be the cause of anything.

'My conclusion is that the cause of the first movement of prime matter is external to matter itself. [Something] set matter in motion. We call this power – which is beyond any human consideration and reckoning – God.'[29]

Meanwhile, to make the friary self-sustaining, Kolbe actively searched for Japanese boys to join the institution. In November 1934, he visited Hisaga-shima, one of the scenic Gotō islands in the East China Sea off the western coast of Nagasaki.

Hisaga-shima was one of the places that the first Portuguese Jesuits had visited in the sixteenth century. Many islanders had become Catholics and later became hidden Christians.[30] In April 1936, Kolbe and Kornel opened a minor seminary at the friary to train young Japanese friars from Hisaga-shima and elsewhere.

During Kolbe's visit to Hisaga-shima, he met two teenagers who would become friars in the spring of 1936. One was Yasugorō Nakamura, then aged fourteen, who became the first child apprentice priest.

'I was only a young boy and was really frightened at the beginning because the friary was very dark inside and all the bearded foreign men looked so alien,' Nakamura recalled. 'When they all gathered to sit at the table and prayed in the evening, I felt out of place and wanted to go home.'

He eventually grew accustomed to religious life and became a core Japanese member of the Militia Immaculatae. Nakamura remembered meeting Kolbe at the entrance of the institution when he visited for the first time.

Kolbe held Nakamura's hands and hugged him tightly, saying: 'You are going to devote your entire life to the Virgin Mary.'

Father Kolbe talking about the Virgin Mary to Japanese workers
who built the church for him in Nagasaki in 1933

Nakamura was taken aback because hugging is not a Japanese custom and he remembered Kolbe's long beard rubbing his cheeks. He was particularly struck by the Polish men's extreme physical labour as they dug into the mountainside with spades and pickaxes to build a minor seminary for the apprentices.[31] Nakamura remained in Nagasaki and died there in February 2015 aged ninety-three.

The opening of the minor seminary was Kolbe's last major accomplishment in Japan. A month later, in May 1936, Kolbe and Father Kornel left the port city aboard the SS *Shanghai Maru* to attend a provincial meeting in Kraków. Kolbe didn't know at the time that Father Kornel feared for his health and didn't want him to return to Japan. A new guardian, Father Samuel Rosenbaiger, was appointed to oversee the Nagasaki community, replacing Kornel.

In Poland, the order asked Kolbe to become head of Niepokalanów again, six years after relinquishing the post to go to Japan. Kolbe, who had said he expected to die in Japan, was surprised and, at first, somewhat upset. 'I had hoped to lay down my bones as a foundation for our Japanese mission,' he told Father Mirochna. 'I had no desire to leave Mugenzai-no-Sono. It was not my will to leave Japan or to remain in Poland, but rather it was the will of the Immaculate. I don't completely understand her.'[32]

Kolbe could look back at his time in Asia with mixed emotions. After arriving in Nagasaki with just two colleagues, he'd built a friary from scratch. Moreover, the monthly magazine he'd started was being distributed throughout Japan and its colonies.

Equally important, the friars' religious devotion had left a positive impression on the Japanese people they met, particularly in Nagasaki, and it inspired several intellectuals, some of whom converted to Catholicism.[33]

Father Hyōzō Umeki, a priest at Ōura Cathedral who took care of the Polish friars in their first year, talked about them with deep reverence. 'I was among many Japanese who felt that for the first time, we were witnessing true devotion to God,' he said. 'We were convinced that Japanese religious figures needed to have similar dignity.'[34]

Outside Mugenzai-no-Sono, Kolbe appeared to realise that his approach of trying to disarm and convert non-Christians with philosophical theories didn't work in Japan. As he matured, Kolbe started listening more to other people's diverse beliefs, particularly those of Buddhist monks.[35]

In Japan, the realities of middle age, most notably his persistent illnesses, had dampened Kolbe's youthful ambitions and dreams. His grand plan to spread Catholicism throughout Asia and then the world was stalled. Perhaps the biggest problem he faced was timing. Kolbe's ambitions clashed with the political tide in Japan, where the authorities were tightening their grip against anyone who didn't willingly worship the 'divine' emperor.

Anti-Catholic sentiment led to the closure of some Catholic schools and the vandalising of churches. In May 1932, an army officer had taken sixty students from Tokyo's Sophia University to Yasukuni Shrine, a sacred place for many Japanese where their war dead are buried. After three Catholic students refused to bow at the altar, Christians were severely criticised throughout Japan for this 'dangerously unpatriotic' act. The Catholic Church in Japan, in trying to avoid further persecution, eventually agreed to accept that praying at a shrine did not conflict with their Christian beliefs.

Still, on the day that Kolbe left Nagasaki, twenty Polish friars – three fathers and seventeen brothers – were living in the mountainside monastery, and nineteen Japanese seminary students were studying there.

Most of the Polish men who bade him farewell were Kolbe devotees and they remained in Nagasaki the rest of their lives. Kolbe, meanwhile, was returning to a Europe in which the threat of war was becoming ever more real.

8. The Emperor or Jesus

1936 – Rason, northern Korea

Kōichi Tagawa didn't like being the smallest boy in his year group at the Japanese elementary school he attended in the port of Rason, northern Korea. Because Korea was part of the Japanese empire, the school year started, as it did in the rest of Japan, in April. Consequently, Kōichi was among the youngest in his class because his birthday was 1 March.

From his earliest days, he thought of himself as a follower rather than a leader. The only time he led the pack was at the school's annual sports day, when Kōichi always won the short-distance running race for his year group. 'That's when I felt like a hero,' he told me. 'I felt really proud when the teacher pinned a yellow winner's ribbon on my chest. I felt like a soldier being given a medal for bravery or heroism. My friends and I always assumed we'd eventually fight in the Japanese army. All Japanese boys in Rason did.'

When Kōichi was seven, in 1935, his father Matsukichi became ill with gallstones. It was just over a year since the Tagawa family had relocated to Rason from Chinhae in the southeast of Korea. They had been hoping to take advantage of the building boom that was transforming the sleepy port into a transit hub between Japan and Manchuria.

At the time, a well-equipped modern hospital was still under construction and there was no proper medical centre in Rason to carry out an operation. Matsukichi developed an infection and became seriously ill. He died at home after a lot of suffering.

A Christian burial was impossible because there was no priest and no church in Rason. Matsukichi's brothers, Fujinosuke and Ikuichi, carried his body in the back of a car to a graveyard in the

Kōichi Tagawa as a boy

nearby mountains. There, they dug a hole and left a raised mound to mark the grave. There was no cross.

Kōichi Tagawa was too young to understand the loss and he retained few memories of his father. But after he died, the boy frequently felt insecure. 'I often got the feeling that someone was peeping through the windows inside the house, watching me,' Kōichi said. 'Years later, I rationalised this as a response to losing my dad.'

Kōichi's mother, Wasa, became more religious after her husband's death. Each evening after school, she made Kōichi sit at a desk and copy prayers into a notebook using a black calligraphic writing brush. He recited these prayers daily, before and after school, in front of the family altar.

Wasa also taught Kōichi the Catechism, a series of religious questions and answers about their Catholic faith. On Sunday mornings, he sat with Wasa, rosary in hand, reciting prayers, frustrated that he was not allowed to meet his friends until he had finished.

Christianity was a burden for the youngster. Kōichi hated the history lessons in which his teacher mentioned Japan's persecution of the Catholics. His parents had repeatedly told him about his family's background, but he did not want his friends to know that his ancestors had been oppressed and discriminated against. 'I felt inconsequential because I was a Christian. I just wanted to be the same as my friends. In that sense, I was a kakure kirishitan, a hidden Christian, myself,' he said.

Wasa had other plans for her only son, and she became ever more determined to ensure that Kōichi grew up as a Christian. Once a year, she arranged for a German missionary priest who was stationed near Pyongyang, 500 miles southwest of Rason, to visit the house for a private Mass. The priest stayed at the house overnight before moving on to meet a handful of other Catholics scattered throughout northern Korea.

After Kōichi's father's death, his bachelor uncle, Fujinosuke, the eldest of the brothers, became a substitute father-figure to the young boy, showering him with Japanese sweets and food. Kōichi's other uncle, Ikuichi, married a divorced Japanese woman with a child whom he had met in Unggi.

Kōichi helped his mother in the family's butcher's shop, which was owned by his uncles who lived in Unggi. In October 1935, a railway line opened between Rason and Unggi that cut the journey to just twenty minutes. It was Kōichi's job, even at the age of eight, to carry the cash from the business to his uncles.

With the money, the men bought cattle and then slaughtered them to sell in Rason. One uncle would haul the cuts of beef on the train to Rason, and Wasa's Korean maid would collect the meat at the increasingly congested railway station.

Rason's metamorphosis from peaceful hamlet to pulsating metropolis owed everything to its strategic location just east of Manchukuo, the puppet state set up by Japan in 1932. The Japanese government entrusted the South Manchurian Railway Company, in which it had a fifty per cent stake, to build the city. Mantetsu, as the company was known, was no ordinary firm. By 1930, it was Japan's largest and most profitable corporation, involved in every aspect of business life in Manchuria, from power generation to soybean research.

Within Manchukuo, for example, Mantetsu built and managed railways, coal mines, iron mills and factories. The company's pride and joy was the Asia Express, the continent's fastest train, which connected Dalian, the southernmost port in Manchuria, with the Manchurian capital, Changchun, after 1934. At the time, that was the quickest route to Manchuria from Japan. Another route was via the southern Korean port of Busan.

Two years later, a railway line connected Changchun with Rason, making this now the fastest route between Japan and Manchukuo. Kōichi would watch as freight trains snaked their way to the port carrying agricultural products and raw materials bound for Japan, a country he had never visited.

Moving in the opposite direction were tens of thousands of Japanese soldiers, en route to joining the Kwantung Army, the Japanese armed forces in Manchukuo. As hotel rooms were in short supply in Rason, the army asked Japanese residents to let soldiers stay in their homes for a few days. At school, Kōichi remembered, children boasted about the ranks of the men who came to stay. A three-star colonel, of course, brought more prestige to a family than an enlisted private.

The Japanese military machine dominated all aspects of life in the port, just as it did throughout Japan. Ever since the Manchurian Incident, most Japanese people had eagerly supported the military's activities, cheered on by the media.

Japan's major newspapers stoked enthusiasm for this Manchurian dreamland at a time when the nation was mired in depression. They screened propaganda newsreels from Manchurian battlefields in city parks, department stores and schools. NHK, the national radio network, first began live broadcasts of troop sending-off ceremonies, funerals and military reviews in 1931.

War songs such as 'Ah, our Manchuria' and 'Manchuria Maiden, My Manchurian Lover' augmented the jingoistic mood and prompted soya and cotton farmers, coal miners and middle-class bureaucrats alike to consider a move to this new western frontier of the Japanese empire.[1]

In 1933, after the League of Nations condemned Japan for its invasion of Manchuria, Japan withdrew from the international body and started down an increasingly solitary path that would eventually lead to the Second Sino-Japanese War of 1937 and beyond. Kōichi and his classmates were excited to be living in a town with so much military activity. 'I admired the soldiers, with their nice clean uniforms and positive attitude. They were making Japan strong at a time when I felt so insecure and weak because of the loss of my father and my religion,' he said.

In Kōichi Tagawa's mind, there was no incompatibility between Japanese militarism and Christianity, even though the Catechism stressed that 'human life is sacred' and one of the Ten Commandments said 'Thou shalt not kill'. But at the age of eleven, Kōichi was forced to confront the most profound spiritual dilemma of his young life.

In February 1940, Kōichi took a written exam that was required to attend an elite Japanese boys-only junior high school in Rason. It was run by the government to educate future leaders of the Japanese empire. The last hurdle was an interview with the headmaster and other teachers.

'So, I hear you are a Christian, Tagawa-kun,' the headmaster began, leaving the sentence hanging. 'Yes, sir,' Kōichi replied in a feeble voice.

'Suppose our emperor's army and Jesus' army fought a war. Which army would you join, Tagawa-kun?'

Decades later, the question still haunted the boy-turned-man. Reliving the scene to me, he said he bit his tongue and his head filled with images of reciting the rosary with his mother.

'I would join Jesus' army, sir,' Kōichi said quietly after a few seconds. He burst into tears. The headmaster stared right through him. The interview was over. He had failed.

Yet to his own and his mother's great surprise, Kōichi was admitted to the school, and he proudly wore the black formal uniform when the term began in April 1940. One day, the headmaster called Kōichi into his office, an unusual occurrence.

'I need to explain something to you, Tagawa-kun,' he began. 'Your written exam was unsatisfactory. But I wanted you to attend my school because of your answer to my question during your interview. You have the guts that all boys need to run our empire. It took courage to say what you said.'

Never had Kōichi felt more delighted. Perhaps it wasn't such a bad thing to be a Christian after all, he told himself.

Rason Junior High School was, like its counterparts throughout the Japanese empire, rabidly jingoistic. Every morning began with a call to worship the emperor. Discipline was paramount. 'Stand to attention!' 'About turn!' the headmaster screamed as the boys looked to the southeast, the direction of the Imperial Palace in Tokyo, and bowed deeply.

Military training in readiness for a stint in Manchukuo began with hours of marching around the school grounds. The adolescents crawled over, under and around strategically placed sandbags. During overnight camps in the frozen north of Korea, Kōichi and his friends walked for miles along deserted mountain paths, each carrying a mess tin, canned food, extra clothing, a sleeping bag and a tent in their oversized rucksacks.

Cooking, eating and sleeping outdoors, away from their parents, Kōichi and his classmates lapped up the chance to act like the proud, clean-cut warriors who had stayed in their homes. They knew nothing about the anti-Japanese guerrillas from China and Korea who lived across the border from Rason, in Manchukuo, and who were intent on killing the well-drilled intruders from the hated Japanese empire.

PART 3

Glory and Defeat, 1936–1945

9. Spiritual Resistance

1936 – Niepokalanów, Poland

When Father Maximilian Maria Kolbe arrived back at Niepokalanów from Japan in the summer of 1936, many friars were shocked at his appearance. He was forty-two years old but looked at least a decade older. His long beard was streaked with white. He stooped and walked with a cane.[1]

For six years, at a heavy cost to himself and his fellow Polish friars, Kolbe had toiled tirelessly to spread the word about the Militia Immaculatae and to build a functioning friary in Nagasaki. His unrelenting pace and fierce discipline had almost killed him and some of his colleagues. Not until Kolbe's superior in Poland, Father Kornel Czupryk, arrived in Japan to address the institution's shortcomings did conditions improve.

Japan had changed Kolbe. Kornel's reforms were a revelation to him. To succeed within and outside the religious community, he realised he needed to become more flexible and understanding towards other people and their culture. That made him determined to institute what he called 'democratic changes' at Niepokalanów and to soften his diehard demeanour.

Back in familiar surroundings, back in the community he had founded, Kolbe appeared transformed. He could talk again in his native language to friends who shared his faith and culture. It was as if an enormous weight had been lifted from his shoulders, allowing him to see MI, the friary and his own reborn country, Poland, in a new light.

Kolbe first scrapped all the inequalities between fathers and brothers. The former were ordained priests while the latter were not and were often treated as inferior. For example, fathers were given better-quality soap and cutlery than brothers. Fathers also

Kolbe, top right, observing a chess game at Niepokalanów

wore a different type of cape during a haircut at the friary's barber. This would be the case no longer.

For rest and rehabilitation, the friars built a recreational lodge in a small pine forest near Niepokalanów. The older men were encouraged to enjoy picnics and walks or simply to relax in the pristine air. The younger friars played football, basketball and table tennis and practised archery. Others created two orchestras and a choir.

Riding a bicycle around the community's seventy-five-acre grounds, Kolbe would frequently stop to talk to the friars and seminary students about his old interests – astronomy, space travel, mathematics and chess. His door, he told them, was always open. No topic was off-limits. No complaints would remain unheard.

The community had grown during Kolbe's absence. At the time of his return, it had 500 friars and 140 seminary students.[2] It had become self-sufficient, with its own farm, bakery, dairy, hospital, fire brigade, barber's shop and machine repair shop. Its reputation as an intellectual hub had also spread, attracting friars from across Poland with a multitude of skills.

Hundreds of these friars were involved in the creation of Niepokalanów's most ambitious and financially risky project – the publication of a new national daily newspaper. The friary had decided to produce a paper after Pope Pius XI sent a letter to Poland's bishops demanding that a daily be established.[3]

The pontiff, who had served as the Vatican's ambassador, or papal nuncio, in Poland from 1919 to 1921, wanted the newspaper to promote Catholic Action. This was a broad movement designed to promote lay Catholics and to counter secular forces that were perceived as a threat to the Church throughout Europe.

Launched in May 1935, *Mały Dziennik*, also known as the *Little Daily*, published articles on politics, current affairs and sport as well as religion.

Many of the friars had worked on some aspect of the monthly *Knight of the Immaculata* (*Rycerz Niepokalanej*) magazine, which had the largest circulation of any periodical in Poland. But expanding from a special-interest monthly to a general-interest daily was a momentous – and costly – undertaking. The paper boosted its circulation by selling for half the price of other dailies.

It was a propitious time to begin such a publication. The Catholic Church enjoyed strong support in Poland during the 1930s, especially after the death of General Józef Piłsudski in May 1935. Piłsudski and his Socialist Party had envisioned a pluralistic Poland, inclusive of minorities such as Orthodox Ukrainians, Jews and Ruthenian Uniates, led by the Polish majority. But after Piłsudski's death, the nation's de facto ruler and head of the armed forces, Marshal Edward Rydz-Śmigły, stressed the benefits of a united state bound together by the Catholic faith.

Poland, which had re-emerged as a nation after the First World War, was struggling economically and politically. Neighbouring countries, particularly the Soviet Union to the east and Germany to the west, again threatened its independence.

The nation needed a thread to bond its thirty-two million people, and in this environment the Catholic faith again became synonymous with Polish identity. Nationalist politicians spread the slogan 'Catholic Poland', openly declaring that if a Polish person was not

Catholic, he or she was not a genuine Pole or a patriot. The *Little Daily* actively promoted this conservative line.

Reflecting the thinking of the Vatican, the *Little Daily* railed against freemasons, Jews, liberals, communists, atheists and other non-believers. Articles frequently pointed out when Jews owned factories and when they were perceived to have an outsized influence on Polish art, literature and films.[4]

Unfortunately, but predictably, such articles probably contributed to the spread of antisemitism. In 1935, Poland's three million Jews constituted almost ten per cent of the population and formed the largest Jewish population in Europe. Right-wing politicians openly criticised Jews for 'controlling' the Polish economy and society. They portrayed Jews in Poland as a 'foreign enemy' and encouraged boycotts of Jewish stores. This led to vandalism and violence in cities with large Jewish populations, including Łódź, Lviv and Kraków.

The *Little Daily*'s editor-in-chief, Father Marian Wojcik, showed little sympathy for Jews or other minorities. Kolbe rarely interfered with the paper's anti-secular editorial stance, but he wrote to Wojcik in July 1935 from Nagasaki, telling him to 'be very cautious neither to arouse nor add to hatred [of Jewish people]'. He added: 'When unnecessary, the writers must avoid condemning individuals, parties or other nations. Our main purpose is the conversion and sanctification of souls, winning them through the Immaculata through love – love for all souls, including Jews, Masons, heretics and all nonbelievers.'[5]

While in Japan, Kolbe had made known his disapproval of an antisemitic article published in the *Little Daily* written by Prelate Stanisław Trzeciak. In June 1937, he banned articles by Trzeciak from appearing in the newspaper, saying that the prelate was 'antisemitic to the point of chauvinism'.[6]

To most readers, promotion of Catholicism and opposition to Jews were two sides of the same coin, but the impact was magnified in Poland because of the size of the Jewish population. Kolbe, as head of Niepokalanów, was negligent in providing sufficient editorial direction that might have tempered the *Little Daily*'s tone. So, too, were Poland's clergy and the Church's leaders in Vatican City. 'In his anti-liberal, anti-masonic, anti-secularist stance, Kolbe typified not only the church in Poland but interwar Catholicism altogether,' wrote Ronald Modras, a professor of theological studies at Saint Louis University.[7]

As the *Little Daily*'s circulation grew, the editorial department set up news bureaus and distribution branches in major Polish cities and subscribed to wire services for general news from around the world. Beginning with a print run of 17,000 copies, the paper was selling 100,000 copies a day by the end of 1935 and soon became Poland's largest-circulation newspaper, with eleven editions. The Sunday edition alone sold 250,000 copies.

The success of the printing division was remarkable. As well as the *Little Daily* and the monthly magazine, the friars also published 180,000 copies a month of the *Little Knight* for youths, yet another version for children under ten, and numerous other publications.

The *Calendar of the Knights of the Immaculata*, which noted important Catholic events and holy dates, was particularly popular, selling more than a million copies a year. The institution also published religious books and a magazine in Latin for priests, and it boasted one of the most technologically advanced printing houses in Poland. One of its three rotary presses could produce 60,000 copies an hour of the sixteen-page daily.[8]

The nationalistic political and social mood not only boosted circulation, it also enhanced the reputation of the friars and their leader, Kolbe, as prominent Poles whose voice could not be ignored.

'Niepokalanów was not a retreat from the world. It was a beehive of activity,' Dr Stefan P. Wilk, who was a seminarian at Niepokalanów in the 1930s, told Kolbe's biographer Patricia Treece in 1982. 'Kolbe was not interested in passive soldiers. The whole friary was organised like a military camp. If Kolbe had not become a priest, he would have been a great general.

'Like Gandhi, Kolbe was a fanatic – a man with an ideal that was his vehicle, his road to perfection – and he wanted to reach perfection,' Wilk continued. 'But Kolbe was also a down-to-earth practical genius. He spent all his years behind the friary walls and yet he knew how to use the press, and later the radio, to get his message out in a country not acquainted with these techniques. This showed enormous ingenuity.'[9]

In spite of Niepokalanów's publishing triumphs, the community operated at a loss. Eager to cut costs, Kolbe worked with a friar who had studied business management in Warsaw and organised the men in line with modern occupational practices familiar in factories. These included round-the-clock shifts, suggestion boxes and daily production reports. Kolbe placed every man into one of twelve divisions, the head of which reported directly to him.[10]

Among the most renowned divisions was the fire department and security brigade, originally formed in 1931 after the community's power plant caught fire and damaged the generators. Even today, the friars still protect the area around Niepokalanów, using an artificial lake in the compound as their water supply.

As the popularity of the friary grew, an average of 200 boys and men travelled to Niepokalanów each year hoping for admission. Most were rejected. In the fortunate few, mostly young Polish peasants and orphans, Kolbe demanded complete loyalty. After meals, one priest recalled, Kolbe would sit with a circle of acolytes around him 'like chicks around the mother hen'.

On the tenth anniversary of Niepokalanów's establishment, in December 1937, Kolbe spoke on Polish National Radio about the community and the twenty-year history of Militia Immaculatae, from its beginnings in Rome to counter masonic attacks against the Church to the Franciscans' Japanese adventures and the success of the publications. The organisation now had 600,000 members, he said.[11]

Kolbe had good reason to be proud of his creation. By the end of 1938, Niepokalanów was one of the largest and most authoritative religious communities in the world. More than 800 men, including over 120 seminary students, lived and worked there, and the friary boasted by far the largest Christian publishing operation in the world.[12]

At the time, Kolbe's 'kingdom' appeared indomitable, and his ambitions were unlimited, though he himself remained as poor as a church mouse. To distribute the publications more quickly, he planned to build an airport at Niepokalanów and sent two brothers to Warsaw to train as pilots. Kolbe also hoped to produce blockbuster religious films starring Poland's leading actors.[13]

Yet even as Kolbe drew up a five-year plan for the community's expansion, he became increasingly concerned that both Niepokalanów and Poland were at risk because of the rapid spread of Nazism in Germany and Europe's deteriorating political situation. Kolbe suspected that Adolf Hitler, who had become the nation's chancellor in 1933, would stop at nothing to expand the Third Reich eastwards and smother Poland.[14]

Niepokalanów's golden age was fast coming to an end. The community's recent growth had occurred in large part because Poland was asserting itself as a staunchly Catholic nation. But as Nazism spread, Niepokalanów's success would soon make it a target for Hitler's henchmen.

On 5 March 1938, Kolbe took a seven-hour train journey from Warsaw to Berlin to attend a Franciscan conference and hear firsthand how the Nazis were persecuting Catholic and Protestant theologians in Germany. He also heard more about Joseph Stalin's purges in the Soviet Union, closing thousands of Catholic churches and exiling clergy to Siberia.[15]

At the Berlin conference, Kolbe also became more aware of the growing tensions between Germany and Poland over the 'free city' of Danzig (present-day Gdansk), 200 miles northwest of Warsaw, and the so-called Danzig Corridor, or Polish Corridor. This narrow strip of land gave Poland access to the Baltic Sea and separated Germany from East Prussia.[16]

No sooner had Kolbe returned to Warsaw, on 11 March, than German troops invaded and annexed Austria. The move yet again underscored the danger to Poland and led Kolbe to start preparing

Niepokalanów for the inevitability of war and the likely closure of the friary.

'My sons, a frightful struggle threatens,' Kolbe said at a conference two months later. 'We don't know yet what will be its details. But here, in Poland, we must expect the worst. War is much nearer than one can imagine and if it comes, that will mean the dispersal of our community.'[17]

Despite the threats from Germany, Kolbe appeared to have made up his mind to become a martyr. He was determined to remain and protect Niepokalanów, no matter what the consequences. 'Whatever happens, everything will be for our good,' he said. 'Persecution purifies. What a privilege to die as a knight in the crusade against evil, sealing our witness with our blood! This is what I wish for you and for myself.'[18]

As preparation for his fight against fascism, Kolbe decided to make a 1,000-mile cross-country pilgrimage in August 1938 to the shrines of the Virgin Mary in four cities – Częstochowa, Kraków, Grodno and Vilnius. To further unify the friary, he selected 232 brothers – about a third of the Niepokalanów community – to accompany him.

Kolbe had visited the Jasna Góra monastery in Częstochowa at several pivotal times in his life. He'd prayed there in 1919 after finishing his studies in Rome, asking the Black Madonna to help MI succeed in Poland. In 1927, he'd called on her to make Niepokalanów a reality. And in 1930, he'd bowed to the monastery from the train en route to Marseilles before leaving for Japan.[19]

Now, with war appearing imminent, Kolbe and the 232 brothers prayed for protection against the Nazis. In Kraków, Kolbe paid a short visit to see his ageing mother, Maria. And in Grodno, he showed the friars the quarters where he had cranked out thousands of copies of the Knight of the Immaculata magazine sixteen years earlier.[20]

The timing of the pilgrimage was fortunate because Poland was plainly in Germany's sights. At the end of September 1938, Germany, France, Italy and Great Britain signed the Munich Agreement, which allowed Germany to annex the Sudetenland in western Czechoslovakia. Part of the Sudetenland bordered Poland.

Back at Niepokalanów, the friars could barely keep up with the demand for its publications as the Polish people tried to stay on top of the fast-changing news. In December 1938, circulation of the *Knight of the Immaculata* magazine topped a million for the first time.

That same month, the men installed a short-wave radio transmitter and antenna after receiving an amateur radio licence from the Polish government. Kolbe, who believed that radio would eventually rival newspapers as a way to deliver his messages to the public, spoke on the first test broadcasts.[21]

As 1939 dawned, it appeared only a question of time before Germany attacked Poland. On 15 March, the Nazis invaded the rest of Czechoslovakia and the following day they made Bohemia and Moravia a protectorate of Germany. Shortly thereafter, Hitler demanded possession of Danzig and a bridge route in the Polish Corridor.

Kolbe himself rarely addressed these political or martial events in his articles, speeches or letters. Rather, as the French author André Frossard noted, Kolbe 'worked in the spiritual gold mine. He did not want the community he had built turned into an ammunition depot, although that was not neutralism. He was anti-Nazi as much as he was anti-Marxist and more of a patriot than ever.'[22]

Nevertheless, Niepokalanów started growing into a centre of quiet resistance against the Nazis. The *Little Daily* newspaper, which was increasingly influential throughout Poland and had a circulation of 300,000 at the end of 1938, began taking a more strident anti-Nazi posture, in line with the general mood within the country. 'All Poles were against the Nazis as a matter of principle,' according to Prince Lubecki, the aristocrat who had donated land to Kolbe to build the friary.[23]

The newspaper's cartoons in particular were striking for their

Z tamtymi daniami poszło dobrze. Apetyt mam nadal wielki, ale obawiam się, że te smakołyki zaszkodzą mi!...

Little Daily, *12 April 1939*

willingness to mock Hitler and to present Poland's case for resisting a German invasion. The 1939 Easter weekend edition, for example, published an irreverent cartoon that showed Hitler relaxing under a tree on the German–Polish border next to three Easter eggs representing Vienna, the Sudetenland and Prague. Behind Hitler, Hermann Göring, the second most powerful man in Germany, talks to a smiling Polish guard across the border. 'Our Führer will be happy to receive something from you,' Göring says. 'Yes, why not?' the guard replies. 'It can be had immediately!!!' The cartoon implied that Poland's 'gift' to Hitler would be far less enjoyable than the Easter eggs.[24]

Four days later, on 12 April, just eight days before Hitler's fiftieth birthday, the *Little Daily* depicted the Führer as an overweight glutton. As a chef removes dishes labelled 'Czechoslovakia' and 'Lithuania' from his table, Hitler looks at a meal of Dutch milk and Swiss cheese and remarks: 'Until now, I have been able to digest my meal. I still have a big appetite, but I'm concerned these tasty dishes might give me indigestion.'

Later that month, on 28 April, Poland's foreign ministry asked Kolbe and Father Wojcik, the editor of the *Little Daily*, to visit Warsaw with other newspaper and broadcast leaders for crisis talks.

Little Daily, *30 April 1939*

The minister in charge appealed to the newspaper and radio editors to inspire the Polish people with patriotic articles or face disaster.

That same day, Hitler unilaterally annulled the 1934 non-aggression pact between Germany and Poland that had helped keep the peace between the two nations.

On the following two Sundays, the *Little Daily* further ridiculed Hitler. One cartoon, captioned 'Hitler's last step', depicted the dictator marching unawares towards a precipice followed by goose-stepping Nazi officers chanting 'Heil! Heil! Heil!' The other showed Hitler, dressed as an overweight street thug, threatening Poland, depicted as a well-dressed nobleman, with the caption: 'Give me your money and your watch, Count, and I won't harass you for a year.'

As the belligerent rhetoric increased, Kolbe's tuberculosis flared up, forcing him to take three weeks' rest in a sanatorium in Zako-pane in May 1939. He asked a loyal but overworked friar called Brother Pelagiusz to accompany him, and they picked up Kolbe's mother in Kraków en route. It was the last occasion on which he spent substantial time with her.

'This trip may prove to be my Palm Sunday before my Good Friday,' Kolbe said before setting off for the mountains, according to Pelagiusz's memoirs. Kolbe also told Pelagiusz that while in Japan he had had a vision in which the Virgin Mary had assured him that he would go to heaven.[25]

At Niepokalanów, the *Little Daily* intensified its criticism of the Nazis. On Friday, 12 May, the paper's front-page headline screamed 'Hitler Lies'. It quoted deserters from the German army saying that Hitler was paralysing the economy. The following day, the *Little Daily* called for a boycott of German newspapers, saying Germany's hatred of Poland and Hitler's tactics bordered on insanity.

'German propaganda is brainwashing people,' another article said. 'It paints the Third Reich as a wonderful country with plenty of food, where everyone is happy and there's no religious discrimination. But the reality is that there is a shortage of food, Catholics are persecuted, and Polish [emigrants'] children are forced to go to mixed religious schools against their parents' wishes.'

A hard-hitting cartoon, published on 24 June, showed a uniformed Hitler brandishing a paint brush in a room containing a map of central Europe. Hitler has painted swastikas on Austria and Czechoslovakia but can't paint Poland because ten swords are sticking out of the country. The caption read: 'I've always dreamed of a room [*pokoj*] with a swastika design.' In Polish, pokoj means both room and peace.

Yet another, on 5 July, showed Hitler being shot out of a cannon and hitting his head against a wall marked 'Gdansk' (Danzig). The caption read: 'We will not allow ourselves to be pushed into the Baltic Sea.'

On 27 July, three months after their first visit, Kolbe and Father Wojcik attended another Polish government briefing for journalists. This time, the official tone was even more strident because the government had learned that the Nazis had completed a strategic plan in June codenamed 'Fall Weiss', or Code White, to invade Poland. The official asked the media leaders to inspire patriotism in their readers and listeners and to tell all Poles that 'they must be prepared for every sacrifice to save the nation'.[26]

Making matters worse was the unexpected news on 23 August that Germany and the Soviet Union had signed a non-aggression agreement, known as the Molotov–Ribbentrop Pact. This essentially meant that Germany could invade Poland without fearing Soviet opposition. Part of the agreement, which wasn't disclosed until after the Second World War, was a secret protocol between the two countries to divide up Eastern Europe.

Six days later, the *Little Daily* showed exactly what the Polish editors thought about the pact. Its back-page cartoon, cynically entitled 'Idealists', depicted Hitler carrying Stalin. Stalin is shaking his fist at the German dictator and shouting, 'Away with Hitler!' Hitler, meanwhile, is screaming at Stalin 'Away with Communism!'

The message to Polish readers was clear – in spite of their superficial pact, Germany and Russia still fundamentally hated each other and were eager to gobble up Poland for themselves. It was a stark and defiant Polish view.

As the head of Poland's largest friary and publishing organisation, Kolbe was clear-eyed about his mission. He must encourage Poles to resist their enemies, just as his father had defied the Russians three decades earlier and as his ancestors had done for several hundred years.

Kolbe's immediate response was to use the million-selling *Knight of the Immaculata* magazine to stir Polish Catholics to action. The cover of the August 1939 edition showed a Polish soldier standing guard as a priest blesses Polish arms. Two eagles, emblems of the nation, flank him. Inside, the magazine carried a stark white map of Poland, sandwiched between swastikas to the west and hammers and sickles to the east.

Meanwhile, Kolbe asked his close friend, Walenty Majdanski, a Catholic activist, to write an editorial for the edition. It began: 'We are a great nation. No country has been more peace-loving, noble and chivalrous than Poland. We are a Catholic nation. Where else is there such an ardent reverence for Our Lady as there is in Poland?'

Illustration in August 1939 edition of Knight of the Immaculata *magazine*

In addressing the struggles ahead, Majdanski fell back on Poland's religious heritage:

> During war, the authenticity of a nation's faith can become fully manifested. When torrents of bullets are aimed at our fathers and brothers, a tide of prayers will flow from children, wives and mothers.
>
> The more devout the nation, the greater its dignity, the stronger its will, the higher its confidence in final victory.
>
> Diligence, patience, self-sacrifice, perseverance and infinite courage are the qualities of a nation of saints. Arming the nation with God's power costs nothing, but that power is of inestimable value for the state.[27]

On 1 September 1939, 1.5 million German troops invaded Poland. From day one, Poland was outmanned and outgunned. The German soldiers were supported by 2,700 tanks, nine times as many as had Poland, and 1,900 aircraft, five times as many.[28]

The *Little Daily*'s editorial line was unbending and upbeat,

Kolbe and other friars started building Niepokalanów on donated land west of Warsaw in 1927
(Courtesy of Niepokalanów MI Archives)

By 1938, the Knight of the Immaculata magazine was selling more than a million copies a month in Poland
(Courtesy of Niepokalanów MI Archives)

Kolbe, second left, and other friars built a wooden friary on a bleak mountainside east of Nagasaki, Japan, in 1931
(Courtesy of the Order of Friars Minor Conventual, Japan Province)

Kolbe in his untidy office in the Nagasaki friary around 1932
(Courtesy of the Order of Friars Minor Conventual, Japan Province)

To typeset the Japanese-language magazine in Nagasaki, the friars bought an old printing press and 145,000 metal characters. Each character needed to be picked out by hand, an extremely time-consuming task
(Courtesy of the Order of Friars Minor Conventual, Japan Province)

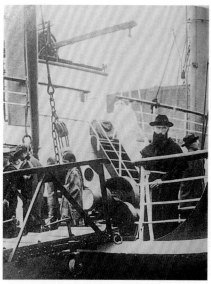

Kolbe left Nagasaki in May 1936 on the SS Shanghai Maru *to attend a meeting in Poland. He never returned to Japan*
(Courtesy of the Order of Friars Minor Conventual, Japan Province)

The Nazis arrested Kolbe and forty-seven Niepokalanów friars in September 1939.
They were sent at first to the Stalag III B Amtitz internment camp
(Courtesy of Niepokalanów MI Archives)

After the Nazis took over Niepokalanów in September 1939, it became a centre of refuge
for several thousand displaced Poles. The banner under the swastika reads 'One
People, One Empire, One Leader'
(Courtesy of Niepokalanów MI Archives)

despite the obvious imbalance in forces. 'We won't give up Gdansk. Keep away from Poland', the headlines screamed in the 2 September edition. 'Poland must win', the story read, and it depicted the Polish people being actively and joyfully mobilised for the military.

The following day, Great Britain and France declared war on Germany and the Second World War began. Two days later, on 5 September, the friars published the final edition of the *Little Daily*.

Correspondence between Poland and Japan continued, although Kolbe, worried about German censors, carefully avoided writing about the situation within Niepokalanów.[29] The Poles in Nagasaki had no real idea what had happened to Kolbe or to their fellow friars.

They knew only that Poland was on course to disappear as a sovereign nation once again. And they sensed that the life of the man who had founded and nurtured the friaries in both countries was in grave danger.

10. Kōichi Tagawa's War

1941 – Nagasaki

On Friday, 1 September 1939, as German panzer tank platoons ploughed through Poland, Japan and the Soviet Union were locked in battle half a world away.

Near a remote border on the Khalkh River between eastern Mongolia and northern Manchuria, the two long-time enemies fought in the air and on the ground in a little-known conflict that left thousands dead or wounded.

The outcome of the four-month fray was an embarrassing defeat for Japan by its historic rival. Japan's loss in what became known as the Battles of Khalkhin Gol was to have major repercussions for the nation's military strategy over the following six years.

Japan's successful invasion of China, six years after occupying Manchuria, had demonstrated the value of the Imperial Japanese Army-led Hokushin-ron, or 'Northern Road Doctrine'. This posited that Manchuria, China and Siberia were Japanese spheres of influence and of the highest value to the empire. The collapse of major cities – Beijing, Tianjin, Shanghai and Nanjing in 1937, followed by Xuzhou and Wuhan in 1938 – had further strengthened the Japanese army's prestige.

But the Soviet victory was a significant setback for the Hokushin-ron. It prompted Japan's leaders in Tokyo to place more emphasis on what was called Nanshin-ron, or the 'Southern Road Doctrine'. Supported by the Imperial Japanese Navy, this asserted the idea of seizing oil, minerals and other resources in the Dutch East Indies (now Indonesia) and elsewhere in Southeast Asia.[1]

Taking advantage of Hitler's occupation of France and Holland (May 1940), Japan invaded Saigon in French Indochina (today's Vietnam, Laos and Cambodia) in July 1941. Infuriated, US President

Kōichi Tagawa in school uniform

Franklin D. Roosevelt imposed a total oil embargo on Japan in August 1941.[2] This was part of a broader series of economic embargoes by the so-called ABCD nations – America, Britain, China and the Dutch – against the Japanese, who railed against what they called the ABCD Line or ABCD Encirclement.

As the Japanese media whipped up support for the military and promoted the dream of a Japanese empire throughout the Asia-Pacific region, war with the Allied forces began to seem increasingly inevitable.

At the elite boys' junior high school in the northern Korean border city of Rason, twelve-year-old Kōichi Tagawa and his classmates could never escape the realities of the war against the Republic of China that had begun in 1937.

Soldiers bound for Manchuria and China often stayed with Tagawa and his mother, Wasa. Other fighters visited his school to build support for the army and to boast of recent victories.

But one day in early 1941, close to his thirteenth birthday, Kōichi's stable schoolboy world collapsed. Skating on a frozen river near his home, Kōichi fell badly on the ice. Pain shot through his lower body. Kōichi stumbled home with help from his friends, but it wasn't long before his hips started to swell and he was unable to walk.

A chiropractor massaged Kōichi's body, but it had no effect. A doctor in the new hospital built for Japanese residents in Rason couldn't understand why Kōichi's pelvis was apparently decaying.

As a frontier town, Rason couldn't attract the highest quality of medical staff. Frantic, Wasa decided to leave her butcher's shop in Rason and take Kōichi by ship to her hometown of Nagasaki. When they arrived, in September 1941, it was Wasa's first trip home for at least fifteen years and Kōichi's first visit to Japan.

Entering Nagasaki Bay, Kōichi saw the Catholic church on the cape of Kaminoshima to the left and Ōura Cathedral's glistening white spire to the right. It was the same scene that had greeted Father Maximilian Kolbe eleven years earlier.

In a taxi from the port to Wasa's sister's home in Urakami, Kōichi clapped with joy as the twin bell towers of Nagasaki's recently built Urakami Cathedral came into view. In Rason, he had always felt an outsider, but he immediately felt a connection with Nagasaki, and he looked forward to becoming part of the Christian community that his mother had frequently talked about.

It was not to be. Kōichi was admitted to the Nagasaki University Hospital. As well as his hip problem, he was diagnosed with pleurisy, an inflammation of the tissues between the lungs and the ribcage. He screamed as a doctor injected a needle between his ribs to drain fluid from his chest.

Kōichi was eventually diagnosed with spinal tuberculosis, or Pott's disease. Every movement of his spine inflamed the vertebrae. The only way to manage the inflammation was to keep the spine immobile in a cast. For the following six months, Kōichi lay motionless in a hospital bed, crying himself to sleep as he wondered why he was suffering so much at such a young age. It was the first of many long periods of solitude and depression that he would endure.

Kōichi remembered one day that remained clear in his mind amid his drug-induced torpor. It was the evening of Monday,

8 December 1941, and he heard the five patients who shared his hospital room shouting and clapping. *'Yattazo, Banzai!'* (They did it, hurrah!)[3] A nurse had told the men that the Imperial Japanese Navy Air Service had launched a surprise attack on Pearl Harbor in Hawaii, destroying much of the US naval base. Although it wasn't known at the time, the torpedoes used in the attack had been made in Nagasaki.

Japan as a whole was jubilant, though apprehensive at how the US might respond. Less than eight hours after the attack, Japan declared war on the US and the British empire. The US, which had officially been neutral, declared war on Japan, as did Britain.

For Kōichi, the Pacific War, as the Second World War is called in Japan, was a sideshow in his fight to recover from his illness. But for the other patients, news of Japan's successful attacks on Malaya, Singapore and Hong Kong in the early stages of the war were greeted with rapture.

Japan was a divine country and would soon rule all Asia, the patients said, echoing the propaganda in the newspapers and on the radio. Kōichi remembered that the teachers at his school in Korea had said much the same thing.

Wasa Tagawa, whose husband had died six years earlier, was penniless and jobless after she and Kōichi arrived in Nagasaki. She couldn't even pay the hospital bills, so in early 1942, shortly after the attack on Pearl Harbor, she agreed for doctors to carry out experimental surgeries on her son in exchange for free medical attention and drugs. It was a precarious situation. In tears, Wasa told Kōichi it was his only chance to become a healthy teenager.

Kōichi was exceptionally lucky. A prominent surgeon called Professor Raisuke Shirabe had just been appointed to the Nagasaki University Hospital faculty after fifteen years of working in China and Korea. A graduate of Tokyo Imperial University's medical college, Shirabe came from a poor farmer's family in the city of Asakura, northeast of Nagasaki.[4]

Confident that he could treat Kōichi, the professor explained to Wasa a new method of treating infected vertebrae. It would mean slicing off about twenty centimetres of Kōichi's shin bone and implanting it next to the contaminated site to keep the spine still and straight. Kōichi, he said, would be the first patient to undergo this surgery.

The surgery, conducted in the spring of 1942, was a success. Dr Shirabe had saved his life. Kōichi was in agony afterwards, but the doctors simply told him to tolerate the pain. 'You are a strong brave Japanese boy of the Japanese empire,' Kōichi remembered one saying. 'Don't be a coward.' Bedridden and with no friends in Nagasaki, Kōichi was miserable and lonely. Wasa was his only comfort. The bond between mother and son grew ever stronger.

Lying in his hospital bed, Kōichi heard his fellow patients eagerly discussing Japan's military successes – the occupation of the Philippines, the Dutch East Indies, Burma and Malaya. But in the year after Kōichi's operation, as he slowly recuperated in the hospital, the tide turned in the war, particularly after the US defeated Japan at the Battle of Midway in June 1942. To prevent morale slipping, that news was kept secret from the Japanese public.

A few miles north of the Nagasaki hospital, at the mountainside monastery built by Father Kolbe, the war had upended the routine of the forty Polish and Japanese brothers and priests who lived and worked there.

During a visit to the friary in 1940, a newspaper reporter, accompanied by a policeman, asked the friars' views about the war. When one of the Poles criticised Germany, the policeman was appalled: 'We cannot allow anybody to criticise our ally!' he shouted. He ordered the man to apologise and retract his comments.[5]

The head of the institution, Father Samuel Rosenbaiger, told the friars to stop talking with outsiders about the war or about politics in general. Since most communication and bank transfers between Japan and Poland had stopped after Germany invaded Poland,

Polish friars were not allowed to leave the friary in Nagasaki during the war

Rosenbaiger went to the US looking for financial help from the Franciscan Church. After Pearl Harbor in December 1941, he was unable to return to Japan.[6] Father Mirochna, whom Kolbe had brought to Japan in 1930 as a seminary student and ordained as a priest, took over as guardian of the community.

Soon after Pearl Harbor, about ten Kempeitai military police officers searched every nook and cranny of the friary and took photos of all the inhabitants. A feared arm of the Imperial Japanese Army, the Kempeitai were as notorious as the Tokkō, the secret police force, for their brutality. Days later, several high-ranking Kempeitai officers arrived to interview Father Mirochna. 'We need to know what you are teaching your seminary students about our emperor,' one asked.

Mirochna chose his words carefully, knowing that an incorrect answer could lead to the institution's closure, the friars' arrest or other punishment. 'We teach them to respect and obey the emperor, because in Japan he is God's proxy,' he said. 'We teach them that God is absolute but has delegated his power to his proxy, who must be obeyed.'

One of the officers smashed his hand on the wooden table. 'That is absolutely wrong!' he screamed. 'Our emperor is not a substitute! He *is* God! He descended from heaven!'

Mirochna said calmly: '*Gomen nasai*. I'm sorry if I offended you. But our mission is to tell the truth. Show us evidence that your emperor came down from heaven and we will believe it.'

'Japanese scholars will prove that soon!' the officer replied, and stormed out of the building with his colleagues.[7]

Soon afterwards, the military ordered the student seminary to close and requisitioned its classrooms and sleeping cells for use as an internment camp. About sixty men and women started living in an area cordoned off from the Poles. Most were British and Canadian missionaries and their families who had been living in or near the cities of Osaka and Kobe. Lacking food and money, the internees reared cows, pigs and chickens on the mountain slopes and grew subsistence crops.

It's unclear why the Polish friars were not put into the internment camp with the other missionaries. After all, Poland was part of the Allied forces until the Nazi invasion and its citizens would have been perceived as Japan's enemies. But the friary was allowed to operate until the end of the war, albeit under strict military restrictions and surveillance.

The military ordered the publishing operations started by Father Kolbe in 1930 to stop, and they took over the printing room as a storage area. Brother Zeno's biographer, Tōru Matsui, speculated that the friars had become so well accepted in Nagasaki that no one wanted to change the status quo.

After two-and-a-half years of bedridden illness, Kōichi Tagawa was able to walk again by the spring of 1944. Shrugging off the occasional pain in his spine, he visited the Lourdes-style grotto above the Nagasaki friary with his mother, to celebrate his recovery.

Kōichi had no idea at the time that this had been Father Kolbe's favourite place to contemplate the world. There, Wasa and Kōichi watched as a group of Japanese seminary students in black uniforms chanted a litany in Latin in front of the statue of the Virgin Mary.

Although the seminary remained closed, the students continued their religious activities.

Kōichi was captivated. It was at that moment, he said later, that he became convinced that his mother had 'given and dedicated her son to the Virgin Mary'.

Wasa and Kōichi, now aged sixteen, had no money and no home. But the hospital in which he'd lived for thirty months found him a job as a laboratory assistant in its otolaryngology department. Kōichi reared rabbits for a military doctor who tested the effects of movement on the rodents' inner ears as part of an air force experiment.

Kōichi slept in a storage closet next to the janitor's office and eventually scraped together enough yen to rent a room near the hospital entrance. He shared it with a woman whose husband was fighting overseas. She was lonely, so female friends often came over to keep her and Kōichi company. After Kōichi told Father Mirochna that he had been sharing a room with several women, the head of the friary told him that it was inappropriate. Brother Yasugorō Nakamura eventually found a small room for Kōichi to rent in a tailor's house nearby.

Wasa, meanwhile, worked as a nursing attendant at the hospital. Every night, she slept in a patient's room and ate the hospital food with Kōichi next to the patient's bed.

On his day off, Kōichi sometimes walked to the friary, occasionally staying overnight and becoming acquainted with Brother Zeno, Father Mirochna and the other Poles. Because of wartime restrictions, the buildings remained dark and quiet, and the friars were prohibited from going out freely.

One exception was Brother Zeno, whose network of friends included some police and military officers. Zeno, one of them told his biographer, Tōru Matsui, was 'much more trustworthy than any Japanese'.[8] Food, clothing and other goods were in such short supply that the Japanese often stole the goods and sold them on the black market.

According to Matsui, the military assigned Zeno to look after their goods in storage at the friary and to work as a liaison between the military and the foreigners in the internment camp. Zeno used his shoe-making skills to repair, without charge, the boots of military and police officers and he was occasionally allowed to visit Nagasaki.

Throughout the war, Zeno sat near the friary's entrance making stone steps out of flagstones that he acquired from a slaughter-house. Whenever locals passed by, including military officers, he'd invite them to visit. If an air raid warning sounded while he was in Nagasaki, Zeno would run into a police station for shelter. The policemen, fearful of being accused of protecting a foreigner, would find him a hiding place until the raid was over.[9]

By mid-1944, despite the upbeat military propaganda, it was clear to Nagasaki residents that the war was going badly for Japan. The Allies were closing in. Thousands of Japanese died during battles with US troops on the Pacific islands of Guam, Saipan and Tinian in July and August 1944. Military leaders in Japan announced that many soldiers there had died 'like shattered jewels' (*gyokusai*). It was a term that idealised death and persuaded the public to revere the soldiers' sacrifice on behalf of the country and the emperor.

The loss of these Mariana Islands meant the US was now able to build airstrips there and to fly B-29 Superfortress bombers directly to Japan and begin strategic air raids over many cities. The US first bombed Nagasaki in August 1944, killing thirteen and injuring twenty-six people. Numerous low-level strafing runs and incendiary bombings on the city of Ōmura, eighteen miles north of Nagasaki, followed.

At the friary, Brother Zeno led a group of men digging an enor-mous air-raid shelter in the mountainside that could hold as many as 200 people. Working with Japanese locals, they also built an underground tank for storing fire-fighting water.

With so many men fighting elsewhere, the government mobil-ised millions of teenagers, women and the elderly to prepare for battles with the US on Japan's main islands. The slogan used to inspire the nation was *Ichioku gyokusai* (100 million shattered jewels).

This meant that in the coming battles, as with the soldiers overseas, everyone should be prepared to die beautifully, like precious gemstones.[10]

Despite his poor health, Kōichi was assigned to join military training exercises. These involved practising bamboo-stick thrusts with an imaginary American enemy. He also learned how to douse fires by dumping buckets of water onto houses.

Kōichi couldn't help but think that bamboo sticks would be no match for American guns. Weaker than friends of the same age, Kōichi knew he'd fail as a soldier if he was drafted. He was desperate to remain with his mother, but didn't want to continue working in the hospital breeding rabbits.

One day in early 1945, shortly before his seventeenth birthday, Kōichi told the military doctor that he was leaving the hospital. He remembered how the Latin litanies of the seminary students at the Polish friary had stirred his soul. 'I want to study theology at a Catholic friary run by foreign missionaries,' he told the doctor.

'Foreigners?' the doctor answered, aghast. 'You want to live in a place run by foreigners? Don't you know we're fighting a war against foreigners? Foreigners in Japan are all spies! You traitor, shame on you!' The doctor punched Kōichi in the face. He screamed and fell over. A few days later, he stopped working at the hospital and resolved to study theology as soon as he had some money on which to live.[11]

Fearful of being sent to a battlefront, Kōichi began job-hunting. He found one immediately, just minutes from Urakami Cathedral in the district of Nagasaki where most Christians lived. The job was in one of Japan's largest arms factories, where 12,000 workers toiled around the clock making torpedoes for the Imperial Japanese Navy.

Nagasaki had long been one of Japan's major centres for manufacturing weapons and warships. At its heart was Mitsubishi Heavy Industries, part of the Mitsubishi conglomerate whose tentacles reached into every corner of the nation's economy.

Even before Pearl Harbor, Mitsubishi was secretly making torpedoes in Nagasaki for the navy. After the attack, the company expanded its operations there, opening the Ōhashi arms factory in May 1942 on a fifty-acre site in north Urakami.

For Kōichi, the job was perfect. With his 100-yen income each month, he was proud to pay the rent for the small wooden house belonging to a relative where he and Wasa lived. Wasa no longer needed to work. Better still, Kōichi could walk to the Ōhashi factory.

From his home, Kōichi could see and hear the B-29 bombers that were targeting Nagasaki and cities nearby. Five US raids on Nagasaki between April and August 1945 led to 330 deaths and 530 injuries.

The military government commissioned Mitsubishi to create six 300-metre-long parallel tunnels inside nearby mountains about half a mile from its main factory in which to make torpedoes. Each tunnel was a maximum of three metres high and four-and-a-half metres wide. As many as 1,000 Korean labourers were conscripted to dig the tunnels. By April 1945 two were complete, connected by thin alleyways, and 1,800 workers were assigned to work in the tunnels, including Kōichi.

In Tunnel 1, teenage volunteers and military draftees produced torpedo body and rudder parts and polished joints. In Tunnel 2, where Kōichi worked, the precision department made propellers, rudders and motion-stabilisation parts. All the finished products were sent to the Ōhashi factory, where about eighty torpedoes were assembled every month.

Some of the torpedoes were placed on *kaiten* submarines that rammed into US and British warships off Okinawa in the spring of 1945. This was part of the military's kamikaze operations, a last desperate effort to counter the Allied offensive at a time when the war was almost certainly lost.

Kōichi tried not to think how the torpedoes would be used. He just wanted to get on with his life and continue to live with his mother.

As the spring of 1945 turned to summer, a few miles from Mitsubi-shi's newly built Sumiyoshi Tunnel arms factory, the Kempeitai were becoming increasingly strict with the remaining men at the friary. Not even Brother Zeno was allowed to leave the premises.

Once, when the men were cooking, smoke billowed from a chimney on the roof. Within minutes, several military police arrived and ordered the friars to congregate outside. Shooting into the air to threaten the men, the Kempeitai officers chastised them for making it easier for the enemy to locate bombing targets.

On 1 August, the military ordered the Polish men to leave immediately for Oyama Inn, a civilian internment camp in a hot springs resort in Tochinoki, Kumamoto prefecture, east of Nagasaki. An American air raid, which killed nearly 200 people, delayed their departure by a day. Only Father Mirochna and Brother Zeno were allowed to remain at the friary to oversee the Japanese brothers and students who were still living there, helping the war effort.

Back in Tunnel 2, Kōichi Tagawa and other workers toiled twelve hours a day, watched by navy guards who brandished bayonet-tipped rifles.

'Conditions were really tough in the tunnel,' he said. 'It was the peak of summer and so it was extremely hot in there. But we had to keep the strictest discipline because senior officers from the navy were always patrolling.'

At 11.02 a.m. on 9 August 1945, just over three hours into his daytime shift, a deafening roar filled the tunnel. It was followed immediately by a violent blast of wind that knocked Kōichi and his work colleagues to the ground. All the lights went out, and part of Tunnel 2's zinc roof crashed down on the machinery.

In an instant, Kōichi Tagawa's life changed for ever.

11. Masatoshi Asari's War

March 1943 – Nanae, Hokkaido

Hirohito, by the grace of Heaven, Emperor of Japan, seated on the throne occupied by the same dynasty from time immemorial, enjoin upon ye, Our loyal and brave subjects:

We hereby declare war on the United States of America and the British Empire.

Two days before his twelfth birthday, on 8 March 1943, Masatoshi Asari stood to attention, head down, in the freezing assembly hall of his primary school in Nanae village, Hokkaido. He listened listlessly as the headmaster read out the Declaration of War that had been released in the name of the emperor after Japan attacked Pearl Harbor on 8 December 1941. (7 December, US time.)

It was the umpteenth time that Masatoshi and his schoolmates had heard their headmaster read out the declaration. It was the umpteenth time that he'd inwardly yawned and tuned out the message.

On the eighth day of every month, head teachers across Japan and its empire were required to read the Declaration of War aloud to their pupils. It was also reprinted on the front page of Japanese newspapers that day to remind an increasingly war-weary nation why they were fighting.

'More than four years have passed since China, failing to comprehend the true intentions of Our Empire, and recklessly courting trouble, disturbed the peace of East Asia and compelled Our Empire to take up arms.'

The US and Britain had obstructed Japan's 'peaceful' trade and severed economic relations, 'menacing gravely the existence of Our Empire', the declaration said.

'The situation being such as it is, Our Empire, for its existence

A military marching exercise at a school in Nanae village

and self-defence, has no other recourse but to appeal to arms and to crush every obstacle in its path.'

As the headmaster droned on, Masatoshi stole a glance at the *goshin'ei*, a sacred portrait of Japan's 'divine' emperor and empress. Masatoshi and his friends found most of the words in the Declaration of War incomprehensible.

'The hallowed spirits of Our Imperial Ancestors guarding Us from above, We rely upon the loyalty and courage of Our subjects in Our confident expectation that the task bequeathed by Our forefathers will be carried forward and that the sources of evil will be speedily eradicated and an enduring peace immutably established in East Asia, preserving thereby the glory of Our Empire.'

As soon as the headmaster finished the reading, Masatoshi drew in his breath, raised his arms and shouted *'Tennō-heika banzai!'* (Long live the emperor!) along with his fellow pupils.

But the principal's talk wasn't quite over. Japan, the headmaster explained for the umpteenth time, was fighting to create a Greater East Asia Co-Prosperity Sphere, free from Western imperialism. This concept was the brainchild of former Prime Minister Fumimaro Konoe, and it was based on the philosophy of Hakkō Ichiu (Eight corners of the world under one roof). The conceit was that the empire of Japan had the divine right to 'unify the eight corners of the world' because the Japanese were a 'chosen race'. The slogan had been popular since Konoe's government first mentioned it in January 1940.

At last, the interminable assembly concluded, and Masatoshi marched back to his glacial classroom. By now, the war permeated every aspect of his education. Fewer teachers offered lessons because most men had been drafted into the military and were fighting overseas.

The emperor's divine power was glorified at numerous other special assemblies at Masatoshi's school. These included Tenchō-setsu, the emperor's birthday; Kigen-setsu, the National Foundation Day; and Genshi-sai, the Shinto Festival of Origins. Each day was supposed to be a national holiday, but children were required to attend school assemblies on those days to 'celebrate' the occasion.

Masatoshi was frustrated and bored. He yearned for normal lessons and to learn in his favourite biology classes about the plants and flowers that he loved. There were so many rules at school to remember. He sometimes forgot to bow deeply when he walked past the *hōan-den*, the small shrine in the schoolyard that normally held the sacred portrait of the emperor and empress.

The shrine's doors were opened only to take the portrait to the hall for special assemblies. Someone was always on duty to guard the shrine. Anyone who didn't bow deeply enough to honour the emperor was punished. Masatoshi was frequently in this group. In the staff room, a male teacher smashed a fist into Masatoshi's face in front of other teachers and screamed at him to mend his ways.

'You were not a human being if you didn't believe in the emperor as a living God,' Masatoshi recalled. Teachers repeatedly told him that the most precious thing one could do was to die for the country. And then you would be worshipped in Yasukuni Shrine in Tokyo as a war hero.

Masatoshi's teachers explained to the pupils that their lives were akin to those of the national flower, the cherry blossom. The boys were told that there was no greater honour than to fall bravely on a battlefield like a cherry blossom petal.[1]

Since the 1930s, cherry blossoms had become a key part of Japan's wartime ideology. It was said that these blossoms lived beautifully for a short time and then fell gloriously. One popular wartime song, 'Cherry Blossom Brothers' ('Dōki no Sakura'), made the analogy clear. 'Having blossomed, we must scatter,' the song went. 'Let us fall magnificently for our country.'

This 'cherry ideology', promoted by the government and the military, focused mainly on the particular variety known as 'Somei-yoshino'. This had been planted en masse throughout Japan in the early twentieth century, to the exclusion of most other cherry varieties.[2]

The cloned, single-petalled 'Somei-yoshino' cherries bloomed simultaneously in a display of youthful vigour. After about eight days the soft pink-white blossoms dropped all at once, in a spectacular image of a mass falling. For the military, there was no more convenient visual tool to evoke the life and death of a soldier.

Even at his tender age, Masatoshi Asari thought this equivalence was bogus, although he kept his thoughts to himself. In Hokkaido, the 'Somei-yoshino' variety had never been popular. In part, this was because the island was mostly too cold for the variety, which bloomed only in some warmer regions. Other cherry species or varieties such as Ōyama-zakura or 'Naden' were more prevalent, and these were not planted en masse. Their flowers blossomed at different times.

At least ten cherry trees grew in Masatoshi's large garden, including the rare 'Kanzan' variety. All were symbols of life, hope and happiness. In fact, Masatoshi didn't recall seeing 'Somei-yoshino' at all in Nanae village. And he had no intention of dying magnificently for anyone.

Sometimes, Masatoshi recalled, soldiers who had returned from the battlefields in China visited his school and boasted to the children of how many Chinese they had killed with their samurai swords. The visits made Masatoshi uncomfortable, but he knew he would be branded a traitor if he voiced any opinion.

It was a different story at home. Masatoshi's mother, Chie, didn't mention any of the belligerent propaganda and slogans that his teachers spouted. Rather, she taught her son to be benevolent and sensitive to others, despite his stubborn and sceptical personality.

One day in the spring of 1943, Masatoshi noticed a ragged young man of about twenty tending the horses and cattle of an impoverished farming couple near his home. The couple bred horses to sell to the military and they needed a helping hand because their only son had been drafted. 'Who's the man?' he asked his mother. 'It's a secret,' she replied quietly. 'If anyone asks, he doesn't exist.'

Soon afterwards, Masatoshi met the man, who went by the Japanese name of Kazuo Takemoto. He had come from Korea, which had been ruled by force since its annexation by Japan in 1910. Takemoto was one of tens of thousands of Korean men whom the Japanese government had forcibly transported to Hokkaido to work in coal mines and on construction sites.

Hokkaido was one of the main energy bases for Japan. Its coal was essential for the power plants that produced electricity for Tokyo and surrounding prefectures. Since most Japanese men had joined the military, the government was now dependent on Korean forced labour.

The Koreans were treated as second-class citizens. In Hokkaido, as elsewhere, they were forced to work long hours without sufficient food or clothing. Often beaten and abused, many died, and others tried to run away. If captured, they were tortured.

Kazuo Takemoto had escaped from a nearby coal mine and taken refuge at the home of Masatoshi's neighbours. It was an extremely dangerous situation. The Japanese police were searching for Takemoto, and it was a crime to hide and protect so-called 'criminal fugitives'. Nonetheless, Masatoshi's mother invited Takemoto for a meal, despite having barely enough food for her daughter and four sons. 'It's not glamorous, but eat as much as you want,' she told him. From then on, Takemoto frequently ate at Masatoshi's home.

For more than a year, Takemoto lived secretly in the neighbours' house. College-educated and fluent in Japanese, he became close with Masatoshi and his older brother, Shōichi. He loved visiting the lively Asari household and everyone treated him as part of the family.

When Masatoshi and Shōichi went swimming with Takemoto in the nearby river, he taught the brothers 'Arirang', a Korean folk song. The boys sang it together and translated the words into Japanese. Takemoto opened up about his life a little, but to protect himself and the Asari family he never told them his Korean name or which part of the country he came from.

In the early summer of 1944, news reached Takemoto through an underground network of fugitives and their protectors that his mother in Korea was extremely sick. He desperately wanted to return home. Shōichi and Masatoshi discussed with their father how to help. At the time, horses from Hokkaido were regularly shipped to Honshu, Japan's main island, for the military, but there was a shortage of men to care for them on board. It seemed like a perfect job for Takemoto as long as no one asked him for identification papers.

The Asaris devised a plan. Step one was to get Takemoto from Hokkaido to Honshu, from where he could travel south and catch a boat to Korea. One day, Shōichi, Masatoshi and their father accompanied Takemoto to Hakodate, the largest port in Hokkaido, and arranged for him to be smuggled on a rail ferry to Aomori, a port on Honshu's northern tip. The rail ferries were a vital lifeline for the military because they carried priceless goods from Hokkaido, such as coal, fish, rice, grain and horses. As the boys said their hasty farewells at the port, Takemoto looked weary but happy, Masatoshi recalled.

For the rest of the war, Masatoshi awaited word that Takemoto had made it home. But none came, and his Korean friend became just one more of the millions who disappeared during the conflict, most likely dead, imprisoned, or captured and sent to fight for the emperor.

'I always wondered if he reached home safely and saw his mother. But I can never forget him,' Asari said. 'His honesty remained with me. As a child, I didn't understand the full circumstances about his life, but I knew he was in a difficult situation and that he'd suffered a lot of injustice in Japan.'

Asari's encounters with Takemoto would drive him in later life to investigate and uncover Japan's inhumane treatment of Korean labourers during the war.

Conditions in Hokkaido largely mirrored those in the rest of Japan throughout the war. In the early days after Pearl Harbor, the island's rich array of agricultural products meant that its 3.3 million inhabitants were well fed. That changed after June 1942, when the US overwhelmed the Imperial Japanese Navy at the Battle of Midway.

For the following three years, Japan mobilised millions of men to fight throughout Asia and the Pacific Islands, and the war effort took priority over every other aspect of life. Food, once abundant, suddenly became in short supply.

The Asari family's life settled into an uneasy pattern. Masatoshi's elder brother, Shōichi, who turned sixteen in 1943, was mobilised as a 'volunteer' worker for the war effort. He worked on road construction sites with several hundred prisoners of war. Mostly British, they had been captured by the Japanese army in Hong Kong or on the Malay peninsula and brought to the main POW camp in Hakodate.

The malnourished men were physically abused if they didn't obey orders. Every evening, Shōichi told his brother stories about the British men. How they were forced to sing military songs in Japanese while marching and were beaten if they didn't remember the words. How they dived into the freezing ocean off Hakodate in winter to clean the keels of Japanese warships. How they ate tiny pieces of dried squid for lunch and then banged on tin cans with wooden chopsticks while singing songs in English.[3]

By 1944, food shortages were the norm in Hokkaido. Most residents in and around Nanae village were farmers. But no sooner were their crops ready for harvesting than the military confiscated large swathes of them to send to Honshu and elsewhere for the troops.

The military pressured the farmers, including Asakichi, Masatoshi's father, to produce ever more rice, wheat, potatoes, corn and other staples to feed the military machine. The local people went hungry, which made them more susceptible to catching beriberi and tuberculosis.

As food became scarcer, Asakichi secretly gave some of his crops to starving locals, which was a crime. Several times, the police hauled Asakichi off to jail for distributing food from his fields.

'I always wondered why my father gave away our crops to other people when we were so hungry ourselves,' Masatoshi said. 'But he grew up in a poor family and he lost everything as an adult in the fire, so he was always sympathetic to anyone who was suffering.'

On 10 March 1945, Masatoshi Asari's fourteenth birthday, the Japan Broadcasting Corporation, better known as NHK, reported that the US Army Air Forces had attacked Tokyo overnight. The firebombing of Japan's capital by 279 B-29 Superfortress bombers from bases in the Mariana Islands turned out to be the most destructive single air attack in human history, killing about 100,000 people.

The US targeted Japanese cities one after another, flying planes from the islands of Guam, Saipan and Tinian to bomb civilian population centres. Japanese military propagandists still crowed that victory was assured because of the emperor's divine power and the people's willingness to fight to the death. At the same time, Masatoshi heard adults whispering that it was only a matter of time before American aircraft would target Hokkaido.

In April 1945, after two years of middle school, Masatoshi started agricultural high school. His brother, Shōichi, was in line to inherit the family farm because he was the eldest boy in the family. But since Shōichi was likely to be drafted into the military, Masatoshi was expected to learn agricultural skills in case anything happened to his brother.

As part of a student mobilisation effort, Masatoshi was deployed to Hokkaido's agricultural experimental centre. Since most workers at the centre had departed for the battlefields, teenagers took their jobs. It was an unusually harsh spring. Freezing air from Siberia blew over the farmland, damaging the rice and corn in the fields. Only pumpkins and radishes survived the raw conditions.

Desperate for food, the military ordered the centre to find ways to improve the crop yields. One of Masatoshi's tasks was to test different kinds of fertiliser.

By now, the scarcity of food had become life-threatening. Along with his brothers, Masatoshi scoured the fields looking for clover, dandelions and other weeds to boil and eat. They caught grasshoppers and locusts, which they killed, dried and ate. They climbed mulberry trees and tore off the young leaves to make tea and to eat. When all else failed, they chewed grass.

At the experimental centre, the instructors told the students that they must be prepared to withstand an American assault. 'But how can we fight if we're so hungry?' Masatoshi wanted to reply. He kept silent, assuming that everyone in Japan was in the same unhappy predicament. In fact, thousands of miles south of Hokkaido, in the Okinawan islands, the situation was far worse.

On 1 April 1945, US troops launched the Pacific War's largest amphibious assault on Okinawa. It was the beginning of an almost three-month-long battle that killed half the islands' pre-war population along with tens of thousands of American and Japanese troops. In response, the Japanese launched waves of kamikaze attacks against American warships.

Scores of tiny aircraft departed from Chiran airbase in southern Kyushu that month, each with a bomb attached to its belly. Many of the kamikaze pilots wrote letters to their parents the night before taking off to die. They wrote that they would 'fall bravely like the cherry blossoms', which were in full bloom at the time.[4]

The kamikaze planes had pink cherry flowers painted on each side of their belly. The explosives they carried were called 'cherry blossom bombs', although the Americans called them 'baka bombs'. (*Baka* means 'stupid' in Japanese.) The cherry-blossom imagery was pure propaganda, designed to rally the population when the war appeared to hang in the balance.[5] One famous staged photo showed schoolgirls standing on a runway waving cherry-blossom branches as the kamikaze pilot took off.

The suicidal attacks continued, even after Germany surrendered on 7 May. Two days later, the Japanese government said that the Nazi capitulation 'would not affect the Japanese Empire's purpose of war'.[6] To most military leaders, defeat was not an option. Indeed, according to the military, the kamikaze campaign had just begun. Soon, they declared, there would be '100 million kamikaze attacks', a hint to the US that the entire Japanese population would commit suicide attacks if America invaded. Throughout the country, everyone feared the worst.

On 15 July 1945, as Masatoshi slept in an air-raid shelter near his home, he was awoken at 5.30 a.m. by the piercing screams of air-raid sirens. Rushing outside as dawn broke, he saw three US Navy Grumman TBM Avenger torpedo bombers fly almost directly overhead en route to Hakodate. They were flying so low that Masatoshi glimpsed the silhouettes of the pilots in the cockpit. The planes had been deployed from US warships anchored off the east coast of Hokkaido.

From the branch of a tall larch tree, Masatoshi watched the Avenger planes and some Curtiss SB2C Helldivers bomb the port town as Japanese anti-aircraft units tried to shoot down the attackers. Bright orange flames lit the sky and jet-black smoke curled into the air. It was like viewing a movie from the treetops, Masatoshi thought.

After the raid ended, Masatoshi ran home immediately, adrenaline pumping. He needed to warn his mother, Chie, and the rest of the Asari family that the Americans had arrived. Inside his house, and in the family's warehouse, more than a dozen strangers were napping on the floor with their children. Since Hakodate was an enemy target, the city had evacuated thousands of people to the countryside. As Masatoshi talked excitedly about what he'd witnessed, Chie shared tiny bowls of wheat and potatoes with their visitors. The mood was quiet and glum. Everyone was resigned to their fate.

Other attacks followed that day and the next. But according to a local newspaper, 'the enemy's raids did not achieve what they wanted. The army and civilians fought back bravely, limiting casualties to a minimum.'[7]

The reality was totally different. The US attacks were aimed at destroying the coal-carrying rail ferries that plied between Hakodate and Aomori. All twelve ferries and more than 150 other ships were sunk or damaged in the raids.[8] Years later, Masatoshi would expose the true picture of what happened during the air raids, which killed as many as 2,900 civilians.

Masatoshi found it hard to concentrate on his job, though it was better than staying at his crowded home. His biggest fear was to be killed or injured in an air raid. This concern intensified in August after he heard that the Americans had dropped a new and more powerful bomb on the city of Hiroshima.

Could anything be worse than the deadly attacks he'd witnessed on Hakodate? he wondered. If so, who would the Americans target next?

12. 'A Rain of Ruin'

August 1945 – above Nagasaki

In the early evening of Tuesday, 7 August 1945, a devout twenty-five-year-old Irish American Catholic from Boston called Charles W. Sweeney borrowed a jeep and drove along the oceanfront on the Pacific island of Tinian in search of an army priest to talk about his upcoming mission.[1]

The day before, 6 August, Sweeney had commanded a B-29 Silverplate bomber called *The Great Artiste* on an historic flight from Tinian to Hiroshima. *The Great Artiste* was an observation plane. It carried the sensitive instruments that measured the destructive impact of the 9,700-pound uranium bomb that its sister aircraft, *Enola Gay*, had dropped on the unsuspecting city.

That bomb, called 'Little Boy', had more than 2,000 times the blast power of the largest bomb ever used previously in the history of warfare. An estimated 140,000 people died before the end of the year.

After *Enola Gay* and *The Great Artiste* returned to Tinian, Sweeney had been told that if Japan didn't surrender immediately, he would command a mission on 9 August to drop another atomic bomb. It was a massive vote of confidence in Sweeney by Colonel Paul Tibbets, the overall commander of the 509th Composite Group. The group was a unit of the US Army Air Forces set up with the sole purpose of dropping atomic bombs.

Tibbets himself had commanded the *Enola Gay* mission, and to Sweeney, the bombing of Hiroshima had been a 'picture-perfect mission from beginning to end'. But he was torn, knowing that the first atomic bombing in history had caused so much death and destruction and that a second mission was a colossal responsibility. 'Jesus taught us to love,' he wrote later. 'He turned the other cheek. Where would He draw the line?'[2]

Charles W. Sweeney

Sixteen hours after the Hiroshima blast, US President Harry Truman had issued a press statement which for the first time offered details of the Manhattan Project, the US's top-secret operation to build and detonate an atomic bomb.[3]

Truman, who had succeeded Franklin D. Roosevelt as president after Roosevelt's death in April 1945, had known virtually nothing about the project when he entered the White House. But in his diary on 25 July, Truman had written chillingly about the planned attacks on Japan.

'We have discovered the most terrible bomb in the history of the world,' he wrote. 'It may be the fire destruction prophesied in the Euphrates Valley Era, after Noah and his fabulous Ark.'[4]

In the press statement after Hiroshima, Truman said it was 'providence' that Germany had not developed the atomic bomb, and his message to Japan's leaders about its possible future use couldn't have been clearer.

'We are now prepared to obliterate more rapidly and completely every productive enterprise the Japanese have above ground in any city. We shall destroy their docks, their factories, and their communications. Let there be no mistake; we shall completely destroy Japan's power to make war.'

Truman added that the 26 July Potsdam Declaration, which

called for Japan's unconditional surrender, had been issued 'to spare the Japanese people from utter destruction. If they do not now accept our terms they may expect a rain of ruin from the air, the like of which has never been seen on this earth.'

The Japanese government had been secretly trying to find a way to end the war since June 1945, but it had failed to agree with the nation's military leaders on the conditions of surrender.[5] After the bomb was dropped on Hiroshima, the government remained silent, and so US plans to drop a second atom bomb continued apace.

The primary target was Kokura, a steel town in the north of the island of Kyushu. The secondary target was the nearby port of Nagasaki, where the Mitsubishi conglomerate made warships and torpedoes.

For the Kokura mission, Sweeney was set to command the strike plane, a B-29 bomber called *Bockscar*. *Bockscar*'s precious cargo was a 10,300-pound plutonium bomb dubbed 'Fat Man' after a character in the novel and film, *The Maltese Falcon*.

Sitting in an open-air theatre where he usually attended Sunday Mass, Sweeney asked the Catholic priest whether it was a sin to wage war and whether any wars could be considered 'just'. In reply, the priest cited Thomas Aquinas, the thirteenth-century Italian philosopher and friar, who had shaped Roman Catholic doctrine for centuries. Aquinas had concluded that war was justified under certain circumstances, such as to secure peace and punish evil in defence of the common good.

Without mentioning Hiroshima or the mission scheduled for 9 August, Sweeney inquired whether weapons of mass destruction could be justified. 'War as we know it today *is* mass destruction,' the unnamed priest told him. 'Will greater weapons bring a quicker end to the war? I don't know. But you must be certain of your cause and your intentions because the nature of modern weapons makes the stakes much higher.'

As darkness smothered the tiny island on that star-filled evening, Sweeney said he felt completely at peace with himself.[6]

America's second atomic bomb mission comprised six B-29s and 65 men. Two planes were for weather reconnaissance and a third was a back-up strike plane that remained at Iwo Jima, an island south of Tokyo, because it wasn't needed. Accompanying *Bockscar* was *The Great Artiste* and a camera plane called *Big Stink*.

The 509th Composite Group was housed in a heavily armed compound on Tinian, completely isolated from the other 40,000 or so US military personnel on the diamond-shaped island. At that time, Tinian was the world's largest airbase, an endless sea of black asphalt and crushed coral from whose four parallel runways planes took off hour after hour to bomb Japanese cities.[7]

Most members of the group were US Army Air Forces crew in their late twenties, but it also included a few men notable because of their unique capabilities.

Perhaps the most noteworthy – and unusual – member was the granddaddy of the mission: a fifty-seven-year-old former Orthodox Jew from a tiny Russian-controlled village called Salantai in Lithuania. His name was Lieb Wolf Siew, or Leyb Ziv.[8]

In 1905, around the same time as Raymond Kolbe (later Maximilian Kolbe) was cheering Japan's military victory over Russia, Siew had his nose smashed in by a Tsarist policeman. He had been protesting Russia's occupation of his exclusively Jewish village.

Fearful of anti-Jewish pogroms that were sweeping through Russia and its territories, the seventeen-year-old Siew made his way to the United States. There, he proclaimed himself an atheist and transformed himself into a bespoke American, changing his name to William Leonard Laurence.[9]

After a stellar education at Harvard University, Boston University and Harvard Law School, Laurence decided to become a journalist. In 1930, he joined the *New York Times*, the world's most influential news source, as a science writer.

On 24 February 1939, after meeting two physicists at Columbia University, Laurence became the first journalist to explain the theory that an atom of uranium's rarest isotope, U-235, could be split in two, unleashing astonishing quantities of energy.[10] In subsequent years, Laurence made a name for himself within the scientific community for his articles about the promise and perils of this energy source.

Laurence himself was deeply – and personally – affected by the war. In 1941, during Operation Barbarossa, Nazi troops massacred most Jewish residents in Salantai, including his mother, brother and sister.[11]

Early in 1945, the US Army's Major General Leslie R. Grove, the director of the Manhattan Project, secretly asked the New York Times for Laurence to join the project as a government-paid publicist and historian.[12] It was a highly unusual assignment for a journalist. Years later, it would raise questions about Laurence's integrity and possible conflicts of interest.[13]

Laurence threw himself into the assignment. He didn't tell his wife, Florence, where he was or what he was doing, although he wrote to a managing editor at the New York Times that he was working on 'a sort of Second Coming of Christ yarn'.[14] Forty years after arriving in the US, on 16 July 1945, Laurence would become the only journalist to witness the test explosion of the atomic bomb in the New Mexican desert. J. Robert Oppenheimer, the physicist who headed the project, called the test site 'Trinity'.[15]

Laurence's descriptions for the New York Times of the beginning of the so-called Atomic Age, a term he coined, won him two Pulitzer Prizes. More importantly, Laurence's writing became the dominant narrative about the atomic bomb, influencing the perceptions of millions of readers around the world.[16]

Particularly potent were the religious analogies and biblical allusions that dotted Laurence's prose, many of which he'd learned at elementary school in Salantai. By the age of eight, Laurence once said, he could recite most of the Hebrew Bible in the original.

Writing with apocalyptic zeal, Laurence captured the scene of the test explosion with spiritual imagery.

There rose from the bowels of the earth a light not of this world, the light of many suns in one. It was a sunrise such as the world had never seen, a great green super-sun climbing . . . until it touched the clouds, lighting up earth and sky all around with a dazzling luminosity.

One felt as though he had been privileged to witness the Birth of the World – to be present at the moment of Creation when the Lord said: Let There Be Light.

On that moment hung eternity. Time stood still. Space contracted into a pinpoint.[17]

After the flash, a hush descended on the desert, Laurence wrote. 'Then out of the silence came a mighty thunder.' It was, he said, 'the first cry of a new-born world'.[18] US Senator Brien McMahon, the son of Irish Catholic immigrants, was equally astonished and overwhelmed by the test, calling the bomb the 'most important thing in history since the birth of Jesus Christ'.[19]

For the bombing mission to Japan, Laurence was assigned to fly in the scientific instrument plane, *The Great Artiste*, commanded by Captain Fred Bock from Michigan, after whom *Bockscar* was named. Set to fly in the third plane, *Big Stink*, commanded by Major James Hopkins from Texas, was an equally exceptional individual: Royal Air Force Group Captain Leonard Cheshire.

Unlike Laurence, the twenty-seven-year-old Cheshire said he 'hadn't the faintest idea' what an atomic bomb was.[20] But what he lacked in knowledge, he more than made up for in experience. Britain's most decorated bomber pilot, Cheshire had been awarded the Victoria Cross, the highest military award, for gallantry after flying at least 100 bombing sorties over Germany. Like Sweeney and Laurence, the mission would change his life for ever.

On 17 July 1945, a day after the US had secretly tested the world's first plutonium bomb, Leonard Cheshire was ordered to meet with Field Marshal Maitland Wilson, head of the British Joint Staff Mission, in Washington, DC.

That same day, Winston Churchill, Joseph Stalin and Harry Truman gathered in Potsdam, Germany, to plan the post-war peace. Before leaving for Potsdam, Churchill and Truman had agreed that

Leonard Cheshire

two British observers would join the US atomic bomb mission to end the war in the Pacific.[21]

One observer was a physicist, William Penney, a thirty-six-year-old mathematics prodigy who had been working in the Los Alamos National Laboratory on the Manhattan Project for a year. The other was Cheshire.[22]

After a thirty-minute meeting, Maitland Wilson commanded Cheshire to fly 8,000 miles west to Tinian. His brief was to take detailed notes about the future implications for aerial warfare of these unknown bombs and to report his findings to the prime minister.[23]

After arriving on Tinian in late July, Cheshire shared a tent with Penney, and the men watched in amazement one evening as 196 heavily laden B-29 bombers took off for Japan in forty-nine minutes – four planes a minute.[24] No other nation had ever boasted such overwhelming firepower.

While awaiting the nuclear mission, Cheshire spent much of his time pondering 'the deeper meaning' of war. Whenever alone, he read *The Screwtape Letters* by C. S. Lewis, an allegorical novel that addressed Christian theological issues and human nature.[25]

Cheshire also found time to attend a wild party for officers after the return of the *Enola Gay*. There, according to Sweeney, Cheshire got into a fight with Sweeney's future brother-in-law, Paul Burns, after the drunken Burns, an Irish Catholic, sang a song which called into question the manhood of the British.[26]

Two evenings later, shortly before midnight on 8 August, Sweeney, Laurence, Cheshire and other members of the mission gathered for customary prayers for the safety of the crew and the return of peace to the world.

The Catholic chaplain was George B. Zabelka, a former farm boy from St Johns in Michigan. Zabelka blessed the 128- by 60-inch bomb, which resembled an oversized squash. His Protestant counterpart, William Downey, a United Lutheran Church chaplain from Wisconsin, also blessed the device.

The chaplains' actions, like the mission itself, would later become controversial, and would divide people when they reflected on the purpose and morality of the atomic bomb.

Shortly before climbing aboard *Bockscar*, Sweeney gave a pep talk to his crew, all of whom had flown with him on the Hiroshima mission. '[Hiroshima] was a perfect mission flown by Colonel Tibbets,' Sweeney said. 'I want our mission to be exactly the same. We will execute this mission perfectly and get our bomb to the target. I don't care if I have to dive the airplane into the target, we're going to deliver it.'[27]

Sweeney's words could hardly have been more amiss. Operationally, the mission was a near-failure from start to finish.

Even before *Bockscar* took off from runway A of Tinian's North Field early on 9 August, the mission to drop a second atomic bomb on a Japanese city ran into a problem that would have severe repercussions later that day.

A defective pump meant that 600 gallons of aviation fuel was trapped in *Bockscar's* reserve tank, leaving the plane with 6,400 gallons for the flight instead of the full 7,000 gallons. That shortfall meant that any delays during the mission could be catastrophic. But Sweeney decided to go ahead rather than postpone the mission, and

Bockscar soared into the Pacific sky at 2.45 a.m., followed by *The Great Artiste*.[28]

Sweeney didn't know about another early problem because the crews observed radio silence. *Big Stink*'s commander, James Hopkins, had ordered the mission's photographic expert, Dr Robert Serber, a key member of the Manhattan Project, off the plane because Serber had forgotten his parachute. Since Serber was the only person who knew how to work the high-speed camera, he had to break radio silence to instruct Hopkins from Tinian during the flight.

Flying at about 7,000 feet, the planes ran into turbulence. Sweeney took *Bockscar* up to 17,000 feet and then to 30,000 feet for a planned rendezvous with *The Great Artiste* and *Big Stink* over the island of Yakushima, 300 miles south of Kokura, the target.

After five hours of flying, *Bockscar* and *The Great Artiste* joined up over Yakushima, but *Big Stink* was nowhere to be seen. According to Cheshire, Hopkins had climbed to 39,000 feet, 9,000 feet higher than the planned altitude, because of the turbulence.

The mission plan called for the planes to wait no more than fifteen minutes at the rendezvous site. Not seeing *Big Stink*, Sweeney flew around for forty minutes, using up precious gallons of fuel, before flying on to Kokura.[29] Later, *Big Stink* also set a course for the primary target.

The orders were for Fat Man to be dropped *only* if the target was visible to the bomb-aimer, a gregarious Texan called Captain Kermit Beahan, after whom *The Great Artiste* had been named. But as Sweeney prepared for the Kokura bomb run, Beahan shouted: 'I can't see [the target].' By now, Japanese anti-aircraft guns were peppering the sky with flak.

After three unsuccessful runs over the intended target, Sweeney decided to fly to the secondary target, Nagasaki. By this stage *Bockscar*'s fuel situation was critical, and Sweeney knew that he had only enough fuel to make one run over the city. 'Can any other god-damned thing go wrong?' he asked his co-pilot.[30]

It could. Cumulus clouds hung over Nagasaki, making a visible drop impossible. *Bockscar* had only 300 gallons of fuel left. In desperation, even though it broke the mission rules, Sweeney decided to drop the bomb using radar.

'It's better than dropping it into the ocean,' he said. 'I'll take full responsibility for this.' But twenty-five seconds before the planned release, Beahan saw a hole in the clouds midway between Mitsubishi's Morichō and Ōhashi armaments factories. It was more than two miles north of the assigned target zone.

At 11.01 a.m. local time, Beahan dropped the world's most powerful weapon on Nagasaki. It detonated at 1,890 feet. 'It was a mesmerising sight, at once breath-taking and ominous,' Sweeney wrote later.[31]

After leaving Tinian in *The Great Artiste*, William Laurence spent much of his time scribbling reams of notes about the flight.

> Somewhere beyond these vast mountains of white clouds ahead of me there lies Japan, the land of our enemy. In about four hours from now one of its cities, making weapons of war for use against us, will be wiped off the map by the greatest weapon ever made by man.
>
> Does one feel pity or compassion for the poor devils about to die? Not when one thinks of Pearl Harbor and of the Death March on Bataan.[32]

'Destiny chose Nagasaki as the ultimate target,' Laurence continued. As the bomb exploded over the city, Laurence wrote in almost evangelical prose about the explosion, seemingly oblivious to the weapon's deadly features.[33]

> Awestruck, we watched a giant pillar of purple fire shoot upward like a meteor coming from the earth instead of from outer space, becoming ever more alive as it climbed skyward through the white clouds. It was no longer smoke, or dust, or even a cloud of fire, it was a living thing, a new species of being, born right before our incredulous eyes.

Its bottom was brown, its center was amber, its top white. But it was a living totem pole, carved with many grotesque masks grimacing at the earth.[34]

When the bomb exploded, *Big Stink* was still fifty miles from Nagasaki, having failed to rendezvous with the other planes. Even so, seated in the cockpit, Leonard Cheshire was overcome – not by the fireball's size but by what appeared to be its 'perfect and faultless symmetry'. 'My whole being felt overwhelmed, first by a tidal wave of relief – it's all over! – then by a revolt against using such a weapon.'[35]

In *Bockscar*, meanwhile, Sweeney transmitted a brief report to his military commanders: 'Nagasaki bombed. Results technically successful.' And he asked the radio operator to call for air-sea rescue. *Bockscar* lacked enough fuel to fly to the nearest US base in Okinawa, let alone Tinian. But by throttling back the propellers and making a gradual descent, the sixty-five-ton aircraft defied the odds and landed at Okinawa. When the plane touched down, seven gallons of fuel remained – less than one minute of flight time.

As *Bockscar* was being refuelled for the flight back to Tinian, Sweeney turned on Armed Forces Radio, hoping to hear that Japan had surrendered. Instead, the main story was that the Soviet Union had declared war on Japan and was preparing to invade Manchuria.[36]

Back on Tinian, the exhausted flight crews were met by one photographer and the ground crew. There was none of the razzmatazz that had greeted *Enola Gay*'s return. But the following day, 10 August, General Curtis LeMay, head of the Strategic Air Forces in the Pacific, asked Sweeney and Tibbets, the commander of the Hiroshima mission, to discuss the latest mission at a press conference.

After addressing the reporters, LeMay met Tibbets and Sweeney alone. Referring to the 9 August mission, LeMay famously said to Sweeney: 'You f—ed up, didn't you, Chuck?', to which Sweeney said nothing. Turning to Tibbets, LeMay said he didn't think an investigation into the operational shortcomings of the Nagasaki strike would serve any purpose.[37]

It was thought best to let sleeping dogs lie. Besides, to most Americans, the mission had been a resounding success. That was the narrative that most Allies wanted to hear and to believe.

When Kermit Beahan, *Bockscar*'s bomb-aimer, released Fat Man over Nagasaki, he could have had no inkling that the failure to hit the designated target would have such appalling unintended consequences. The target was Tokiwa Bridge, the heart of Nagasaki's commercial and administrative district, including the port, the railways and Mitsubishi's factories.

Instead, the bomb detonated almost directly over the district of Urakami. As intended, Nagasaki's port and factories were largely destroyed. But so too was Japan's largest Christian community and Urakami Catholic cathedral.

About 8,500 out of a total of 12,000 Nagasaki Catholics died instantly, incinerated by temperatures of several thousand degrees centigrade. In all, about 74,000 Nagasaki residents died before the end of 1945, with 75,000 injured. Thousands more would succumb in the coming years to burns, other injuries and radiation poisoning. The deaths continue. More than 190,000 have died as a result of the bombing as of August 2022, according to Nagasaki city's statistics.

The Nagasaki strike was, concluded Barry Scott Zellen, an American research scholar, the greatest irony of the Second World War. 'We [Americans], the liberators and defenders of freedom, fought what, to most historians, was the textbook definition of a *just war* for four long, hard-fought, and bloody years against a global alliance of totalitarian dictatorships,' Zellen wrote. 'And yet our final act of combat would be to drop the deadliest bomb ever devised by man onto Japan's most Christian of communities – one that shared a closer historical and religious connection with our country than any other city in Japan.'[38]

The mission, commanded by a Catholic and blessed by Catholic and Protestant chaplains, devastated the long-suffering Catholic neighbourhood just seventy-two years after Japan's 240-year ban on Christianity had been lifted.

For Kōichi Tagawa, who was making torpedoes in a tunnel when the bomb detonated, the Nagasaki blast was the start of an apocalyptic nightmare that would last more than seven decades.

PART 4

Cries and Whispers, 1945

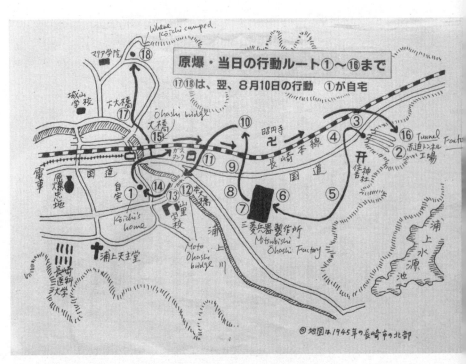

Kōichi Tagawa drew a map of his journey across Nagasaki on 9 & 10 August 1945. Drawn by Kōichi Tagawa, with English-language annotations by the author.

13. Torment

9 August 1945 – Nagasaki

Kōichi Tagawa sat up in the pitch-black tunnel where, just a few seconds earlier, he'd been making parts for airplane torpedoes. His ears were ringing, and he could barely see his hands in front of his face.

Shouts and screams rang through the tunnel as his colleagues came to their senses and tried to comprehend the magnitude of the force that had knocked everyone to the floor like bowling pins. 'What happened?' Kōichi cried out. Out of the darkness came a reply from a co-worker: 'Maybe Mitsubishi detonated dynamite outside to make another tunnel?' (See point ② on map, opposite.) It seemed unlikely.[1]

Kōichi stumbled towards an emergency exit, where he knew there were supplies for use in a crisis. He found an oil lamp and lit it. In the distance, towards the entrance of the tunnel, the ghost-like shadow of a teenage girl staggered inside.

He slowly made his way towards her, stepping over workers lying distraught on the floor, and carefully avoiding the machinery. The girl's straight black hair was frizzled. Wisps of smoke curled from the top of her head. Her face and arms were badly burnt, her red skin was peeling. He couldn't help but stare at this strange apparition.

The girl, a fellow worker, had stepped outside the tunnel to pick up lunch packages for the staff. She was crying softly, clearly in shock. She looked at Kōichi. 'When I was waiting for the lunch truck, I heard a roaring in the sky and a huge white flash like lightning struck the city,' she said. 'The next thing I knew I was all burnt . . .' She collapsed to the floor and whimpered.

A score of injured people trickled into the tunnel, their clothes ripped and askew. Some were drenched in blood. Others dragged their legs or clasped their head in their hands. A man without an arm zig-zagged inside and fell. A young woman followed; she collapsed and Kōichi watched in horror as her guts burst out from an open wound.

The tunnel filled with the ceaseless howls of the dying and injured. A naval officer on patrol bellowed: 'Everybody, get out! Immediately! Anyone who's not injured.' He pushed Kōichi and a few other boys outside with his bayonet. It was about noon, less than an hour after the blast.

Kōichi was stunned at the sight outside. The sky high above was as black as death. Underneath this pall sat a layer of yellow smoke. Beneath, the landscape was a mix of red and orange – fire after fire shooting into the air, burning everything in its path.

The entire world was in ruins. There were no houses, no roads, no cars, no people. Nothing. Just devastation.

At 11 a.m., lush green hills and mountains had surrounded the beautiful port of Nagasaki. Now, shortly after noon, the mountain surfaces were almost bare and grey smoke rose from the crooked trunks of a few leafless trees.

In a field across from the road that ran in front of the torpedo factory tunnel, a taxi burned. (④ on map.) Its driver sat close to his vehicle, which was upside down, his shirt torn, his arms burnt red-raw. Nearby, a man covered in mud lay next to a crumpled bicycle, gasping for air. He too must have been blown into the field from the road.

A luxurious mansion near the tunnel was on fire, flames leaping through the roof. Nobody was trying to put the fire out. (③ on map.) Why, Kōichi wondered? Everyone had been trained in the basics of quenching fires. What had caused this annihilation? Had the earth exploded from within? Kōichi felt as if he had slipped into a dystopian nightmare.

As a Bible-reading Catholic growing up in northern Korea and Nagasaki, he was aware of Heaven and Hell. In his mind, he'd always assumed that Heaven was far above the clouds. That Hell was deep down below. No more. He was witnessing Hell on earth.

In shock, Kōichi and a couple of other boys from the tunnel

climbed a nearby hill to get a clearer view of their city. From the top they could see across central Nagasaki and beyond. (⑤ on map.) Kōichi looked towards his home in the Urakami district, where the Catholic cathedral was the dominant landmark. The whole area was a blanket of fire. The cathedral was nowhere to be seen.

Only then did Kōichi awaken to the reality of the destruction. His house was amid those flames. His mother, Wasa, was at home. Alone. His only thought was to save her.

His mind flashed to earlier that morning. He'd woken at 7 a.m. on a typical humid summer's day. He'd changed out of his *yukata* and pulled on a clean white shirt and baggy work trousers. Then he'd eaten breakfast with Wasa – a tiny portion of strained soybeans and a bowl of brown rice. 'I'm off to work now. See you later,' he'd said. His mother hadn't replied. As he closed the front door, he turned around and shouted: 'See you later, mum!' She was standing in the kitchen, washing up. Through the open window, she smiled at him.

Where was she now? Kōichi's legs began shaking. 'I'm going home,' he told his colleagues and darted down the hill.

Kōichi walked alone among the dirt and the dust of the demolished buildings. There were few signs of life. He reached Mitsubishi's Ōhashi plant where he had worked before moving to the tunnel factory. (⑥ on map.) It was a mass of smoking rubble. Mud-covered corpses littered the site. 'I would have been one of them had I been working here,' Kōichi thought.

He heard a shout. 'Come and help!' A middle-aged man was calling to him. A few survivors were trying to rescue a teenage girl trapped underneath piles of debris from the factory. After about twenty minutes, they pulled her out and put her on a makeshift stretcher. With three other men, Kōichi carried the girl towards a railway track that ran through Nagasaki, hoping that a rescue train would come and pick her up. (⑦ on map.)

In the sweltering heat of the midday sun, sweat poured down Kōichi's face. While carrying the stretcher, he saw the owner of a lavish two-storey house squatting on stone stairs at the entrance. (⑧ on map.) His hair was burnt. The skin of his half-naked body was inflamed. He couldn't move.

Kōichi saw the man a few days later in the same position. His corpse had already started to decay. 'Life is fickle,' Kōichi thought. 'All humans are fragile, no matter how wealthy.' The thought remained with him the rest of his life.

One of the stretcher bearers heard the growl of a plane in the distance. 'The enemy! Another bomb! We'll all be killed!' The men placed the stretcher on the ground and fled, abandoning the injured girl. Kōichi later learned that it was a US reconnaissance plane, taking photos of the damage. (⑨ on map.)

Alone again, Kōichi crossed the railway tracks and walked into the woods. (⑩ on map.) Scores of severely injured people lay on the rough ground, most unable to move. Some screamed in agony. Others were already dead.

Among the injured, Kōichi spotted a familiar face. It was a young man who had worked with him at the Ōhashi factory. The man had bullied Kōichi because he was small and fragile. After work one day, he had beaten up Kōichi for no reason. The man was lying on the ground clutching his belly. His intestines were spilling out of an open wound.

Kōichi had no pity. 'It serves you right!' he told him. 'Damn you . . .' the man replied feebly. There was no chance that he could have survived. The memory of this incident would torment Kōichi for life.

Fleeing from the scene, Kōichi walked into a bomb shelter in the woods. Enemy planes flew overhead but dropped no bombs. He rested for a while with a couple of strangers. No one spoke. In the eerie silence, he thought about his mother. 'What am I doing here? I need to find her.'

It was about 3 p.m., four hours after the blast. Leaving the woods, Kōichi approached the Urakami district, where fires were still raging. He crossed the railway tracks next to a gas tank that had been completely crushed. (⑪ on map.) A dead horse lay near the destroyed tank, along with many mud-covered corpses. Kōichi wondered whether the people had died from the blast or the gas explosion. But what did it matter?

He wandered towards the Moto-Ōhashi Bridge that crossed the

Urakami River. There was no bridge. Scores of corpses floated on the water's surface, their black hair swaying in the current. Naked bodies – old and young, men and women – littered the river banks, some on top of each other. A burnt and half-naked mother clasped an infant.

Kōichi heard feeble cries. 'Help . . . water . . . give me water!' They didn't sound like human voices, more like shrieks from Hell, from far beneath the earth.

Years later, Kōichi learnt that the Moto-Ōhashi Bridge was less than a kilometre from the bomb's epicentre. Anyone living near the Urakami River would have been exposed to temperatures of several hundred degrees. Severely burned, the residents had dragged their bodies towards the river to deaden their pain. They died a cruel death in the cool, quiet water.

Kōichi removed his *geta* clogs and walked barefoot through a narrow stretch of the river. He heard a shrill voice. 'Please help me . . .' (⑫ on map.) Behind Kōichi, a boy of about ten was struggling to stand because his legs were badly injured. 'I was with my uncle in Urakami when the blast hit,' the boy explained. 'My uncle is dead, and I fled here, but I can't move. Please take me somewhere.'

'I can't help you,' Kōichi replied. 'All of Nagasaki has been destroyed. Stay here until somebody comes to rescue you.' Kōichi left the boy, ignoring his shrieks. He crossed the river, carefully avoiding the floating bodies, and climbed the riverbank.

He found it difficult to breathe because of the persistent smoke. He stepped over the debris of houses, where the lifeless bodies of children and their mothers lay in pools of black mud. A distraught infant girl sat in front of a collapsed house, screaming. 'My mummy is in the debris! Please help!' Kōichi saw strands of dark hair under some burning timber. (⑬ on map.) Again, helpless, he left.

It was late afternoon by the time Kōichi reached the vicinity of his home. (⑭ on map.) A walk that usually took thirty minutes had taken about five hours. His home was in flames. It was impossible to approach the scalding fire. (① on map.) It wasn't just his house; the entire neighbourhood was burning. His home had been only 500 metres from the bomb's epicentre. '*Okaa-chaa—n!*' (Mummy!)

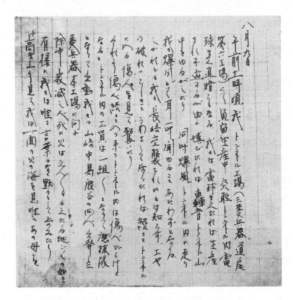

*Kōichi Tagawa's handwritten diary entry on the
atomic bombing day, 9 August 1945*

he screamed. '*Okaa-chaa—n! Okaa-chaa—n!*' No one answered.
'*Okaa-chaa—n!*'

Kōichi wandered in a trance back towards the tunnel factory.
He had not eaten since the morning. He propped himself up near
the tunnel entrance, exhausted. Amid the black smoke, an orange
sun set into the mountain to his far right. It felt strange that on
a day when his known world seemed to have vanished, the sun
remained, slowly sinking beyond the horizon. As darkness fell, he
sat cross-legged, arms around his head, and watched his hometown
burning.

Kōichi lit an oil lamp that was lying near the tunnel and pulled a
dusty pocket diary from his trousers. He began to write in precise
kanji and *hiragana* characters with a pencil. 'Something inside me
urged me to write,' he told me. 'Was it my mother? God? Another
force? I don't know, but the words flowed.' For two months, the
teenager scribbled notes in his journal, recording the unprecedented horror. He shared his diary with me in 2019.

Diary, 9 August 1945: Oh, what a tragedy. My home has disappeared, engulfed in endless fire.

I look around the sea of fire and smoke across the sky. At the far end of the horizon, there's a blood-curdling scene.

I think only of my mother but could not find her injured body or corpse.

I am covered in choking smoke. What a horrendous battlefield.

With a couple of other workers, he crept into a room for machine-tools in the tunnel factory and lay down to sleep. The tunnel was full of injured people groaning and crying. As he drowsed, Wasa, his mother, appeared. 'Where are you, mummy? I need you.' She smiled sweetly and was gone.

The following morning, 10 August, Kōichi again returned home. The fire had burned itself out. Only smoke remained. He trod carefully as he entered the site where his house had stood twenty-four hours earlier.

It was a mere blackened piece of land. There was no house, no roof, no furniture, virtually no debris. Kōichi found it difficult to imagine what kind of monstrous blast had swept everything, including his mother, away in an instant.

There was no sign of Wasa, not even bones or ashes. He stood speechless. It began to sink in that he would never see his mother again. She had been his sole anchor for ten years, since his father died, nurturing and supporting him through his difficult teenage years. Now, in a split-second, he had become an orphan. The tears wouldn't stop. Where am I going to go now, how am I going to live?

Diary, 10 August 1945: My house, which stood problem-free until yesterday, left no sign of existence today. My mother has gone, even her body . . .

Kōichi heard a desperate voice. 'Can you come and help?' It was Shūichi Yamaguchi, who lived in an adjacent house. The Yamaguchis were Wasa's relatives. Wasa and Kōichi were renting an annexe of their house.

Like Kōichi, Shūichi had survived the blast because he had been at work. He'd rushed home to find his house in flames. Four members of his family were missing, but he had rescued six others, including his three daughters, aged four, six and ten. His father and two of his younger brothers also survived but were badly injured.

Worried about another bomb attack and with nowhere to sleep, Shūichi and Kōichi decided the family should head towards Mount Shiroyama, a wooded mountain to the north. (⑱ on map.) Shūichi put his youngest daughter, Rumiko, on his back and grabbed the hands of the other girls, Reiko and Kumiko. All the girls appeared to be in good health.

During the uphill climb, Kōichi saw a scene that would haunt him for ever: a standing corpse. (⑰ on map.) When the blast hit, the man had apparently been walking. Now he was simply a piece of charcoal with blackened eyeballs and an equally blackened tongue that protruded from his head.

The eight-person group decided to camp on flat, sheltered land near the mountaintop, where it was relatively cool. As soon as Kōichi laid a blanket on the ground, he collapsed on it and slept for hours. For the following eighteen days, he lived on the mountainside, scavenging for food and water, tending the injured – and watching agonised children and adults die.

Shūichi's daughters appeared unharmed. But it wasn't long before they fell ill. First, six-year-old Kumiko's hair started falling out and purple spots spread over her body. Her gums started bleeding. After suffering from extreme diarrhoea, high fever and fatigue, she died on 13 August, four days after the blast. Four-year-old Rumiko died the next day, showing the same symptoms.

Kōichi collected three wooden drawers from the remains of a house nearby. He placed Kumiko in one and Rumiko in another. He left the third for ten-year-old Reiko, knowing she would be next.

Kōichi collected old newspapers, straw from tatami mats and wooden sticks to create a pyre, on which he placed the drawers.

'I kept saying *"gomen-ne, yurushite"* [I'm sorry, forgive me] to the girls while burning them,' he said. 'That was the first and only time I burnt human flesh like that. It took me all day. Body parts such as heads, arms and legs burn quickly and easily, but the bellies don't because there are organs inside. Lots of fluids came out and I had to poke the bellies with a bamboo stick to let the water out.' After the bodies were burnt, Kōichi picked up the bones, put them in a bucket and accompanied Shūichi to the Yamaguchis' family grave in Urakami to bury them in the typical Japanese manner.

That same day, Shūichi's youngest brother, thirteen-year-old Katsumi, developed the same symptoms. He died in Shūichi's arms on 15 August, the day that Japan surrendered and the Pacific War ended.

At the family grave, Shūichi and Kōichi prayed for the souls of those who had died, including Kōichi's mother. The Yamaguchi family were all Catholic descendants of Nagasaki's hidden Christians, like Kōichi.

It was soon the turn of Shūichi's other brother, Eiji. His diarrhoea was so intense that Shūichi thought he might have contracted typhus. It is known now that heavy diarrhoea is a typical symptom of radiation sickness, but very few people in Nagasaki knew what kind of device the Americans had dropped. They simply called it 'a powerful new bomb'.[2] Shūichi and Kōichi carried Eiji to a mountainside air-raid shelter to isolate. He died alone in the shelter on 16 August, a day after his brother.

Only three of the eight survivors – Kōichi, Shūichi and Shūichi's father, Kōhei – were now alive. But it wasn't long before Kōhei became sick. Desperate to save him, Shūichi and Kōichi wheeled him on a trolley to a makeshift hospital in a school near Nagasaki railway station. It was packed with injured people, most with severe burns, many already losing their hair. In a second-floor classroom, Kōichi spent the night with Kōhei. While watching the injured people, Kōichi wrote snippets in his diary about the war. He was dejected at the nation's defeat.

Diary, 17 August 1945: The 'Greater East Asia War' has ended. Ah, Japan, you have at last given in. When we think of the past, we are filled with sad emotions and regrets.

When Kōichi awoke, the young man sleeping next to him lay in a pool of blood. He had cut his throat with a knife, unable to bear his pain any more. That same day, Kōhei died, aged fifty-eight.

Diary, 18 August 1945: Kōhei has gone to heaven today. He has died a glorious death. He was an earnest Catholic. He went to Mass every day and received Communion. I am convinced he has gone to a good place. I would like to die like him.

Kōichi had no more will to live. He felt that death was stalking him. Trying to shake his despondency, he walked along the ash-strewn streets to the hill where Urakami Cathedral had stood. Now, only a few tree stumps remained, smouldering in the heat.

Kōichi had been to Mass at the cathedral dozens of times since he and Wasa arrived in Nagasaki from northern Korea four years earlier. The cathedral was the pride of all descendants of the hidden Christians in Nagasaki. It symbolised their endurance, resilience and survival after 240 years of persecution.

During the Mass, Kōichi had always felt hopeful about the future for himself, his mother, fellow Catholics and Japan. Now everything was in ruins. Even the food that the military had stored inside the spacious cathedral during the war was burned to a crisp.

Kōichi sat on a hill near the cathedral for several nights and watched the embers in the darkness. He cried alone. His dreams for life had been shattered. Only the stars were unearthly bright and sparkling with life. Nothing was real any more. He poured his soul into his diary.

Diary, 23 August 1945: The enemy planes dropped just one newly created bomb. What an absurd power it had. Look at the ghastly damage it brought. Not a single house undamaged, as far as I can see.

I've been left alone in this world. No longer can I see my mother, my only consolation.

Within a few seconds, I lost my mother and home. I have no clothes, no possessions. My mother looked after me for three years when I was sick, never losing hope, always giving warmth and light. Without her, life is meaningless, nothing to look forward to.

How am I going to live from now on? All that beckons is a mountain of hardships. My head is all hazy. All I see is endless destruction and death. I feel like a total fool.

By 23 August, two weeks after the blast, the local government was distributing rationed food at a school near the foot of Mount Shiroyama. Kōichi was given some rice and tinned food.

The Ōhashi Bridge (⑮ on map) over the Urakami River, which hadn't collapsed from the blast, became an information centre for Nagasaki survivors. Families searching for relatives and friends attached small pieces of paper to the bridge railings. But beneath the bridge, scores of bloated corpses still floated in the water, a macabre reminder of the tragedy.

Diary, 27 August 1945: How I hate my misery. The world where I had some freedom has gone for ever and turned into darkness. Looking at the moon, I yearn for my mother. Everything else – water, mountains, trees, the sky – remind me of her. Why did I live? Why couldn't I have gone with her?

On 29 August, Kōichi obtained a certificate of death for Wasa at the Nagasaki police station. Even after the horrors of the bomb, the Japanese bureaucracy continued to function. Certificate in hand, Kōichi decided to leave Nagasaki. There was nothing left for him there, only painful memories.

Twenty-five miles northwest of Nagasaki, Kōichi's father's brother, Manjirō Tagawa, lived in a small coastal town called Kurosaki. It was in the Sotome region of Nagasaki prefecture, an area where many hidden Christians had lived secretly for centuries.

It was stiflingly hot and raining hard when Kōichi began to walk over the mountains to Kurosaki, a journey of more than twelve hours. He was hopeful that his uncle would offer him shelter and food for at least a few days. As the eldest of four boys, Manjirō had inherited all his father's farmland and remained in Japan when his brothers left for northern Korea in the mid-1920s.

Manjirō welcomed his nephew and offered him work on the farm. For a few days, Kōichi weeded the fields and planted potatoes. But he felt unwell and uncomfortable most of the time. The scenes of devastation that he'd witnessed recurred as flashbacks, preventing sleep.

Kōichi was also dejected because Japan had lost the war. He had always felt weak, inconsequential and excluded. And although he wasn't as unashamedly patriotic as many of his colleagues, he was proud to have been born in a Japanese colony, Korea, and to have met some of the soldiers who went to fight in Manchuria. But now the country was in ruins and under foreign occupation. Many American soldiers had already arrived in Nagasaki.

Diary, 24 September 1945: Poor Japan. Small Japan. Our first-class nation has been crushed back to its imperfect past. Only heaven knows where we are going from now.

As Kōichi dug up the weeds, he noticed that his hands had developed pimples and sores. He suffered headaches and constantly felt tired. Manjirō and his family said nothing, but it became clear that they did not want a sick teenager living among them. 'Thinking back, those were typical symptoms of radiation poisoning,' he said. 'Which isn't surprising. Considering that I was exposed to high levels of radiation for eighteen days, it's miraculous that I survived.'

Alone in the fields and at night, Kōichi started experiencing a deeper agony. The sights and sounds of the victims that he had failed to help on 9 August loomed ever larger in his mind. There was the face of the young woman on a stretcher whom he had abandoned. The agonising cry of the man who had bullied him. The voice of the helpless boy by the river.

'Why didn't I help them? These people must all be dead now.

Nagasaki bomb survivors made shacks using debris from buildings that were levelled by the atomic blast, 4 September 1945

How could I have said "It serves you right!" to a dying man? How can I face up to my ugly side? I can't bear it.'

The questions tormented him. He ran to a nearby beach and watched the tidal pull of the waves. He felt an urge to stride into the water and be swept away. He'd never been more alone.

> Diary, 2 October 1945: I wish I could go somewhere. To live a lonely life by myself. But without my mother, how shall I live? Where are you wandering, dear mother?

Desperate to discard his persistent thoughts of ending his life, Kōichi tried to concentrate on happier times. He remembered his visits to the Polish friary in Nagasaki in the spring of 1944 and his plan to study theology there as soon as the war ended.

Well, that time had now arrived. His main fear was that the buildings might have been severely damaged or demolished.

On 8 October 1945, Kōichi left his uncle's house, caught a boat along the coast to Nagasaki, and walked up the steep hill to the friary. He'd expected to see blackened ruins, like those in Urakami where his mother died. It was a revelation to see the buildings almost intact. The friary had been shielded from the blast by the mountains.

Kōichi knocked on the wooden door and waited. Brother Zeno, Father Maximilian Kolbe's long-time confidant, undid the latch and smiled. 'Where is your sister?' Zeno asked in his crude Japanese, meaning Kōichi's mother. 'She died in the bombing,' Kōichi replied.

Zeno thrust out his arms and embraced the boy. Zeno began to cry, telling Kōichi that he could remain at the friary as long as he wanted. Tears of relief, pity, happiness and sorrow streamed out of Kōichi. After a month of tension and terror, Kōichi had found a new home.

It had been nine years since Father Kolbe had left the Nagasaki monastery that he, Zeno and other Polish friars had built with their bare hands in the early 1930s. Now that the war was over, the ten Poles whom the military had sent to an internment camp had returned to their friary home.[3] And the sixty Allied civilian internees who had been imprisoned there had finally been repatriated.

As he settled into the community, Kōichi learned that the friars had preserved Kolbe's tiny living quarters and office exactly as it had been in 1936, when he had returned to Poland. The men told Kōichi that Kolbe had apparently died during the war, but they had no details of how, when, where or why.

It would be some time before that mystery would be solved.

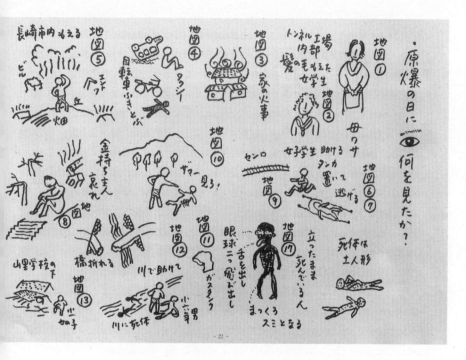

What Kōichi saw. Drawn by Kōichi Tagawa

14. MacArthur and the Emperor

August 1945 – Nanae, Hokkaido

Twelve hundred miles northeast of Nagasaki, at the same time as Kōichi Tagawa was mourning the death of his mother in the atomic bomb blast, Masatoshi Asari was trying to absorb the significance of the four-minute speech that he'd just heard on the radio.

Japan, Emperor Hirohito had told the nation, had surrendered. The war was over.

The head of the agricultural experimental station where the fourteen-year-old Masatoshi was working, Mr Suzuki, tried to placate his labourers. 'Remain calm, everyone. The enemy is not going to kill us. Don't do anything rash. We're going to survive.'

No one spoke. Masatoshi ate a meagre potato and soybean *bento*, or packed lunch, and walked silently back to the rice paddy to trim insect-infested leaves off the plants.

Even on a day when the world had turned upside down, the employees were ordered to continue working. Masatoshi's mind was racing. He couldn't get the word 'defeat' out of his head. What will the surrender mean for my future?, he wondered. He kept his focus on the rice plants, not wishing to make eye contact with his colleagues, who also appeared deep in thought.

Something inside Masatoshi had changed that lunchtime. For most people, defeat was deeply shocking and humiliating. For Masatoshi, the shock soon turned to feelings of relief. He was now free. Free from war, free from the fear of being bombed, free from having to listen to government propaganda about Japan's 'inevitable victory'.

More than anything, he realised, he was free from the pressure of dying for the emperor and the country. Free to pursue his interest in flowers, trees and plants. 'Now I can live,' he told himself. 'Now I may be able to fulfil my dreams.'

Homeless families huddled in a Tokyo subway station, October 1945

That evening, inside the family home, his father, Asakichi, said not one word. Throughout the war, Asakichi had read the local newspaper from beginning to end and found comfort in stories that explained how Japan was winning the war. Head down, hands on his forehead, he was clearly in shock at the emperor's statement. By contrast, his mother, Chie, was calm. 'Things will take their natural course,' she told her children. 'Let's just follow the instructions of our leaders. The Americans won't murder us.'

In the following days, a mood of despondency, distress and disbe-lief hung over the adults at the agricultural station. Without the government's belligerent encouragements to keep fighting, no one knew what to do. The defeat was total, and the surrender was unconditional. By now, most Japanese knew that the 'new bombs' dropped on Hiroshima and Nagasaki were powerful atomic devices.

After eight years of conflict, first in China and later in the Pacific, the Japanese population was exhausted. In the previous fourteen months alone, incessant Allied bombing had destroyed large swathes of more than 200 cities. More than three million Japanese military and civilians had died during the war. At least nine million people in Japan were homeless. Japan's fighting spirit had long since disap-peared. In short, people were simply tired. And hungry.

In the early hours of 15 August, after signing the surrender document, Japan's War Minister Korechika Anami performed *seppuku*, slitting his belly with a samurai sword at his home. His abstruse suicide note said: 'I – with my death – humbly apologise to the emperor for the great crime.' Following Anami's death, at least 600 military officers and soldiers took their own lives, along with scores of civilians in Japan and overseas.[1]

Some years later, when Masatoshi learned of Anami's suicide note, he wondered what 'great crime' Anami was referring to. The crime of starting the war, the crime of giving up or the crime of losing? He was confused.

His father had said: 'Anami took responsibility for the entire army. They wanted to continue to fight. He was apologising to the emperor for not achieving victory.'

His father had told him that army officers had planned a *coup d'état* in protest at the decision to surrender. Anami's death had calmed them down and the coup hadn't happened. Masatoshi remained unconvinced about the 'great crime'. Surely, he thought, it referred to the question of who led the country to war.

General Prince Naruhiko Higashikuni, who became prime minister on 17 August, said that the whole nation was to blame for the war – the military, government officials, industrial leaders, civilian bureaucrats and the people at large. The only way for the nation to survive and resurrect itself, Higashikuni said, was for *Ichioku sōzange*, meaning 100 million acts of repentance, referring to the number of people who lived in Japan and its empire.

On 30 August 1945, just two weeks after Japan's surrender, the nation's new ruler, 65-year-old General Douglas MacArthur, flew to Atsugi airbase southwest of Tokyo. MacArthur had been named Supreme Commander for the Allied Powers, also known as SCAP, by US President Harry Truman.

MacArthur oversaw the US-led Allied military occupation of

Japan, which would last almost seven years. It was the first time ever that Japan had been occupied by a foreign power.

The following day, Masatoshi and his father looked studiously at a photograph of MacArthur's arrival in a Hokkaido newspaper. They couldn't help but comment on his height – at six feet, he was eight inches taller than the average Japanese man – and his confident bearing as he strode down a ramp from a US Air Force plane in his well-pressed khaki military uniform.

MacArthur set up the so-called GHQ, or General Headquarters, of the occupation forces in central Tokyo. He told the Japanese media that his job was to 'demilitarise' and 'democratise' the nation so that Japan would never again be a threat to the world.

MacArthur immediately dissolved the Imperial Japanese Army and Navy and ordered the arrests of thirty-nine former military and government leaders as suspected war criminals. This was the first of four sequenced arrests of more than 100 suspected 'class A' war criminals – men who were alleged to have committed 'crimes against peace'. Across Asia and the Pacific, hundreds of other former Japanese military were imprisoned as suspected 'class B' and 'class C' war criminals. They were accused of 'conventional war crimes' and 'crimes against humanity'.

MacArthur also ordered the Japanese Education Ministry to eradicate any trace of militarism from textbooks. He banned every description claiming Japan's ambitions for its empire and the emperor's divinity. He also banned the nation's creation story from being taught as history rather than myth.

By the end of 1945, more than 450,000 American soldiers were stationed throughout Japan, and there were widespread concerns about how they would treat the local people.

One day in early September, the Asari household received a community notice. It read: 'When the Americans come, be very cautious, especially young women. Stay at home as much as possible. If you run into them outdoors, do not look them in the eye.' In Nanae village, some fearful wives and daughters hid in the nearby mountains.

Returning to school later that month, Masatoshi was handed a calligraphy brush and an inkstone. His first task in the classroom was *suminuri*, which means 'to blacken over'. In this government initiative, children across Japan had to paint over all passages in their textbooks that were perceived as militaristic or otherwise inappropriate.

Suminuri left a deep scar in Masatoshi's mind. 'Imagine being told that everything you have been learning at school was wrong,' he recalled. 'I felt shattered. We were taught lies. It was as though the values and morals that I'd held in life suddenly crumbled and I didn't know what to believe any more'. Masatoshi vowed to himself then that nothing in life was absolute.

More than 7,500 US troops connected to the 11th Airborne Division arrived in Hakodate in early October. It wasn't long before they were driving jeeps through Nanae and living in the town hall and on the campus of Hokkaido University's fisheries college. But contrary to the prevailing fears, the GIs were friendly and non-threatening.

'We children loved them because they gave us candies, juice, sugar, chocolates and chewing gum,' Masatoshi recalled. He also saw them giving food to the liberated Chinese and Korean labourers who had been treated appallingly by the Japanese during the war. By year's end, the Americans had won over even the most sceptical Japanese with their generosity and good humour.

The feelings of relief were mutual. Before landing in Japan, the US soldiers had been fearful that they would encounter fierce resistance. Instead, they were shocked to see the extent of the devastation from their bombing campaigns, and it was immediately apparent that the general population was in no condition to fight.[2]

Besides peace, everyone wanted food. Hunger and malnutrition were pervasive. Food imports no longer arrived from China or Korea. Poor weather in 1945 and the lack of a domestic farming labour force caused the worst crop since 1910. More than 1,000 people died from malnutrition in Tokyo alone during the three months after the war ended. To survive, most people resorted to the black market.[3]

In Hokkaido, where food was usually plentiful, Masatoshi and his brothers continued to forage for clover, dandelion and mulberry leaves, which Chie boiled in a rice soup to help feed the family. The gnawing hunger lasted for four more years, Masatoshi remembered.

In early November 1945, the deputy headmaster of the school that Masatoshi had attended until the age of fourteen, suddenly showed up at his home. He was desperate, and begged Masatoshi's father, Asakichi, to give him some rice in exchange for a broken clock.

The deputy head, the headmaster and several other senior teachers had been fired from their jobs by MacArthur's GHQ. They were part of the purge of teachers who had been labelled 'militaristic' for inciting young children to fight in the war. Nationwide, out of 450,000 teachers, 5,200 were expelled and 115,000 resigned voluntarily.

The ousting of the teachers was the beginning of a sweeping reform programme that would quickly target virtually every aspect of Japanese society. The GHQ's goal was to transform the former aggressor into a totally new democratic nation that supported the Allies. There was little resistance. The country's devastation – materially and psychologically – was so comprehensive that almost everyone desired a new start.

'It was a time of great confusion, but at the same time, a time of great liberation,' Masatoshi told me. 'I, as a teenager, felt a sense of hope for a new future for myself and Japan.' It would be a democratic future, he hoped, in which all people were equals and in which any individual could voice their opinion without fear of criticism.

Governing indirectly through the Japanese government, MacArthur dismantled the powerful industrial conglomerates, called *zaibatsu*, that dominated the business world. He stripped land from large landowners to give to farmers and abolished the hated Tokubetsu Kōtō Keisatsu, or secret police.[4]

On the religious front, MacArthur dismantled State Shintoism. This had been the nation's core ideology promoting the war machine, with the divine emperor at its head. Shinto was no longer a national religion. To get the message across, the emperor announced publicly on New Year's Day 1946 that he was no longer a 'living god', simply a human being like everyone else.

Shortly afterwards, MacArthur purged former military, political, economic and media leaders, removing more than 210,000 high-level people from their jobs.

In spite of these seismic events, MacArthur declined to pursue one question that was on everyone's mind – that of the emperor's war responsibility. As the supreme commander of the Japanese military, Emperor Hirohito had signed and issued the Imperial Rescript to start the war in December 1941.

Within the Allies, there were incessant cries to prosecute the emperor. A Gallup poll conducted six weeks before the war ended showed seventy per cent of Americans favoured executing or harshly punishing him.[5] Even within Japan itself, the public mood called for the emperor to resign to acknowledge his culpability.

MacArthur wasn't swayed. Indeed, he vowed to protect and preserve the forty-four-year-old emperor. MacArthur's views echoed those of Joseph C. Grew, a former ambassador to Japan, who had told the US Congress that the emperor functioned like a queen bee. If removed, he said, the entire bee colony might collapse.[6]

MacArthur convinced Washington that if the emperor were prosecuted, Japan would riot and the occupation force would need at least one million more soldiers to deal with the expected chaos.[7] The GHQ also wanted to make sure that the Japanese would not resent their occupiers.[8]

MacArthur's intent was to create a new image for the emperor – that of a peace-loving and benevolent man. To promote this well-scripted public relations campaign, the GHQ encouraged the emperor to travel around Japan to meet and talk to his people.

Guarded by American GIs, Hirohito travelled the length and breadth of Japan for 165 days over more than eight years. Dressed in a tailored Western suit, a soft felt fedora atop his head, the uncomplaining emperor drew massive and adoring crowds, many of whom felt sorry for the former deity and accepted his new 'peaceful' image.[9] Speaking in a high-pitched voice and peering through thick glasses, the emperor sought to connect with his people. But in truth, he had little to say to them, so different were their worlds.

This epic pilgrimage ended in Hokkaido in August 1954, more than two years after Japan had regained its independence. By then, the emperor had become a symbol of a new nation emerging from the ruins of a military-promoted war.

The US authorities had successfully convinced the Japanese that their emperor was almost blameless for the war. But had he now become a pawn in the occupiers' power game, honour-bound and indebted to the GHQ and to MacArthur for saving his life and the imperial dynasty?

At that time, Masatoshi Asari was too young to understand the GHQ's intentions. But this question and many others would rankle in him over the years as he researched Hokkaido's wartime history and mulled the significance and consequences of the atomic bomb strikes in Hiroshima and Nagasaki.

In Hiroshima, the public actively demanded that the dead victims be remembered and that the survivors receive as much help as possible to relieve their suffering from radiation and other diseases. In Nagasaki, the predominant sound was silence.

15. Silence

Autumn 1945 – Nagasaki

At the time of the Nagasaki atomic bomb blast on 9 August 1945, the head of the Mugenzai-no-Sono community, Father Mirochna, and several Japanese seminary students were mustered in the wooden building's small library. Apart from broken windows and damage caused by falling debris, the friary survived in its sheltered location.[1]

That good fortune enabled the Franciscan sanctuary to play a key role in the city's reconstruction efforts, and its reputation in Nagasaki changed almost overnight. During the war, the Japanese authorities had considered the friary to be a den of enemies and foreign spies. Now, it became known as a charitable relief centre.

After the Japanese surrender on 15 August, the Polish brothers watched in amazement as US military planes parachuted relief supplies onto the mountainside compound to aid foreign nationals who had been interned there. The supplies were so abundant that the friars donated them to Japanese survivors at help centres throughout Nagasaki.

Injured and sick civilians whose homes had disappeared struggled up the hillside seeking food, clothing, accommodation and medicine. Homeless soldiers returning from Asia's battlefields also sought shelter there.[2]

With the arrival of Allied occupation forces in Nagasaki in September 1945, the friary was inundated with even more supplies, some of which were stolen by starving citizens. Yet even as Nagasaki began to rebuild, the city faced another hardship. On 17 September, one of the most powerful typhoons in Japanese history barrelled through the city, washing away bridges, railway tracks and makeshift homes.[3]

Kōichi Tagawa, who had arrived at Mugenzai-no-Sono on 8 October after two months of hell, slowly settled into a daily monastic lifestyle of prayer, meditation, study and cleaning duties.

For the first time since losing his mother, Kōichi felt protected and loved. He knew instinctively that he would spend the rest of his life there, and he dedicated himself to becoming a Catholic priest or brother, like the twenty or so Polish men who lived in the institution.

On trips into Nagasaki, Kōichi watched the city's stoic survivors, known in Japanese as *hibakusha*, begin to clear the debris from the nuclear explosion and the typhoon.[4]

Week by week, maimed and tormented men, women and children emerged from air-raid shelters, tents, hillside caves and crude backyard shelters to start rebuilding their homes and cremating the bones of their dead. Other citizens who had fled Nagasaki trickled back to their stricken neighbourhoods.[5]

Besides food and shelter, the biggest problem the survivors faced at first was sickness. Most of Kōichi's relatives in the Yamaguchi family had died from radiation poisoning after suffering a combination of bloody diarrhoea, nausea, anaemia, gangrene, vomiting, high fevers, internal bleeding and loss of hair, among other diseases and infections. Thousands of Nagasaki residents were similarly afflicted.

Before the US exploded the atomic bombs, American scientists had focused little attention on the side-effects of radiation poisoning. In the immediate aftermath of the detonations, the US government downplayed reports that people were dying from radiation-related sicknesses.

Indeed, after the September typhoon and other torrential rain, there were reports that fewer people were showing symptoms of radiation illnesses. The storms appeared to have literally washed away a large part of the radiation from the topsoil.[6] That prompted some doctors and scientists in Nagasaki to encourage people to return to their homes. Among them were the few survivors who had lived in the city's Urakami neighbourhood, home to Japan's largest Christian community.

Most of these Urakami residents hadn't just lost their families, friends and homes. They'd also lost the lofty symbol that represented their victory over centuries of persecution – Urakami Cathedral.

On the morning of Friday, 23 November 1945, Kōichi Tagawa and several Polish brothers descended the steep hill from their friary to attend a requiem Mass in front of the ruins of Urakami Cathedral. It was the first Mass to be held in the neighbourhood since the atomic bombing fifteen weeks earlier.

The keynote speaker that day was a renowned doctor, Takashi Nagai, dean of the radiology department at Nagasaki Medical University Hospital. His wife Midori, a descendant of a leader of the hidden Christians, had burned to death in their home when the bomb exploded. Amid the white ash and broken roof tiles, Nagai had found only the charred remains of Midori's skull, hips and backbone, along with her rosary beads.[7]

Nagai had been asked to speak at the Mass as a representative of all the Catholic survivors of the blast.

The doctor himself was fighting for his life. Just two months before the explosion, Nagai had learned that he had no more than three years to live because he had contracted incurable chronic myeloid leukaemia from radiation poisoning while working at the hospital.

At the time of the explosion, at his hospital 700 metres from the epicentre, flying glass severed an artery in Nagai's head. The head injury and the radiation poisoning left Nagai weak and incapacitated. But for weeks he worked around the clock treating the injured.

The toil took its toll. On 20 September, the doctor collapsed and began slipping in and out of a coma. In a moment of lucidity, he wrote a final haiku:

Into the high and shining
Autumn sky
I am leaving this world

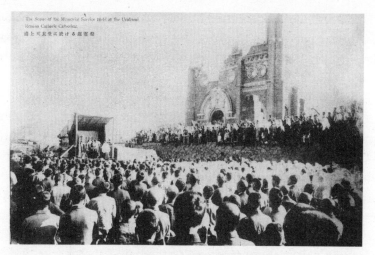

The requiem Mass held at the ruins of Urakami
Cathedral in November 1945

Later, while in the coma, Nagai said he felt cold water on his lips and heard an old lady whisper: 'This is from the Lourdes grotto at Mugenzai-no-Sono.' He said he had a vision of the Virgin Mary at the grotto and heard a voice telling him to ask Father Maximilian Kolbe for help. He later credited Kolbe's mediation and the Lourdes water for his speedy recovery from the coma.[8]

Father Kolbe and the Polish religious brothers knew Dr Nagai well. After returning from military service in Manchuria, Nagai had been a frequent visitor to Mugenzai-no-Sono in 1935 and 1936, treating Kolbe's tuberculosis. When the men first met, Nagai had been surprised to discover how badly Kolbe was suffering. He wrote that eighty per cent of Kolbe's lungs were not functioning and that most people in this condition would be bedridden.

Nagai was mobilised as a military surgeon in 1937 and sent to China until 1940. After the 1945 bombing, he spent several nights sheltering at the friary.

By late morning on 23 November, a crowd of about 600 burned, bandaged and debilitated Catholic survivors had gathered on a site next to the cathedral's rubble awaiting the Mass and Dr Nagai's address.

Undeterred by his sickness, Nagai had crafted a meticulous ora-
tion for the gathering. Looking like an ancient mountain shaman,
with uncut hair and a long beard, he slowly made his way to a temporary stage.[9]

Few in attendance that day would forget the doctor's words.

'At 11.02 a.m. on 9 August 1945, an atomic bomb exploded above
Urakami and the souls of 8,500 Catholics were called by the hands
of God instantly,' Nagai began. 'Raging flames turned this Oriental
holy place into ashes in a few hours. I heard that the second atomic
bomb was destined for another city. But because of clouds, the
Americans headed for the secondary target of Nagasaki. In Nagasaki, the bomb was dropped further north than planned and ended
up bursting right above Urakami Cathedral. If that is true, we can
say that God's Providence chose Urakami. It was not because the
American pilots targeted our neighbourhood.'

Hearing the words 'God's Providence', the assembled Catholics
fell silent and strained to hear Nagai's next words.

'Was not Urakami – the most sacred place in all Japan – chosen as
a victim, a pure lamb that had to be slaughtered and burned on the
altar of sacrifice to expiate this sin of humanity, the World War?'[10]

Nagai answered his own rhetorical question.

The sacrifice, he said, was a case of *hansai* (a burnt sacrifice). All
the survivors were sinners who had not sufficiently repented, he
added. Each sinner now faced a period of trial and tribulation, of
suffering and misery. The dead had been chosen as a pure redemp-
tive sacrifice to God. That sacrifice had brought peace to Japan. The
bomb victims had not suffered or died in vain.

'How noble, how splendid, was that holocaust of midnight on 9
August, when flames soared up from the cathedral, dispelling darkness and bringing the light of peace,' Nagai concluded.[11]

As the doctor finished talking, Kōichi began to sob, along with
many others in the crowd. Here, at last, was an explanation as to
why Japan's largest Christian community had felt the full impact of
the atomic fireball.

The 3,500 or so Catholic survivors of the Nagasaki bomb had
long felt stigmatised because of their religion. After the explosion,

they felt even more outcast from Japanese society. Non-Christians in Nagasaki whispered that Japanese Shinto gods had punished Urakami residents because they believed in a 'foreign god'.[12]

Many Catholics in Nagasaki viewed the atomic bombing as the 'fifth persecution' of their beliefs. It was, they told one another, undoubtedly the most severe torment since almost 700 Christians died or were killed between 1867 and 1873.

Kōichi himself had no doubts about God's Providence. 'You could not imagine the level of our agony at that time. We were all in unimaginable despair,' he told me. 'Many people not only lost everything but had to cope with the criticism that they had been punished because of their religion. Doctor Nagai's true intentions were to say that the Catholics had overcome the persecutions because they believed in God's Providence. He was simply conveying the message that we needed to move forward, just like our ancestors, and focus on rebuilding our lives.'

In public, the Catholics remained largely silent about their predicament. They didn't want to aggravate tensions with other Nagasaki citizens or in particular with the GHQ, the MacArthur-led Americans who directed the occupation forces.

Confronted with the scale of the devastation and concerned about a backlash, the GHQ had suppressed any discussion and publications about the bombs' impact on Hiroshima and Nagasaki. The GHQ also confiscated documentary footage of nuclear destruction filmed between August and November 1945 by a team of thirty Japanese cameramen.[13]

Nagai's narrative was convenient for the GHQ because it lessened the blame on the US for dropping the bomb and quieted the victims' anger. Nagai's theory also played a role in enabling the public to turn a blind eye to Japanese leaders' war responsibility, which had ultimately led to the dropping of the atomic bomb.[14]

Not all the Urakami Catholics took solace in the doctor's conclusions. Many people, especially the most severely injured residents, could not accept the thought that the bombing of the Urakami district was God's Providence and that they were sinners for having survived. Some Catholics renounced their religion.

Nagai's theory explained a saying that became common in Japan: '*Ikari no Hiroshima, inori no Nagasaki*' (Hiroshima rages, Nagasaki prays). The phrase highlighted the willingness of Hiroshima victims to speak out about the consequences of the atomic bomb, especially after censorship ended in 1952 when the Allied occupation forces left. Hiroshima survivors were said to be angry, noisy, highly political and anti-American.[15]

In contrast, most Urakami Catholics remained silent, reflective and non-political for thirty-five years until the 1980s, accepting Nagai's challenging theory. They quietly internalised their sufferings, wrapping them up in their religious faith, even as their bodies were racked by radiation-related diseases. While many non-Catholic hibakusha in Nagasaki spoke out about their grief and anger, their voices were largely drowned out.

In both Hiroshima and Nagasaki, thousands contracted thyroid cancer or cancer of the blood. The hibakusha also found it difficult to keep jobs or to find marriage partners because they frequently fell ill. Prospective spouses feared that their offspring might be contaminated with irradiated genes.

To this day, almost eighty years later, the few bomb victims still alive bear a stigma and often feel discriminated against by fellow Japanese.

Set on a hill, Urakami Cathedral had towered over Nagasaki since its completion in 1925, and most residents of the city could see its twin towers. They could also hear the two enormous Angelus bells in its towers. These rang out three times a day – at 5.30 a.m., noon and 6 p.m. – as though hailing the Christians' triumph over oppression and discrimination.

Yet when the atomic bomb exploded, the 210-foot-tall red-brick structure, which could seat 5,000 worshippers, was almost completely demolished. One of the bronze bells fell into a stream next to the cathedral. The other tumbled, unbroken, onto the debris.

A week before year's end, a group of young Christian men dug the bell from the rubble and hung it on a tripod of cypress logs.[16] At 6 p.m. on Christmas Eve, 1945, as Kōichi and the brothers prepared for Mass at the friary, a startling sound rang through Nagasaki's crisp early-evening air.

It was the peal of the cathedral bell, tolling for the first time in 137 days.

'The bell represented the Catholics' will to live again, so it was hugely symbolic,' Kōichi told me. 'My mother and I had always listened to the bells. And at the sound of the Christmas bell, I resolved to live without my mother.'

The following summer, Dr Nagai finished writing a book called *The Bells of Nagasaki*. It was a vivid record of everything he had seen and experienced as a doctor, from 9 August to Christmas Eve 1945. But the GHQ refused to allow its publication because it contained too much detail about the level of destruction in Nagasaki and graphic accounts of people's illnesses.

In the final chapter, Nagai recounted his speech at the requiem Mass outside Urakami Cathedral. The book ended with the cathedral bell ringing again on 24 December.

The bell rings out, calling for peace. From now on, with atomic bombs at hand, war can only mean suicide for the human race. Weeping people in Urakami's atomic fields cry out to the world: 'No more war.' 'Do not plan war.'

The Nagasaki bell is ringing, saying 'please make Urakami the last atomic wilderness in the history of the world.'[17]

The GHQ finally allowed *The Bells of Nagasaki* to be published in January 1949 and it immediately became a bestseller. It was turned into a movie the following year and the title song became a huge hit in Japan.[18] 'The Japanese people rediscovered in this book something that had long lain buried under war – love!' the author Shūsaku Endo wrote.[19]

Nagai continued to write about the bombing even after he

became bedridden in a tiny hut called Nyoko-dō that he shared with his son and daughter.[20] Well known in post-war Japan, the doctor was visited by Helen Keller, the American deaf and blind author, in October 1948 and by Emperor Hirohito in May 1949.

A more frequent but unknown visitor to Nyoko-dō was Kōichi Tagawa, who had attended Nagai's biology classes within the seminary for about six months in 1948. The doctor then had to stop teaching because he was so sick. Kōichi was always eager to talk to Nagai about his beliefs and about the doctor's friendship with Father Kolbe.

As well as an author, Nagai was also an artist, and he showed Kōichi many black-and-white *sumi-e* ink paintings of the cathedral ruins and other grim landscapes depicting the aftermath of the bombing.

Kōichi, who was also an artist, painted replicas of some of Nagai's drawings. But he later burned these pictures because the GHQ wanted to erase images of the bombing. 'I regret this now,' he said later. 'I should have kept them.'[21]

Dr Takashi Nagai's controversial theory about God's Providence dominated his speeches and writing in the three years after the bombing. In March 1948, he presented a song to Junshin Girls' High School, a Catholic mission school in Nagasaki near the explosion's epicentre. There, 214 girls and staff had died, the largest number of casualties among Nagasaki's high schools.

Nagai's wife, Midori, had taught at Junshin, and his daughter Kayano would later attend the school. The song was originally a poem that Nagai had written a couple of years earlier, with music by a Nagasaki composer, Fumio Kino.

The title, predictably, was 'Hansai no Uta' (The Hansai Song):

> Maidens like white lilies
> In the raging flames of Hansai
> They were devoured
> Singing in the fire[22]

Nagai and his children, Makoto, left, and Kayano

At the time, Nagai himself was slowly dying from leukaemia. But he continued treating patients until 1948, by which time he was unable to move. Nagai also continued his research on radiation and wrote innumerable books and articles, primarily about the need to renounce war.

In *Itoshi-go yo* (My Precious Children), published in 1949, Nagai asked his children to 'stand up and scream about the importance of peace'. Makoto, who was ten years old in August 1945, and his three-year-old sister, Kayano, survived the bombing because they had been evacuated to their grandmother's house four miles outside Nagasaki.

'We, the Japanese, have pledged to remain a peaceful nation for ever. In the future, depending on international circumstances at the time, some people may advocate annulling these peace principles,' he wrote. 'If that happens, you must keep fighting to prevent war. Don't give up, no matter what curses or violence you might encounter, even if you become the last two people on earth standing up for these principles. Guard yourselves with love, guard Japan with love and guard the entire human race with love. That's when a peaceful and beautiful world will be born.'[23]

In the spring of 1948, the doctor used the proceeds from some book sales to buy and plant more than a thousand young cherry trees surrounding the ruins of Urakami Cathedral. They were known as *Nagai senbon-zakura*, or 'Nagai's 1,000 cherry trees', and they became symbols of peace and renewal.

For three successive springs, Nagai enjoyed the sight from Nyoko-dō of the wispy pink and white blossoms on the so-called 'Hill of Flowers'.[24]

When Nagai died, in May 1951, aged forty-three, about 20,000 mourners crowded into and around the ruins of Urakami Cathedral for his funeral. They included, of course, Kōichi Tagawa and the men from Mugenzai-no-Sono.

PART 5

The Aftermath, 1946–1951

16. The Reading

1946 – Nagasaki

Every morning at 5.30, a stalwart of the Mugenzai-no-Sono friary in Nagasaki, Brother Romuald Mroziński, rang a small bronze bell to wake the twenty Japanese seminary students who were sleeping on straw mattresses in their second-floor dormitory.

Among the young men was Kōichi Tagawa, now eighteen years old. He'd been living in the compound since October 1945 after being orphaned in the atomic bomb blast.

Brother Romuald, tall and stocky, had arrived in Japan from Poland in March 1931, less than a year after Father Kolbe had set up a branch of the Militia Immaculatae in Nagasaki. Romuald had helped build the friary from scratch, and he'd worked day and night to help write, publish and distribute the monthly magazine in Japanese. As the seminary's housemaster, Romuald tried to ensure that the teenagers under his care were trained properly so that they could eventually become clerics.

'Non nobis, Domine, non nobis, sed nomini tuo da gloriam' ('Not unto us, O Lord, not unto us, but unto thy name give glory'), Brother Romuald called out to the students. 'Deo gratias' ('Thanks be to God'), Kōichi and his colleagues replied in unison before kneeling by their thin mattresses to pray.

After prayers, the teenagers ate a breakfast of sweet potatoes and miso soup prepared by Brother Kasjan Tetich, another friar who had helped Kolbe establish MI's Japanese headquarters.[1]

Kōichi still had diarrhoea and fatigue related to the radiation, but he was eager to spend time with his friends at the seminary, which had reopened in April 1946. Before its reopening, Kōichi had attended a local private junior high school outside the friary grounds for several months with other seminary students.

'We had a clear aim that we would become Catholic friars in the future at a time when other Japanese youngsters were searching for a purpose in life,' he recalled. The friary boys were revered at the junior high school because they had contacts with the occupation forces. 'We also had better bento lunches with tinned beef from the Americans, which brought us some respect,' Kōichi laughed.

Kōichi's health had slowly improved over the previous twelve months. He accompanied Brother Romuald and the other boys twice a week on hikes into the nearby mountains, often to glistening waterfalls or dense forests.

Yet no matter how much he prayed or enjoyed the natural environment, Kōichi was still haunted by what he had experienced on 9 August.

The faces of the dying kept re-emerging – the injured young woman he'd abandoned on a stretcher by the railway, the suffering colleague who had bullied him, the little boy who had begged for help at the river.

Feelings of guilt and disgrace tormented him at unexpected times. His heart would beat rapidly, and these recurring panic attacks left him with uncontrollable anxieties and a sense of melancholy. Deep down, Kōichi was grappling with existential questions about his own being and worth. He felt that his ego and self-centred nature had prevented him from helping others when they were most in need.

To overcome these dark moods, Kōichi took refuge in the routines of his cloistered life, which also bolstered his confidence as a young adult.

'I had lost my father in Korea to illness and my mother in Nagasaki to the bomb. I was a lonely orphan. The Polish friars saved my life,' Kōichi said. 'They raised me when I had nothing and no one.'

Kōichi remembered Brother Romuald with particular affection, and he kept a letter from him, written in crude Japanese, until the end of his life. It read: 'I love all my students, but I think of you especially with a mother's heart. Remember, in this world, I am your mother. Don't forget it. Child, give everything like loneliness, hunger, to the mother [Virgin Mary].'

One day in mid-1946, Kōichi Tagawa's bachelor uncle showed up unannounced at the friary's main entrance. The last time Kōichi had seen Fujinosuke Tagawa, his father's elder brother and closest living relative, was in September 1941 in northern Korea. That was when Kōichi and his mother had left the Japanese colony for Nagasaki because of Kōichi's illness.

For six years after Kōichi's father died in 1935, Fujinosuke had been a surrogate father to the young boy. During the war, Fujinosuke and his brother had run a successful butcher's shop near Korea's northern border with China and Siberia.

But the brothers' fortunes had changed dramatically when the war ended, as they did for millions of Japanese living outside the island nation.

With the end of Japanese rule in Korea, local Koreans were intent on revenge over their hated colonial settlers.[2] Feeling it was no longer safe to remain there, Fujinosuke disappeared into the mountains for six months as he sought a way to return to Japan. Eventually, he reached the south coast of Korea and hitched a ride on a boat bound for Nagasaki. There, he travelled to his eldest brother Manjirō's house in nearby Kurosaki village, where Kōichi had stayed for a few weeks after the bombing.

Seeing his nephew at Mugenzai-no-Sono, Fujinosuke broke down in tears – of joy mixed with anger.

'I came back to Japan looking forward to seeing you,' he told Kōichi as they sat in a reception room. 'But my brother told me that you had left to join the religious order without even discussing this idea with him. How could you be so selfish?'

Kōichi remained silent.

After a pause, Fujinosuke continued: 'You've clearly made up your mind about what you want and have started a new life. But this

Father Mirochna, the head of Mugenzai-no-Sono

isn't going to be an easy path. Are you sure you have the commitment to lead a religious life?'

Kōichi nodded. 'Uncle, I am devoting my life to the Virgin Mary,' he said. 'OK,' Fujinosuke replied. 'I have lost both your mother and now you. But I swear that I will be as committed to my new life in Japan as you are to yours.'

Before Fujinosuke left the friary, he had a long talk with Father Mirochna. It's unknown what was said, but Mirochna later told Kōichi that 'family is the most dangerous hindrance to a friar's calling'. 'Child, leave everything to the Virgin Mary,' Mirochna told him. 'You are under her protection. Being her child, you have no reason to fear anything.'

After their reunion, Kōichi often visited his uncle when the seminary was on holiday. Fujinosuke lived alone in a house next to his brother Manjirō for the following five years. He died in 1951, aged sixty-four.

In early September 1946, a long-awaited letter arrived at the Nagasaki community from Poland. It was the first missive from Niepokalanów since the end of the war. The friars were eager to learn how the Polish friary had fared during the German occupation – and the fate of Father Kolbe, the founder of Mugenzai-no-Sono.

Kōichi was already intrigued by Kolbe's life, and he peppered Brother Romuald with questions about the institution's genesis and its printing business. Kōichi was especially interested in writing and art, and he enjoyed hearing stories about how Kolbe and his colleagues had laboured day and night at the printing and typesetting machines to publish their Japanese-language magazine.

Other Polish brothers talked with Kōichi about the size and reputation of Niepokalanów before the war, as well as its influential newspapers and magazines. The friars knew that Father Kolbe had died during the conflict, but they didn't know how, or the current state of the institution.

All, they hoped, would be revealed in the letter.

Gathered in the dining hall after lunch, the friars sat expectantly as Father Mirochna read out the contents, first in Polish and then a Japanese translation. It didn't take long.

During the war, the Nazis arrested and killed many Polish priests and brothers.

Our churches were destroyed and the Polish people's freedom to practise their faith was taken away from them.

Father Maximilian Kolbe, the founder of the Niepokalanów friary, died a martyr's death in place of somebody else at Auschwitz concentration camp.

That was it. Three sentences. Nothing more. The men were silent, confused and frustrated.

What did it mean that Kolbe had 'died a martyr's death in place of somebody else'? Who? Why? When? How? And what had the Nazis done to stop the Polish people from practising their faith?

There were far more questions than answers.

Two weeks later, on 21 September, a thicker envelope arrived from Poland. Inside were the November and December 1945 issues of the *Knight of the Immaculata* (*Rycerz Niepokalanej*) magazine published by Militia Immaculatae.

Once again, Father Mirochna asked the men to remain in the dining room after their lunch. He began to read out the November issue. The following afternoon, he read out the December issue.

This time, the articles explained how the Nazis had mistreated and abused Kolbe at Auschwitz. How Father Kolbe had volunteered to take the place of another prisoner who was about to be sent to a starvation chamber. How the Nazis had murdered Father Kolbe with an injection in his arm.

The articles had been written by Father Conrad Szweda, a twenty-four-year-old associate pastor, who was at Auschwitz at the same time as Father Kolbe. The authenticity of the information was not in doubt.

After each reading, the Polish friars' tears ran unashamedly onto their beards and dark cassocks. Kōichi and his fellow Japanese seminary students didn't understand all the context of the articles, but it was clear immediately that Kolbe had suffered a horrifying death.

Kōichi was traumatised. Over the past year, he had witnessed a lifetime of suffering. Yet not since the death of his mother, Wasa, had he felt as shaken up inside as he did when the readings ended.

One question kept recurring to him. How could Kolbe have given up his life to save somebody when he, Kōichi, had neither the courage nor the commitment to help the dying in Nagasaki? Kolbe had shown that pure selfless love for others could conquer ego and hate. He'd shown that light and love could emerge from even the darkest sides of humanity.

Yes, Kolbe's death was just one more excruciating event in a war that had shattered millions of lives. But this was a man who had built the friary where Kōichi was now living. A man who had eaten in the very dining room where he was now sitting. A man whose very presence pervaded the mountainside building.

Towards Kolbe, a man he had never met, Kōichi felt an immutable bond.

The confirmation of Kolbe's death, however sparing in detail, seemed to give Kōichi's life purpose after a year in the wilderness.

Even at his tender age, he knew instinctively what steps he must take to survive and thrive.

He pledged to himself to explore Kolbe's life and try to understand where this Polish priest drew his strength and character from. Kolbe had placed his faith in the Virgin Mary to guide him. Now, Kōichi placed himself in Kolbe's hands.

The quest that would dominate the rest of his life began that cool autumn afternoon.

17. 'The Truth'

August 1939–May 1941 – Poland

In the months after Kōichi Tagawa learned about Father Kolbe's death, the young scholar began to take copious notes about every aspect of the Polish priest's life.

Day after day, Kōichi quizzed the friars who had known Kolbe during his six years in Japan. He sat in Kolbe's small cell at the friary, which had been left intact. He climbed the steep stone steps to Kolbe's favourite spot – the tranquil Lourdes grotto above the religious buildings. He ruminated in the printing room where Kolbe and the Polish priests had laboriously published the Japanese-language newspaper.

Was Kōichi obsessed? Perhaps, he told me one day, but he wanted to understand what had made Father Kolbe tick and why he had made certain judgements.

Kōichi had always believed that at the extremities of human suffering, it would be natural for someone to become self-absorbed and to fight to survive. But not Kolbe. He had appeared content, indeed almost relieved, to sacrifice his life for that of a stranger. What had led him to make such a heroic decision?

Over the following years, during ten visits to Poland, Kōichi tracked the life of his guru, from Kolbe's birth in the Russian-controlled area of Poland in 1894 to his death in Auschwitz forty-seven years later.

Kōichi was particularly interested in Kolbe's final years between 1 September 1939, when Germany invaded Poland, and 14 August 1941, when he was murdered.

Kōichi made it his mission to investigate and examine the events leading up to Kolbe's death, no matter how painful the truth. This is what is now known, based on research by Kōichi and others.[1]

On Monday, 28 August 1939, Father Maximilian Kolbe called together the inhabitants of Niepokalanów to discuss their collective future. It was already clear that Germany was set to invade Poland and that the world's largest friary would become caught up in the hostilities.

Kolbe was in no doubt about what this would mean for him. As a Polish patriot, an intellectual and head of a Christian institution that published the popular *Little Daily* newspaper, he was convinced he would be arrested and probably tortured.

'Suffering will be my lot shortly,' he told the assembled priests and brothers. 'By whom, where, how and in what form this suffering will come is still unknown. However, I'd like to suffer and die in a knightly manner, even to the shedding of the last drop of my blood in order to hasten the day of gaining the whole world for God through the Immaculate Mother. I wish the same for you as for myself.'[2]

Four days later, on 1 September, the Nazis attacked Poland from the west and north. Poland's civil authorities ordered the friary's 622 brothers, thirty-seven seminarians and thirteen priests to seek safety as soon as possible.

Kolbe encouraged the brothers to serve in the Polish Red Cross, to care for the wounded and dying in hospitals, or to simply spend time with their families at home. 'Wherever you go, in all that you do, don't forget love,' he told them.[3]

Before the friars left the community, Kolbe told them to burn all copies of the *Little Daily* newspaper, fearing its contents would anger the Nazis.[4] The editors of the paper went into hiding or fled the country because they were on lists for immediate arrest by the Gestapo, the Nazi secret police.[5]

As the men departed, Kolbe repeated to them individually: 'Do not forget love.'

Kolbe himself vowed to remain within the compound along with several dozen priests and brothers. After the friars departed, one brother shaved Kolbe's long, greying beard to avoid provoking the Germans and to prevent easy recognition.[6]

The following two weeks were chaotic. On 7 September, Luftwaffe planes bombed the small town of Teresin, where the friary was located, for the first time. This was part of Germany's strategy to encircle Poland's capital, Warsaw, just thirty-four miles to the east. Some bombs slightly damaged a few buildings within the compound.[7]

On 8 September, armoured units reached Warsaw's suburbs, presaging the Nazis' siege of the capital. On 17 September, the Soviet Union invaded Poland from the east.

And at 10 a.m. on 19 September came the event that everyone was expecting, but dreading – the arrival of rifle-toting Wehrmacht officers at Niepokalanów to arrest Kolbe and the remaining Franciscan friars.[8]

Dressed in their black habits with white-corded waistbands, Father Kolbe and forty-seven priests and brothers clambered into four trucks bound for an internment camp. On the way, the Franciscans stopped at Częstochowa, where the brothers could see the steeple of the Jasna Góra monastery, and prayed to the Black Madonna, 'the Queen of Poland'.

Eventually, as part of a steadily growing batch of prisoners that included Polish soldiers, Jews and Ukrainians, the priests were herded into cattle boxcars on a train west to Lamsdorf (present-day Łambinowice). A couple of days later, the bedraggled 600-person group arrived at a village near the Polish–German border called Amtitz (now Gębice) where they slept in leaky tents inside the heavily guarded Stalag III B Amtitz camp. Within a month the internment camp held 25,000 prisoners.[9]

On 28 September, while Kolbe and the friars were in captivity, Warsaw capitulated after sustaining heavy damage from air attacks and artillery shelling.

Within days, Kolbe's beloved Polish Republic disappeared and was split into three zones. In the west was the area annexed by the Nazis. In the centre was the so-called General Government, a German zone of occupation whose capital was Kraków rather than Warsaw. In the east was the area annexed by the Soviet Union after its invasion on 17 September. This included the city of Lviv (known at the time as Lwów).

Almost twenty-one years of Polish sovereignty had vanished in little more than twenty-one days.

Hitler considered Poles to be racially inferior to Germans and he envisioned Poland's peasants and workers labouring on behalf of his 'superior' German race. To achieve this, he had launched a campaign of terror intended to destroy the Polish nation and culture and to 'Germanise' the country.

The terror campaign began in the former capital, Warsaw. Beginning on 8 October, hundreds of Polish teachers and Catholic priests were detained, arrested and sent to two notorious detention centres – Pawiak and Mokotów Prisons – where many were tortured. In all, the Nazis killed 61,000 Polish intellectuals between September 1939 and spring 1940 in a campaign known as the Intelligenzaktion.

For Kolbe and the thousands of prisoners at Amtitz, conditions steadily deteriorated as the Polish winter set in. 'A whole potato was a rare culinary treat,' Brother Juventyn said. 'Insects and filth tormented us, but Father Maximilian bore it all with joy. It was a way he could show his love for God,' Brother Jerome Wierzba added.[10]

After six miserable weeks in Amtitz, the Franciscans were transferred to a new camp. It was in the basement of a converted secondary school in Schildberg (present-day Ostrzeszów).[11]

The school was dry, warmer than Amtitz, and local people often brought food to the Franciscans. Moreover, the German commandant of the internment centre, Hans Mulzer, was a Protestant pastor. Mulzer allowed a few friars to visit Schildberg to beg for food and medicine on the condition that they would work in the kitchen and not steal the scarce provisions.[12]

Finally, on 8 December 1939, after eighty days as prisoners, Kolbe and the other Niepokalanów friars were released. It remains unclear why the Nazis let Kolbe go at such a time.[13] After boarding a train to Warsaw, the friars tried to persuade their leader to go into hiding or to escape to another country. But Kolbe was adamant. His home was at Niepokalanów.

Kolbe refused to change his mind even after his superior, Father Provincial Madzurek, told him about atrocities that the Nazis were inflicting on Polish intellectuals. At the nation's most prestigious seat of learning, Jagiellonian University, for example, the entire Polish teaching staff had been arrested and sent to concentration camps.[14]

Back at Niepokalanów, the brothers were horrified at the friary's condition. Kitchenware and tools had been stolen and religious symbols desecrated. The Germans had sealed the printing presses with lead, and Wehrmacht administrators had taken over the main buildings.

To complicate matters, 3,500 displaced civilians, including 1,500 Jews, arrived at the compound two days after Kolbe's return. They came from Poland's Poznań region in the western part of the country. The Nazis had expelled these families in the early stages of their invasion.

Kolbe immediately decided to turn Niepokalanów into a centre of refuge. This marked somewhat of a shift in his philosophy. Until then, Kolbe had focused on disseminating Christian principles through the mass media. But at this time of national emergency, he reverted to the traditional Franciscan practice of directly helping people in need.

'Our mission now is, in the name of the Immaculata, to work for the benefit of these souls,' he told the friars. 'We must house them, feed them, and provide for their spiritual and physical needs.'[15] Kolbe insisted that they should help everyone, regardless of religion or ethnic identity, because they were all Poles.

Kolbe organised the men and women into work groups. One repaired farm machinery, watches, bicycles and other items. Another grew food and took care of livestock. Others focused on the community's safety and healthcare. He wanted Niepokalanów to

function as a self-sufficient entity as it had before the war, dependent on no one.

This arrangement was highly convenient for the Nazis at the
time, as it meant they didn't have to take care of the forcibly displaced families. And so they allowed Niepokalanów to remain open
and encouraged friars to return there even as they shut down friaries and convents elsewhere in Poland. The friars celebrated
Christmas 1939 with the families. Kolbe gave a Mass, and the choir
sang carols. Kolbe also organised a separate celebration in the new
year for the Jewish civilians, including a party for their children.[16]

Encouraged that the friary was still functioning, Kolbe conceived
an audacious plan. He asked the German authorities for permission
to resume publication of the *Knight of the Immaculata* magazine.

The purpose, he told the authorities in December 1939, was 'to
disseminate love' for the Virgin Mary. Later, in a prepared message
to officials, he said: 'You can see from this mission that we're not a
centre of hate against anyone, nor do we preach political
revolution.'[17]

The application ended up in the office of the Governor General in
Kraków, which, surprisingly, approved the request. Predictably, however, the Gestapo refused to unseal the printing machines, making
publication impossible.[18] It was back to square one.

The new year began with more bad news. In early January 1940,
Kolbe was informed that some journalists from a new German-
language newspaper in Warsaw, *Warschauer Zeitung*, wanted to
write an article about the friary.

The reporters' visit was a disaster. On Saturday, 3 February 1940,
the headline on the front page of the newspaper, widely read by the
occupation forces, screamed: 'A Visit to the Hotbed of Extreme
Hatred'. Another headline read: 'Friary Publishes Inflammatory
Polish Newspaper'.

The article itself said the *Little Daily* had been 'one of the more
vitriolic anti-Third Reich newspapers', and dismissed it as a 'venom-
ous hate sheet' printed 'in a place in which the patrons hypocritically
proclaim that they stand for morality'.

The story explained how, in a tour of the institution, the

Kolbe in 1940 after his beard and hair were shaved

reporters had found old copies of the *Little Daily* on Kolbe's bookshelves. This contradicted Kolbe's statement to the German authorities that all copies had been burnt for fuel.

The article also noted that the unpublished cover for the 1940 calendar, confiscated by the Germans in September 1939, showed the Virgin Mary gazing down on a white eagle, the Polish symbol. Below the eagle was a helmeted soldier with a rifle, looking at a map of Poland.[19]

Although Kolbe went to Warsaw to complain about the damning article in *Warschauer Zeitung*, it was impossible to deny that many articles in the *Little Daily* had been critical of, and a potential threat to, the occupying forces.

Many friars believed that the newspaper article appeared to seal Kolbe's fate, and they pestered him to go into hiding. Again, he refused.

As the noose tightened around Niepokalanów and its leader, the authorities ordered the Poznań families who had arrived in December to leave. Yet within weeks, a second wave of about 1,500 displaced people arrived. This group came from Pomerania, a region on the Baltic Sea west of Danzig.[20]

Most were either elderly or very young. Many were sick, forcing the understaffed infirmary to provide care to sixty or seventy people a day. Thirty more displaced civilians occupied a small hospital above the kitchen.

By now, about 200 friars – a quarter of the pre-war population – were running the friary's operations at full stretch. As well as making meals for the families, they operated various repair shops, a tailor's, a bakery and a vegetable garden.[21]

By July 1940, most Pomeranians had left the friary, which had been draped with a large swastika flag and a banner that read 'Ein Volk, Ein Reich, Ein Führer' (One People, One Empire, One Leader). Many families were placed in sealed trains heading for forced labour camps in Germany. Only those with some German ancestry were allowed to stay in the new German territories.[22]

Around that time, ironically, a Gestapo officer visited Niepoka-lanów and offered German nationality to Kolbe if he agreed to cooperate with the Nazis. As he was one of Poland's most influen-tial citizens, this would have been a coup for the Nazis. As a Polish patriot, Kolbe said no.[23]

To the outside world, Poland's subjugation by 1940 had become just another chapter in the broader litany of Nazi aggression. Hit-ler's European ambitions had escalated through the year with the conquest of Norway and Denmark in April, the Netherlands, Bel-gium and Luxembourg in May, and France in June.

When the Nazis invaded Poland, millions of Poles felt betrayed by Britain's and France's failure to intervene, as promised in their defence pact. Going it alone, exiled Poles set up an influential government-in-exile in France and later London, which helped organise the Polish Underground State and the Armia Krajowa (Home Army) resistance.

These efforts, no matter how heroic and courageous, fell far short of what was needed to fight the Wehrmacht.

In the occupied territories, Nazi atrocities became ever more extreme. All Poles – the elite, farmers and workers alike – were in constant danger of being abducted, arrested or assassinated.

In a campaign called AB-Aktion, the General Government had begun in May 1940 to systematically eliminate Polish leaders and the social elite.

At least 30,000 citizens were arrested in Polish cities and some 7,000 were murdered. Thousands were sent to concentration camps. The Nazis also rounded up thousands of Polish workers and sent them to Germany as slave labourers.

In mid-November 1940, against all the odds and out of the blue, a piece of unexpectedly good news arrived at the embattled Niepokalanów community. Because of confusion within the bureaucracy, the General Government's propaganda division approved – with strict conditions – the publication of the *Knight of the Immaculata* magazine. This time, the Gestapo hadn't been asked for approval, and its officers became furious after they found out.

In agreeing to the publication, the propaganda board specified three things: the magazine would be a one-off publication; circulation would be limited to no more than 120,000 copies; and it would be distributed only in Warsaw.

Kolbe was determined to take advantage of the situation. He immediately began to write an article for the publication and commissioned a drawing for the cover. He was desperate to publish by 8 December, the Feast of the Immaculate Conception, which celebrated the belief that the Virgin Mary was free of original sin from the moment of her conception.

The cover's defiant design depicted the Virgin Mary standing on a globe that was entwined by a serpent. Mary's left foot was crushing the serpent's head.

To most Poles, the message was clear. The serpent represented the Nazis, who were strangling the Polish people and the wider world. Their evil could only be stamped out if people kept their faith in Poland's Queen, the Immaculata.

Inside the magazine, written in veiled language to evade the German censors, Kolbe penned an article, which he called 'The Truth'. It was a concealed condemnation of the Nazis' propaganda lies.

'There is only one truth,' Kolbe wrote. 'Truth is powerful. No one can change any truth. One can only seek the truth, find it, recognise it, conform one's life to it, and advance on the road of truth in every question. There is not a person in the world who is not seeking enduring happiness. [Yet] happiness that is not built on truth cannot be lasting, just as untruthfulness cannot be durable. Whether for individual men, women or children, only truth can be and is the unshakeable foundation of happiness.'

The magazine was distributed by hand to its Warsaw subscribers on and after 8 December. Kolbe thought it was too risky to post the issue because the Gestapo might confiscate the magazines.[24]

'The Truth' was Kolbe's last message to his readers. Although he asked the authorities for permission to publish more issues of the magazine, none was approved, and it became clear to the friars and Kolbe himself that his arrest was imminent.

Nevertheless, Kolbe didn't alter his schedule, and he continued to reply to the letters of individual clergy in Poland and Japan. One letter, sent to Father Donat Gościński at the Nagasaki friary, on 17 January 1941, showed how much he had changed since leaving Japan.[25]

Responding to trivial complaints that some Polish friars in Japan were growing their hair and smoking cigarettes, he was surprisingly calm. 'Sanctification doesn't depend on hairstyle . . . although a uniform hairstyle is in the spirit of the rule, and I don't believe Father Francis [of Assisi] possessed either comb or mirror,' he wrote. 'It's more useful for the soul to set aside such trifles. It's only with great difficulty that one can imagine St Francis with a cigarette in his mouth. The idea is absurd. Besides, tobacco costs money and the spirit of poverty is stronger when we use the money that would be spent on cigarettes to offer to the needy.'[26]

In another letter to a depressed Pole in Japan, written two weeks before his arrest, Kolbe was sanguine. 'There's no reason to be sad. The sufferings you describe must not rob you of a tranquil mind. When peace returns, we shall go about the task of establishing Niepokalanóws everywhere in the world. At that time perhaps I'll be able to travel to Japan to visit you. Who knows where, one day, the Immaculata will decide where I will leave my bones.'[27]

Ten weeks after publication of the *Knight of the Immaculata*, at 9.50 a.m. on Monday, 17 February 1941, three black limousines pulled up at Niepokalanów, and four uniformed Gestapo officers arrested Kolbe and four other black-habitted priests.

Their destination was the Pawiak Prison in Warsaw, where generations of Polish patriots had been imprisoned, tortured and often executed.

In the six months after his arrest, Father Maximilian Kolbe would endure several lifetimes of suffering in Pawiak and, later, Auschwitz. His ordeals were just beginning.

18. The Final Days: Six Months in Hell

February 1941–August 1941 – Pawiak Prison; Auschwitz

The eighty-foot European white elm tree outside the entrance of Pawiak Prison stood stark and grey as a Gestapo officer ushered Father Maximilian Kolbe into the four-storey detention facility on a freezing afternoon in February 1941.

At the time, the leafless tree had little to distinguish it, though years later it became a focus of attention in Warsaw. For after the elm tree finally withered, it was replaced in 2005 with an imposing bronze copy that was covered with scores of name plaques.

Each was a testament to someone who had died – usually murdered – in the prison. An estimated 100,000 people were imprisoned at Pawiak between 1939 and 1944. Some 37,000 of them were executed by firing squad and 60,000 more were transported to Nazi concentration camps. Among the latter group were Kolbe and four fellow priests from Niepokalanów.

As well as political prisoners who formed part of the resistance movement against the Germans, most other Pawiak inmates were Poland's social elite, including priests, lawyers, teachers and other influential leaders whom the Nazis regarded as their enemies.

Predictably, the Gestapo ignored a petition signed by twenty brothers at the friary offering to take the place of Kolbe and his colleagues. Instead, Niepokalanów's founder and leader was separated from other priests and thrown into cell 103 in Block 6, along with other intellectuals.

About twenty men were crammed into the cell, which was designed for three or four. Food – a hunk of bread in the morning, a bowl of watery beetroot or swede soup at lunch – was inadequate. The groans of the men inside the cell were often punctuated by the screams of those in the torture rooms and the sound of the firing squad's rifles.

One day, according to multiple reports, an SS officer wandered into cell 103 and became enraged to see Kolbe wearing his Franciscan habit. Grabbing the priest, the officer tore off his crucifix and rosary beads, then punched him hard in the face.

'Do you still believe in Christ?' the officer screamed. Bleeding from the nose, Kolbe replied: 'Yes, I believe.' The officer repeatedly punched Kolbe's face until the priest lay motionless in a corner of the cell.

Following the beating, Kolbe developed a high fever and pneumonia and was confined to the prison hospital. On 4 April, the other four priests from Niepokalanów were transferred to Auschwitz.[1] Kolbe, after being released from the infirmary, was assigned to work in the prison library, a relatively benign task.

There, and in his cell at night, Kolbe gave clandestine communion services to fellow Polish patriots using wafers smuggled into the prison by Polish guards. He also conducted confessions and offered religious advice to other inmates. All these acts were banned within the prison. Polish guards and inmates who were found to have breached the rules were either executed or sent to a concentration camp.

Kolbe wrote six postcards from Pawiak – five to the friary and one to his mother, Maria. In his final postcard dated 12 May 1941, he asked his former colleagues to send him a suit of civilian clothes as soon as possible, including a jacket, vest and woollen scarf.

Kolbe and his fellow inmates knew that they would soon be transferred to a concentration camp, though this didn't appear to make him fearful. Rather, he wrote, 'Let's determine to permit ourselves to be led more and more by the Mother of God, however and to wherever she wills to lead us.'[2]

Two weeks later, on 28 May, Kolbe and 304 other ill-clad prisoners were jammed into a cattle car on a train bound for Auschwitz. As the train left Warsaw, Kolbe quietly started to sing a Polish hymn.

> Beloved mother, protectress of the nation
> Hear, lend ear to our supplication

One by one, other prisoners joined in, and the hymn spread through the train like ripples on the ocean.

> Thy loving children from country and city
> We bow before thee, imploring thy love and pity

At the time, Kolbe had no way of knowing that one of the singing prisoners aboard the train was Innocenty Protalinski. He was a 'Siberian orphan' who had been repatriated to Poland from Vladivostok via Japan in 1922. During the Nazi occupation, he had become a resistance fighter and was arrested by the Gestapo in Warsaw.

On the highway due west from Kraków to Auschwitz these days, the past is virtually invisible. Billboards advertise Burger King, Toto Sushi and a dinosaur theme park called Zatorland. On the forty-five-mile journey, my luxury coach passed all the trappings of a prosperous industrial society – a Lidl supermarket, a Renault dealership, a drive-through McCafé and well-lit shopping centres with large car parks.

Yet at Auschwitz, the past has a forbidding presence. Because of the global pandemic, there were relatively few visitors when I arrived on a warm October day in 2021. Many of the exhibits were closed, yet I couldn't shake off a sense of dread as I entered a place whose very name was synonymous, like Hiroshima and Nagasaki, with mass death and destruction.

Auschwitz, after all, was the first Nazi concentration camp founded in German-occupied Poland. Established in June 1940 on the grounds of a pre-war Polish army barracks in the suburbs of a town called Oświęcim, it grew into the largest of all the Third Reich camps.

Auschwitz was originally intended to be just one of many concentration camps set up to house the rising number of Polish men being arrested and imprisoned by the German police, including

Oil painting of Kolbe at Auschwitz

Father Kolbe. By May 1941, over 16,000 men, mainly sent from prisons in Polish cities, were living there. A majority were either intellectuals or members of the Polish resistance.

Yet beginning in 1942 Auschwitz became the largest centre for the mass extermination of Jews. More than 1.1 million men, women and children were murdered there, including 960,000 Jews, 74,000 ethnic Poles and thousands of Roma, Soviet prisoners of war and other Europeans.

My private guide at Auschwitz was Teresa Wontor-Cichy, a Polish researcher into Kolbe's life in the concentration camp. Walking alongside her, I was able to follow in Kolbe's footsteps and imagine the kind of torturous life he had lived for eleven weeks in the summer of 1941.

Like Kolbe eighty years earlier, I walked under the arching main gate at Auschwitz, with its ironic inscription '*ARBEIT MACHT FREI*' (Work sets you free). For a majority of Auschwitz prisoners, freedom came with death attached.

The new arrivals limped into the camp to the sound of a military march played by the camp's orchestra. The twenty or so orchestra members were predominantly Polish, selected from the prisoners. The precision of the military marches enabled the guards to more easily count the prisoners entering and leaving Auschwitz and to hurry them along.

On the evening of Kolbe's arrival, the 305 new inhabitants – mostly Poles, and a dozen or so Jews – were jammed into a shower room. The next morning, 29 May, after being sprayed with disinfectant and having their heads shaved, they were given torn and blood-stained blue-and-white striped serge uniforms to wear.

During the registration process, Kolbe and the other men received numbers. Kolbe's was 16670. These were stamped on a scrap of cloth, which the prisoners sewed onto their clothes. From that moment, the prisoners were all but nameless, reduced by their SS guards to digits.

Later, in the spring of 1943, when tens of thousands of Jews were sent to Auschwitz, the inmates who survived the initial selection process, and other deportees, had their numbers tattooed on their left forearm.

In the assembly yard that day, Auschwitz's deputy commandant Karl Fritsch, the son of a Bohemian stove builder, gave his usual sadistic and sardonic 'welcome speech' to the men.

You have come to a concentration camp, not a sanatorium. There is only one exit from here, up the crematorium chimney. If you are displeased, you may leave at once by walking into the electrified fence. Jews in this transport may expect to live two weeks, priests one month, all others three months.[3]

Over the following two weeks, Kolbe and other newcomers were forced to participate in what the SS guards called 'sport'. No matter how sick, the inmates repeated countless physical exercises, including high-tempo squat thrusts, frog-marching and prolonged rolling on the ground. The goal was to terrorise and subjugate the men, forcing total compliance.[4]

At night, exhausted by these exertions, Kolbe slept fitfully on straw that had been thrown on the cold floor of a crowded concrete room in Block 18 (later renamed Block 25) of the camp.

No one had time to rest. Auschwitz was in the midst of a dynamic expansion in 1941. Almost immediately, the men were assigned jobs on construction sites, building accommodation for more prisoners and the future importation of thousands of Jews.

For several weeks, Kolbe removed gravel and stones from a quarry. The gravel was needed to build a fence at a crematorium. It was back-breaking work for a man in his state of health.

On Sunday, 15 June, Kolbe wrote a letter in German to his mother, Maria – the last letter he ever wrote – that betrayed no hint of any suffering.

My Dearest Mother, At the end of May, I was transported to the Auschwitz camp. I'm well, because our dear God is everywhere and thinks of everyone with great love. Don't be concerned about me or my health.[5]

At the end of the letter, Kolbe told his mother not to write back as he didn't know how long he would be living in the camp.

Just a week later, on 22 June, a news bulletin spread through Auschwitz like wildfire – Germany had invaded the Soviet Union.

Over the following five months, the largest force in the history of warfare – some 3.8 million personnel from the Axis powers – occupied parts of the western Soviet Union. Operation Barbarossa, as the invasion was codenamed, was a dramatic escalation of the Second World War, and it caught Stalin largely by surprise. Hitler simply ignored the non-aggression pact he had signed with Stalin in August 1939.

As details of the invasion circulated through the camp, the inmates speculated that they would be sent to the battlefields as cannon fodder because Germany would find it difficult to sustain fighting on two fronts. Others believed that they'd have to work even harder as forced labour for the Axis war effort.

Either way, their future appeared bleak. For Maximilian Kolbe, conditions were about to deteriorate further.

Like most Nazis, Auschwitz's deputy camp leader, Karl Fritsch, abhorred the Polish clergy, regarding them with the same disdain that he showed Jews. A member of the Nazi Party since 1930, Fritsch had worked in the SS's first concentration camp in Dachau in 1934, where thousands of political opponents were incarcerated.

In late June 1941, Fritsch decided to heap even more work on the hapless priests, including Kolbe. During a visit to Block 18, Fritsch ordered all the priests to step forward and assigned them to a construction project in the village of Babice, about two-and-a-half miles from Auschwitz. The group was called the Babice commando, and it was supervised by a notoriously brutal *kapo*, Heinrich Krott, whose nickname was Krott the Bloody. A kapo was a prisoner, often a former German criminal, assigned by the SS to oversee forced labour in exchange for food and other privileges.

The work was gruelling. For two weeks, Kolbe walked to the village from the camp, where Krott made the frail father carry heavy logs almost a mile from a forest to a field. After Kolbe dropped the logs in the field, Krott ordered him to run back to the forest and return with another one and yet another, for hours on end.[6]

Worn out from lack of food and weak from his tuberculosis, Kolbe staggered under the weight of the load. When he couldn't run any more, Krott slashed him with an ox-hide whip. Eventually, Kolbe collapsed, motionless.

Believing that Kolbe was dead, Krott kicked his body into a marsh and covered it with branches. Later, when the day's work had ended, other inmates carried the barely conscious Kolbe back to the camp and tried to get him admitted to the infirmary.

It was impossible. More than 100 sick or injured inmates were gathered in front of the hospital waiting to be examined. The infirmary was always full and new patients weren't admitted until someone died.

'The hospital wasn't really a place to treat the sick,' according to Wontor-Cichy, the Kolbe researcher at Auschwitz. 'It was more a way for the Nazis to prevent infectious diseases from spreading to the SS staff and the rest of the inmates.'

Hearing that Kolbe was in dire straits, an influential former Polish army physician called Rudolf Diem examined the priest and found him a bunk bed in the infirmary. Like Dr Diem, many of the medical staff were Polish prisoners who clandestinely tried to help the sick.

In fact, Diem belonged to a military resistance group inside Auschwitz set up by Captain Witold Pilecki. A member of the Secret Polish Army (Tajna Armia Polska or TAP), Pilecki deliberately joined a group of Poles being arrested during a round-up in Warsaw and was deported to the camp in September 1940. There, he established a network of small units that acted independently of each other.[7]

Kolbe knew several of these TAP patriots, but it's unlikely that he was aware of their links to Pilecki or to each other. According to Wontor-Cichy, the commanders of this network of several hundred Polish inmates were looking far into the future. 'They knew that when the war eventually ended, Poland would need leaders and intellectuals to rebuild the country,' she said.

Key doctors such as Diem and Władysław Dering, a Pilecki confidant in TAP, played 'hide and seek' with the Germans and tried to protect influential prisoners, Wontor-Cichy said. Many professionals survived the camp thanks to their help and daring.

For most of July 1941, Maximilian Kolbe lay in a bed at the Auschwitz infirmary under Diem's supervision. While the injuries from Krott's beating slowly healed, his tuberculosis flared up. Three X-rays showed that he had pneumonia. Yet although Kolbe was by no means well, the clandestine Polish doctors' network arranged for him to be discharged from the infirmary.

There was a good reason. The resistance network inside Auschwitz had learned that a German euthanasia commission was set to visit the camp. The commission would be selecting patients in the infirmary to send to the Sonnenstein Euthanasia Centre in Saxony, one of six 'death institutes' set up by the Reich to 'eliminate life unworthy of life'. Most patients were gassed to death.

After the commission arrived, on 28 July 1941, members selected 573 prisoners from the infirmary, most of them Poles. Many patients volunteered to leave after they were falsely told that they would be transferred to another camp for lighter work or were being moved to a sanatorium to improve their health.

The prisoners' network knew better, essentially saving Kolbe's life. They also arranged that he be moved to a quarantine block for suspected typhus patients and placed in a group that repaired camp uniforms.

Later, Kolbe was transferred to the kitchen, where he peeled potatoes and vegetables together with influential Polish writers and scientists. After regaining some of his strength, he was moved to Block 14 (later renamed Block 19).

No matter where a prisoner worked, life at Auschwitz was endlessly dehumanising and humiliating. Beatings, kickings and curses were the daily norm, as was hunger. Diseases such as dysentery and typhus were rampant. Death stalked the men.

Worse, trust and human dignity were too often disregarded as prisoners fought for survival. For many, including some priests, hope and faith disappeared, replaced by despair and doubt. Many prisoners, overwhelmed with gloom and anger, simply ran to the 220-volt electrified barbed-wire fence that ringed Auschwitz and ended their ordeal.

Kolbe was an exception. In the eleven weeks that he lived in Auschwitz, he was the personification of decency and morality. Kolbe was never aggressive or outraged at the Nazis' cruelties. Moreover, his faith in God never wavered.

This meant that he had an extraordinary influence on the lives of scores of men that he met there.

His impact extended far beyond his religion. For while Kolbe was well known as the founder of Niepokalanów and its publishing empire, the concentration camp inmates all saw different qualities in him. Beaten down and beleaguered, they needed some form of leader, spiritual or otherwise, to look up to at a time when they could fall no further. Kolbe often provided that inspiration.

The testimonies of those who knew Kolbe in Auschwitz depict a man of remarkable maturity, sensitivity and empathy. Knowing his days were numbered, he offered his fellow inmates comfort, erudition and hope at the most desperate time of their lives.

Kolbe believed with total conviction that God, led by Poland's queen, the Virgin Mary, would ultimately sweep humanity to victory. He said repeatedly: 'Do not counter violence with violence. Hatred is not creative. Only love is creative. Never forget love.'

'Never forget love' wasn't a trite slogan to Kolbe. It was a profound exhortation that he expected everyone to follow.

'It was he who encouraged me [to talk] and we finished by his hearing my confession,' said Dr Joseph Stemler, a First World War veteran and director of the Polish Education Department. Stemler had been sent to Auschwitz in April 1941 and met Kolbe in the infirmary after contracting severe diarrhoea. 'I was so unhappy and desperate. His words, on the other hand, were simple and scholarly. He urged me to have firm faith in the victory of good.'[8]

On the southern edge of Auschwitz, close to the Sola River, a corridor of silver birch trees ran along the inside of the electrified fence. Some of the trees, or their offspring, still stand to this day. Here, in the evenings after work and after their sparse meal – often just a tiny piece of bread – the Auschwitz inmates were allowed to meet with fellow prisoners for between several minutes and half an hour.

This was almost the only occasion that prisoners could mix with those outside their work detail. During these brief moments, many survivors testified that Kolbe listened to prisoners' confessions, which was, to the Nazis, a treasonable act.

In the shade of the trees, a twenty-year-old student called Ladislaus Lewkowicz frequently sought out Kolbe after evening roll call. Lewkowicz had spent a year at Niepokalanów when he was sixteen. 'He was my confessor,' Lewkowicz recalled. 'He was always serene; his spirit was at peace.'[9]

Repeatedly beaten by the prison guards, Lewkowicz asked Kolbe's advice on how to handle the cruelty. 'Never respond with violence,' Kolbe told him. 'Instead, focus your mind on how to survive. In the end, if you survive, you will have won the battle for life.'

Kolbe's words marked a turning point in Lewkowicz's life, and he held out at the camp, later becoming a veterinarian in the Polish city of Poznań.[10]

For many prisoners, survival meant finding a few scraps of food to fend off the gnawing hunger. Not Kolbe, who would frequently offer his meagre portions of bread and soup to others.

'Take it. Eat it. You are younger than me. You, at least, must live,' Kolbe told one young prisoner, according to a tailor, Alexander Dziuba, who had been in Auschwitz since September 1940. At other times, Kolbe would take his bread rations, bless them and give pieces to the inmates to symbolise communion.[11]

To Mieczysław Kościelniak, a renowned Polish painter who was sent to Auschwitz in May 1941, it was Kolbe's patriotism that shone through the gloom. 'He made us see that our souls were not dead, that our dignity as Catholics and Poles was not destroyed,' Kościelniak said later. 'Uplifted in spirit, the men returned to their blocks repeating his words: "We will not break down. We will survive. They will not kill the Polish spirit in us." '

After the SS spotted Kościelniak's talent as an artist, he was assigned to work for the Nazis, producing posters and paintings for the camp's administrators. At Kolbe's request, Kościelniak drew him a picture of Christ and the Virgin Mary. It was sketched on paper the size of a postage stamp, which Kolbe placed in a hidden pocket sewn inside a wide belt.[12]

In one of their clandestine meetings, Kolbe told Kościelniak: 'I will not survive the camp, but you will. Remember that you will have an obligation as an artist to convey the truth to the world.'

With these words in mind, Kościelniak portrayed Auschwitz's terrifying reality in about 300 drawings that depicted beatings, abandoned corpses, murders and multiple other atrocities and war crimes. Most drawings were smuggled out of the camp in loads of dirty linen by the underground resistance network.[13]

Kolbe's love for others in Auschwitz was unconditional. Sigmund Gorson, a Polish Jew, was just thirteen years old when he arrived at the camp. His parents and three sisters were all murdered there, leaving Gorson as the sole survivor of his immediate family. Many traumatised boys of Gorson's age in the camp ended their lives on the electrified fence.

Father Kolbe was the reason Gorson did not follow them. 'He [Kolbe] was a refuge from insanity, an escape from madness,' Gorson recalled. 'Like a mother hen, he took me in his arms. He used to wipe away my tears. He knew I was a Jewish boy. That made no difference. He dispensed love and nothing but love. His lips were swollen from hunger, but he was always smiling, always cheerful, the only one. God spoke through him.'[14]

One of Kolbe's most unusual friendships was with Warsaw's bantamweight boxing champion, Tadeusz 'Teddy' Pietrzykowski, who was a member of Pilecki's resistance organisation within the camp. Deported to Auschwitz in 1940 as a twenty-three-year-old political prisoner, Pietrzykowski took part in boxing matches on Sundays. These were arranged by a kapo and former German middleweight champion, Walter Dunning, for the entertainment of the Gestapo and other German officers. The fights usually involved some of the German criminal kapos and the camp inmates. Volunteers were often given extra bread rations. In the first of more than forty boxing matches in the camp, Pietrzykowski fought the much fitter and heavier Dunning, yet the Pole landed a left hook that bloodied the German's nose. The fight ended after Dunning threw down his gloves and offered Pietrzykowski some bread and meat.[15]

According to numerous sources, Pietrzykowski once gave Kolbe some bread, which was then stolen from the priest. Outraged, Pietrzykowski seized the thief, but Kolbe interceded, telling the boxer not to hurt the man. He then gave the thief the bread, saying: 'He is also hungry.'

'He [Kolbe] had too great a heart,' Pietrzykowski was quoted as saying about this incident. 'It was against all reason.'[16] Yet to Kolbe, the gift of bread to a desperate man was not only reasonable, it was a selfless obligation.

Just a few weeks later, another act of altruism would turn Kolbe into a martyr.

At about three o'clock one afternoon during the week of 28 July 1941, Auschwitz's sirens began to shriek. One of the 600 or so prisoners housed in Father Kolbe's block had escaped.[17]

The German guards immediately began to count the prisoners and started searching the fields and buildings for any sign of the escapee. Outside the camp, the police set up roadblocks.[18]

After work, the inmates from Block 14 were forced to stand at attention, without food, until bedtime, according to Ladislaus Swies, a friend of Kolbe's who had been in the same boxcar that had carried them to Auschwitz two months earlier. Also among the men was prisoner 16658, Innocenty Protalinski, the Siberian orphan, who welcomed his job cleaning the Nazi guards' toilets because in return he received extra margarine and potatoes.[19]

The following morning, everyone in Block 14 lined up in ten rows of about sixty men each, with the shortest inmates at the front. For hours, the men stood at attention in the boiling summer sun, with only a break for soup at noon. 'Quite a few keeled over and were left lying where they fell,' recalled Thaddeus 'Ted' Wojtkowski from Poznań.

Near the end of the day, deputy commander Karl Fritsch appeared and announced that the fugitive had not been found. 'In reprisal,' he said, 'ten men will die by starvation. Next time it will be twenty.'

Fritsch started walking among the rows of terrified men, accompanied by Gerhard Palitzch, an SS officer known for conducting many inmate executions at Auschwitz's so-called Death Wall. Palitzch had arrived at the camp in May 1940 and brought with him thirty German convicts to work as kapos.

The SS officers chose ten victims at random. All were quiet until one of the chosen men cried out: 'My wife and my children!' The cries came from a thirty-nine-year-old former Polish army sergeant called Franciszek Gajowniczek, who had been captured by the Nazis during the invasion and had been living at Auschwitz since October 1940.

A few moments later, there was a murmuring among the men as one of the prisoners pushed his way to the front of the line-up. 'I would like to take the place of this prisoner,' he said in flawless

Oil painting of Kolbe volunteering to take the place of a fellow Polish prisoner

German, pointing to Gajowniczek. 'I have no wife and children, and I am old.'

'Who are you?' the stupefied Fritsch asked. 'A Catholic priest,' the man replied. After a slight hesitation, Fritsch said, 'Request granted', and kicked Gajowniczek away, snarling: 'You, back to ranks!'

The priest, Father Kolbe, staggered with the other nine inmates along a path towards Block 11, the camp jail, which housed a starvation bunker in its basement. Along the way, Kolbe grasped the skeletal body of one of the men who could no longer walk under his own strength.

'I could only try to thank him [Kolbe] with my eyes,' Gajowniczek said later. 'I was flabbergasted. The immensity of it. I, the condemned, was to live and someone else – a stranger – willingly and voluntarily offered his life for me. Was this a dream or reality?'[20]

'Strip.'

The ten Polish men who had been condemned to die cast off

their dirty striped uniforms at the command of an SS guard. Apart from Kolbe, the other men have never been named.

After descending some narrow stairs in the penal block, the men were flung into cell 18, a white, rectangular basement room about ten foot by eight foot six. A tiny window near the ceiling allowed a few shafts of light into the gloom.

There was no furniture, except a urine bucket in one corner. The men sat naked on the cold concrete floor. 'In a few days, you'll all dry up like tulips!' an SS guard shouted as he slammed and locked the door.

From then on, the prisoners were given no food and not a drop of water.

The extraordinary account of the men's final days was recorded by several witnesses. The most detailed came from a German-speaking Polish prisoner from Silesia called Bruno Borgowiec, who was the interpreter for the Germans in the penal block.

Once a day, Borgowiec entered the bunker with the SS to inspect the men and to translate from Polish to German whatever the prisoners said. He also recorded the prison numbers of the dead and carried away the bodies.

Borgowiec wrote down in detail what he saw in the bunker and sent two statements to Niepokalanów in December 1945.[21]

Kolbe, according to Borgowiec, spent hours trying to pacify and placate the terrified men who were screaming and cursing in despair at their hunger, thirst and overall weakness. Borgowiec wrote:

The stench was overwhelming. I never needed to empty the urine bucket. It was always empty and dry. The prisoners drank its contents to satisfy their thirst.

To keep up their spirits, he [Kolbe] encouraged them that the escapee might still be found and they would be released . . .

He prayed aloud. The cell doors were made of oak. Because of the silence and acoustics, Father Kolbe's voice in prayer was diffused to the other cells, where it could be heard as well. These prisoners joined in . . .

From then on, every day from the cell, one heard the recitation of prayers, the rosary, and hymns. Father Kolbe led while the others responded as a group. As these fervent prayers and hymns resounded in all corners of the bunker, I had the impression I was in a church.

Father Kolbe never asked for anything, and he never complained.

Whenever the SS guards opened the bunker door, Borgowiec wrote, Kolbe was either standing or kneeling on the floor leading the prayers. He would then look up and peer directly into the guards' eyes. His glance was so penetrating that the SS men yelled: 'Look at the ground, not at us.'

According to Borgowiec, most prisoners in the starvation cell would perish in just a few days. Those with Kolbe lived much longer. But as the dog days of August 1941 dragged on, the men's prayers and hymns became gradually weaker until they were merely whispers. One by one, the men fell silent.

After about two weeks, several men were still breathing, including Kolbe. But the SS needed the bunker, as they now had other plans. The Nazis were preparing for the mass murder of Jews and the arrival of Russian prisoners. To clear the bunker, the SS decided to kill the remaining Polish prisoners.

They sent a German criminal, Hans Bock, from the infirmary to inject the men with carbolic acid. Borgowiec accompanied Bock to the cell.

Kolbe, deep in prayer, held out his arm to the executioner, Borgowiec said. But Borgowiec left the bunker because he could not bear to look. He returned after the injection to see Kolbe sitting upright, leaning against a wall, his head tilted a little to one side, his eyes wide open.[22]

Kolbe's body was carried out of the basement the following morning, 15 August, in a trough-like wooden box. He was cremated that day in the Auschwitz crematorium.

In that same basement, just weeks after Kolbe's murder, the Nazis carried out the first trial of Zyklon B, a cyanide-based gas. On that occasion, in September 1941, the SS gassed about 600 Soviet prisoners of war and 250 Polish prisoners, foreshadowing the Holocaust that would follow.

19. The Awakening

1946–1950 – Hokkaido

Four weeks after Japan's surrender at the end of the Second World War, on 11 September 1945, the militarist who had ordered the attack on Pearl Harbor in December 1941 shot himself in the chest at his Tokyo home.

Former Prime Minister Hideki Tōjō, sixty-one, who oversaw the war in the Pacific until mid-1944, had tried to commit suicide to avoid being arrested by the Allied occupation forces as an alleged war criminal.

He failed. When a team of US Army counterintelligence officers burst into Tōjō's home, they found him lying on a couch, his shirt splattered with blood, a pistol in his right hand. The team quickly found a doctor to staunch the wound.[1]

Tōjō's capture made headlines around the world because he was the Allies' number one enemy. His inability to kill himself – and then to be saved by his enemy – damaged his already scarred reputation in Japan. After all, Tōjō himself had issued the military code called Senjinkun that said: 'Never live to experience shame as a prisoner.' There was no better scapegoat than Tōjō for Japan's humiliating defeat.

Barely eight months later, Tōjō was the key defendant at the International Military Tribunal for the Far East, better known as the Tokyo Trials. The tribunal had been set up to put on trial Japanese individuals responsible for violations of international law, beginning with Japan's 1931 invasion of Manchuria.

Tōjō was one of twenty-eight 'class A' suspects charged with crimes against peace. The trials were modelled after the International Military Tribunal, or Nuremberg Trials, begun in November 1945, in which the Allies brought charges of crimes of

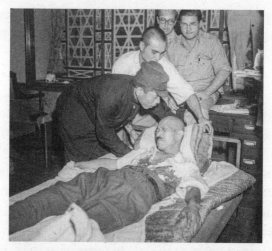

Tōjō after his failed suicide attempt in September 1945

aggression and crimes against humanity against Nazi leaders and organisations.

After the Tokyo Trials began in May 1946, Japanese newspapers reported for the first time graphic descriptions of the Nanjing Massacre, the Bataan Death March, the Manila Massacre of February 1945 and reams of other atrocities.[2]

Sitting in his parents' home in Nanae village near the southern tip of Hokkaido, the precocious fifteen-year-old Masatoshi Asari devoured the local newspapers' accounts of the trials with fascination and revulsion.

Asari had returned to his junior high school in September 1945 to catch up with the studies he had missed while working at the agricultural experimental station for the Japanese war effort. He found it impossible to ignore the accounts of the abominations that were a staple of the prosecution's testimony against Japan's leaders.

For millions of readers and radio listeners, including Asari, the trials were a powerful indictment of the nation's political and military leaders, stirring contempt for those who had led Japan during the 1930s and 40s.

Yet for other Japanese, and indeed for some Allies, the trials were simply an exercise in revenge, or victors' justice. Still others passively accepted the findings, viewing them as a consequence of the nation's defeat. Many Japanese saw themselves as victims of their leaders' excesses and had no sense of collective responsibility.[3]

Under the strict censorship rules of the Allied occupation forces, it was prohibited to criticise the tribunal or to defend the war criminals. And at the tribunal, to Asari's chagrin, one other topic was taboo – the war responsibility of the emperor.

In mid-June 1946, the chief prosecutor, Joseph Keenan, announced that the emperor would not stand trial. This was a major victory for Douglas MacArthur, the Supreme Commander for the Allied Powers. MacArthur believed that putting the emperor on trial might destabilise post-war Japan at a time when the occupation forces were concerned about a famine and possible civil disorder.

To Asari, the wartime belief that Japan had been fighting a 'sacred war' on behalf of a divine emperor was absurd. The truth, he came to realise, was that Japanese soldiers had slaughtered tens of thousands of innocent people in China and throughout Asia in the emperor's name.

'I'd always believed, as did most of my schoolmates, that Japan had a mission to rule other Asians and to liberate them from "Western imperialists,"' he said. 'But it was quickly apparent from the Tokyo trials that Japanese soldiers often became killing machines of civilians and Allied prisoners of war.'[4]

Asari became convinced that the Japanese had blindly pursued a fanatical war ideology based on an imperial system in which the emperor was 'God'.

'It was a cult,' Asari said. 'We were all led to believe that we were superior to others because we were the emperor's children. And this conviction led to countless people dying on the battlefields. Millions perished for this ignoble cause and yet the emperor, who was the supreme commander of the Army and Navy, was spared his responsibility. Everyone wanted to believe that the emperor wasn't culpable, that the only really bad guy was Tōjō.'

At the same time as the Tokyo Trials were prompting a reckoning with Japan's wartime past, another momentous event was taking place in the nation's capital that would have ramifications for generations to come.

Determined to eradicate 'war' from Japan's vocabulary, MacArthur's occupation forces in early 1946 pieced together a draft of a revolutionary document designed to make Japan the most non-violent major nation on Earth. The draft was passed back and forth between the Americans who directed the occupation at the General Headquarters, and Japanese government officials.

The document outlined a new democratic Constitution to replace the charter that the Meiji government had enacted in 1889. That old charter had cast the emperor as Japan's 'divine' head of state. In the new Constitution, the emperor's role was largely ceremonial and symbolic.

The most striking part of the document was a directive called Article 9, in which Japan renounced its right to wage war and to maintain any armed forces. The Constitution, which came into force in May 1947, also made it clear that Japan would explicitly pursue the notions of human rights, popular sovereignty and pacifism.

For a country that had been at war less than two years earlier, this was an extraordinary metamorphosis. Predictably, it shocked Japan's conservative elite, who wanted to preserve the emperor's sovereignty as head of state. In contrast, the public at large, eager to embrace peace and democracy, widely accepted the new Constitution.

So, too, did the nation's left-leaning intellectuals, who dubbed the document the 'Peace Constitution', which remains its informal name. They vowed that they would never again allow militants to take control of the nation and lamented that most intellectuals had supported the military government during the war. The only group of people who had consistently opposed the war were communists, many of whom had been imprisoned and tortured, some of them to death.[5]

For Asari, the new Constitution was not only a much-needed change of direction for the country. It would also change his life.

Shortly after his seventeenth birthday, in April 1948, Masatoshi Asari took a local train through the late-winter snow to a teacher training university in the port town of Hakodate, Hokkaido, for the start of the new Japanese academic year.

He couldn't have been prouder. Asari was the first member of his family to attend any kind of further education. He was one of just five students in the region to win a place at the university. Most of his friends had stopped going to school at age seventeen or even earlier.

Disillusioned with those who had led Japan to war, Asari was convinced that the nation's only hope lay in teaching its children. His goal was to become a science teacher, focusing primarily on botany and nature, influenced by Chie, his flower-loving mother.

But first, Asari was required to take a series of liberal arts courses, including one on the new Constitution. This was part of MacArthur's educational reform programme that was trying to shake up the nation's schools and universities.

By chance, Asari's professor was an idealistic young man called Tōru Ukita, who had just arrived from Tokyo with his new bride. Ukita, who was twenty-six, was a graduate of Tokyo University's Law School, the most prestigious educational establishment in Japan. Ukita had volunteered to teach in the remote city of Hakodate to pass on his passion for the new Constitution. He also wanted to give something back to Hokkaido, where he had grown up.

Ukita couldn't have wished for a more enthusiastic student. Seated in the front row of the classroom, Asari hung on Ukita's every word as the professor discussed the importance of human rights, pacifism and the equality of individuals – the key principles behind the Constitution.

Every evening after class, Asari immersed himself in the translated works of influential Western philosophers. There was Baron de Montesquieu, whose theory of the separation of powers – legislative, executive and judicial – had been widely adopted in many nations' constitutions. There was Friedrich Nietzsche, the German philosopher who wrote that humans must craft their own identities through self-realisation, a view that Asari applauded. There was Johann Wolfgang von Goethe, the poet and scientist who also wrote about Asari's first love, botany. Above all, Asari adored the writings of Jean-Jacques Rousseau, the eighteenth-century French thinker whose political philosophy influenced the Enlightenment in Europe. In particular, Asari admired Rousseau's *Emile, or On Education*, a book that stressed the importance of free expression to produce well-balanced and creative children.

'Professor Ukita's course turned on a light switch,' Asari told me. 'I learnt that the new Constitution was all about individual rights, regardless of gender, race or faith, which had been totally ignored under the old Constitution.'

Asari concluded that Japan's path forward needed to be based on the principles of freedom and human rights. And he resolved that as soon as he became a teacher, he would instruct children about civil liberties as well as about the futility of war.

Most of Japan's seventy-five million people would have agreed with those sentiments. Struggling to make a living in the aftermath of war, their goal was to escape poverty and to move ahead, rather than reliving the past. Indeed, their desire for closure was reflected in declining public interest in the Tokyo war crimes trials, which ended in November 1948.

Throughout 1948, reports about the trials diminished substantially as more pressing issues took centre stage, particularly the moribund economy. After thirty months of trials, twenty-five class A defendants were found guilty of war crimes. (Two others died of natural causes, and one was ruled unfit to stand trial.)

Seven men, including former Prime Minister Tōjō, were sentenced to death and executed at Tokyo's Sugamo Prison in December 1948. Sixteen others were sentenced to life imprisonment. Many prisoners were later quietly released as post-war realities supplanted the Allies' appetite for justice and as millions of Japanese explored new ideas, values and faiths at this time of transition.

One warm weekday evening in mid-1949, Masatoshi Asari stayed behind after class for a lesson he would never forget. A couple of

American children drinking Coca-Cola in occupied Japan

Americans were visiting his university to demonstrate 'modern' dances to the students, such as the boogie-woogie.

Even in rural Hokkaido, Western customs and lifestyle – mostly American – permeated many people's daily lives for the first time since the war. Baseball, which had become popular in the 1930s, supplanted the martial arts as a sporting pursuit.

Anything from the West, including Hollywood blockbusters that spread messages about democracy and humanism, appeared fresher and more appealing than stolid Japanese alternatives. One particularly popular film was MGM's *Madame Curie*, a love story starring Greer Garson and Walter Pidgeon about the Polish-born scientist and her ill-fated husband.[6]

Asari himself had more interest in botany than in baseball and was more curious about live bugs than the jitterbug, but he and his friends were intent on experiencing different activities.

'It was a time of new beginnings for me, and for Japan,' Asari said. 'Everyone had to find their feet, to find a direction in which to tread.'

For example, one of Asari's close friends, Etsuo Yusa, invited him to a Catholic church in Hakodate, run by a French missionary. There, Asari saw for the first time an edition of *Seibo-no-Kishi*, the

Japanese-language *Knight of the Immaculata* magazine, which Father Kolbe had started in 1930.

The Polish friars in Nagasaki had resumed publishing the magazine after the war. Asari later recalled that even though the magazine looked shoddy, it contained appealing articles about the importance of serving others and support for the downtrodden. He returned to the church several times in 1949 to read the Bible and to discuss religious principles, although he said he never felt the urge to be baptised.

On the train to and from university, Asari and five or six fellow students had friendly but heated discussions about religion, freedom, human rights and competing philosophies.[7] But one day in early 1950, midway through his studies, Asari's lively world collapsed.

His heart began palpitating as he left the train to walk to his classes. He started coughing violently and found himself breathless, unable to move.

The diagnosis was bad. Asari was suffering from tuberculosis and heart disease. For the following two years he had little choice but to quit his classes and stay at home, to be nursed by his mother.

Masatoshi Asari couldn't remember a time when he hadn't been busy. Even while studying at the university, he had helped his father and brother Shōichi in the family's rice paddies and with the sale of hōzuki cherries.

Now he had no option but to rest, and to read. Asari spent most days engrossed in different religions, philosophies and ethics. He pored over the translated works of European writers, especially those of Albert Camus, the young French philosopher and fellow tuberculosis sufferer.

Critical of the Soviet Union and worried about the consequences of totalitarianism, Camus' writing taught Asari that life was a perennial search for meaning and that he must never give in to hopelessness. One of Camus' most notable sayings – 'Peace is the only battle worth waging' – written on 7 August 1945, the day after the Hiroshima atomic bombing, also resonated with the young man.

'Camus gave me deeper insights into the human condition and provided a foundation for my future,' Asari said. He added that his lifelong research into cherry blossoms and part of his quest for humanity and peace stemmed from these two years of concentrated reading.

At the same time as Asari's awakening in Hokkaido, the outside world was changing dramatically. In March 1946, former British Prime Minister Winston Churchill had declared that an 'Iron Curtain' had descended across Europe.

The following year, US President Harry Truman announced policies that became known as the Truman Doctrine. These were designed to contain the Soviet Union and to aid any democratic nation threatened by totalitarianism.

In Asia, that meant Korea. Just thirty-five miles from southern Japan at its closest point, Korea had been divided along the 38th Parallel in 1945. Three years later, Kim Il-Sung became leader of the Soviet-occupied North Korea, and a US-backed politician, Syngman Rhee, was elected president of the South.

Japan was well positioned strategically to help the Americans, and as tensions rose on the Korean peninsula, the euphoria and idealism that had helped create a pacifist Japan in the late 1940s began to dissipate.

When North Korea invaded South Korea in June 1950, it was immediately clear to Asari that MacArthur's occupation forces would use Japan as a bulwark to defend the South and to prevent the creep of communism in Asia.

The course of Japanese 'democratisation' had taken a sudden shift to the right, even while the country was tying up loose ends left over from the Second World War.

One of these unresolved problems was the plight of thousands of Japanese orphans whose parents had died during the war. Over the following three decades, Father Maximilian Kolbe's disciple, Brother Zeno Żebrowski, would spearhead a movement on behalf of the orphans that would draw nationwide attention to the Nagasaki friary.

20. No Time to Die

1946–1950 – Nagasaki

Unexpected visitors, usually homeless, jobless and penniless men, often came knocking at the wooden door of the Nagasaki monastery seeking help. But the trio who clambered up to the mountainside cloisters one day in early 1946 were far from the norm.

One was an elderly Yamabushi monk, a hermit wearing white leggings, a colourful surplice and a broad, conical straw hat. He usually led a solitary life in the mountains. The other two were ravenous and near-naked brothers.

The ascetic monk, a follower of the Shugendō religion, had come across the boys – thirteen-year-old Iwao and nine-year-old Hitoshi Morita – living in a remote air-raid shelter on the side of a mountain. They were orphans whose parents had died in the bombing of Nagasaki in August 1945.

Concerned for their well-being, the grey-bearded monk asked his Polish Catholic counterparts to shelter and feed the brothers. There was never any doubt about the answer.

Iwao and Hitoshi's arrival marked the beginning of a new phase at the Mugenzai-no-Sono friary, during which several hundred orphans came to live there. Some arrived by themselves, struggling up the hill and begging for food. Others were dropped off by relatives unable to feed and clothe their distant kin.

As word spread that this Christian community was a haven for orphans, the Nagasaki police and local government officials also began to bring more parentless boys.

At first, lacking a place to accommodate the orphans, the friars gave up their rooms and slept in a shed outside. But as the numbers swelled, Dr Takashi Nagai and two other Japanese Catholic educators

The Yamabushi monk who brought the
first orphan boys to the monastery, January 1946

who were staying at the friary discussed with the Poles how to care
for the children over the longer term.

Father Mirochna, the head of Mugenzai-no-Sono, temporarily
designated part of the friars' former dormitory as an orphanage,
calling it Seibo-no-Kishi-en, the Knights of the Immaculata Children's Home. By the end of 1946, about 100 boys lived there.

But as this was still clearly too small, Mirochna tapped his favourite can-do friar – Brother Zeno Żebrowski – to provide a solution. It
was an inspired choice.

Brother Zeno, now in his late forties or early fifties (no one,
including Zeno himself, knew exactly when he'd been born), had
been Father Kolbe's trusted adviser and confidant since he showed
up at Kolbe's monastery in the town of Grodno, Poland, in 1925.

Resourceful and devoted, Zeno had helped build Mugenzai-no-
Sono and used his charm, guile, abundant energy and appalling
Japanese to achieve his goals. For Zeno, every human being was the
same and he cared little for status, wealth or reputation.

At the General Headquarters offices in Nagasaki, Zeno demanded
food and sweets for the boys from the American occupiers. At food
wholesalers, he solicited donations of bread and other staples.

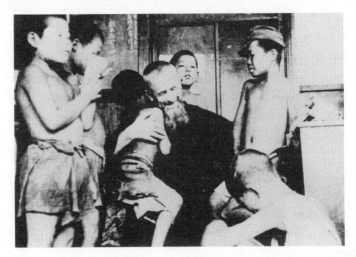

Zeno and the orphans

Elsewhere, Zeno asked for used clothes, shoes, blankets, lumber, cement, soap, medicine and any other products that the orphans might need.[1]

Whomever he met, Zeno stroked his beard, smiled, bowed and handed out his business card. It read, in Japanese: 'I am Brother Zeno. I am working to help poor children. Please contact me.'

Within weeks, Zeno had sweet-talked government and company officials into allowing the orphans to move into a large dormitory once inhabited by Mitsubishi Heavy Industries workers. To fill the hostel, Zeno searched former air-raid shelters, burnt-out houses and demolished factories looking for young atomic bomb survivors. These 'street children' had been abandoned by the overstretched authorities and by their relatives.

Showing up in disused buildings where the lice-ridden boys lived, Zeno would pull sweets and bread out of a battered black leather bag. At the time, some orphans survived by cleaning shoes, selling newspapers and helping vendors shift black-market goods. Others worked for *yakuza* criminal gangs, looting properties and robbing residents of anything that had value.

'Most orphans had no shoes, no clothes and were really starving when they arrived,' a Japanese nun who belonged to the Militia

Immaculatae recalled. 'There was scarcely any rice in our large rice chest. We just prayed for a miracle so that we could feed the boys.'[2]

That miracle worker was usually Zeno, who used his sixteen years of connections in Nagasaki to aid his orphan-rescue campaign. When asked whether he needed a break from his exhausting routine, Zeno always answered in his heavily accented Japanese: 'Zeno is so busy, he has no time to die.'

In early May 1947, one of America's most famous educators and social welfare experts arrived at the Nagasaki friary at the request of General Douglas MacArthur.

Father Edward J. Flanagan was a superstar in the US, largely because a movie about his life, called *Boys Town*, had been an Oscar-winning hit nine years earlier. One of Hollywood's biggest stars, Spencer Tracy, played Flanagan. Another celebrity, Mickey Rooney, took a boy's role. Tracy and Rooney reprised their roles in a sequel, *Men of Boys Town*, in 1941.

Boys Town was a centre set up in 1921 west of Omaha, Nebraska, for homeless and delinquent boys aged ten to sixteen. MacArthur had invited Flanagan, an Irish-born Catholic priest, for a two-month visit to Japan and Korea to give advice on how conditions for children could be improved.

Nagasaki was on the agenda so that Flanagan could meet Brother Zeno, Father Mirochna and other priests at the friary to gain their insights on child welfare in the aftermath of the nuclear bombing. Flanagan had been shaken by Japan's suffering, which, he said, 'was most evident by the great number of homeless and abandoned children roaming the streets, the alleys, the depots and other places, seeking whereon to lay their little heads'.[3]

Before the war, few children had been abandoned because Japanese family ties were so close. But in 1947, Flanagan witnessed 'a great lack of social consciousness on the part of the public', as well as an absence of training, inadequate child protection laws and economic instability. Overall, he said, it was a 'deplorable situation'.

Inspired by Flanagan, who later wrote a report entitled 'Children of Defeat' for President Truman, Zeno and Mirochna decided to expand their fledgling orphan-rescue programme beyond Nagasaki.

At first, Zeno visited other parts of Kyushu island. Later, the campaign expanded to the main island of Honshu, including the most populated cities of Tokyo and Osaka.

Once again, Zeno cajoled government authorities and company executives to fund the orphan programmes. At every train station, he went immediately to the specially designated entrance for the GHQ's American staff to secure a free travel pass.[4]

Whenever he saw a devastated area through a train window, he would jump out of his carriage at the next stop in search of street children to take back to the Nagasaki orphanage. Zeno brought back only boys, but he arranged for girls to go to other Catholic institutions in Nagasaki and Tokyo.

Zeno's crusade was just a drop in the ocean compared to Japan's needs. Officially, there were 123,500 street children in Japan as of 1948.[5] But his audacity and eagerness to help the dispossessed soon made headlines in the nation's newspapers.[6]

'Zeno made full use of being a blue-eyed *gaijin* [foreigner],' his biographer, Jin Ishitobi, told me. In post-war Japan, the rulers were the Americans. And so Zeno behaved as though he was an American, rather than a Pole.

Zeno embraced the mass media to highlight the plight of the nation's orphans and other deprived children. He made friends with newspaper reporters and editors, and he always asked them to bring a photographer to his rescue sites to generate more publicity. Whenever a journalist wrote a story, Zeno would clip the article and proudly show it to company and government leaders to procure more money and resources.

Zeno's public-relations campaign was almost too successful. Hundreds more orphans arrived in Nagasaki from throughout Japan, prompting some friars to ask him to stop actively recruiting children. The orphanage itself was overflowing, and more volunteers were needed to look after them.

Father Mirochna's solution was similar to that followed by Father

Kolbe when setting up Niepokalanów in 1927. Twenty-five miles northeast of Nagasaki, amid cedar woods near a town called Konagai, Mirochna secured 200 acres of donated land for a Militia Immaculatae complex. There, having received approval from the Vatican in 1950, he began to build MI's first Japanese convent – the Franciscan Sisters of Militia Immaculatae.

On the same site, Mirochna built a permanent home for 140 orphan boys, who moved there from Nagasaki. Both the convent and the boys' home opened in May 1953, with seven Japanese nuns trained to look after the orphans. Eventually, Mirochna also built a primary and junior high school, a church, a small friary and a care home at Konagai.[7] The convent later opened branches in Poland.

Zeno's activities, encouraged by Father Mirochna and watched by seminary student Kōichi Tagawa, underlined the weakness of the Japanese welfare system after the war and the disconnect between helping one's immediate family and taking care of the broader society. Zeno and the Polish friars were doing what the Japanese authorities were neglecting to do. Indeed, while Zeno was rescuing orphans, the Japanese police and local authorities began rounding them up.

The government passed a Child Welfare Act in May 1948 that legalised the setting up of children's homes. But these institutions were like internment camps or prisons, fenced off from society and sporting iron-barred windows in the dormitories to prevent the children from escaping. Physical punishment was rampant.

Zeno, Mirochna and the other Polish friars in Nagasaki believed that saving the orphans was a Christian obligation. But there were other reasons for their benevolence. In particular, the friars remembered how the Japanese had helped save Polish orphans in Siberia in the 1920s, and they wanted to reciprocate.

'We Poles learnt about the Japanese for the first time when we heard these stories,' Zeno said in 1955. 'In the early 1920s, Polish bishops encouraged the Poles to pray for the Japanese. All this left a deep impression on Father Kolbe and the Polish Knights.'[8]

Another reason for the friars' dedication to the Japanese orphans was Kolbe himself. Those who had known him in Nagasaki and who had spent the war in the city were loyal admirers and followers. To these men, Kolbe's willingness to give up his life to save another human being was an exceptional act of selflessness. They agreed that his sacrifice was precisely what John the Evangelist had meant when he wrote: 'Greater love has no one than this, than to lay down one's life for his friends.'[9]

The loss of their spiritual leader at the age of just forty-seven weighed heavily on the friars, and they resolved to burnish Kolbe's legacy in Japan in whatever ways they could.

As the men became more involved in welfare activities and resumed publication of the *Seibo-no-Kishi* magazine, Kolbe's name and the Conventual Franciscan philosophy and spirit blossomed in post-war Japan. In the 1950s and 60s, Father Mirochna expanded the friary's well-being activities, building a kindergarten, schools and a care home in the Nagasaki area.

Zeno, meanwhile, continued his rescue campaign into the 1960s even though there were no more war orphans and Japan's economy was booming. In November 1950, Zeno had met Satoko Kitahara, a twenty-one-year-old professor's daughter and descendant of ruling samurai warriors. Kitahara had renounced her Shinto upbringing after reading about Japanese war atrocities and had been baptised as a Catholic.[10]

Zeno introduced Kitahara to a dark side of Japanese society, taking her to a crowded community of ragpickers, known as *bataya*. Many of the ragpickers lived in holes dug into the bank of the Sumida River in Tokyo, in which they spread cardboard and newspapers on the damp soil to stave off the cold. They survived by scouring the capital for rubbish that could be sold for recycling.[11] Their community, formed in 1950, was called Ari-no-machi, or Ants Town, and Zeno worked there throughout that decade to improve the lives of the 'ants'.

'Brother Zeno, a man without formal education, bridged a chasm separating two nations and two cultures,' Kitahara wrote. 'He discovered a part of Japan I did not know existed, where thousands lived in unbelievable destitution. This unlettered foreigner worked without thought of self in a world of painful reality.'[12]

Kitahara moved to Ants Town and lived among the ragpickers until she died of tuberculosis in 1958. Zeno, meanwhile, worked on other projects, visiting slums in large cities and helping victims of areas stricken by typhoons, earthquakes and volcanic eruptions.

Zeno's work made him a national celebrity and he often appeared on TV and in newspapers to promote his activities and occasionally to talk about Father Kolbe and the Nagasaki friary. For his dedication, the emperor awarded Zeno the Order of the Sacred Treasure in 1969, a rare commendation for a foreigner in Japan.

At a press conference in front of scores of journalists, Zeno placed the medal in his trademark black satchel and said with a grin: 'Thank you very much, but I won't need this medal in heaven.'

In July 1978, Brother Zeno's biographer, Jin Ishitobi, tracked down the orphan brothers who had been brought to the friary by the Yamabushi monk thirty-two years earlier. Iwao Morita, now forty-five, had operated a successful painting business in Nagasaki for the previous two decades. Hitoshi, forty-two, was working for a painting firm in Tokyo.

As a surprise, Ishitobi arranged for the brothers to meet Zeno at a friary in Tokyo where he was spending his final years. Now in his eighties and confined to a wheelchair, Zeno's blue eyes sparkled when he saw the orphans.

Tears ran down Zeno's face as the men stroked his straggly white beard, just as they had done in 1946. 'Thank you. Thank you,' the Morita brothers said to their rescuer as they handed him a bouquet of white lilies and some sweet cakes.

Zeno's love affair with what he and other Poles called 'the cherry blossom country' ended when he passed away on 24 April 1982. It was fifty-two years to the day since he had arrived in Japan with Kolbe. On that very day in Hokkaido, Masatoshi Asari was admiring the early blossoms on the cherry trees that he'd begun creating three decades earlier.

PART 6

Repentance and Discovery, 1951–1970

21. The Children's Cherries

1950s – Matsumae, Hokkaido

'Go on without me. I don't think I can make it.'

Masatoshi Asari, twenty-five, called out to the men ahead of him who were scrambling on all fours over boulders and outcrops to reach the 3,500-foot summit of Mount Daisengen in southern Hokkaido.

The view from the mountains over towering birch trees towards the Matsumae peninsula was stupendous. But Asari was too exhausted to appreciate the scenery. 'I thought I was going to die,' he said later.

It was July 1956, and Asari was part of a seven-man group on a two-day plant-hunting expedition. The goal was to find a specific wild cherry that grew in the mountains.

Asari's tuberculosis, which had forced him to remain at home for two years after 1950, had long since disappeared, cured with antibiotics. But even after he resumed college and became a teacher at a primary school in Matsumae, a small port in southwest Hokkaido, his heart disease lingered.

Anaemic and suffering from palpitations, Asari had deep doubts whether he could keep up with his colleagues on the strenuous hike. Typhoon Marie had pummelled Hokkaido in September 1954, knocking down thousands of birch and beech trees and forcing the men to use hatchets and knives as they struggled up the mountain.

Accompanying Asari, who was considered a cherry-tree expert by then, were another tree specialist, three bureaucrats from Matsumae and two armed bear hunters. Their job was to protect the group against attack from eight-foot *higuma* brown bears, Japan's largest land mammal, which roamed the Hokkaido mountains.

Asari, aged twenty-four, as a teacher in Matsumae and his
future wife, Kuniko

The wild cherry trees that Asari sought were called 'Chishima-zakura', or Kurile cherry. They were a variant of 'Takane-zakura', or Japanese Alpine cherry, which is one of the eleven known wild cherry species in Japan. These trees grew in northern Hokkaido and in the freezing Kurile Islands north of Japan but were unknown elsewhere. Asari knew that if any Chishima-zakura trees grew on Mount Daisengen, they would be near the peak.

A driving rain from a passing typhoon soaked the men, who were tired and eager to return home. But as Asari approached the group, he spotted a thin grey tree about eight feet tall swaying in the bitter wind. Scattered beneath the tree were some sodden pale-pink blossoms. A few feet away stood a similar tree. And yet another. After examining the trees' bark and leaves, Asari was convinced that as many as fifty Chishima-zakura trees were growing atop the cold mountain.

Exultation replaced exhaustion. This was Asari's first major discovery. How good it felt!

As the group descended, Asari experienced an unfamiliar feeling. 'I felt an inexplicable energy within myself,' he told me. 'The cherry trees seemed to possess a mysterious power. Amazingly, after the expedition, I was able to stop medication, and my dizziness and palpitations disappeared. The sakura goddess saved me.'

Ancient Japanese believed that animistic gods lived in the mountains and that one of them was a 'cherry goddess' who protected and gave strength to people.

Asari had long scorned myths about the emperor's divinity, believing that these had led Japan to war. But the legend of the sakura goddess had a special meaning for him. Indeed, he said that the Chishima-zakura discovery prompted him to dedicate his life to researching, collecting, cultivating and distributing cherry trees.

Asari had caught the plant-hunting bug after returning to his Hakodate college in 1952, following his illness, and taking a botany class from an elderly lecturer.

Shigezō Sugawara was the opposite of Tōru Ukita, the young elite professor whose course on Japan's new pacifist constitution had captivated Asari in his first college year. Seventy-six years old, Sugawara was a self-taught botanical pioneer, a plant and tree lover who had lived in South Sakhalin since 1921. North Sakhalin was occupied by the Soviet Union.[1]

In 1944, sensing that it was only a matter of time before Japan lost the war, Sugawara fled South Sakhalin with his family, bringing with him a mountain of research material.

In Sugawara's botany class, Asari studied the flora of Sakhalin and Hokkaido, constantly referring to the professor's 1937 book, *The Plants of Sakhalin*.

Sugawara also taught his students about the characteristics of different wild cherry trees, some of which grew in Asari's childhood home in Nanae village. From an early age, Asari had played in and among the cherry trees, but he knew little about their specific differences. Fascinated, he became Sugawara's most committed student and his successor in the study of sakura.[2]

Sugawara's research style was simple. He told his students: go 'plant hunting', find cherry trees, collect their leaves and blossoms, and compare species and varieties. Asari took this method to heart, never judging a tree until he had witnessed it with his own eyes.

Sugawara encouraged his disciple to become a cherry tree specialist, giving Asari a trove of all the specimens he had collected in Hokkaido, together with his notes. Sugawara also gave him his prized possession. It was a ground-breaking book about cherry trees, written in German in 1916 by Professor Manabu Miyoshi of Tokyo Imperial University.[3] Asari taught himself German so that he could read the book.

After moving from his home in Nanae to Matsumae in 1953 to teach, Asari and an agricultural adviser to the town, Makoto Tanaka, began hunting cherries every weekend, taking notes about the shape, colour and other features of their branches, leaves and blossoms.

For surprising historic reasons, there were few better places in the world than Matsumae to conduct this research.

Sixty miles south of Hakodate city, the town of Matsumae had become a depopulated backwater by the mid-twentieth century. Yet throughout much of the Edo period between 1603 and 1868, the port was a thriving mini-metropolis. At that time, Ezo, as Hokkaido was then known, wasn't part of Japan, although Ezo's southern region was controlled after 1590 by a feudal lord called Yoshihiro Matsumae, who pledged allegiance to Japan's ruler, the shōgun.

From Matsumae, merchant ships transported herring, seaweed and other seafood products to Osaka, a major commercial centre in Japan. On the return journey, the vessels brought food, clothing and manufactured goods.

The ships occasionally carried another prized product – ornamental cherry trees. These cherry imports became even more prominent at the start of the seventeenth century when some high-ranking imperial court nobles from the then-capital city of Kyoto were exiled to Matsumae. The emperor had punished them for having affairs with his ladies-in-waiting.[4]

Not all the trees from central Japan survived in the cooler Hok-kaido climate. But over the centuries, some adapted to the climate and rooted.

Cherry hunting and teaching left Asari with little time for other activities, but in 1954 he became attracted to a fellow teacher at his rural primary school.[5] Two years younger than Asari, Kuniko Satō was the industrious eldest child of a carpenter from a village close to Matsumae. Right after the war, the family scraped together enough money to send her to Shirayuri Girls' School, a Catholic boarding school in Hakodate, set up by three French nuns in 1878.[6]

An independent young woman, Kuniko followed Christian principles and subscribed to the *Seibo-no-Kishi* magazine, but she declined to be baptised, saying she could not accept the Adam and Eve creation story.

After graduation, unable to pay for college, Kuniko obtained her teacher's qualification through a correspondence course.

At the primary school, Asari was impressed with how tenderly Kuniko treated her pupils, and he asked her for a date to see *Roman Holiday*, the popular film starring Audrey Hepburn and Gregory Peck. After a short courtship, the couple had a simple marriage ceremony in the presbytery of an historic Catholic church in Hakodate in the spring of 1955.

The couple wore their work clothes at the wedding and invited only their parents. 'We didn't take photos because we were too poor. And we didn't have a honeymoon,' Asari told me. 'We just pledged our love to each other in front of a charming French priest, Father Pierre Einshardt. He made me say that I would protect my wife all my life and that we would help each other. The next day, we went back to the school and worked.'

Kuniko bore three children – two sons, Toshihiko and Masahiko, and a daughter, Setsuko – between 1957 and 1961. The family lived with Kuniko's parents, who looked after their grandchildren while their daughter and son-in-law continued to teach.

As a teacher, cherry grower and researcher, Asari was totally absorbed with his work and did little to help with housework or child-rearing. That was the norm for Japanese husbands at the time, although Setsuko remembers her father putting her and her brothers to bed and reading them folk tales.

On dark winter evenings, Asari and Kuniko would read the *Seibo-no-Kishi* magazine together. They learned about Father Kolbe's life in Japan, about hidden Christians in Nagasaki, and about how Brother Zeno had saved Japanese orphans after the war.

'We admired Zeno because we'd often seen war orphans who were living on the streets outside Hakodate station and we knew how difficult life was for them,' Asari said. 'But it wasn't until much later that I found out about the circumstances of Father Kolbe's death.'

In April 1959, Asari was transferred from his school on the fringes of Matsumae Town to Matsushiro Primary School, close to the dilapidated Matsumae Castle. That same month, he joined a local-history society, one of whose members, Tomitomo Nagata, was researching a virtually unknown topic – persecuted Christians in Hokkaido.

Hundreds of Christians had fled there from Japan's main islands of Honshu and Kyushu at the start of the seventeenth century to escape abuse and discrimination by the Tokugawa shogunate, which ruled Japan. Many had ended up living on the densely forested slopes of Mount Daisengen near Matsumae, the mountain where Asari had discovered the Chishima-zakura trees. The Christians survived by panning for gold in the freezing rivers and streams.

The shōgun had banned Christianity throughout Japan in 1614 and expelled all missionaries. But after gold was discovered on Mount Daisengen in 1616, Japanese speculators hired Christians to toil in the snow-swollen rivers. Here they could practise their religion in secret.[7]

At first, the Matsumae daimyō, Kinhiro, turned a blind eye to the Christians in his domain. But by the late 1630s, the shōgun had begun a brutal crackdown across Japan after a series of revolts by Christian peasants. In Matsumae, the daimyō placated the shōgun in 1639 by arresting and beheading 106 hidden Christians on Daisengen. He chose the poorest of the poor to die, many of whom were relatively new arrivals from Honshu.[8]

In August 1959, after an exhausting hike and an overnight camp, Asari, Nagata and twenty Catholic men from Hakodate including Father Einshardt arrived at a plot of land halfway up the mountain slope where Nagata believed the Christians had been murdered. Three hundred and twenty years after that barbarism, the group chopped down a beech tree and fashioned it into a crude cross to commemorate the martyrdom of the Christians as well as the 100th anniversary of the French church in Hokkaido.

The event made a lasting impression on Asari, whose sympathies towards the oppressed and persecuted would later be expressed in several initiatives. This was just one of many topics that absorbed his attention at a time of colossal political and social change in post-war Japan.

Following Japan's fraught 1940s, dominated by the Second World War, the nuclear denouement and the Allied occupation, the nation's eighty-four million people were no doubt hoping for a more tranquil and less frenetic decade. It wasn't to be. The 1950s were barely six months old when North Korean forces, supported by China and the Soviet Union, invaded South Korea.

The ambitions of China's new leader, Mao Zedong, and the Soviet Union's old warhorse, Joseph Stalin, shattered General Mac-Arthur's dreams of a peaceful Japan. Mao had emerged victorious over China's Nationalist government in 1949. This was followed by the creation of the communist People's Republic of China. The US now needed Japan to become a strategic shield against communism and an anchor for US interests in the region.

With that in mind, the US and Japan signed a security treaty in 1951 that allowed the US military to maintain bases in Japan without charge in return for protecting the country. The US also kept its bases in the southern island of Okinawa.

The seven-year Allied occupation ended in 1952 and Japan again became independent when the San Francisco Peace Treaty came into effect. Most Japanese were delighted to regain their sovereignty.

But more than a million people, including Asari in Hokkaido, demonstrated on May Day 1952 to protest that the security and peace treaties gave the US too much power and made it impossible for Japan to be neutral and pacifist.

Washington now pressed Japan to rearm. It was a dramatic shift in US policy. Purged wartime political and military leaders were hurriedly rehired to oversee the nation's rearmament.[9] To circumvent the Constitution, the government established in 1954 what it called 'Self-Defence Forces'.

Asari was disillusioned. 'I was boiling with anger when rearmament happened,' he said. 'What had happened to the passion and euphoria for Japan to remain a peaceful nation? The Self-Defence Forces were nothing but a violation of the Peace Constitution.'

Asari concluded that the lessons of the war were being deliberately set aside because of the new conflicts in Asia. Japan's leaders also wanted to take advantage of the procurement boom ignited by the Korean War. Japan used the Cold War mentality as an opportunity to recover economically and to bury its history.[10]

Against this tide, Asari was more determined than ever to remember the war and to fight injustice. Quite how he would do this, he wasn't sure. But an occasion soon arose that would enable him to combine his love affair with cherry trees with his passion for peace.

Like countless communities across Japan whose youngsters had left to live in big cities, the town of Matsumae was desperate to revive the declining port's economy at the end of the 1950s. Among the job-creation projects that town officials suggested was the formation of an educational botanic garden. They asked Masatoshi Asari, now twenty-eight, to supervise the garden's development.

Asari said no. He was unimpressed at the small scale of the project. Instead of a vapid garden, Asari proposed the development of one of the largest cherry parks in the world, on the site of the old castle. He suggested bringing together cherry species and varieties from all corners of Japan. With support from Hokkaido's new governor, Kingo Machimura, the ambitious project was given the green light, along with millions of yen in funding.

The first step was to reconstruct the castle, originally built in 1606 as the home of the Matsumae daimyō. Much of the castle had burned down in 1949. But by 1960, an imposing 100-foot-tall concrete replica was in place, and the city had started to develop some forty acres, equivalent to about twenty football fields, for the cherry park. Overlooking the Tsugaru Straits, which connects the Sea of Japan with the Pacific Ocean, the land stretched from the castle to the mountains.

As part of the ambitious plan, Asari had insisted that the park promote diversity of cherries. Over the previous 2,000 years, Japanese gardeners had created close to 300 different varieties. But after the latter half of the nineteenth century, many of these had been forgotten and had gone extinct.

In their place, Japan's cities and towns had planted hundreds of thousands of the new 'Somei-yoshino' variety. These cloned cherries had become synonymous with Japanese militarism during the war, as soldiers were encouraged to fall for the emperor like these short-lived blossoms.

Asari was fiercely critical of this warped symbolism. He had always believed that the blossoms were emblematic of peace and life, not war and death. He also believed that cherry blossoms were the domain of ordinary people, not just of the rich and powerful.

Ultimately, Asari's lofty vision was for Matsumae Park to become a symbol of world peace where people from different parts of Japan and overseas could meet to view an abundance of species and varieties.

Asari threw himself into this task. On weekends, he travelled to other parts of Hokkaido and brought back scions, or small branches, of wild and cultivated cherries to graft onto the rootstock of another kind of tree. During longer school holidays, he travelled as far as Kyoto and Osaka in search of traditional varieties.[11]

While most cherry experts in Japan focused on the identification and classification of cherries, Asari sought to unfold the mysteries of how different varieties had evolved in Japan over the previous two millennia.

Asari and the children of his Sakura Club observing a cherry tree

Asari decided to involve children in the process, including his two sons and daughter. He believed that it would be an excellent occasion to teach youngsters about the rhythms of life by collecting, growing and hybridising cherry trees. At his school, Asari launched the Matsumae Sakura Children's Club, whose members were pupils aged eight to twelve.

One summer, Asari and club members collected 500 seeds from temple gardens and streets. These were seeds of a double-flowered cherry of the 'Naden' variety, the most prevalent cherry in Matsumae.[12] About fifty seeds germinated the following spring. After moving the saplings to the cherry park, fifteen trees blossomed after two years. The most prominent had a large darkish-pink blossom with over twenty petals, twice the number on the mother tree. It was clearly a different cherry from the parent.

It was believed that double-flowered cherries couldn't produce offspring, but Asari proved for the first time that this was a fallacy. He named this unique cultivar 'Aya-nishiki', or twilled brocade, because the blossoms resembled woven fabric.

Encouraged by this success, Asari and his pupils created 116 varieties over the following twenty years. Some came from seeds, others by artificial cross-pollination. As a group, these are known as

'Matsumae-zakura' or Matsumae cherries. All were planted in the cherry park. No one in the world has created so many new varieties of cherry trees.[13]

Among the most popular was a double-flowered crimson blossom that Asari called 'Beni-yutaka' (abundant crimson). It was created by hybridising the 'Naden' artificially with 'Beni-yaezakura'.[14]

Asari taught his sons, Toshihiko and Masahiko, how to graft cherry trees, and because his daughter, Setsuko, liked sketching, she would draw the flowers in great detail. One day, she told her father that one of his unnamed cherry creations looked like the planet Venus. That became the cherry's name.

'By tending the cherries, the children came to understand how precious life is,' Asari said. 'Equally important, they learnt how precious it is to live in peace, so that trees can flower, and people can appreciate their beauty.'

These were sentiments that he would repeat many times over the following four decades, when he began to send cherry trees to countries whose people had been maimed and killed during the Second World War. Among these countries was Poland, where Father Kolbe had died a martyr's death in 1941.

22. A Friar's Secret Love

1950s – Nagasaki

When Agnes cleans my body, her hands and mine touch. What a
pleasant feeling.

I have learnt from Agnes that a happy and joyful life can only be
achieved when one loves someone and is loved in return.

Tōmei Ozaki diary entry, May 1954

Tōmei Ozaki was the name that Kōichi Tagawa gave himself in
1949 when he began his novitiate training to become a priest. It
was based on the Christianised name Tomas Kozaki, given to him
by the friary head in Nagasaki. Kozaki was a fifteen-year-old Christian martyr who had been crucified in Nagasaki in 1597 along with
twenty-five other Catholics.

Tōmei Ozaki was dying.[1] Shortly after beginning the novitiate with
eight other Japanese men in the spring of 1949, he'd suffered a series
of excruciating illnesses that had left him incapacitated and melan-
cholic. Doctors had removed his right kidney in January 1950 after
he caught tuberculosis. But later that year, the TB had spread to his
left kidney, bladder and spine.

Worse, the scar from an operation on his left ribs in 1941 had ruptured. Every day, Ozaki passed blood in his urine and yellowish pus
leaked from his chest wound. Every day, he ran a high fever. Every
day, he cried out in pain and pondered his fate.

Lying immobile in a tiny cell at Mugenzai-no-Sono, Ozaki could
do little except think about his life as a Catholic boy growing up in

Tōmei Ozaki in his Franciscan habit

northern Korea, his return to Nagasaki because of his sickness, and the aftermath of the atomic bomb.

On 1 March 1951, his twenty-third birthday, Ozaki's depression deepened when Father Mirochna, the Polish head of the friary built by Father Kolbe, had told him to give up his novitiate training due to his illnesses.

Mirochna's successor, Father Justin Tadeus Nazim, made matters worse by asking Ozaki to leave the institution. He had nowhere to go until Mirochna offered him a place in the small friary he was building at Konagai, northeast of Nagasaki, next to a convent and a boys' home.

Ozaki was still officially a trainee priest. But his dream of becoming a priest and of following in Kolbe's footsteps were all but shattered. Haunted by questions about why he had to suffer so much after surviving the atomic bomb, he began to question God's existence. His only close friend was Mirochna, who had come to Japan in 1930 to join Kolbe and had stayed on after Kolbe left.

Sitting by Ozaki's bedside, Mirochna told the young man that Kolbe had frequently assured him that 'illness is a blessing and suffering is a treasure. Your sufferings are proof that God loves you.' Mirochna himself had been very sick after he came to Japan.

'I was touched and comforted by Father Mirochna's love,' Ozaki told me in 2019. 'But deep down, I was sceptical that illness was a blessing from God. I was young and seriously ill. It was hard to accept.'

At the time, Ozaki said, he felt as though another self was watching him through his window. That self was mocking him, telling him that his life had no meaning.

Ozaki was desperately lonely, unable to breathe properly or to move his limbs without help. Too often, the day of the nuclear destruction came to his mind. He could never forget the faces of the dying. Why didn't I help them? Is it God's punishment, rather than his blessing, that I will soon join these people in death because I was so weak? How could Father Kolbe be so unafraid of suffering, so loving to others?

In Ozaki's prayers, he told Kolbe: I cannot be as selfless as you, but please help me. Now, more than ever, I need your support.

At the new convent, nestled among cedar woods in the mountains, a young Catholic sister who had trained as a nurse was assigned to aid the helpless Tōmei Ozaki.

Sister Mitsue Nagamatsu had grown up in Kawaguchi, a city just north of Tokyo, and was the eldest of five children. The daughter of a bicycle shop owner, Mitsue excelled in traditional Japanese cultural pursuits, from *ikebana* (flower arranging) and playing the *koto* (Japanese harp) to *sado* (the tea ceremony).

As a youngster, Mitsue had developed severe abdominal problems. After a successful operation, she decided to study at a nursing school in order to help others with their illnesses.

Mitsue became friendly with a Catholic surgeon, who often had his bike repaired at her father's shop. Over time, he talked about his faith with Mitsue, who was by now working at a hospital in Kawaguchi.

Sometime in the early 1950s, Mitsue took her religious vows to become a nun and moved to the Militia Immaculatae convent in Konagai. She was given the Catholic name of Agnes, after Agnes of

Mitsue Nagamatsu, aka Sister Agnes

Rome, a third-century virgin martyr. Her parents, who had hoped their daughter would marry an ambitious Japanese man, were appalled and cut off their ties with her.

Twenty-five years old in 1953, Mitsue was the same age as Ozaki, and the pair quickly developed a special bond. The only other person who had showered him with as much attention was his mother.

Mitsue cleaned his entire body, disinfected his scars and changed his dressings. She washed his blood-stained underwear and sweat-drenched garments. She massaged his painful back and limbs, kneading her hands and fingers into his muscles and ligaments to relieve his suffering.

Mitsue fulfilled Ozaki's yearning for intimacy with warmth and good humour, and it wasn't long before he found himself smitten with this empathetic nun.

The feeling was mutual. Mitsue would place wild pansies from the fields in a vase at his bedside. One day, she left an intricate lily-shaped piece of origami in his medicine box. Other days she wrote him short letters with comforting words such as 'Do not give up. God is with you', and 'I am thinking of you'.

These were potent missives for the dispirited Ozaki, who thought of her night and day. 'Agnes has beautiful eyes,' he wrote in his diary. 'Her smile and her round cheeks, full of youth, are lovely.'

By necessity, the incipient romance was clandestine. Mitsue, after all, had taken vows of poverty, chastity and obedience to become a nun. As a trainee friar, Ozaki was on a similar celibate path.

In the strict and strait-laced world of the Franciscan order, any attachment between a friar and a nun would have been scandalous. Both would likely have been ejected from the religious order.

Mitsue's immediate goal was to save Ozaki's life by finding appropriate medicine for him. She contacted an American military priest who was stationed at the US naval base in Sasebo, fifty-six miles north of Nagasaki. This was one of many bases that remained after the Allied occupation forces left Japan, as stipulated in the US–Japan Security Treaty.

In May 1954, the priest helped Mitsue obtain a powerful new antibiotic for tuberculosis, called isoniazid, which had been approved in the US in 1952. He also procured a recently developed TB drug called PAS (para-aminosalicylic acid). It was extremely expensive in Japan and usually not available from Japanese doctors.

The combination of the drugs had an almost immediate impact. Ozaki's temperature fell, he stopped passing blood in his urine and the pus from his scar ceased.

Day by day, Ozaki began to feel better. By October 1954, for the first time in eighteen months, he was well enough to get up and sit outside. After everything he'd suffered, Ozaki felt like he'd been the beneficiary of a miracle performed by Mitsue, his guardian angel.

Ozaki no longer needed Mitsue's thrice-daily care, but the couple continued to meet covertly. Their hiding place was usually the sacristy of the church, a room behind the altar where the priests kept their vestments and church equipment. When they met, they sat on high-backed chairs in their long black tunics and talked quietly, enjoying each other's company.

One day, an intense storm passed over the mountains while the couple were in the vestry. Torrential rain pounded on the roof. A flash of lightning was followed seconds later by a gargantuan thunderclap. Frightened, Mitsue clutched Ozaki. He held her tight, clasping his arms around her warm habit. They looked at each other and for a few seconds their lips touched.

'I love you, Kōichi. Let's live together somewhere,' Mitsue whispered.

Silence.

'I love you, Kōichi. Let's live together somewhere,' she repeated with more intensity.

The silence lingered. Ozaki heard a sniffle and a sob. Tears fell onto his habit.

Ozaki pulled away. After a few seconds, he looked her in the eyes and said simply, 'I would love to be with you, Agnes. But I am just recovering from a long illness. And I don't have any money to live with you.'

Mitsue recoiled. These weren't the sentiments she had longed to hear. Without looking back, she ran out of the vestry. Cast out from her family, spurned by some Japanese for joining a foreign religious order, she now felt rejected by the man she loved.

What happened next? Ozaki wasn't sure. Most likely, Mitsue asked to leave the convent, or she mentioned the incident to her superior, which prompted her departure.

Shortly afterwards, Mitsue left to work at a Catholic clinic on a remote island northeast of Nagasaki. A year later, in 1956, she became a nurse at a Catholic care home in Nagasaki, followed by a few years as the head nurse at a home for the severely handicapped.

Ozaki went to see Mitsue several times, but she tried to avoid him. Finally, the couple agreed that he would not visit her again.

'Perhaps it was God's Providence,' Ozaki told me. 'Maybe God was testing us. And in the end, we both realised we each had a mission – as a nun and as a brother.'

Mitsue was Ozaki's first love, and his last.

'She saved my life. And I loved her,' he said. 'But I do not regret our mutual decision to part, despite the pain at the time.'

For eleven more years, until 1965, Ozaki remained at Konagai, occasionally helping the orphans at the children's home while slowly recuperating. He was now thirty-seven years old. He could no longer become a priest because there was an age limit of thirty at that time.

Nevertheless, Ozaki decided to return to the religious life in the Mugenzai-no-Sono friary in Nagasaki. He would not be allowed to conduct a Mass, preach a sermon or listen to confessions as an ordained priest. But he was allowed to continue the novitiate training to become a religious brother that he had begun sixteen years earlier.

Once again, Ozaki committed himself to learning more about Father Kolbe's life and began writing regularly for the *Seibo-no-Kishi* magazine. However, he could never forget – nor did he want to forget – the days he had spent with Mitsue.

In 1968, Ozaki heard that Mitsue had been hospitalised with a heart problem. It was sadly ironic, he thought, how the tables had turned. He was now quite healthy while she was gravely sick, depressed and alone.

Apart from other nuns, Ozaki was Mitsue's only visitor at the hospital where she spent her final years. Her family never came because she had become a nun against their wishes. She died in October 1968 at the age of forty and was buried in the grounds of the convent in the Konagai mountains. Her father was the only family member to attend her funeral.

In 2000, thirty-two years after Mitsue's death, Ozaki travelled from Nagasaki to Tokyo and visited each of her brothers and sisters individually at their homes. He talked with them about reconciliation and invited them to a special Mass.[2]

Time had healed the wounds of Mitsue's siblings and other relatives. More than thirty family members gathered at a Franciscan church in Tokyo, followed by a feast at a nearby Chinese restaurant.

For fifty-one years, Ozaki travelled to Mitsue's grave on the anniversary of her death to pay tribute to his beloved. Only the pandemic in 2020 prevented him from leaving his care home to make the hour-long journey.

On one occasion, in 2006, Mitsue's youngest sister accompanied Ozaki to the convent grounds. It was raining hard when they approached her tomb and read the simple inscription. It said: 'Sister Agnes Maria Mitsue Nagamatsu's grave'. It was the first visit by anyone in Mitsue's family since her funeral.

'I finally felt that Mitsue's soul had been comforted,' Ozaki told me. 'For all those years after she passed away, she continued to live in my heart.'

23. Peace Offerings

1960s, 1970s – *Matsumae, Hokkaido*

After six years of preparation, Masatoshi Asari's cherry park opened in the spring of 1965 in the tiny port of Matsumae in southwest Hokkaido. It was a massive achievement for the thirty-four-year-old schoolteacher and sakura lover. Within a generation, the park would become the largest of its kind in the world, boasting more than 10,000 trees. Many were Asari's own creations, belonging to a group of cherries now known around the globe as Matsumae cherries.

Crowds of Hokkaido residents thronged the park each spring, inhaling the soft scent of the cherries and taking photos on newly purchased Canon, Nikon and Pentax cameras. Surveying these sakura enthusiasts, many of whom drank sake under the trees at hanami parties, Asari reflected that the flowers seemed to project an aura of happiness and love.

Everyone was smiling. Everyone was in awe of the blossoms' beauty. Where else, he thought, could one enjoy such a feeling of contentment?

Among the sixty trees that grew in the park when it first opened was a Chishima-zakura, or Kurile cherry. The tree had been grown from seeds that Asari had collected atop Mount Daisengen during one of his cherry-hunting expeditions. It was this wild cherry, Asari believed, that had revitalised him after the illnesses that had disrupted his college education.

Enchanted by his cherries, Asari began to wonder how he could use the soft power of his delicate creations to help spread his intangible messages of friendship and harmony around the world. It wasn't long before several opportunities arose unexpectedly.

Asari aged forty checking one of his cherry trees

On the fringes of Matsumae, close to the primary school where he taught, Masatoshi Asari began talking to an elderly resident about a deep overgrown ditch that stretched eastwards for more than a mile. The ditch had no apparent purpose, but the man told him that it had been the roadbed for a planned extension of a wartime railway.

'Hundreds of skinny young Koreans dug that ditch,' the man said dismissively. 'I heard some of them died.'

Shocked, Asari immediately thought about 'Kazuo Takemoto', the pseudonym for the young Korean who had escaped from hard labour during the war. 'Takemoto' had lived secretly in Asari's neighbour's home for a year.

In the late 1960s, Asari began collecting testimonials from Matsumae residents about the forced labour of Koreans who had worked on this abortive railway project. He also searched for documents about the Koreans at the Matsumae library and in its town hall.

There were none. The Koreans appeared to have been airbrushed from history.

In 1971, Asari decided to work with fellow teachers in his local-history group to investigate this enigma. What they found was unnerving, although it fitted into a wider pattern of well-known wartime Japanese atrocities and abuse throughout Southeast Asia.

It turned out that construction of the railway connecting Matsumae and Hakodate had begun decades earlier but had been abandoned in 1930. After Japan attacked Pearl Harbor in 1941, the government had hurriedly restarted it, along with an extension, because the military urgently needed manganese – used in batteries, steel and other war products – from Hokkaido's mines.

Since most young Japanese men had been mobilised, the government scoured Korea, its colony, for cheap labour. As many as 150,000 Koreans were shipped to Hokkaido to work as miners, farmers and construction workers. Most came from poor farming areas and were promised three yen a day (about seventy-five US cents at the time).

The conditions in Hokkaido were appalling. In Matsumae, Asari found, the Koreans worked minimum twelve-hour shifts, often barefoot in the freezing winter, digging tunnels through the mountains and cuttings into the hills. The men were overseen by a baton-wielding Japanese *bōgashira*, or supervisor.

The Koreans lived in barracks of about 140 men each, with iron bars on the windows to prevent escapes. They slept in long lines on thin straw mattresses with a log for a pillow. Meals usually consisted of watery miso soup and a fist-sized *onigiri* ball of rice, potatoes and wheat.

Many labourers tried to escape these harsh conditions. If they failed and were captured, they were severely beaten or even killed. And although some Japanese residents, like Asari's parents and neighbours, were sympathetic to the men's predicament, any family caught harbouring an escapee was heavily fined.

Interviewing Matsumae residents in 1971, twenty-six years after the war had ended, Asari faced a wall of embarrassed silence when he asked questions about Japanese morality and, worse, brutality. One man, who had recruited labourers in Korea in 1942, screamed at Asari: 'Why are you dredging up the past, asking me these stupid questions?' He brandished a stick and pushed Asari out of his house.

When the local-history group published its findings in 1972, it was the first time that the Koreans' plight in Matsumae had received attention. But few Japanese residents had any interest in exploring the past. In contrast, Hokkaido's small North Korean and South Korean communities were all ears.[1]

Shortly after publication, the principal of the North Korean school in Sapporo, Hokkaido's capital city, contacted Asari to say thank you for shining a light on such a controversial issue. Most pupils at his school were second-generation Koreans whose parents had been born in the north of the country before the beginning of the Korean War in 1950.

In response, Asari sent twenty of his cherry creations, including 'Beni-yutaka' and 'Benigasa', to the school as a sign of atonement and conciliation. And with the students from his Sakura Club, he planted about 300 trees in a half-mile-long 'cherry blossom tunnel' along both sides of the Matsumae to Hakodate railway line.[2]

Soon afterwards, a South Korean executive contacted Asari about his findings. In turn, Asari sent sixty cuttings of his double-flowered cherry creations and other varieties, such as 'Ukon' and 'Fugenzo', to South Korea, along with an apology.[3]

These gifts marked the start of Asari's 'peace offerings' to countries that Japan had invaded during the war, or whose people had suffered and died during the conflict. 'The cherries were all symbols of peace,' he told me. 'If they bloomed in places where people had been tormented because of aggression, I felt that I was fulfilling my responsibilities.'

A few weeks later, Asari switched his one-man cherry blossom diplomacy to another Asian country where the Japanese were despised because of their wartime activities: China.

In February 1972, US President Richard Nixon flew into Shanghai, the first American head of state to visit communist China while in office. A few days later, the US and Chinese governments laid out the principles for normalisation of the nations' relationship after a quarter-century without diplomatic ties.

Nixon's visit paved the way for China and Japan to normalise ties in September 1972. As part of the process, Japan cut its diplomatic links with Taiwan, which China claimed as its own territory.

To mark this new era, China sent two giant pandas – Kan Kan and Ran Ran – to Japan. After Ran Ran died in 1979, Asari created a 'Ran Ran' cherry variety, which now thrives in Matsumae Park and in Windsor Great Park in the UK. Japanese Prime Minister Kakuei Tanaka reciprocated by sending China 1,000 Sargent cherry saplings from Hokkaido, along with 1,000 larch trees.

One day late in 1972, a pupil in Asari's cherry blossom club politely asked him why the ever-expanding Matsumae cherry park wasn't participating in this official gift to China.

It should have been, Asari conceded, and he proposed, via the Hokkaido prefectural government, that his club would send saplings to China to complement the government's present. To Asari's delight, the Tokyo authorities approved a 'private gift' of fifty cherry saplings to be sent to a Beijing elementary school under the name of Chief Cabinet Secretary Susumu Nikaidō.

The Chinese children planted the young trees in Tiantan Park near the Temple of Heaven, one of the city's major visitor attractions. The donation set in motion another round of Asari's 'peace offerings' at a time when many Japanese were suspicious of Mao Zedong's regime.

Asari's gift prompted a teacher at the Beijing primary school to compose a 'flower of friendship' song in Mandarin. The chorus noted how cherry blossoms were the prime connection between Chinese and Japanese children. The Sakura Club later recorded the song in Chinese and sent a tape recording to their Beijing counterparts. Over the following decade, Matsumae and Beijing children created and exchanged poems, songs, paintings and other artwork.

Groups that were making friendly visits to China frequently asked Asari to provide his Matsumae cherry creations to them as gifts. Asari himself joined an official delegation from Hakodate to China in 1979. At the Beijing elementary school where he had sent his saplings, Asari sang the 'flower of friendship' song together with the teacher who had composed it.

The trip was an eye-opener, especially a visit to the National

Museum of China in Tiananmen Square. There, Asari watched groups of primary school children learning about the Sino-Japanese War of 1937–45. In Japan, most children were taught little about the war. On his return home, he decided to examine the history of Chinese prisoners of war who had been shipped to Hokkaido in 1944 and 1945 to work in mines and on building sites.

As with his research into the Korean labourers, Asari focused on the construction of a railway line, this time near the house where he'd grown up, in Nanae. Predictably, he found that the conditions the Chinese endured were little different from those of the Korean labourers – back-breaking jobs, a scarcity of food, abysmal accommodation and frequent punishment.

At a Buddhist temple in Nanae called Myōrin-ji, the elderly chief monk told him about burial ceremonies that he had conducted for at least nineteen Chinese labourers and one Japanese man who had starved to death in the final days of the war.

At another temple in Nanae, called Sen'nen-ji, Asari found burial records for thirty-seven Korean labourers, most of whom were in their early twenties. Their cause of death had been recorded as 'acute pneumonia' or 'indigestion'.[4] In all, Asari concluded that at least 150 young Korean and Chinese workers had died during construction of the railway lines in southwest Hokkaido. The actual number was probably much higher.

How many others had suffered in Hokkaido during the war, he wondered? Determined to uncover the island's hidden history, Asari asked his elder brother, Shōichi, to remind him about the stick-thin Allied prisoners of war whom he had occasionally seen in Hakodate in 1944.

Thousands of young British, American, Australian and Dutch soldiers captured by Japan in the Malay peninsula, Java and Singapore were shipped to prisoner-of-war camps in Hakodate after 1942.[5]

Shōichi Asari had worked as a seventeen-year-old volunteer for the military in 1944 and had witnessed the Western prisoners sitting next to a road-construction site, chewing boiled squid to stave off hunger. The camp where they lived was considered 'a notorious hell-hole even amongst the Japanese'.[6]

The dreadful conditions in the camp were no different from those endured by the Koreans and the Chinese, Asari found. He also came across the burial permits of fourteen British soldiers.

To find out more, Asari visited the British consul-general in Tokyo, Edward Ripley, in the early 1980s. 'History is like broken glass, Asari-san,' Ripley told him. 'You need to collect as many shattered pieces as possible. Only when you put them together can you get a true picture of what really happened.'

Six months after their meeting, Ripley sent Asari some UK government records about the British POWs who had lived in the Hakodate camp. A decade or so later, in 1993, Asari made a 'peace offering' to the UK, sending the scions of fifty-eight different Matsumae cherry varieties to Windsor Great Park, one of the homes of the royal family. After the scions arrived in England, they were grafted by Britain's foremost cherry-blossom expert, Chris Sanders.

'I have a strong personal wish to present sakura trees to the people of the UK,' Asari wrote to John Bond, the Keeper of the Gardens at Windsor. 'I sincerely hope that the blossoms will give pleasure and consolation to all who see them, including those bereaved families of the war dead.'

As well as Windsor, many Matsumae cherry varieties also thrived in major UK horticultural parks such as Kew Gardens, RHS Wisley and the Oxford Botanic Garden and Arboretum. Dozens more Matsumae trees were subsequently sent from the UK to Belgium, France, Germany and the Netherlands by British horticulturist Chris Lane.

Meanwhile, the US also became part of Asari's 'peace offering', thanks to a prescient African American botanist who travelled to Hokkaido several times in the 1980s.

Roland Jefferson, the first Black botanist employed by the US National Arboretum, was a renowned authority on cherry trees who had helped look after the 'Somei-yoshino' blossoms along the Potomac River in Washington, DC for many years.

These were trees that Japan had given to the US in the early twentieth century as a gesture of friendship. By the 1970s, many of the cherries were in decline. The following decade, Jefferson travelled to Japan, Korea and Taiwan to collect sakura seeds that he hoped would grow in both warm and cold US states.[7]

In Hokkaido alone, Jefferson collected more than 50,000 cherry seeds which were sown in the National Arboretum. The seedlings were then sent to Oregon, North Dakota, Louisiana and other parts of the US.[8]

For Jefferson, the prime goal was to ensure the preservation of the famous Potomac cherries by diversifying their varieties. For Asari, the mission was more esoteric. He saw it as part of his global peace initiative at a time when US President Ronald Reagan was promoting his controversial Strategic Defense Initiative against the Soviet Union.

'I wanted to tell the world that after the Second World War, we Japanese had been reborn as a peaceful nation,' he told me. 'My trees were all gifts of reconciliation. Cherry blossoms have been symbols of goodwill in Japan since ancient times. Our earth will not survive unless everybody collaborates with one another. Cherry blossoms make everybody feel cheerful and contented. This may be a small thing in the big picture of life, but it's what has always driven me on.'

Indeed. In the 1970s and early 80s, Asari sent cherries – always gratis – via the Flower Association of Japan to Japanese communities in Argentina, Brazil and Uruguay. He sent 300 trees to Munich when it became Sapporo's sister city, and several hundred Chishima-zakura seeds to Halifax, Nova Scotia on Canada's eastern seaboard when it became Hakodate's sister city.

Altogether, Asari's seeds and saplings ended up in gardens, parks and nurseries throughout Europe, Asia and the Americas. Asari received scant recognition for these little-noticed donations.

At the beginning of the 1980s, during his self-styled cherry peace initiative, Masatoshi Asari was transferred from his school in Matsumae to another in the Aoyagi district of Hakodate. On his way to and from the new school, he passed the monument to one of Japan's best-known poets and humanists, Takuboku Ishikawa.

Takuboku, the pen name by which he was known, was a brooding, impoverished non-conformist, who described himself as 'a useless key that does not fit' in society.[9] Takuboku had worked as a young substitute teacher in Hakodate in 1907 but lost the job when the school burned down. The monument bore one of Takuboku's lyrical *tanka* poems about cornflowers.

Using seeds from his mother's garden, Asari and his class planted blue cornflowers in the schoolyard and studied the author's poetic style and themes. To Asari's surprise, Takuboku's writing in the early twentieth century was riddled with anti-imperialistic comments and analogies at a time when Japan was expanding its empire.

For example, most Japanese applauded their nation's annexation of Korea in 1910, which followed Japan's victory over Russia in 1905. Yet Takuboku, Asari discovered, was fiercely opposed to this landgrab. Asari believed the annexation marked the beginning of Japanese aggression towards Asian countries, which eventually led to the invasion of China and the Second World War.

Asari saw in Takuboku a fellow idealist and anti-war crusader who sympathised with the downtrodden and the weak. One poem, written days after the annexation, showed sympathy towards the Korean people and anger towards the Japanese government.

I hear the autumn wind
As I brush away, with black ink
The nation of Korea

The poem referred to new maps of Japan's empire, on which Taiwan, the southern part of Sakhalin Island and Korea were covered in black ink. The 'autumn wind' was Japan's show of force.

Delving further into Takuboku's work, Asari found a series of

Asari at the monument of Takuboku's poem in Hakodate, November 2018

newspaper columns that commiserated with the Polish people because their country had been wiped off the map in 1795 by Austria, Russia and Prussia.[10] Takuboku was impressed by the novels of the Polish patriotic writer, Henryk Sienkiewicz, especially *Quo Vadis*. That book, also a favourite of Father Kolbe's, was about Christian resistance to the Romans. It made Asari think deeply about Christian persecution in Japan, as well as the plight of Poland and its people during the Second World War. It was a topic that would soon become a major part of his life.

Asari's research into the lives of Korean and Chinese labourers and Allied soldiers in Hokkaido during the Second World War was but a sliver of the well-documented story of Japan's ill-treatment of non-Japanese labourers and prisoners of war. His research was conducted before these topics became thorny diplomatic issues with foreign governments in the 1990s.

'The mentality that we were the chosen race led some Japanese to mistreat the Koreans as well as the Chinese and the Allied POWs,' Asari told me. 'Isn't this the same thinking as the Nazis? They regarded the Jews, the Poles and other Slavic peoples as inferior. I can't help but draw parallels between these situations.'

To make amends for the abuse, Asari constructed a cenotaph at the Sen'nen-ji temple. A plaque on the monument was unveiled on 3 May 1985, the thirty-eighth anniversary of the day the Peace Constitution came into effect. It reads:

> This monument is to express our thoughts of gratitude to Korean, Chinese and Japanese who died in their work during the construction of the Matsumae Line railway from 1941 to 1945. They never returned to their native land.
>
> Forty years have passed since that time. Now all of us thank them for their hard work and pray that their souls may find peace.

Every year on 3 May, Asari and monks at the temple conduct a memorial ceremony, which is attended by Chinese, North Korean and South Korean residents from the Hakodate area of Hokkaido. They far outnumber the Japanese attendees.

PART 7

Towards the Light, 1971–1989

24. The Bunker

1971–1983 – Auschwitz; Nagasaki

Clutching a posy of white chrysanthemums, forty-three-year-old Tōmei Ozaki stood at the entrance of Block 13 in the Auschwitz concentration camp and slowly descended the stairs into the basement. His heart was pounding.

At the bottom of the stairs, he turned right and walked along a dimly lit corridor to the underground dungeon in which the man he revered, Father Maximilian Maria Kolbe, had been murdered thirty years earlier. In this dark and tiny cell, Kolbe and nine other Polish inmates had lived without food or water until they starved or were put to death. The atrocity was beyond Ozaki's comprehension.

Ozaki was visiting Auschwitz for the first time, along with Brother Zeno Żebrowski and a small group of Japanese Catholics. It was October 1971, and the men were en route to Rome for the beatification of Father Kolbe, one of the formal steps towards canonisation.

After his companions had left the bunker, Ozaki remained. He stared at the small window near the top of the room. He touched each wall. He knelt on the floor. And as the tears flowed, he contemplated the unimaginable ordeal that the men had had to endure.

In his mind's eye, Ozaki could see their agonised faces and hear their cries. He didn't understand Polish, but it was clear to him what they were saying: 'Please help me! Give me water, please!'

As he listened, his thoughts flashed back to 9 August 1945 in Nagasaki, the day of the bomb. Burnt and tortured faces stared at him. He heard the harrowing pleas of the dying: 'Please help me! Give me water, please!'

Auschwitz. Nagasaki. At that moment, these places were one and

The starvation bunker where Kolbe died.
The central pole was placed there by Pope John II

the same to Ozaki. Two parallel living hells. Two tragic symbols of war's cruelty. Two evils caused by mankind. Yes, by mankind, not by God.

For the first time, Ozaki questioned his belief that the Nagasaki bomb was 'God's Providence'. This was the controversial theory that Kolbe's friend, Dr Takashi Nagai, had outlined at a requiem Mass to the city's Catholic community after the bombing.

At the time, Nagai's speech had soothed Nagasaki's Catholics by explaining that God had chosen the victims as a sacrifice that had brought peace to Japan. Most survivors, including Ozaki, had quietly accepted Nagai's thesis and they had suffered in silence for the following quarter-century.[1]

The starvation chamber where Ozaki now knelt, and the radiated Japanese city where his mother had died, were now firmly and unexpectedly connected in his mind.

Out of nowhere, Ozaki heard a faint noise. It sounded like hymns and religious chanting.

The choruses ceased. A voice. It was Father Kolbe's. Kolbe had left Nagasaki in 1936, nine years before Ozaki had joined his friary. But the Japanese friar had no doubts about who was speaking. The

Polish voice was calm, clear, comforting. 'You must live,' it said. 'God is always with you.'

The dungeon fell silent. Ozaki lay prostrate on the concrete floor. I now understand, he thought, how easy it is for man to desire death, to want to escape his unrelenting pain.

And yet here, in this ungodly extermination camp, Kolbe had been totally oblivious to his own needs. His only aim was to care for his nine compatriots.

'In that starvation cell, I finally grasped the true meaning of Father Kolbe's actions,' Ozaki told me. 'He left hope that humans are still worth believing in, and that life is still worth living no matter how dire the circumstances.'

The realisation was a hammer blow to Ozaki's psyche. Tormented by guilt since the day of the Nagasaki bomb, he'd spent twenty-six years lamenting the selfish and ugly side of mankind. But at Auschwitz, in this unlikeliest of places, he grasped the truth. If a human being can be as admirable as Kolbe in such an extreme environment, perhaps humanity and love can, after all, triumph over evil.

As he mounted the stairs out of Block 13, Ozaki took several deep breaths to steady himself. He felt energetic. He felt enlightened. And he felt elated that his mission to trace Father Kolbe's footsteps was transforming his own life.

Over the following twenty years, Ozaki would visit the Auschwitz bunker nine more times as part of a ritual pilgrimage to Kolbe's homeland. The next stop on his journey was Rome, where Kolbe had formed the Militia Immaculatae organisation fifty-four years earlier and where Pope Paul VI was preparing to beatify the Polish priest as a 'martyr of charity'.

From the high altar of St Peter's Basilica in Vatican City, the city state that is home to the hierarchy of the Catholic Church, Pope Paul VI told a vast audience on 17 October 1971 that Father Maximilian Kolbe was 'perhaps the brightest and most glittering figure to emerge from the darkness and degradation of the Nazi epoch'.[2]

Seated alongside Ozaki and his Japanese colleagues at the ceremony were as many as 2,000 Poles, all wearing red and white badges to symbolise their nationality. A delegation of former Auschwitz inmates included Franciszek Gajowniczek, sixty-nine, whose life Kolbe had saved. Gajowniczek sobbed into a handkerchief as he led the offertory procession.

In his homily, the Italian-born pontiff highlighted Kolbe's patriotism, calling him 'a son of noble Catholic Poland'. 'As a Pole he was condemned to that unhappy concentration camp. And as a Pole he was willing to give up his life for that of a fellow countryman.'

'The circumstances of his departure from this life are so horrible and harrowing that we would prefer not to speak of them in order not to see the depth of inhuman degradation to which the abuse of power can lead,' the Pope continued. 'Millions of victims [were] sacrificed to the pride of force and the madness of racism. Nevertheless, it is necessary to scan this dark picture again in order to pick out the gleams of surviving humanity.'[3]

In the decade following Kolbe's beatification, while living in Nagasaki as a religious brother, Ozaki interviewed people who had known Kolbe and began writing articles for the *Seibo-no-Kishi* magazine, published by the friary. These later became a book.

As a Kolbe devotee, Ozaki was thrilled when one of the Polish priest's greatest admirers, Cardinal Karol Wojtyła, the Archbishop of Kraków, was named Pope John Paul II in October 1978 following the deaths of Pope Paul VI and Pope John Paul I.[4] Known as 'the Pilgrim Pope', John Paul II visited 129 countries as pontiff, including nine trips to Poland and several to Kolbe's death cell in Auschwitz.

For Ozaki, the Pope's arrival in Japan in February 1981 – the first-ever papal visit to the country – had special significance. He and other descendants of Japan's hidden Christians viewed the visit as nothing less than a miracle, given their history of persecution.[5]

At the Hiroshima Peace Memorial Park, in a speech broadcast throughout Japan on 25 February, the Pope began his address with three short sentences:

War is the work of man.
War is destruction of human life.
War is death.

He continued:

> Two cities will forever have their names linked together, two Japan-
> ese cities, Hiroshima and Nagasaki, as the only cities in the world
> that have had the ill fortune to be a reminder that man is capable of
> destruction beyond belief.
> Their names will forever stand out as the only cities in our time
> that have been singled out as a warning to future generations that
> war can destroy human efforts to build a world of peace.

Bomb survivors in Hiroshima and Nagasaki reacted differently to these words. The Hiroshima survivors had long talked openly about their distress, and many were members of anti-nuclear movements or engaged in anti-war activities. Moreover, the city of Hiroshima had chosen to permanently preserve the ruined dome that had survived the bomb as a symbol of peace.[6]

In contrast, as we have seen, most Catholic survivors in Nagasaki had remained mute, believing in the 'God's Providence' theory. Even though the ruins of Urakami Cathedral were emblematic, the Catholic community asked the city government to tear down the remains. They argued that the cathedral had been built as a symbol of triumph and victory over their ancestors' agony. In late 1959, a new reinforced concrete cathedral was opened.

For Nagasaki's Christians, the Pope's first words in his Hiroshima speech – 'War is the work of man' – were revelatory. The pontiff was clearly implying that the atomic bomb was not a result of God's will.

This was a watershed moment. After thirty-six years of silence, the city's surviving Catholics began discussing their experiences in public for the first time. Ozaki himself said the Pope's message enabled him to view the world – and the Second World War – more realistically and with more clarity.

'We survivors needed to ask for forgiveness for what the Japanese had done at Pearl Harbor as well as from the Chinese and other Asian peoples. We must not forget what we did as aggressors, not just talk about how miserable we are as atomic bomb survivors,' Ozaki said.[7]

It was snowing hard when the Pope arrived on 27 February to visit Mugenzai-no-Sono. Earlier that day, throngs of citizens had witnessed the papal visits to the peace park, memorial museum and Ōura Cathedral, where the hidden Christians had been discovered.[8]

Within the friary, a planned twenty-five-minute visit was extended to sixty-five minutes so that the pontiff could hear more from Ozaki and other friars about Kolbe's activities. Before he left, the Pope placed wreaths of red and white flowers near Kolbe's statue.

While in Japan, the Pope also met the ailing Zeno Żebrowski, Kolbe's compatriot, who had been living in a Catholic hospital in Tokyo since 1978. Brother Zeno arrived in a wheelchair, and burst into tears when the Pope stroked his head and praised his activities in Japan, particularly his dedication to helping war orphans.[9] Zeno passed away fourteen months later.

Maximilian Kolbe was canonised in Vatican City and formally named a saint on 10 October 1982, less than six months after the death of his most dedicated friend, Brother Zeno. Sainthood was the ultimate accolade for a man born in a poor Polish textile town who had sacrificed himself for another at Auschwitz.

'Maximilian did not die but gave his life for his brother,' Pope John Paul II told the crowd of at least 150,000 people who filled St Peter's Square. Among them were Ozaki and other friars from Nagasaki.

The three-hour ceremony was even more lavish than Kolbe's beatification eleven years earlier, and the film director Franco Zeffirelli oversaw its live broadcast throughout Italy. The crowd included thousands of Poles waving national banners and wearing badges in support of the Solidarity trade union, which the Polish government had banned just two days earlier.

At the time, Solidarity had about nine million members, or a quarter of the population. Poland's Soviet-backed communist government had declared martial law in December 1981, deploying tanks on the streets and imprisoning thousands of activists without trial.

Raising his voice, the Polish Pope pleaded with the crowd 'on this solemn day' for 'all men of goodwill throughout the world to pray for the Polish nation'.[10]

At Niepokalanów in Poland, meanwhile, the Archbishop of Warsaw, Jozef Glemp, delivered an outdoor address to more than 10,000 people that described Kolbe's faith and hardship. He also noted, in a reference to the ban on Solidarity, his own shared 'bitterness with those who were or are deprived of freedom'.[11]

Yet even as Catholics honoured their new saint, some others challenged Kolbe's rectitude. A small number of individuals questioned some of his writing and made the grave charge that he had been antisemitic.

An article in the *New York Times* in November 1982 claimed that Kolbe's collected works 'contain a number of comments that indicate that the Polish priest may have shared in the antisemitism current in the Polish Roman Catholic Church in the 1920s and 1930s'.

However, the article continued, Kolbe 'opposed the most violent antisemitism of the period'. An examination of a 3,200-page collection of his writings showed 'that he tried to discourage it in the columns of the two newspapers published by an organisation [MI] he founded'.[12]

The accusations against Kolbe had first appeared during the canonisation process in an Austrian periodical, *Wiener Tagebuch*, an arm of the Austrian Communist Party. After its assertions were reported in an American newspaper in June 1982, two scholars at Saint Louis University, a Jesuit research university in the US, labelled the charges 'false'. The scholars – Daniel L. Schlafly Jr and Warren Green – noted that Kolbe's writings contained a few references to Jews that reflected common antisemitic beliefs propagated in the *Protocols of the Elders of Zion*. Published in Russia in 1903, the *Protocols* purported to describe a Jewish plan for global domination, and added credence to conspiracy theories about a Masonic–Jewish alliance. Even though the *Protocols* was exposed as a fraud in 1921, antisemites continued to translate and distribute the text for decades.

During the beatification process, numerous Polish witnesses testified that Kolbe had sheltered as many as 2,000 Jewish displaced civilians at Niepokalanów at the outbreak of the Second World War. Kolbe didn't distinguish between Germans or Poles, Christians or Jews, they said. All the families were given food, fuel and clothing, no matter their faith or nationality.

'His image of the Jews, as of all who did not share his faith, was of people who were prisoners of error, not objects of hatred,' Schlafly and Green concluded.[13] Indeed, Kolbe was proud to be known as a zealous Catholic, always trying to convert others to his religion. But there's no evidence that he expressed hatred towards Jews, and the charges of antisemitism failed to gain traction.[14]

As soon as Pope John Paul II finished the canonisation service for St Maximilian Kolbe in Rome in 1982, he walked over to a person whom the *New York Times* described the following day as 'a haggard, tall, grey-haired Polish peasant'.[15]

He embraced the eighty-year-old man, whose forearm was tattooed with the number 5659. It was Franciszek Gajowniczek, whom Kolbe had saved in 1941.

Gajowniczek was a mystery to Tōmei Ozaki, who had long wondered how 'the Polish peasant' had felt about sending another man to his death. 'I needed to talk to him urgently,' he told me. 'I wondered if he had undergone psychological trauma like I had after I ignored the dying people in Nagasaki.'[16]

In 1983, Ozaki made a pilgrimage to Poland. He took a two-hour taxi ride from Kraków to the medieval town of Brzeg, where Gajowniczek lived in an old, detached house. His two sons, aged fifteen and eighteen, had been killed in a Soviet bombardment in 1945, and his wife, Helena, had died just a few months before Ozaki's visit.

Gajowniczek and Ozaki's first meeting in 1983

When the taxi entered Brzeg, Ozaki was struck by the number of tanks and military vehicles on the tranquil tree-lined road. 'Russian military', the driver said matter-of-factly to Brother Roman Kwiecień, a Polish friar at the Nagasaki friary who was accompanying Ozaki as an interpreter.

Ozaki hadn't told Gajowniczek that he was coming. But as soon as Ozaki, dressed in his Franciscan habit, said the words 'Japan' and 'Kolbe', Gajowniczek ushered the men inside and began to tell his dramatic life story, as if for the first time.

Born in a village east of Warsaw in 1901, Gajowniczek had joined the Polish army as a professional soldier at the age of eighteen. At the beginning of the Second World War, in September 1939, he was captured by the Gestapo while crossing the border into Slovakia. Sentenced to hard labour, he was sent to Auschwitz with a group of 1,700 Poles in October 1940. He lived in the camp for more time – over four years – than all but a handful of prisoners.

Gajowniczek said he talked to Father Kolbe in person for the first time in May 1941, most likely in Block 14, where the two lived. After Kolbe's death, he contracted typhus and was admitted to the camp hospital.

He was due to be sent to a Nazi gas chamber in the same block where Kolbe had been murdered, but he was saved by Dr Władysław Dering, the prisoner-doctor who was part of a Polish resistance network at the camp. Dering convinced the Nazis to move Gajowniczek out of the hospital. In October 1944, Gajowniczek was transferred to Sachsenhausen concentration camp, north of Berlin, and was liberated there by the Allies. He was eventually reunited with his wife, and they started a new life in Brzeg.

As Gajowniczek finished his story, Ozaki asked the question he'd been longing to raise. How did he feel that Kolbe had died instead of him?

Gajowniczek started to well up. 'I was in agony for a long time,' he said. 'I kept asking myself: Why did I send such a great priest to his death? A great leader was lost.'

Gajowniczek said that he suffered after the war because some people accused him of being responsible for Kolbe's death. But he eventually decided it was his mission to tell as many people as possible about Kolbe's life. He began travelling and gave scores of talks in France, Italy, Germany, the US and elsewhere, telling the story of Kolbe in Auschwitz.

As they parted, Gajowniczek said to Ozaki: 'Please spread my message to young people in Japan that war is avoidable. Nobody should have to go through what we had to endure.'[17]

Gajowniczek's determination to speak out impressed Ozaki, who years later became a professional storyteller. Never again would Ozaki be silent about his experiences on the day that the atomic bomb destroyed the lives of so many Nagasaki citizens.

25. Encountering Kolbe

1980s – Nanae, Hokkaido

Masatoshi Asari rarely missed an opportunity to spread the word about the horrors of war using the 'weapon' with which he was most familiar – the cherry blossom.

On Monday, 8 June 1987, NHK, Japan's national broadcaster, aired a thirty-minute documentary about Asari, the world's most prominent cherry tree creator. Filmed in Hokkaido's sprawling Matsumae Park under blossoming cherries, the programme focused on one class of forty-three children whom Asari had taught fifteen years earlier.

At that time, Asari had asked each twelve-year-old child to choose and plant a specific cherry variety. These saplings grew on the side of a mountain adjacent to the park, and the documentary showed the young adults' glee as they recalled planting the trees.

'Every tree brought back so many memories,' a teary-eyed Asari said. 'Every tree had a unique drama, just like every pupil's life. And the trees helped the pupils bond, connecting their lives to each other – and to me – over the years.' Sadly, one of the boys, a fisherman, had recently drowned after a collision at sea. In his memory, Asari had created a pale-pink cherry cultivar called 'Asami', named after the man's daughter.

The documentary also mentioned that Asari had sent cherry trees to Korea, China and elsewhere to make amends for Japanese wartime atrocities and as symbols of peace for the new generation.

Among the millions who watched the broadcast that evening was a sixty-nine-year-old war widow called Haruko Fujishima, who lived in central Japan. Fujishima, a Catholic, was an admirer of Father Kolbe, who had been canonised five years earlier. He was known as 'the saint who left his footsteps in Japan'. Kolbe's sainthood prompted a surge of interest in Japan in the 1980s, during which several biographies were published, including one by Tōmei Ozaki.

Inspired by Kolbe, Fujishima visited Niepokalanów in Poland shortly after the NHK programme. She described it as austere and forbidding because the communist government had severely restricted the friars' activities, and money was scarce. In a letter to Asari, whom she didn't know, Fujishima said that the Poles would appreciate some flowering blossoms to brighten their surroundings. She also included a copy of Ozaki's book about Kolbe.[1]

Fujishima's letter and gift provided another 'unexpected connection' to Kolbe, Asari said later. The book reminded him of evenings when he had sat with his wife, Kuniko, reading the *Seibo-no-Kishi* magazine published by the Nagasaki friary. Ozaki's book placed Kolbe's life in perspective, describing his six years in Nagasaki from 1930 to 1936 and continuing until his death in 1941 in Auschwitz.

The narrative about Kolbe's final year deeply shocked the cherry creator. Giving up his life for another man was the ultimate defiance against Nazi atrocities, Asari thought. What had he, Asari, done for mankind?

Yes, he'd researched and written about Japan's atrocious treatment of Koreans and of Chinese and Western prisoners of war in Hokkaido. He'd created cherries as 'peaceful weapons' to assuage his guilt and show remorse towards war victims. But all this was nothing compared with Kolbe's humanitarian actions.

When Germany invaded Poland, Japan was linked to Berlin via the Anti-Comintern Pact of 1936, the forerunner of the Axis Alliance. Didn't that make Japan indirectly complicit in Germany's aggression towards Poland? Did any Japanese protest or resist the war in the same way as Kolbe? Not a chance.

Asari believed that the emperor bore culpability for the war, though he remained the nation's symbolic head. Even though Mac-Arthur had decided not to pursue the emperor's responsibility, the Japanese should have questioned that decision more loudly.

Japan drifted along in the Cold War because it was convenient to focus on economic recovery, Asari thought. Now that it was a wealthy country, it had become triumphalist and arrogant, he said.

Asari was proud that Japan had a 'No War' clause in the Peace Constitution, but he was disturbed that its Self-Defence Forces had become among the largest in the world.

Asari felt empty and worthless. His country had let him down. Equally, he felt that he had let down his country by his passivity and indolence. It was time to make amends. But how?

Now fifty-six, he was famous in Hokkaido for creating his signature Matsumae cherries. But as a low-paid primary school teacher living in a remote Japanese city, he was still all but unknown in Japan outside sakura circles.

He felt he had but two gifts to offer the world – an intense desire to atone for Japan's wartime cruelty and a stubborn craving to create beautiful blossoms.

Asari pondered what the people who had most influenced his life would encourage him to do. From his idealist university professor, Tōru Ukita, he'd learned the importance of Japan's Constitution and of the rights of individuals. From the humanist writings of Takuboku Ishikawa, he'd learned to be more sympathetic to the oppressed. From his mother, Chie, he'd learned compassion and honesty, and had inherited her love of plants.

He could imagine this trio calling on him to create something special to celebrate Father Kolbe and the Polish people. And so, during the summer school holidays of 1987, Asari jumped on a bus to the Hakodate central library and checked out as many books on Poland as he could carry.

He began with a history of the Polish–Lithuanian Commonwealth, a multi-ethnic, multi-religious kingdom for 409 years until 1795. The size of Texas and California combined, the Commonwealth included most of today's Ukraine. Reading how Poland had been wiped from the map in 1795, he thought of Korea's similar fate at the hands of Japan. He moved on to biographies of Polish heroes, including Chopin and Madame Curie. Then he switched to histories of Polish resistance against their Russian, German and Austrian occupiers. He ended his reading binge with books about the resistance movement during the war, culminating in the 1944 Warsaw Uprising.

'The books I read made it clear to me that Poland had always produced outstanding people with a broad outlook on humanity,' he said. 'Kolbe and the Polish resistance forces sent the message that there were many causes worth fighting for. That was exactly what I had been searching for.'

Humbled, Asari resolved to commemorate Kolbe's life with yet another cherry-blossom 'peace offering'. He vowed to send hundreds of 'Kolbe cherries' from Hokkaido to Niepokalanów. This gift would be greater and more meaningful than his previous donations to Korea, China and elsewhere. It would include some of Japan's most famous varieties, such as a weeping tree called 'Beni-yae-shidare'. This was a grandchild of a 1,000-year-old tree, a national treasure called 'Miharu Takizakura' from Fukushima prefecture.

'This would become the most profound project of my life,' he said. It would also become the most difficult because of Poland's unstable political environment during the 1980s.

Poland's communist government had imposed martial law on the country in December 1981 following years of recession, strikes and demonstrations. Apart from church attendance, gatherings were banned and all existing unions and organisations were suspended.

Although martial law was lifted in July 1983, many restrictions remained in place throughout the 1980s, and an economic crisis led to more rationing of food and other products in the one-party state. The trade union Solidarity, which had been banned in 1982, gained influence during the decade as an underground organisation, eroding the power and legitimacy of the ruling Polish United Workers' Party.

Cherry trees had always been a safe gift from Japan as symbols of international friendship. But at a time when the Marxist-Leninist regime was imploding, it was unclear to Asari whether Poland would allow the importation of trees destined to commemorate a man who had fiercely opposed everything the government now stood for, especially its ties to Russia and communism.

Undaunted, Asari pressed on. With help from Haruko Fujishima, he contacted Brother Roman Kwiecień, one of the Polish friars who had known Kolbe and who was now living in a Tokyo friary. Roman briefed his Niepokalanów counterparts about Asari's proposal. The Polish friary, it turned out, owned a small field in which cherries could be planted, but the men had no expertise in caring for them.

On land near his home and on his youngest brother Shigeru's two-and-a-half-acre farm, Asari was growing at least 1,500 trees as 'peace offerings' for foreign countries and for projects within Japan. Out of this collection, he chose twenty hardy, disease-free saplings to send to Kolbe's friary.[2]

This was a test run to ensure that the trees would survive Poland's winter, where temperatures often fell to minus 20 degrees Celsius. He also needed to check that the cherries would grow in Poland's alkaline soil, which differed from Hokkaido's more acidic conditions.[3] Provided the trees lived, he planned to send 360 more the following spring.

Asari's diary entries showed the rigour of his preparation and his enthusiasm for the Kolbe project.

Diary, 16 October 1987: Rose at 5 a.m. to wash cherries' roots and trunks in preparation for quarantine inspection. Wrapped the roots in sphagnum moss [to retain moisture]. Took trees to quarantine office in Hakodate after school. Officer asked why I'm sending them to Poland. Explained about Father Kolbe. He seemed pleased. Trees all passed inspection.

Diary, 19 October: Got up in the dark again to re-wrap roots in fresh sphagnum moss. Covered them with water-logged, torn newspaper pieces. Wrapped them in plastic bags so that moss sticks to roots. Wrapped trees in glass wool [an insulating material]. Put them in long, thin boxes. Continued packing all evening. Made labels for each tree, wrote Japanese name and Latin name on each tree. Finished packing at 1 a.m. Woke in middle of night worrying about the trees. Will they get to Poland safely?

Diary, 21 October: Sent trees to Sapporo via Nittsu [Nippon Express, a global logistics company]. Trees on plane to Nagasaki.

Diary, 22, 23, 24, 25 October: Didn't sleep well.

Diary, 26 October: Fujishima-san phoned. Trees arrived in Warsaw. Slept well.

That was the last that Asari heard about the trees in his pilot project. He assumed that they had been delivered to the friary and planted, so he moved ahead with the plan to send more trees. By now he was obsessed with the idea that the project in Poland would be the ultimate triumph for Kolbe and the Polish people as they sought to extricate themselves from the grip of the Soviet Union.

Diary, 4 November 1987: This is the project of my life, and I must succeed. Father Kolbe and the Polish friars such as Brother Zeno gave a lot to Japan, but we have not done anything in return. To achieve peace, the most important ingredients are empathy and solidarity. My cherry relay is a relay for peace.

In December 1987, Masatoshi Asari buried 360 saplings in the frozen grounds of his brother's house in Hokkaido, to protect them from frost.[4] There were 305 cherries. Accompanying them were twenty-five ornamental plum trees and thirty dogwood trees, grown from seeds given him by Roland Jefferson of the US Department of Agriculture.[5]

Asari was well aware of the project's difficulties. He had no idea who would pay to ship the trees to Poland. He didn't really know whether the friary owned enough land on which to plant such a large number.

Diary, 21 December 1987: The obstacles to tackle are the severe Polish climate, the different soil and the social environment under Soviet suppression. The Poles' circumstances are totally different from Japan. I must keep track of the political situation there and judge what I can do. This project is a fight within myself.

While Asari fretted, Brother Roman and Haruko Fujishima looked for ways to transport the trees from northern Japan to central Poland. Their first stop was a meeting in Tokyo with Poland's ambassador to Japan, Ryszard Frąckiewicz, a loyal communist and former student of the famed neo-Marxian economist Oskar Lange. As expected, Frąckiewicz said he needed to talk with his bosses in Warsaw about whether the project could move ahead.

Throughout the winter of 1987–88, some two feet of snow and ice covered the buried saplings, but in mid-March Asari determined that they were still alive.

In early April 1988, Haruko Fujishima and Brother Roman flew to Hokkaido to meet Asari and inspect some of the plants. Brother Roman was a rare living link between the Polish and Japanese friaries. He'd lived with Kolbe in Nagasaki for two years, helping create the Lourdes grotto above the friary. He'd then lived alongside Tōmei Ozaki, Brother Zeno and other Nagasaki friars for more than four decades after the war. He had also accompanied Ozaki to Poland in 1983 as his interpreter.

Despite Asari's excitement for the project, the timing couldn't have been worse. On 21 April, a wave of strikes hit Poland that quickly spread through the nation's coal mines and shipyards, destabilising the government. That left Ambassador Frąckiewicz in a precarious position. But after consulting his Warsaw bosses, Frąckiewicz agreed not only to pay for the trees' transportation but also to accompany them to Poland along with Brother Roman. It was a magnanimous gesture, although it was becoming clear to most Poles that communism's days were numbered.

Diary, 27 April 1988: Arose at 4 a.m. Dug up the cherries. Delighted to see new roots growing. Ordered most expensive sphagnum moss from Sapporo nursery.

Diary, 29 April: National holiday. Washed all the saplings. Worked until 9 p.m. without a break. Wrote lists of all the cherries and other trees.

Diary, 1 May: May Day. I view my trees as 'memorial blossoms' for all the war dead, including the Jewish people killed by the Nazis.

At Narita airport in 1987. From left: Brother Roman, Mrs Fujishima and the Polish ambassador Frąckiewicz with his wife

Father Kolbe gave up his life to save the lives of innocent people. His spirit will appreciate these different blossoms.

On 2 May, a quarantine officer certified that the plants were disease-free. Asari worked until midnight, wrapping the trees' roots with moss, attaching name tags and packing them in ten boxes.

This lonely labour of love left him exhausted but exhilarated. 'I protected the roots as if I was wrapping a new-born baby in a blanket,' he wrote in his diary. Two days later, the boxes were sent to the friary in Tokyo where Brother Roman was living.

Ambassador Frąckiewicz, his wife and Brother Roman left Narita International Airport in Tokyo on 10 May 1988 on a plane bound for Warsaw that contained the 360 saplings in its refrigerated hold.

Accompanying the trees were two letters. One contained Asari's instructions for tending the trees: 'Give fresh soil to each sapling. Leave no air between the soil and the roots. Plant them at least five metres apart.' The second was a heart-warming letter to the head of Niepokalanów. It read in part:

The Polish people . . . have produced a splendid culture and arts with sincerity and diligence, thus achieving respect from people all over the world. These achievements came about because they hold principles based on Christian love and a spirit of service to others.

St Maximilian Kolbe, whom we Japanese deeply admire, was the highest practitioner of these principles. Through his love, he maintained the dignity of human life, showed the ideal of peace to all humankind, and manifested justice with his death. His noble spirit will live on for generations as a precious heritage for humankind.

Poland and Japan alike were devastated by the Second World War and both countries rose from utter ruin. Both nations have shared hardships and hold a strong desire for peace. We need to teach and lead our children towards a future free from wars, which are the worst of all human crimes.

If these flowering trees could be planted not only at Niepokalanów but also at other places associated with St Kolbe, such as Warsaw, Auschwitz, and Kraków – places where there were many victims during the Second World War – the Japanese people's wishes would be even more fulfilled.

On 14 June, Asari heard from Brother Roman that the trees had arrived and had been planted at Niepokalanów near the end of an unusually dry spring.

Diary, 14 June: Dry weather can be fatal to young cherry saplings after being planted. Quite a few may wither.

This wasn't quite the start that Asari had expected, but there was nothing he could do about it. Asari's work in Poland was now complete, or so he thought. The fate of his trees lay in the hands of Polish friars, many of whom had never seen flowering cherries, let alone planted or cared for them.[6]

Little did Asari realise that within a year, his international initiatives would lead the Japanese security services to investigate him as a possible communist collaborator or a spy. Whom did they think he was spying for? Not Poland, but Kim Il-Sung's North Korea.

26. The North Korean 'Spy'

1988–1989 – Hokkaido

Sometime in late 1988, Masatoshi Asari received an unexpected phone call from North Korea's de facto embassy in Japan. The rogue state of North Korea and Japan had been at loggerheads almost since the end of the Second World War and had no diplomatic relations.

In Japan, an organisation known as Chōsen Sōren, or the General Association of Korean Residents in Japan, acted officially on the North Korean government's behalf. It also operated schools, banks and *pachinko* gambling parlours throughout the nation.

Sixteen years earlier, in 1972, Asari had published a booklet about Japan's abysmal treatment of Koreans in Hokkaido during the Second World War. He'd subsequently donated twenty cherry trees to a Korean school in Hokkaido, the first of his 'peace offerings' to atone for Japanese atrocities. Later that year, he'd sent fifty cherry saplings to Beijing after Japan and communist China normalised diplomatic ties.

Mr Son, the Chōsen Sōren chief in the city of Hakodate, had known Asari since 1972 and the two men had discussed the idea of Asari donating cherry trees to Pyongyang, the North Korean capital, to commemorate the fortieth anniversary of the communist nation's founding in 1948.

Asari, now fifty-seven years old, didn't belong to any political party. He considered himself a maverick, proud to plough his own furrow and beholden to no one. But ever since the Second World War, when a young Korean runaway had secretly stayed with a neighbouring family, he had sympathised with the Koreans' plight in Japan.

He told Son that he would donate fifty-seven cherry trees, mostly of the Chishima-zakura species, and three apple trees to the North

Korean capital as a gesture of friendship.[1] Asari included apple trees because he had read that the malnourished Korean labourers had enjoyed eating Hokkaido apples while working on railway construction sites near his home between 1943 and 1945. Many Japanese were anti-North Korean. But Asari didn't care about what they or the government might think.

At 10.30 a.m. on Wednesday, 29 March 1989, Son called Asari again. A ship was departing from the Japanese port of Niigata for North Korea on 7 April. Asari confirmed that the cherries would be ready to sail.

Diary, 30 March 1989: I feel it is my destiny to send Japanese cherry trees to North Korea at such a difficult time between the two countries.

Asari was referring to diplomatic talks that month between North Korea and Japan to solve what was known as the 'Dai-18 Fujisan Maru problem'. In 1983, North Korea had arrested and imprisoned for fifteen years the captain and chief engineer of a Japanese cargo ship named *Dai-18 Fujisan Maru*. Pyongyang alleged that the two men, who were from Hakodate, had helped a North Korean stowaway flee to Japan.

As Asari prepared the cherries for shipment, he began to worry that his gift to Japan's long-time adversary might prove controversial.

Diary, 31 March 1989: [Government] negotiations surrounding the Dai-18 Fujisan Maru appear to be making progress. My cherry gift might attract positive interest from both the Koreans and the Japanese, or it could lead to further animosity. If the media report about the cherries leaving for North Korea, what would the family of Isamu Beniko, the ship's captain, think? How will people in Hakodate react? They might welcome my act, or perhaps the opposite.

The following afternoon, a reporter and photographer from the *Hokkaido Shimbun*, the most influential newspaper in the region, showed up at Chōsen Sōren's office to interview Asari. Asari told

Asari with the cherries that were sent to North Korea, and Mr Son (right)

the journalists that it was wrong to believe that all North Koreans were 'terrorists', and that he was donating the cherries as 'an act of goodwill'.

Only when the newspaper article appeared, four days later, did Asari realise that his largesse was no small matter for the Japanese authorities.

Diary, 5 April: Snow. First day of new school year. *Hokkaido Shimbun* evening edition carried an article about the cherries going to Pyong-yang. I will not bend my beliefs about my peace offering. But I'm sure the security police will come to interrogate me.

Asari was spot-on. At 10.35 a.m. the following day, an officer from the security division of the Hakodate police force called his school. He questioned Asari on why he was sending cherries to North Korea and pointedly reminded him that he'd been investigated before for his sakura gifts to China. Asari was clearly on a list of pos-sible communist sympathisers – or worse, possible spies.

At the time, Japan's security services were under pressure to report any seemingly unusual dealings with North Korea, following several incidents. In November 1987, a North Korean female secret agent, Kim Hyon-Hui, had blown up a Korean Air passenger jet, killing all 115 people on board. Captured in Bahrain, Kim was put on trial in Seoul in early 1989 and was sentenced to death. She was later pardoned.

Kim had been taught to impersonate a Japanese tourist by a bar hostess, Yaeko Taguchi, whom the North Koreans had abducted in Tokyo.[2] Taguchi was one of at least seventeen Japanese known to have been abducted by North Korea between 1977 and 1983.

At 4.30 p.m. that same day, 6 April, two policemen, neither wearing a uniform, arrived at Asari's school. One was a 'soft man' in his forties from Hakodate. The other was 'an arrogant, tough guy' in his fifties from Hokkaido's capital, Sapporo. Both were 'former Tokkō', Asari wrote cynically in his diary, referring to Japan's feared secret police force during the war. Asari refused to meet them alone and asked his headmaster to attend the meeting.

The 'soft man' and the 'tough guy' went through an elaborate 'good cop, bad cop' routine, Asari said, as 'they tried to find out whether I was a spy'. 'The Tokkō believe that anyone who deals with communist countries is a traitor. I taught sixth graders who were twelve years old, so they were particularly nervous that I might be teaching them communist ideas.'

While Mr Soft Man smiled, took notes and made polite comments about cherry blossoms, Mr Tough Guy was 'high-handed and intimidating', Asari recalled. It was the same man who had questioned him in 1972 about his gifts to China.

'Do you have links with North Korean politicians?' he shouted. 'Who are your collaborators in sending cherry trees to North Korea? Who paid to send the cherries there?'

'I paid everything myself,' Asari answered. 'I don't smoke or drink, so I have extra money to send the cherries. What's wrong with sending beautiful cherries to North Korean children? I treat every child equally, whether Japanese or Korean.'

Mr Tough Guy continued: 'Do you understand what communist countries are like? Are you telling your children that it's OK to demonstrate against Japan? What else are you hiding?'

Asari was shaken.

Finally, the headmaster intervened, telling the men that Asari was trustworthy and very popular with his pupils.

Diary, 6 April: I told the Tokkō I had done nothing wrong and asked: 'Why do you need to investigate this act of friendship?' I told the police about the spirit of the new 'Peace Constitution' because they didn't seem to understand it at all. Their intention is clear: They want to suppress me.

The following day, one of Japan's leading newspapers, the *Asahi*, phoned to ask him about his donation to North Korea. 'Japanese cherries', the *Asahi* reported, 'were regarded as a symbol of aggression before and during the war. But Mr Asari notes that "sakura don't bear any responsibility for Japanese wrongdoings. They are symbols of peace now." '[3]

Diary, 7 April: The security police are really sly. Why do they investigate someone's goodwill? Their attitude is linked to the emperor system, which lies deep within our society. They think communist states are the enemy. And yet they violate human rights with their power, just to show off their influence.

Unnerved by Mr Tough Guy's questions and manner, Asari started fearing that he might be fired as a teacher. With three children to support, he put money aside. 'I half-jokingly told my wife that I would open a mobile *ramen* [noodle] shop if need be,' he said.

According to Asari's diaries, the cherries arrived safely in North Korea sometime in April 1989. This was the same time as some senior Japan Socialist Party members of parliament were visiting Pyongyang and as the *Dai-18 Fujisan Maru* dispute headed for a solution.[4]

'The timing [of my gift] seems to be supernatural, designed by divine power,' Asari wrote in his diary. 'All I want is for my cherries to warm people's hearts.'

Asari never found out what happened to his sixty trees after they arrived in Pyongyang, and the Japanese security police never again called to investigate him.

Indeed, within weeks, he'd moved on from this North Korean escapade. Once again, Asari plunged into the 'project of his life' – the creation and delivery of even more 'Kolbe cherries' to Poland.

Several months before Masatoshi Asari became an unsuspecting cog in Japan's diplomatic dispute with North Korea, a Japanese nun called Sister Iida phoned him long-distance from the southern island of Kyushu. Sister Iida was the deputy head of the MI convent and orphanage complex northeast of Nagasaki where Tōmei Ozaki had lived for eleven years while recuperating from illness.

As usual when friars and nuns contacted Asari, the topic was cherry blossoms. Sister Iida's convent, dedicated to Father Kolbe, was building a sister convent in southeast Poland in a village called Strachocina.

Her request was simple. The new convent wanted to plant cherry trees in a Japanese garden on its grounds to symbolise Kolbe's Japanese–Polish links. The opening ceremony was set for September 1989.

Asari was tired. Creating and sending trees to Niepokalanów in 1988 had exhausted him. After teaching all day, he tended his cherries at night and on weekends. But in his few spare moments every evening, he read in the newspapers about Poland, which was fast embracing democracy. In February 1989, the communist regime had agreed to hold so-called 'round table' talks with the Solidarity opposition movement, led by Lech Wałęsa.

> Diary, 16 March 1989: I wonder why God told me to send cherries to Poland? At present, the creation of a new country by Solidarity is progressing really well. I've learned a lot from Poland about their desire to create their own country. I hope this new project doesn't cause trouble for anyone.

In mid-April, days after his cherries departed for North Korea, Asari committed himself to the Strachocina project. His detailed diaries showed, as always, his meticulous preparations to ensure the cherries would survive both Poland's winters and its alkaline soil.

As an experiment, Asari poured well-watered slaked lime onto half of his farm to replicate Strachocina's soil, and he transplanted wild Ōyama-zakura and other double-flowered cherries there. As the saplings grew, he checked the trees' roots and trunks daily, and he trimmed their small, thin branches. He added nitrogen fertiliser to turn the leaves a darker green. By early September, the trees were ready.

> Diary, 10 September: Rained all day but I had to dig up all the cherries to send to Strachocina. My experiment over the past year has proven that cherries can grow healthy new roots in nutritious soil, whether it's acidic or alkaline.
>
> I chose forty cherries to send to Strachocina and ten grams of Shidare-zakura seeds. I chose the trees with the healthiest roots. I pray that these cherries will arrive and settle in well in Strachocina as 'peace offerings' and friendship cherries.[5]

The following day, Asari took the saplings and seeds to the Hakodate quarantine office. His diary entries were lively and upbeat.

> Diary, 11 September: The officer was a young chap. He didn't find any disease or insects apart from some grasshopper larvae in one of the boxes. How did that get there?! Received a certificate of safe, clean trees and left the office at 5.20 p.m. After dinner, wrapped roots of each tree with sphagnum moss and covered them with plastic. Finished after midnight. It certainly takes a lot of effort to send sakura abroad!

> The sun is in the sky
> Flowers are in the ground
> People's kindness and love are everywhere
> I've lots to be thankful for!

> Diary, 12 September: Rose very early to pack the trees for Poland. Taught all day. I feel supported by many people with conscientious

Brother Roman and the parish priest, Father Niżnik, planting
cherries in Strachocina convent

and noble minds. I get strength from them to move ahead with my small initiatives.

Diary, 13 September: Took the 5 a.m. train to Hakodate, carrying the trees. The Nittsu delivery service said the boxes were too big. Pleaded with them that these trees are on a special mission of international friendship. Nittsu finally accepted them. Very relieved. Went to school to teach.

Sister Iida will travel with the trees (as well as Brother Roman). Wrote details about how to care for them during the winter and spring. I pray they will grow well at the convent.

It wasn't until November 1989 that Asari heard from Sister Iida, who was still in Poland, that the trees had been planted in the convent grounds at Strachocina. After that, apart from a photograph showing one small blossom-bearing tree, Asari had no idea whether his Kolbe-inspired gifts were alive or dead.

On New Year's Eve 1989, as 108 bells chimed in temples throughout Japan to welcome in a new decade, Masatoshi Asari reflected on one

Nagasaki friary in 1932
(Courtesy of the Order of Friars Minor Conventual, Japan Province. Colourised by Uwe Pleban)

Kolbe in Zakopane circa 1936–39
(Courtesy of Niepokalanów MI Archives. Colourised by Uwe Pleban)

Zeno in later life
(Courtesy of the Order of Friars Minor
Conventual, Japan Province)

Asari's cherries planted at Niepokalanów
friary in 1988
(Courtesy of Masatoshi Asari)

Asari's cherry in blossom at Strachocina in 1993
(Courtesy of Masatoshi Asari)

Ozaki in 2020
(Courtesy of Tōmei Ozaki)

Surviving 'Beni-yutaka' cherry tree in Strachocina
(Courtesy of Sister Klara Machulska)

Matsumae cherry park
(Courtesy of the author)

Masatoshi Asari in 2019
(Courtesy of the author)

The statue of the Virgin Mary in Strachocina
(Courtesy of the author)

of the busiest and most memorable years of his life. As usual, his year had begun with cherries (for Pyongyang) and ended with cherries (for Strachocina). In between, as well as his regular day job teaching twelve-year-olds, he had built a memorial in Hakodate for people who had died in US air raids near the end of the war.

What drove him? 'I'm not sure,' he said. 'But when I sent the cherries to North Korea, I was in the midst of the Polish cherry project. I was still full of admiration and reverence towards Father Kolbe. He taught me that hatred does not produce anything, that only love is creative. And I always believed we should not hate North Korea, as many people did. I was aware that I might be put on a bed of nails for my actions, but I was also aware of the risks I was taking.

' "International friendship projects" and "peace offerings" are not always as straightforward as they sound. But I felt I was led by something supernatural, a force that pushed me irresistibly to fulfil these projects. You really need to be strong to pursue what you believe in.'

Thousands of miles from Hokkaido, in the US state of Michigan, another man – the Catholic military chaplain who had blessed the atomic bomb before it was dropped on Nagasaki – had also found the strength to follow his convictions.

27. 'I Said Nothing'

1980s – Michigan, US; London, UK

'If a soldier came to me and asked if he could put a bullet through a child's head, I would have told him, absolutely not. That would be mortally sinful. But in 1945 Tinian Island was the largest airfield in the world. Many planes went to Japan with the express purpose of killing not one child or one civilian but of slaughtering hundreds and thousands and tens of thousands of children and civilians – and I said nothing.'[1]

It was August 1985, the fortieth anniversary of the Hiroshima and Nagasaki atomic bombings, and the seventy-year-old speaker from Michigan was addressing a Pax Christi USA conference about the morality of the nuclear detonations.

In the years after the Nagasaki bombing, George Zabelka, the Catholic military chaplain who had blessed the world's most destructive device on Tinian Island, had suffered a crisis of faith. Zabelka had concluded that he must speak out regarding his own 'about-face' because Jesus had preached the importance of non-violent love towards friends and enemies alike.[2]

The Hiroshima and Nagasaki bombings generated more controversy and attention than any other events in the Second World War save for the murder of millions at Auschwitz and other concentration camps. Zabelka was just one of the military personnel involved in the bombings who later questioned his actions, although this was by no means a frequent occurrence.

Zabelka's transformation from military chaplain to peace activist had begun in the 1950s in Flint, Michigan, where his parish contained a large and poor Black population. Zabelka marched with Martin Luther King Jr and thousands of civil-rights demonstrators in Selma, Alabama, in 1965. By the early 1980s, Zabelka had turned

George Zabelka

his attention to the atomic bombs, making a pilgrimage from Hiroshima to Nagasaki to ask forgiveness.

'I was brainwashed!' he told the conference. 'I was told it was necessary – told openly by the military and told implicitly by my church's leadership. I made a terrible mistake.

'As Catholic chaplain for the 509th Composite Group, I was the final channel that communicated this fraudulent image of Christ to the crews of the *Enola Gay* and the *Bockscar*. I watched as *Bockscar*, piloted by a good Irish Catholic pilot, dropped the bomb on Urakami Cathedral in Nagasaki, the center of Catholicism in Japan. I knew that St Francis Xavier, centuries before, had brought the Catholic faith to Japan. I knew that schools, churches, and religious orders were annihilated. And yet I said nothing.'[3]

Zabelka's words were like a red rag to a bull for the Protestant chaplain who had also blessed the Nagasaki bomb and its crew on Tinian all those decades earlier. William Downey became a Lutheran pastor in Milwaukee, Wisconsin, after the war and later moved to Florida. After Zabelka decried the nuclear attacks, Downey called him 'either a fraud or mentally affected' and 'an itinerant priest' who hadn't been on Tinian day-to-day with the 509th Composite Group, as he had.[4]

Until the end of his life in 1994, Downey never wavered in his support of the bombings and in his disdain for Zabelka and the Japanese.

'In my view, there's very little difference between killing a Jap soldier in the jungles of Burma with a rifle bullet, and killing Hiroshima off. It's just a matter of quantity, not of quality,' he said in an oral history interview in 1987.

'The Jap was a barbarian. They like to think that they're the cultured people of the world, and all that manure. Look what they did at the Bataan Death March, look what they did all over Asia, in an exercise of cruelty and inhumanity.'

He continued: 'This business of war is an evil, terrible thing. It's very easy to complain and criticise and exercise judgment upon what happened forty-plus years ago. They [critics of the bomb] weren't there, their ass was not on the line, they didn't have to hear shots fired in anger, and they didn't have to risk their life on an invasion.

'We were going to invade Japan. This was going to be one of the bloodiest things in the history of the world. It's not unreasonable to suppose there would be three million or more Japanese casualties.'

Downey's support for the atomic bombings echoed that of a majority of Americans in the half-century after the war. They believed that the nuclear strikes had prevented tens of thousands, if not millions, of deaths.

That viewpoint would later be denounced by leading US and Japanese historians.[5] The American government itself, in a report released on 1 July 1946, less than a year after the bombings, was unequivocal. 'It seems clear that, even without the atomic bombing attacks, air supremacy over Japan could have exerted sufficient pressure to bring about unconditional surrender and obviate the need for invasion,' the US Strategic Bombing Survey concluded. 'Based on a detailed investigation of all the facts and supported by the testimony of the surviving Japanese leaders involved, it is the Survey's opinion that certainly prior to 31 December 1945, and in all probability prior to 1 November 1945, Japan would have surrendered even if the atomic bombs had not been dropped, even if Russia had not entered the war, and even if no invasion had been planned or contemplated.'[6]

J. Samuel Walker, chief historian of the US Nuclear Regulatory Commission, echoed that conclusion. 'The consensus among scholars is that the bomb was not needed to avoid an invasion of Japan and to end the war within a relatively short time. It is clear that alternatives to the bomb existed and that Truman and his advisers knew it. The hoary claim that the bomb prevented 500,000 American combat deaths is unsupportable.'[7]

About six weeks after the Japanese surrender in August 1945, another of the men involved with the Nagasaki mission knocked on the door of 10 Downing Street in London, home of the British prime minister.

Group Captain Leonard Cheshire was there to offer the premier his conclusions about the bomb.[8] Cheshire had flown on the mission in *Big Stink*, the camera plane, and had watched transfixed as the 'beautifully sculpted nuclear cloud climbed into the air'.[9]

Winston Churchill had instructed Cheshire to go on the mission as one of two British observers. But Churchill had been heavily defeated in a general election in July 1945 and Clement Attlee's Labour Party was now in power. At Number Ten, Prime Minister Attlee listened intently as Cheshire explained that if both sides in a conflict have atomic bombs, there is military stalemate.

The mission had exhausted Cheshire. After meeting Attlee, Cheshire said, he 'felt lost and empty' and had begun to 'feel compassion for the people under this vast boiling cloud'. Diagnosed with psychoneurosis, he retired from the Royal Air Force in January 1946. 'I think, perhaps, it had all been a bit much for me,' he wrote later.[10]

Yet Cheshire couldn't get the bombing of Nagasaki out of his head, and it stoked his interest in the question of whether it was morally acceptable for nations to possess a nuclear deterrent, let alone explode a bomb. 'The [Nagasaki] atom bomb did not influence the war one way or the other for, politically speaking, the war was already over,' he said in 1950. 'What is more, this was known to the Allies at the time.'[11]

After the war, Cheshire became a practising Catholic, although he said this had nothing to do with witnessing the atomic explosion or his other wartime experiences.[12]

'It is a sad reality that man is capable of killing on a huge scale without nuclear weapons,' Cheshire wrote in 1983. 'Twenty million people were exterminated in Hitler's concentration camps with nothing more powerful than bullets, Zyklon B gas, doctors' scalpels and the like.

'The Soviet Revolution and its aftermath have accounted for an estimated fifteen million, and conventional wars and conflicts since 1945 at least another ten million. This is by no means to argue in favour of powerful armaments, only to re-state that it is out of man's heart rather than the weapon that the evil comes.'[13]

After years of study, Cheshire concluded that it was illogical to call for unilateral nuclear disarmament while upholding the right to armed self-defence 'since once nuclear arms have been renounced there remains no effective defence against a determined nuclear aggressor'.

'A policy of deterrence is a means of saving lives and of preserving freedom and it thus cannot be held irreconcilable with man's divine calling to love all his fellow men,' he said.[14]

Cheshire's wartime experiences prompted him to set up a charity in 1948 called Cheshire Homes, to help disabled British military veterans. The charity later became international, opening several homes in Japan, and it now focuses on people with severe learning disabilities.[15]

For the commander of the second atomic bomb mission, Charles W. Sweeney, the post-war years were bittersweet. In the US, he was lauded at first for dropping the bomb that many believed helped bring the war to a swift conclusion.

But Sweeney's command of *Bockscar*, the strike plane, became embroiled in controversy after numerous crew members wrote autobiographies or were quoted in magazines and books contradicting his account.[16]

Paul Tibbets, the overall commander of the 509th Composite Group who had chosen Sweeney to lead the mission, was bitter about the flight for years to come. Sweeney, he said, 'was the only bad mark on the whole 509th Composite Group all the time it existed'.[17] He was particularly scathing about Sweeney delaying the mission while waiting for the camera plane at the point where the three B-29 bombers were supposed to rendezvous. Because *Bockscar* was running short of fuel, Tibbets felt that the delay had put the mission in jeopardy.

The *New York Times'* star science reporter who had flown on the Nagasaki mission also faced a reckoning. The newsroom greeted William L. Laurence as a hero when he returned from the Pacific, and he won a second Pulitzer Prize for his reporting.[18] But journalists later roundly criticised him, as well as the *New York Times*, for ethical conflicts of interest because the US Army had paid his salary while he was seconded to the Manhattan Project. His positive reports about the bomb and the future of atomic energy also made him appear as a propagandist for the military establishment.[19]

Years later, Beverly Ann Deepe Keever, a University of Hawaii journalism professor, correctly claimed that Laurence's stories about Nagasaki had omitted or covered up the harmful effects of radiation and radioactivity on bomb survivors.[20] Indeed, it was a Black American reporter, Charles H. Loeb, writing in the *Atlanta Daily World* in October 1945, who showed how radiation was sickening and killing Japanese citizens, contradicting the US War Department, the Manhattan Project and the *New York Times*.[21]

For Tōmei Ozaki and thousands of Nagasaki residents who had been underneath the bomb on 9 August, the radiation poisoning was, of course, no secret. Radiation sickness killed thousands. But the reluctance of most Catholic survivors to talk about their experiences until the 1980s meant that far less attention was given to the impact of the Nagasaki bomb than to Hiroshima's. It was a situation that Ozaki sought to rectify as a professional storyteller.

PART 8

Blossoms of Hope, 1990–2023

28. The Storyteller

1990 – Niepokalanów; Nagasaki

The sky is clear blue
But my heart is filled with deep sorrow
Within the ever-changing human world
I am just a short-lived wildflower
Comforting, cheering
The bells of Nagasaki ring

Arms outstretched, palms raised upwards, sixty-two-year-old Tōmei Ozaki stood in front of more than 200 Catholics at a gathering in the Niepokalanów friary in Poland and belted out three verses of 'The Bells of Nagasaki' in Japanese with the musical backing of a karaoke machine.

The song had been a massive hit in Japan in 1949, telling the story of the grief felt by Father Kolbe's friend, Dr Takashi Nagai, after his wife died in the atomic blast. Nagai was comforted by the bells from Urakami Cathedral that had been rung again on Christmas Eve 1945. The song was the offshoot of a book written by Nagai, which had been made into an equally popular film in Japan in 1950.

Few of the Polish men listening to Ozaki on that summer's day in 1990 had any idea what their Japanese colleague was singing about. It mattered not. Ozaki's tenor voice echoed through the conference hall. When he finished, the audience applauded with gusto, as if they had understood the song's meaning of hope and consolation.

Ozaki gave a short bow, briefly recalling the isolation he'd felt on the day of the bomb, a lone orphaned flower in a field of ruins. Just like the lyrics in the song, he had been stricken for years, long after the dark skies became blue.

How unexpected and gratifying it was, he thought, that he should be singing this Japanese ditty at Kolbe's friary in Poland. He was sure that Kolbe was humming along.[1]

Equally surprising was the sight of hundreds of small cherry trees growing in a field close to the hall where he had performed. At the time, Ozaki knew nothing about the 380 trees that Masatoshi Asari had sent from Hokkaido to Niepokalanów as a peace offering for Kolbe and the Polish people.

In the nineteen years since Ozaki's first pilgrimage to Poland, the Warsaw Pact country had undergone seismic political changes along the bumpy road to democracy. The Franciscans lauded these developments, which were fast bringing an end to half a century of authoritarian rule by the Nazis and then the communists.

Niepokalanów's dynamic pre-war development, spearheaded by Kolbe, had ended with the Nazi invasion and occupation. The friary was still the largest religious community in the world at the end of the war, housing about 300 Franciscans. But the conflict took its toll, as it did on all religious institutions in Poland. Soviet bombings on 16 January 1945 destroyed several buildings within the compound, killing seven friars.

As soon as the Nazis left, the communists took over.[2] The friars set about making Niepokalanów self-sufficient and helping the local community. Those not involved in the publishing operation made shoes and sweaters and operated a sawmill and power plant. Others tended the beehives, bred silkworms, milked cows and acted as firefighters in the voluntary fire brigade.[3]

Yet at almost every turn, the leaders of the Soviet satellite state of Poland tried to limit the friary's influence and to undermine any activities that appeared threatening, especially its publications.[4] The authorities allowed the monthly *Knight of the Immaculata* (*Rycerz Niepokalanej*) magazine to resume publication in July 1945 with a circulation of just 80,000, but its success spooked the censors, who claimed that the friars were spreading anti-communist propaganda.

Bureaucrats scrutinised each issue before publication, deliberately causing delays. Certain topics, particularly those concerning how to raise children, were prohibited. And in 1949, after the government nationalised the printing industry, Niepokalanów's printing presses were confiscated.

In 1952, publication of the magazine stopped altogether.[5] It didn't appear again until 1971, when frustrated Franciscans published an edition in Italy and secretly sent copies back to Poland via Japan. Not until 1982 was *Knight of the Immaculata* again published in Poland.

The communists used other techniques to thwart the community's ventures. All typewriters had to be registered. Friars were forced to submit handwriting samples. Paper for publications was rationed and quotas set, which were reduced year after year.

The government's Office for Religious Affairs also closely monitored the instructors, students, curriculum and individual lessons at the minor seminary. The government had closed the minor seminary in 1954 after six years of operation, then reopened it in 1957 following protests. Books that contained allegedly anti-Soviet material were confiscated from its library.

Construction of Niepokalanów's new church, which had begun in 1939, was delayed time and again after requests for bricks, concrete and other building materials were rejected. The church was finally consecrated in 1954. Niepokalanów also found itself in debt because of disputes with the authorities about its ownership of the land and government demands for income and property taxes.

Despite this continual harassment, Niepokalanów's influence in Poland was largely undiminished. 'Camouflaged' pilgrims arrived in coachloads after telling their bosses that they were visiting Warsaw on official business. Thousands of others came to watch the friars' Passion Plays.[6] And the beatification and canonisation of Father Kolbe led to ever more visitors during the communist era.

Between 1945 and 1953, about 30,000 people attended services at Niepokalanów each year. That number rose to 100,000 in 1966 and almost 200,000 in 1978 as the Polish people showed their support for Catholic institutions, and in protest against the state.

By 1990, when Ozaki visited Poland for the fourth time, the friary's prestige as a religious institution both domestically and internationally was undisputed. That year, some 500,000 pilgrims, including many from outside Poland, visited Niepokalanów.

Inside the grounds, the friars were buoyed by Mikhail Gorbachev's *glasnost* and *perestroika* policies in the Soviet Union and by the fall of the Berlin Wall in November 1989. The following month, as democratic forces gained momentum, Marxist references were removed from Poland's Constitution and the country's name was changed back to the Republic of Poland.

In a matter of months after Ozaki's visit, the communist president, Wojciech Jaruzelski, would be replaced by the Solidarity leader, Lech Wałęsa, following the first free presidential elections since 1926. By then, Poland's peaceful democratic transition was almost complete.

The friars, and the rest of Poland's thirty-eight million people, could finally breathe sighs of relief. Bonded by faith, Niepokalanów – and the Catholic Church at large – had largely held firm through fifty years of suppression and oppression.

Franciszek Gajowniczek, the man whose life Father Kolbe had saved, turned eighty-eight in November 1989. He suffered from cataracts and other minor illnesses yet was still extremely active for his age, travelling around Europe and the US to give speeches about life in Auschwitz.

Fearing that Gajowniczek didn't have long to live, Tōmei Ozaki visited him for a second time in August 1990. Acting as his interpreter was a Japanese-speaking Polish man, Konrad Wierzbicki. The two took a taxi from Kraków to Gajowniczek's home in the town of Brzeg. The cost, Ozaki noted, was 50% higher than on his first trip in 1983 because of inflation, but at least the Russian tanks that he'd witnessed then had vanished.

In 1988, Gajowniczek told Ozaki, he had faced death once again and had Kolbe to thank for his survival. Severely bitten by a dog at a conference in Zduńska Wola, Kolbe's birthplace, he underwent successful emergency surgery at a local hospital but fell into a coma after receiving an antibiotic injection.

While unconscious, he said, he awoke in a heavenly setting and saw an image of Kolbe in his Franciscan habit. 'Your wife is worried about you. Talk to her,' Kolbe told him. 'This is a happy place, without suffering, but you should not be here yet. Go back.' After hearing three claps of thunder, he stirred from his coma and soon felt well enough to continue giving his speeches.[7]

Ozaki visited Gajowniczek for a third time in 1993. By then, the Auschwitz survivor was extremely frail. As Ozaki prepared to leave, Gajowniczek took his right hand and looked him solemnly in the eyes. 'I want you to know,' he said, 'that I did not live my life with my own will. I feel that something supernatural gave me this life and kept me alive. I have treasured the fact that my life had meaning. You, Mr Ozaki, have also survived hardships. Let us aim to achieve peace in the world together.'[8]

Ozaki himself said he experienced that same mystical power. 'Time and again, on all my visits to Poland, I made sure I visited the Auschwitz bunker where Father Kolbe died. His spirit repeatedly called me back there,' Ozaki said. The bunker became almost like a sanctuary to Ozaki because he knew it contained 'an invisible light of humanity'.[9]

Gajowniczek died at his home in Brzeg on 13 March 1995, aged ninety-three. As soon as he heard the news, Ozaki knew that he needed to continue Gajowniczek's mission. He viewed his friend as a comrade who, like him, had witnessed utter evil and its opposite – undiluted love. It was imperative, he concluded, to tell as many people as he could about these contrasting sentiments.[10]

For several hundred years, beginning in the eighth century, storytellers at Japan's imperial court had memorised and recited the nation's history from a book called the *Kojiki*. These narrators were called *kataribe*, and they related folk stories, myths and heroic events as a way to pass on knowledge about the past and to aggrandise the emperor. This storytelling tradition diminished over the centuries, but it was revived by some atomic bomb survivors in Hiroshima

Ozaki as a kataribe in June 2018

and Nagasaki who were concerned that Japan's youngsters knew too little about their ordeal.[11]

Determined to spread Franciszek Gajowniczek's message far and wide, Tōmei Ozaki decided to become a kataribe and to tell his story to children and any adults who would listen. Ozaki chose to make his debut on 9 August 1995, the fiftieth anniversary of the bombing and of his mother's death, to a group of 660 primary school children in Nagasaki.

Half a century after the war's conclusion, a majority of Japan's population had no direct experience of the Second World War and children at Japanese schools were taught little about the nation's recent history.[12] As a kataribe, Ozaki decided, his focus would be on two topics he knew intimately – the bombing of Nagasaki and the bounties of Father Kolbe.

Ozaki had given numerous spontaneous speeches about Kolbe since becoming head of the St Maximilian Kolbe Memorial Museum in Nagasaki in 1991. He had returned to Nagasaki permanently that year after spending six years as headmaster of the MI primary and junior high schools in the mountains of Konagai. He lived at that complex, built by Father Mirochna, for more than twenty years, mostly recuperating from illness.

Located next to Mugenzai-no-Sono, the Kolbe museum housed a replica of Kolbe's cell, along with his original writings, his habit and hat, and the printing press that the Polish friars had used to publish their monthly Japanese-language magazine.

The role of the kataribe was more formal and official than Ozaki was used to, which made him nervous. To calm himself, he placed a photo of his mother, Wasa, in the chest pocket of his jacket before addressing his youthful audience.

Speaking in simple words that children would understand, Ozaki poured his soul into his talks. He spoke slowly and emotionally, as if reliving his experiences on the day of the bomb. He told the startled children how he had abandoned a young woman on a stretcher and shown no sympathy to the man who had bullied him. He told them that human weaknesses surface in extreme situations. But so too, he explained, do human strengths and valour, as exemplified by Father Kolbe.

As the children – and many of their teachers – squirmed or wept at his recollections, Ozaki ended his talk with a powerful anecdote. In 1955, while recuperating from his illness at the friary north of Nagasaki, he had confessed to a visiting priest that he had deserted a woman on a stretcher and left her to die. The priest shook his head. By chance, he said, he had recently met two sisters and the younger one had told him how she had been rescued while lying on a stretcher. She was alive and working in Nagasaki.

Desperate to apologise, Ozaki arranged to meet the woman, who was now twenty-seven years old. She told him that after Ozaki left her, an elderly man carried her on his back to the railway tracks and told her to wait for a rescue train. She was eventually hoisted aboard a train that took her and others to a temple. After six months of painful recuperation there, she was reunited with her family. A few years later, she married and had two children. She died, aged eighty-nine, in 2017.

Ozaki always ended his talks with this story of determination and deliverance. 'In my talks, I wanted to emphasise the values I had come to admire through my decades of suffering – the joy of living, the importance of unconditional love and the courage to fight against evil,' he told me. 'Together, these three can put us on the path to peace.'

Ozaki delivered his kataribe talks for twenty-four years until November 2019. In hundreds of speeches, his passion never flagged. Yet neither did the guilt he felt for his actions on 9 August 1945. To his dying day, his five-hour walk from the Nagasaki munitions tunnel to his pulverised home defined his life.

29. End of an Era

2008–2021 – *Nagasaki*

Tōmei Ozaki blog entry, 1 August 2014: I woke up in the middle of the night and thought about what kind of family I would like if I had another life. I have had a solitary existence, being born as an only child, losing my father to illness at age seven and my mother to the atomic bomb at age seventeen.

I would have loved to have been born into a family with many siblings, a household full of life and vigour, children playing and fighting with each other.

I did not make a family myself because I chose to become a Catholic brother. Although I have no regrets, I still dream of being part of a lively family.

Shortly after his eightieth birthday in 2008, Tōmei Ozaki began to write a blog. Like Father Maximilian Kolbe, the spiritual guide he'd never met, Ozaki strove to use the latest technology to reach as broad an audience as possible with his musings about life, love and Kolbe.[1]

In the 1920s and 30s, eschewing monastic tradition, Kolbe had communicated via magazines and the radio. Eight decades later, Ozaki's blog enabled him to write to, and read comments from, several hundred people who read Japanese around the world. It was a perfect form of communication for a man with limited mobility but unlimited energy.

Ozaki continued his talks as a kataribe, speaking about his atomic bomb experiences and about Father Kolbe. His audiences were mainly children and teenagers who were visiting the Kolbe museum or the Peace Museum in Nagasaki on school trips.

But in April 2009, just after his eighty-first birthday, Ozaki was diagnosed with bladder cancer. Despite a successful operation and treatment, he could feel that his body was deteriorating. Three years later, his remaining kidney stopped functioning. Sixty years earlier, one kidney had been removed when he was suffering from tuberculosis. An infection in the remaining one had been cured with the antibiotics that his 'true love', Sister Agnes, had obtained from a US military doctor in 1954.

Ozaki's Japanese doctor inserted a ureteric stent between the kidney and the bladder, but this needed replacing every four months through a surgical procedure in a hospital. During a general check-up, his doctor told him that his lungs weren't functioning properly and this made him more prone to bronchitis and pneumonia.

Bowing to the inevitable, Ozaki moved out of the Nagasaki friary in October 2014 to a care home for both Catholics and non-Catholics run by the Franciscans on the outskirts of the city. He stepped down as head of the Kolbe museum, aged eighty-seven. And for the first time in more than fifty years, Ozaki stopped wearing his Franciscan habit.

This was a traumatic psychological experience. 'I was very depressed when I took the habit off and just wore normal clothes. It felt as though I'd lost my entire identity,' he said. 'Being a brother helped me overcome many obstacles and kept me going. I had neither a job nor a family. All I had now was plenty of time and it seemed eternal.'

To make matters worse, one of his closest friends, Brother Roman, died a month after Ozaki moved to the care home, aged 100. Roman had been living in the care home for six years and was its oldest resident.

Brother Roman had come to Japan in 1934 to work alongside Kolbe in the last group of Polish friars to arrive in Nagasaki. He was one of the first Polish clergy that Ozaki met. In 1943, while recuperating from illness, Ozaki had visited the friary and helped Roman to clean stone statues that the brother had skilfully carved. A keen gardener, Roman became friendly with Masatoshi Asari in the 1980s and accompanied the cherry creator's trees to Niepokalanów and Strachocina. His death signalled the end of an era.

The author interviewing Ozaki in 2019

As Ozaki became accustomed to life at the care home, small things comforted him. He became more optimistic after seeing cosmos flowers in the fields outside his room, their red, orange and white blossoms glowing in the autumn sunshine. The flowers sent Ozaki a message, he said: 'Life is precious. Never despair.'

Sitting in the garden one day, a dragonfly flew gracefully by, its four wings whirring in the breeze. Like the dragonfly, Ozaki decided to let nature take its course and to live in the moment as though he was 'on a boat which drifts wherever the current takes it'.[2]

Ozaki decided to wear his Franciscan habit whenever he felt like it. He arose daily at 5 a.m., donned the black habit, walked to a church next to the care home and attended the 6 a.m. Mass. After the service, he usually removed the garment and began his daily routine. When I met him for the first time in 2019, he wore the habit specially to greet me.

With more time on his hands, Ozaki pondered his life in blog postings that frequently focused on the day that had transformed his life – 9 August 1945. All the suffering he had faced stemmed from that one day.

> Blog, 28 May 2016: I can never forget the day of the bomb. What a
> shock when I left the tunnel. The green mountains, the farmland,
> the houses which I saw that morning. All gone. A totally different
> scene – mountains on fire, burning houses, dead and injured people.
>
> I kept walking through the destruction, the fires and smoke, filled
> with fear. Such a horrendous scene should never recur.

And yet, he noted, in the years since the war, millions had died or
been injured in regional conflicts, suffering continued, and there
was little evidence that humankind would ever learn to stop fighting. Had civilisation learned nothing from its past? The painful
answer was no.

Perhaps the only positive was that nuclear weapons had not been
deployed since 1945 and that the memory of both the Hiroshima
and Nagasaki atrocities contributed to keeping the bombs at bay.
That's why I should continue my kataribe work as long as I possibly
can, he thought.

2018 began with a surprise. The Polish government awarded the
eighty-nine-year-old Ozaki the Bene Merito decoration for strength-
ening bonds between Poland and Japan. They cited his two books
about Kolbe, numerous articles in Catholic publications, and his
talks as a kataribe.[3]

At the awards ceremony on 29 January, held at the Peace Museum
in Nagasaki and attended by Japanese and Polish dignitaries, Ozaki
said: 'In the darkness of the war, Father Kolbe lit a light of hope in
the form of love. I want to continue telling young people that here
was a man who clung firmly to the principles of love and peace.'

> Blog, 29 January 2018: Maybe it's not bad living so long. But I want
> to stress that rather than me helping Poland, the Polish people
> helped me. They saved my life when I became an orphan.

On the seventy-fifth anniversary of the Nagasaki bombing, 9 August
2020, Japan's NHK television broadcast a one-hour programme
about Ozaki, titled *Kokoro no Jidai: Shūkyō, Jinsei* (The Age of the
Mind: Religion and Life). A TV crew had filmed Ozaki over six

months, focusing on his dedication towards Kolbe and desire for peace.

Ozaki wanted NHK to film him in the Lourdes garden above the Nagasaki friary. But because of his various illnesses and weakening muscles, he couldn't climb the 107 steps easily. Early one morning, he took a taxi from the care home to the friary. Knowing it would be the last time he would see the garden, he hauled himself up the steps and collapsed happily next to the grotto that Kolbe and the Polish friars had carved out of the cliffs eighty-eight years earlier.

As the coronavirus pandemic raged around the world, Ozaki was diagnosed in February 2021 with pancreatic cancer. He was just short of his ninety-third birthday. Because of his age, neither an operation nor chemotherapy treatment were possible. After several weeks in hospital, Ozaki was moved to a hospice.

The cancer progressed quickly. Strict pandemic rules meant few visitors were allowed to see him. Day by day, he became a little weaker. He lost his appetite. Any pain that he felt was tempered by drugs.

Yet through it all, Ozaki's mind was clear. Lying in bed at night, he thought about the trio of people who had taught him most about the significance of life.

He'd had many close friends and confidants in Korea, Japan and Poland, from his bachelor uncle, Fujinosuke, to Father Mirochna and many friars, including Brothers Roman and Zeno. But when he meditated on the meaning of unconditional love and hope, three people – his mother, his lover and his spiritual teacher – sprang to mind.

His mother, Wasa, had raised her only child to become a thoughtful Christian. He recalled the day when she first took him to Mugenzai-no-Sono, aged fifteen. 'It was thanks to my mother that I later joined the friary,' he told me. 'My mother gave her son to the Virgin Mary on that day.'

The woman he loved, Sister Agnes, had rescued him from depression and years of illness with her care and attention. 'Agnes saved my life in the mountains when I nearly died from tuberculosis. We were in love. But I have no regrets that we parted.'

His religious guide, Maximilian Kolbe, had provided him with a spiritual path to follow. 'For years I had been tormented by negative experiences on the day of the bomb. Father Kolbe taught me it was possible to overcome human shortcomings to achieve love,' he said.

As he prepared for the end, Ozaki continued to write his blog, focusing on the people he had known.

Blog, 12 February 2021 (viewed 1,435 times): There are many people I want to meet when I die. My father and my mother. My aunties and cousins. Also, Father Mirochna and Sister [Agnes]. And the Polish friars. Above all, Father Kolbe.

I would also like to meet again the young lady whom I abandoned on a stretcher on the day of the bomb. I feel that the deceased are somehow connected to the living. Likewise, the living are linked to the dead. That's what makes life so thrilling.

During Ozaki's final days, I talked to him frequently on the phone from England. He would always pick up his smartphone in his hospice bed and talk happily about what he was thinking at that very moment. 'I am observing how I am withering away,' he told me on 22 February 2021.

Ozaki took a breath. 'There is one thing that I have never talked about, Abe-san. Something that I have had buried deep inside me. I need to confess it before I am gone.'

I waited as he gathered his thoughts. 'When I was walking among the dead and the injured, I felt superior to everybody. Nobody was walking in the ruins besides me. Everyone was dead or had collapsed. Except me. I hate to say it, but true human nature surfaced that day.'

'I've talked so often about how I did not help people that day. The truth is, on top of all that, I had a "chosen" feeling. For all these years, I have never talked about this because I have felt so ashamed to feel that way. But now I need to lift this burden off my shoulders.'

The phone line purred. Seconds ticked by. I heard Ozaki choke. I didn't know what to say. He came back on the line. 'Soon I'm going to talk about all this publicly in a Zoom talk.'

On 25 February 2021, on a Zoom link set up by the hospice, a tearful Ozaki confessed to the staff at the Nagasaki Foundation for the Promotion of Peace about the 'elite and chosen' feelings he had felt on the day of the bomb. It was the last public talk Ozaki gave. A few days later, he told me how well the talk had gone, and how happy he was to have finally confessed.

On Monday, 1 March, I called Ozaki on his ninety-third birthday. More than 1,700 people viewed his blog that day. Still mulling over his life, he was eager to explain his views on suffering, repentance and love.

'Humans are inherently sinful and need to repent,' he said. 'Repentance is often manifested in some form of suffering, which God asks you to go through. In my case, I have undergone a lot of suffering, but not enough repentance. Now, I am going through the final stage of suffering.'

He continued: 'Father Kolbe also suffered. He suffered painfully while in Japan. He was very much a human being with shortcomings.'

'What do you mean?' I asked, surprised at this comment.

'Well,' he answered, 'other friars in Nagasaki told me that he complained a lot in Japan because he didn't have enough money to spread Christian teachings. But I think his suffering in Japan changed him and later elevated him from being an ordinary priest to becoming a saint.

'In the starvation chamber at Auschwitz, Father Kolbe made sure that he sent everybody to heaven first before he died. You don't normally see God but when you start showing deep love towards other people, you begin to see him. I think Father Kolbe saw the Virgin Mary in the starvation bunker and ascended to heaven with her. Faith steers you to a wondrous state.'

I spoke with Ozaki on 24 March for what turned out to be the last time. That day, he appeared relaxed and somewhat indulgent. He knew that I loved and wrote about cherry blossoms, but he'd never spoken to me about sakura before. That early spring day, he couldn't stop talking.

'I can see a cherry tree in the hospice garden, Abe-san. It's in full bloom,' he said as soon as he answered his phone. He talked about the blossoms he had seen as a child in the early 1930s while living with his parents in the southern Korean town of Chinhae. He still had a vivid memory of the Japanese and Koreans he had seen drinking, singing and dancing together at a hanami flower-viewing party.

'I used to see a single cherry tree from the friary in Nagasaki,' he said suddenly. 'It stood on a small hill, all alone. But it had a very strong presence. It was as though the tree was saying "I am here!" For some reason, I saw Father Kolbe in that tree. I felt that he was there.'

Ozaki reminded me that in the Lourdes garden above the Nagasaki friary, where Father Kolbe used to sit, there grew at least ten cherry trees. Two were the offspring of cherries planted in the garden of a primary school near the bomb's epicentre.

The school had been used as an administration office for a weapons factory during the war. On the day of the bomb, 138 people, mostly young women who had been mobilised to work there, were killed. The mother of one of the victims, fifteen-year-old Kayoko Hayashi, donated fifty cherry trees to the school after the war to commemorate her daughter and other victims. These became a symbol of peace, named 'Kayoko-zakura'. Six of these trees still blossom at the school. Others have been propagated and planted elsewhere, including at the friary.

I told Ozaki that I had been talking extensively to a cherry expert in Hokkaido called Masatoshi Asari, who had read his book on Father Kolbe and then decided to send cherry trees to Niepokalanów and to the Strachocina convent in the late 1980s. I mentioned that I was trying to track down what had happened to those trees to see how many were still blossoming.

'That's a wonderful story,' Ozaki replied. 'I recall seeing lots of small trees when I visited Niepokalanów. I hope some are still living and will continue to keep Father Kolbe's flame alive. The light he lit should never be allowed to fade.' Those were the final words he spoke to me.

Ozaki continued to write short entries in his blog.

12 April: I am sleeping all day.

13 April: I slept well last night. Bright morning.

14 April: Small happiness is everywhere. You just don't realise it because you are looking for a much bigger happiness.

15 April: I have no more strength to live. Please pray for me.

Ozaki passed away peacefully at 6.48 p.m. on 15 April 2021 after writing his last blog entry.

On 9 August 2021, the seventy-sixth anniversary of the Nagasaki bomb, the city's mayor, Tomihisa Taue, noted at the annual Nagasaki Peace Memorial Ceremony that an atomic bomb survivor, Tōmei Ozaki, had passed away earlier that year.

Speaking in front of dignitaries including Japanese Prime Minister Yoshihide Suga, the mayor quoted from an essay that Ozaki had written in 1999: 'Nuclear weapons are no ordinary bombs. In order not to repeat the nuclear disaster, I will keep saying "No, No, No" to nuclear weapons and will keep crying out for their abolition.

'We who have survived nuclear hell would not want to die before witnessing a peaceful world without such arms.'[4]

30. The Martyr and the Red Kimono

2018–2023 – Poland

In November 2018, when Masatoshi Asari told me that he had once sent hundreds of cherry trees to Poland, his memories of the event had long since faded. At my request, he patiently pored through decades of diaries, resurrecting his life day-by-day as he recalled cherished friends – and cherished cherries – that had meant most to him.

His journey down memory lane revealed his 'peace initiatives' of the 1980s and 90s, when he had sent trees to North Korea, China, England and elsewhere to atone for Japan's wartime atrocities. However, the Poland initiative, which Asari called 'the project of my life', was different. It commemorated Father Kolbe, the martyr who had given up his life for another, and the Polish people who had resisted foreign oppressors for centuries.

Asari, then aged eighty-seven, painstakingly copied out his diaries for me. Unlike Kolbe and Ozaki, Asari was a technophobe. He disdained computers, didn't own a mobile phone and knew nothing about social media. Using a ballpoint pen, he re-wrote years of diary entries and sent me swathes of paper in thick envelopes.

In all, his diaries showed, Asari had dispatched 420 cherry trees of various types to Poland: twenty to Niepokalanów in October 1987, 360 more in May 1988, and forty trees to the Strachocina convent in September 1989. It was quite an achievement and yet virtually no one knew anything about it.

As far as Asari was concerned, these projects were complete. Like most Japanese, who don't speak another language, Asari thought of his 'foreign' projects as out of sight, though not out of mind. The cherries lived on in his imagination even though he had no way of finding out what had happened to them. He thought incorrectly that some had found their way to Auschwitz.

The Miyama-zakura tree with Sister Agata and Sister Mediatrix

In one envelope from Hokkaido, Asari enclosed three colour photographs to prove that the cherries had been planted. One, taken in 1988, showed two friars – Brother Roman Kwiecień and Father Fabian Stefan Piętka, the head of Niepokalanów – standing amid rows of planted trees. The second pictured Brother Roman and Brother Maciej Szymkowski, who was in charge of the institution's gardens. A third man in the snap, Brother Francisco Yasugorō Nakamura from Nagasaki, was visiting Niepokalanów at the time.

To Asari, the photos appeared to show that the trees were in good hands, although he had heard little more about them since June 1989 when he'd been informed that the cold-resistant Chishima-zakura had blossomed beautifully in the spring. He'd grown these trees from seeds he had collected with his brother, Shigeru, near the peak of a Hokkaido mountain.

Some four years later, in May 1993, Asari unexpectedly received a letter and photograph from the Strachocina convent. The photo showed a small tree bearing white blossoms, surrounded by five smiling nuns.

The letter said simply: 'Your tree has blossomed!' In his diary, Asari noted how delighted he was to know that at least one of his trees – out of forty that he had sent to the convent – was growing.

After that, nothing. The cherry trees appeared to have fallen into an historical black hole, their existence forgotten. That, of course, is the fate of virtually all living things. But as I read Asari's diaries from three decades earlier and thought about his passion for the 'Kolbe cherries', I wanted to learn their fate.

The Polish project was the embodiment of everything Asari believed in: his desire for peace and his belief in the goodness of humanity. Had all the trees, their blossoms and their leaves – the result of years of dedication – simply died or decayed and become mulch? I told Asari that I was determined to find out.

He wasn't optimistic. Haruko Fujishima, who had first proposed sending trees to Poland, and Brother Roman, who had taken them, had both died. I called the Polish embassy in Tokyo because its last communist-era ambassador, Ryszard Frąckiewicz, had also been on the plane with the trees. The embassy had no documents about events that had taken place before 1990.

I had more luck with Niepokalanów, where a friar connected me on the phone with an Italian American woman from Connecticut, Annamaria Mix. A devout Catholic and follower of Father Kolbe, she had worked in the archives there since 1997 and often liaised with non-Polish-speakers inquiring about Kolbe.

After hearing my lament, Annamaria vowed to 'help solve this great cherry mystery'. In the archives, she found a note dated 11 May 1988 saying that Brother Roman had arrived from Japan, and he had 'brought fourteen cherry bushes that Brother Maciej planted near the beekeeping hives'. The current hive keeper, Brother Stefan, confirmed that ten trees were still growing there. Finally, a breakthrough.

My joy was short-lived. Looking at old photos of the flowering trees, UK cherry expert Chris Sanders identified them as apple blossoms, not cherries. Two other elderly friars told Annamaria that fourteen cherry trees brought by Brother Roman had withered and died. No one knew what had happened to the original twenty trees or the other 346 saplings.

I ran into a similar dead end after contacting nuns in Strachocina, where Asari had sent his third batch of trees in 1989. The Strachocina convent has close contact with four other convents in Poland, as well as with nuns at the Japanese convent north of Nagasaki set up by Father Mirochna. The Japanese convent is the headquarters of Militia Immaculatae convents around the world. There are five branches in Poland and one in South Korea.

The sixteen nuns who lived at Strachocina knew nothing about events that had taken place more than thirty years earlier. But by chance, the former Mother Superior of the Nagasaki convent, Sister Kazuko Nishimura, had lived at Strachocina in the late 1980s as a young nun. Among her few possessions were photographs that showed Brother Roman and Father Józef Niżnik, the parish priest of the Strachocina church, planting cherry trees in the convent garden.

Sister Nishimura also found a photo of a cherry tree in blossom, with five beaming nuns gathered around it. It was the same photo that Asari had received in 1993.

The photos were heart warming. But I was still no closer to discovering whether any of the cherry trees at Niepokalanów or Strachocina were still living. It was time to find out for myself.

The global coronavirus pandemic put paid to my plans to visit Poland in 2020. So it wasn't until September 2021 that I finally arrived at Niepokalanów after an hour-long ride on a packed commuter train from Warsaw. The friary is just a five-minute walk from Teresin-Niepokalanów station.

Niepokalanów's most impressive feature is its white basilica, a spotless shrine to Kolbe and the Virgin Mary that can hold up to 5,000 people. Every year, thousands of pilgrims and tourists take guided tours of the friary that include the St Maximilian Kolbe Museum, the Franciscan Firefighter Museum and a sanctuary chapel. The friary still publishes an impressive array of magazines, books and brochures, and Radio Niepokalanów broadcasts programmes on two channels and over the internet.

Yet despite this activity, Niepokalanów's finest days are clearly behind it. In late 2022, only 113 men – thirty-nine priests and seventy-four friars – were living within its cloisters, compared with almost

800 at its peak in the late 1930s. At that time, just before the war, demand for MI's publications was so great that Father Kolbe had planned to set up an airport to distribute almost sixty million magazines a year.

Niepokalanów suffers from the same social crises that afflict Catholicism throughout Poland and much of the world. About ninety per cent of Poland's thirty-eight million population are registered Catholics, but there's been a 'devastating decline' in religious practices among the young since the 1990s.[1] Consumerism, corruption, lack of leadership and entrenched views on abortion and LGBTQ rights have harmed the Church's credibility. Fewer Poles attend church, still fewer view the priesthood as a path in life.

It's a similar situation in Japan, where the number of Catholics had fallen to just 0.34 per cent of the nation's 126 million population by 2021 – one Catholic for every 300 people. While the highest percentage of lay Catholics – 4.4 per cent – lived in Nagasaki, the facility built by Kolbe there attracted ever-fewer friars.[2]

My guide, Annamaria, confirmed the location in the photos where Brother Roman and others had planted Asari's trees in the late 1980s. Sadly, there were no signs of any cherries. Another blind alley. Next stop, Strachocina.

At the Strachocina convent, I had been told, no one spoke English, let alone Japanese. But from his care home in Nagasaki, Tōmei Ozaki had put me in contact with a Japanese-speaking Polish nun whom he knew well. She had lived in the Konagai convent for thirty-one years and always met Ozaki at the convent on the anniversary of the death of Sister Agnes, the Japanese nun he had loved.[3]

Sister Mediatrix, who turned seventy-one in 2023, had worked as an architect in the city of Szczecin before deciding to become a nun. During Pope John Paul II's visit to Niepokalanów in 1979, she had met Father Mirochna, the Polish head of the Nagasaki friary who had built the Militia Immaculatae convent. He'd invited her to go to Japan, where she learned the language and dedicated her life to helping children from broken families and the severely disabled. Rarely had I met a more positive person.

These days, Sister Mediatrix tends to the elderly and sick at a nursing home close to Rzeszów International Airport in southeast Poland. Sister Mediatrix and a fellow nun picked me up at the airport and drove for two hours along country roads to the village of Strachocina, close to the southern border with Ukraine.

Only then did the final pieces of the 'Kolbe cherry' jigsaw start to fit into place. Anxious to find any living trees, I walked around the convent gardens with Sister Mediatrix and other black-veiled nuns, none of whom knew what a Japanese cherry tree looked like.

There were scores of mature trees in the convent grounds but none that resembled a cherry. It was disheartening. But on a road next to the convent's guest house, I noticed a triple-trunked tree, about twice my height, whose spindly branches bore yellowish leaves. It looked out of place among the evergreens. Convincing myself that it was a cherry, I removed several leaves and placed them carefully in an envelope.

Then, we walked over to the convent's Japanese garden. There, another tree came to my attention. It was perhaps nine feet tall. Its multiple trunks bore ringed bark, often a sign of a cherry tree, and its branches rose into the sky in the shape of a vase. It was another sakura, I thought. I couldn't be sure because a typical cherry tree planted thirty years earlier should have been much taller and thick-trunked. Another set of leaves in an envelope.

Buoyed by these discoveries, Sister Mediatrix led me to an iron fence in front of the St Catherine of Alexandria church, adjoining the convent grounds. Only then did I know for sure that I'd found one of Masatoshi Asari's creations.

About sixteen feet tall, its branches spread in all directions and its large, dark-green leaves seemed to possess a spirit of confidence, as if to say, 'I belong here. You can never destroy me.' I placed several leaves into a third envelope.

The following morning, with Sister Mediatrix as an interpreter, I sat down with Father Józef Niżnik, who had been Strachocina's parish priest since 1984 and was one of the few living people who knew about Asari's cherries first-hand.

Over coffee and cakes, Father Niżnik recalled that Brother Roman and Sister Iida, a nun from the Konagai convent, brought forty cherry trees from Japan in September 1989 for the opening ceremony of Poland's first MI convent. Earlier plans to build a convent had been stymied by the communist regime.

'We were delighted to receive cherry trees from Japan at the opening because the convent had such close ties with Nagasaki,' he told me. 'The blossoms epitomised the friendly relationship between the two countries based on Father Kolbe's life, and they also celebrated Poland's new start as an independent nation.'

Father Niżnik, Brother Roman, several nuns and village volunteers had planted the trees in the hard soil near the vicarage and the church. But it wasn't long before some trees started dying because they couldn't withstand Poland's freezing winters.

In 2001, Father Niżnik continued, Militia Immaculatae leaders decided to build a Japanese garden at Strachocina to commemorate Kolbe and his links to Japan. A plan to build such a garden at Niepokalanów had earlier been voted down.

After the garden was completed, Father Niżnik moved some of the remaining cherry trees there. But every year, fewer blossoms bloomed on ever-fewer trees. Only the tree that grew in front of the church appeared to be totally healthy. Its crimson flowers blossomed every May, and villagers often snapped photos of themselves underneath the blooms, just as hanami-lovers did in Japan.

After our discussion, Sister Mediatrix led me towards a square wooden gazebo.

And there she stood, upon a circular pedestal. The Virgin Mary in a red kimono, her hands raised in the universal gesture of gratitude, greeting and reverence. A halo shone above her long, jet-black hair. Beneath the pink cherry blossoms on the kimono, green and red leaves adorned her *furisode* sleeves.

While researching Father Kolbe and the cherries, I had heard about this statue and seen her photo on a website. But I wasn't prepared for the effect she had on me – a Japanese madonna far from home.

I looked up at her dark brown eyes. I felt strange kindred feelings towards this Japanese Virgin Mary, a statue conceived in Japan during Poland's political and social turmoil. She stared directly ahead, surveying the trees and the convent in front of her. At the same time, her eyes seemingly peered far into the distance, across continents, across time and space, across humanity. No one – and nothing – escaped her gaze.

In Polish, the statue was called 'Matka Boska Japońska' (Our Lady of Japan), and one of the nuns explained that for them she symbolised Kolbe's desire for world peace. How she'd ended up in Strachocina was an unlikely story in itself, which had taken almost twenty years to unfold.

In 1982, during the communist era, the Polish Academy of Sciences invited a professor of structural engineering at Tottori University in western Japan to Poland for two weeks of seminars. Nobuyoshi Takaoka, a bridge specialist, happened to be a member of the Japanese Militia Immaculatae and had become acquainted with the Polish friars in Nagasaki.

As an admirer of Father Kolbe, Takaoka proposed making a statue of a Japanese Virgin Mary to send to Niepokalanów. He raised money for the statue in Japan and commissioned it from a sculptor in Nagasaki.

Sadly, Takaoka died of cancer in 1990, aged fifty-four. But members of MI in Japan continued the project, and the sculptor completed the statue. Eleven years after Takaoka's death, the brothers in Nagasaki arranged for the statue to be sent by plane to Poland. She was placed in the convent ground on 1 September 2001, the sixty-second anniversary of Germany's invasion of Poland.

On my final evening in Strachocina, the Polish nuns cooked me a feast of soup, fish and home-grown vegetables. After the meal, the nuns brought out some photos of the trees in blossom, taken in the spring. I sat next to the head of the Polish MI convents, Sister Klara Machulska, and explained in detail how and why Asari had sent trees to Niepokalanów and Strachocina.

Sister Klara listened quietly, frequently near tears, as Sister Mediatrix translated. 'I had no idea of this history,' she said. 'It's our responsibility and delight to cherish and treasure the cherries from now on.'

After returning to England, I called Asari to tell him about my visits to Niepokalanów and Strachocina. There was no sign, I told him, of the 380 trees that he'd sent to the friary thirty years earlier.

As for the forty cherries he'd sent to the convent, I had better news. I was convinced that at least one tree had survived, and was cautiously confident that two other smaller trees were from Hokkaido. A fourth tree, I told him, had been struck by lightning in 2019 and died. I put the leaves from the three trees into an airmail letter and awaited his verdict.

A week later, I called Asari. As usual, his daughter, Setsuko, who lives with her parents, answered the phone. She screamed at her father to come quickly to talk to 'Abe-san from England'. Asari was excited. 'These are definitely leaves from the trees I sent,' he shouted down the phone. 'How wonderful. One is a Miyama-zakura, and a second is a Chishima-zakura. Wild mountain cherries. I chose both of these because I thought they would be able to withstand the severe cold in Poland.'

The Chishima-zakura, or Kurile cherry, was especially close to Asari's heart. It was the tree that he had found atop Mount Daisengen in 1956 and which he credited with giving him strength and hope after years of illness. Indeed, it was the discovery of the Chishima-zakura that had led him to devote his life to cherry blossoms. The sakura goddess who had protected Asari in the 1950s in Japan was now guarding Father Kolbe and the Polish people in a remote European outpost in the 2020s.

But what about the other leaves I sent you, the dark-green ones, I asked? I could imagine Asari smiling broadly as he answered. 'My creation,' he said proudly. ' "Beni-yutaka".'

Among the most famous of Asari's creations, the umbrella-shaped 'Beni-yutaka' tree produces large, fragrant semi-double blossoms. In the autumn, its leaves turn red. This was the mature tree that now graced the front of the church in Strachocina. There could be no doubt.

I offered Asari my congratulations. He was silent for a few seconds. Then he said: 'Frankly, I never dreamt that anyone would discover the cherries' fate. Of course, I'm disappointed that the bulk of the trees I sent to Poland didn't live. But I have to look at the positive side: Three trees did survive. That is amazing. Father Kolbe must have protected them. I'm delighted about that!'

Epilogue

July 2023 – Strachocina

Seventeen miles due east of Rzeszów airport in southeast Poland, the Franciscan Sisters of the Militia Immaculatae work around the clock caring for the aged and infirm at a secluded nursing home in the village of Kosina. But in February 2022, the solitude of their convent, where Sister Mediatrix has lived since 2017, was shattered by the turmoil of war.

Russian President Vladimir Putin's invasion of Ukraine placed Poland in the international spotlight as the US and its NATO allies scrambled to help Ukraine with weapons, medical aid and supplies. Inside the Kosina home, the nuns' softly spoken prayers were frequently drowned out by the noise of US, Canadian and UK military cargo planes landing and taking off from the Rzeszów airport.

In an unprecedented operation, NATO used the airport, about sixty miles west of the Ukrainian border, as the staging post for tons of equipment. From there, the goods were trucked over land into Ukraine to help the embattled country fight Putin's invaders. It was from there that US President Joe Biden made his first visit to Ukraine in February 2023.

Inside Ukraine, the city of Lviv, where Maximilian Kolbe had studied at a minor seminary more than 110 years earlier, became a gathering place for Ukrainians departing for Poland, forty miles to the west. Most Poles, whose families had suffered for centuries as part of Tsarist Russia and then as a Soviet satellite state, empathised with Ukraine.

Two hours south of Rzeszów, in the village of Strachocina, where Masatoshi Asari's three surviving cherry trees grow, the sixteen nuns at the remote convent suddenly found themselves in the eye of a storm after the Russian aggression. For weeks, they carried donated food, clothes, medicine and money to a makeshift refugee centre in Przemyśl, a town on the Polish side of the border, about fifty miles northeast of Strachocina. Tens of thousands of Ukrainians, mostly women and children, had crossed the border there, en route to cities in Poland, Germany, France, the UK and elsewhere.

By mid-2023, more than a million Ukrainians had settled in Poland, though Strachocina itself was relatively quiet again, aside from an increasing number of pilgrims who arrived at the St Catherine of Alexandria church to pray for an end to the hostilities.

Within the convent, Father Kolbe's portrait hung in countless corridors and rooms, just as it does at Niepokalanów and at Catholic institutions throughout the world.

Outside, behind the guest house, the statue of the Virgin Mary, sporting her sakura-studded kimono, stood tall and serene. But as I reflected on her presence and on the unexpected exodus to Poland of fearful Ukrainian women and children, I couldn't help but feel anxious about the future of our planet.

Putin's war continued unabated. People on both sides of the conflict were dying daily in large numbers. Putin's threats to use nuclear weapons against the people of Ukraine no longer seemed like empty warnings. Kolbe's high hopes for the future of humanity, embraced by Tōmei Ozaki and Masatoshi Asari, were clearly in retreat.

It wasn't just the Ukraine war. Around the world, it seemed more than likely that our collective failure to halt and resolve conflicts would mean that tens of thousands of people were destined to die in the decades ahead. This made me feel physically sick.

And then there were the cherries, and all that they represented. I had been dismayed that my journey to find the 420 trees that Asari had lovingly sent to Poland in 1988 and 1989 had concluded with a grand total of only three living plants. In July 2023, I was pleased to discover, that trinity of trees was thriving. The 'Beni-yutaka' cherry stood firm in front of the church. The wild cherries – Miyama-zakura and Chishima-zakura – were taller and more robust than when I'd visited two years earlier. The nuns had laid protective pebbles around the trees' roots and their blossoms had been unusually abundant and colourful in the spring of 2023.

The statue of the Virgin Mary at Strachocina

Still, I wondered, should I, like Asari, be applauding this trio, or lamenting the 417 that had perished? Was it a hollow victory to salute the survivors?

Asari had found disease-free trees resistant to the harsh Polish climate. He'd given clear instructions about how to care for them. But for whatever reason – lack of knowledge, lack of water, lack of interest, climate change – ninety-nine per cent of the Hokkaido trees had died.

Poland's political tumult in the late 1980s undoubtedly played a part in their demise. The trees arrived at Niepokalanów and Strachocina at a time when everyone in Poland, friars and nuns included, was trying to shift from the strictures of communism to a democratic society. People were simply too busy building their new lives to care much for cherry trees.

To me, however, the fragility of the cherries seemed to reflect the fragility of our planet. It was a discouraging reality. But one day, I received a poetic message from Annamaria Mix, the archivist at Niepokalanów, that brightened my mood. Annamaria, who had shared my cherry-hunting passion, noted that although the trees no longer thrived at the friary, they still lived.

'After quietly sleeping beneath the blanket of time, Mr Asari's

Asari and the author at the Matsumae cherry park in May 2023

colourful scented blossoms are sending messages of truth, peace and joy throughout the world,' she wrote to me. 'Please thank him. His saplings, many of which seem to have withered in the Polish winter, will sing every spring, even if only in our minds.'

And then I realised: it didn't matter that most of the cherries had died. That was the way of all life. It mattered only that they had lived, many for just a few months or years, spreading happiness to those who sowed them, watered them, watched them grow and swooned over their beauty.

The fact that they had been created by Asari, witnessed by Ozaki and commemorated Kolbe was almost beside the point. All the trees had carried the message of the three men who had lived through the hell of war and in one case been destroyed by it. That message was clear: Stop Killing.

I thought how remarkable it was that two men living on opposite sides of Japan with little in common should have ended up honouring Kolbe – and in such different ways. One by visiting his Auschwitz starvation bunker ten times and dedicating his life to the saint. The other by sending cherry trees to Poland.

To the nuns, the Japanese garden at Strachocina was mainly a way of giving thanks to one special person: Father Kolbe. I saw it differently. To me, the garden was a secret gathering place for everyone that Kolbe, Ozaki and Asari cherished, a cast of characters spanning 130 years, from their mothers – Maria, Wasa and Chie – and their families to the friars, nuns and friends who had shaped their lives.

In one corner of the garden, I saw Brother Zeno, Father Mirochna and Doctor Takashi Nagai talking with Kolbe about patriotism, Christianity, the publishing industry and Kolbe's appalling health. Nearby, I spied St Thérèse of Lisieux admiring some roses. In another corner, I saw Sister Agnes grasp Ozaki's hand as Franciszek Gajowniczek explained to him how Kolbe had taken his place at Auschwitz.

Among the evergreens, I saw Kazuo Takemoto, the Korean runaway, describing to Asari's university professor, Tōru Ukita, how he'd escaped from Hokkaido during the war. Lounging on the grass, I saw George Zabelka, the US military chaplain at Tinian Island, and British Group Captain Leonard Cheshire deep in discussion about the impact of the Nagasaki bomb on their lives.

I heard laughter as I watched the still-vibrant ninety-two-year-old Asari explain to his Matsumae Sakura Children's Club how to gather seeds from tall cherry trees. I heard singing as choirs from schools bearing Father Kolbe's name in Canada, the UK and the US, among other countries, sang hymns and Christmas carols. I heard silence – precious silence – as visitors prayed for peace in Marytown, a national shrine to Kolbe in Libertyville, Illinois, and at Kolbe missions in Argentina, Brazil, Italy and elsewhere.[1]

The departed cherry trees at Niepokalanów and Strachocina – of multiple varieties and species, ages, shapes and colours – represented everyone who had died in Auschwitz, in Nagasaki, in countless cities, towns and villages, in conflicts through the ages.

The living trees, few in number but strong in spirit, represented hope that future generations would somehow learn to live without war. They embodied the indefatigable truth that wars don't just destroy people and places. They destroy dignity, integrity and humanity.

Maximilian Kolbe, a true Polish patriot and inspirational religious leader, had defied his totalitarian aggressors by giving up his life for a fellow man.

Tōmei Ozaki had used his experiences as an atomic bomb survivor to highlight the pain of war and the moral bankruptcy of using nuclear weapons.

Masatoshi Asari had spread the gospel of peace in the only way he knew how – by creating cherry trees with stunning blossoms that left admirers flushed with the wonders of life.

What more could I do? It was a question that still haunted me as I thought about the kimono-clad statue at the convent and wondered how many more years she'd gaze at the cherry trees from Japan, and far beyond.

List of Illustrations

Bibliography

Abe, Naoko, *'Cherry' Ingram: The Englishman Who Saved Japan's Blossoms* (London: Vintage Press, 2020)

Akizuki, Tatsuichirō, *A Memoir of the Nagasaki Atomic Bomb* (Tokyo: Nihon Book Ace, 2010)

Akizuki, Tatsuichirō, *Nagasaki Genbaku-ki* (Nagasaki Atomic Bomb Record) (Tokyo: Heiwa Bunko, 2010). Akizuki's book was originally published by Kōbun-dō in 1966.

Asari, Masatoshi, *Oshiete Kudasai, Hakodate Kūshū o* (Please Tell Me About the Hakodate Air Raids) (Hakodate: Genyō-sha, 1991)

Asari, Masatoshi, *Shōgen – Nihon Saigo no Gakudō Shūdan Sokai* (Testimonies – Japan's Last Children's Group Evacuation) (Hakodate: Genyō-sha, 1994)

Asari, Masatoshi and Noro, Kiichi, *Sakura* (Kyoto: Seisei-sha, 2008)

Brackman, Arnold C., *The Other Nuremberg: The Untold Story of the Tokyo War Crimes Trials* (London: Fontana Paperbacks, 1990)

Cheshire, Leonard, *The Nuclear Dilemma, a Moral Study* (Abbots Langley, Herts: Catholic Information Services, 1983)

Cheshire, Leonard, *The Light of Many Suns: The Meaning of the Bomb* (London: Methuen, 1985)

Chiba, Shigeki, *Korube Shinpu: Tomo no Tame ni Sasageta Inochi* (Father Kolbe: a Life Sacrificed for a Friend) (Tokyo: Joshi Paulo-kai, 1982)

Chinnock, Frank W., *Nagasaki: The Forgotten Bomb* (London: George Allen & Unwin Ltd., 1970)

Deepe Keever, Beverly Ann, *News Zero: The New York Times and the Bomb* (Monroe, Maine: Common Courage Press, 2004)

Dewar, Diana, *Saint of Auschwitz* (London: Darton, Longman & Todd Ltd., 1982)

Diehl, Chad R., *Resurrecting Nagasaki: Reconstruction and the Formation of Atomic Narratives* (Ithaca, New York: Cornell University Press, 2018)

Doak, Kevin M., 'Hiroshima Rages, Nagasaki Prays', in *When the Tsunami Came to Shore*, ed. Roy Starrs (Leiden: Brill, 2014)

Dower, John, *Embracing Defeat: Japan in the Aftermath of World War II* (London: Penguin, 1999)

Edami, Shizuki, *Kagirinai Ai – Zeno no Shōgai* (Endless Love – Zeno's Life) (Tokyo: Shimizu Kōbundō, 1980)

Endō, Shūsaku, *Onna no Isshō – Sachiko no Baai* (Sachiko – A Novel) (Tokyo: Shinchō-sha, 1986)

Fairweather, Jack, *The Volunteer: The True Story of the Resistance Hero Who Infiltrated Auschwitz* (London: W. H. Allen & Co., 2019)

Foster, Claude R., *Mary's Knight: The Mission and Martyrdom of Saint Maksymilian Maria Kolbe* (West Chester, Pennsylvania: West Chester University Press, 2002 and 2013)

Frankl, Victor E., *Man's Search for Meaning* (London: Rider, 2011)

Frossard, André, *Forget Not Love* (San Francisco: Ignatius Press, 1991)

Glynn, Paul, *The Smile of a Ragpicker: The Life of Satoko Kitahara* (Hunters Hill, NSW: Marist Fathers Books, 1992)

Glynn, Paul, *A Song for Nagasaki: The Story of Takashi Nagai: Scientist, Convert, and Survivor of the Atomic Bomb* (San Francisco: Ignatius Press, 2009)

Green, Michael J., *Japan's Reluctant Realism: Foreign Policy Challenges in an Era of Uncertain Power* (New York: Palgrave, 2001)

Handō, Kazutoshi, *Shōwa-shi* (History of Shōwa) (Tokyo: Heibon-sha, 2004)

Handō, Kazutoshi, Katō, Yōko, and Hosakas, Masayasu, *Taiheiyō Sensō e no Michi* (The Road to the Pacific War) (Tokyo: NHK Shuppan, 2021)

Harder, Robert O., *The Three Musketeers of the Army Air Forces. From Hitler's Fortress to Hiroshima and Nagasaki* (Annapolis, Maryland: Naval Institute Press, 2015)

Heibon-sha Editorial Department, *Dokyumento – Shōwa Sesō-shi* (Document – Social Conditions of Shōwa Period) (Tokyo: Heibon-sha, 1976)

His Majesty's Stationery Office, *The Effects of the Atomic Bombs at Hiroshima and Nagasaki, Report of the British Mission to Japan* (London: His Majesty's Stationery Office, 1946)

Ishitobi, Jin, *Kaze no Shisha Zeno* (Zeno, A Messenger of the Wind) (Tokyo: Shizen-shoku Tsūshin-sha, 1998)

Katō, Yōko, *Manshū-Jihen Kara Nicchū Senstō e* (From the Manchurian Incident to the Second Sino-Japanese War) (Tokyo: Iwanami Shoten, 2007)

Katō, Yōko, *Tomerarenakatta Sensō* (The War Which Could Not be Stopped) (Tokyo: NHK Shuppan, 2011)

Kawashimo, Masaru, *Korube* (Kolbe) (Tokyo: Shimizu-Shoin, 1993)

Kōdan-sha (publisher), *Shōwa: Niman-nichi no Zen-kiroku* (Shōwa: The Entire Record of 20,000 Days) (Tokyo: Kōdan-sha, 1989)

Kolbe, St Maximilian, *The Writings of Fr. Maximilian Kolbe (Pisma o. Maksymiliana M. Kolbego)* (Niepokalanów: Niepokalanów Publications, 1970). Seven volumes.

Koskodan, Kenneth K., *No Greater Ally* (Oxford: Osprey Publishing, 2009)

Kuwabara, Kazutoshi, *Tenshi no Zeno-san* (The Angel Zeno) (Nagasaki: Seibo-no-Kishi sha, 2002)

Lukas, Richard C., *The Forgotten Holocaust: The Poles Under German Occupation 1939–1944* (New York: Hippocrene Books, 1990)

Matsui, Tōru, *Zeno Shinu Hima Nai* (Zeno Has No Time to Die) (Tokyo: Shunjū-sha, 1998)

Matsumoto, Teruo, *Sensō to Senryō* (War and Occupation) (Tokyo: Iwanami, 1989)

Matsumoto, Teruo and Theiss, Wiesław, *Shiberia Koji* (Siberian Children) (Warsaw: Wydawnictwo Sejmowe, 2018)

McClelland, Gwyn, *Dangerous Memory in Nagasaki* (London: Routledge, 2020)

Merklein, Iwona, *Brat Zeno Żebrowski. Polski Misjonarz w Japońskich Mediach* (Warsaw: Wydawnictwo Trio; Oblicza Japonii series, 2006)

Miyazaki, Kentarō, *Kakure Kirishitan* (Hidden Christians) (Tokyo: Kadokawa, 2018)

Miyazaki, Kentarō, *Senpuku Kirishitan wa Nani o Shinjite Itanoka* (What Did the Hidden Christians Believe?) (Tokyo: Kadokawa, 2018)

Modras, Ronald, *The Catholic Church and Antisemitism: Poland, 1933–1939* (New York: Routledge, 1994)

Mori, Reiko, *Gotō Kuzure* (Crackdown in the Gotō Islands) (Tokyo: Ribun Shuppan, 2019)

Nagai, Takashi, *Nagasaki no Kane* (The Bells of Nagasaki) (Tokyo: Hibiya Shuppan-sha, 1946)

Nagai, Takashi, *Itoshi-go yo* (My Precious Children) (Tokyo: San Paulo, 2014; reprint of the 1949 original)

Nagata, Tomitomo, *Ezo Kirishitan* (Ezo's Christians) (Tokyo: Kōdan-sha, 1972)

Nagai, Takashi, *Kono Ko o Nokoshite* (Leaving These Children Behind) (Tokyo: San Paulo, 1995)

OFM Conventual, *Patavina seu Cracovien. Beatificationis et Canonizationis ven. Servi Dei Maximiliani Mariae Kolbe, Sacerdotis Ordinis Fratrum Minorum Conventualium* (Patavina or Krakow. Beatification and Canonization of the Servant of God Maximilian M. Kolbe, Professed Saint of the Order of Friars Minor Conventual) (Rome: OFM Conventual, 1965)

Okagami, Riho, *Chūō no Fushichō* (The Phoenix in Central Europe) (Tokyo: Demado-sha, 2019)

Oku, Takenori, *Rondan no Sengo-shi* (A History of Post-war World of Criticism) (Tokyo: Heibon-sha, 2018)

Onodera, Yuriko, *Baruto-kai no Hotori nite* (By the Baltic Sea) (Tokyo: Kyōdō Tsūshin-sha, 1985)

Ozaki, Tōmei, *Nagasaki no Korube Shinpu* (Father Kolbe in Nagasaki) (Nagasaki: Seibo-no-Kishi sha, 1983, republished 2010)

Ozaki, Tōmei, *Migawari no Ai* (Love as Sacrifice) (Nagasaki: Seibo-no-Kishi sha, 1994)

Ozaki, Tōmei, *Jūnana-sai no Natsu* (His Seventeenth Summer) (Nagasaki: Seibo-no-Kishi sha, 1996)

Ozaki, Tōmei, *Haru Itsumademo* (Spring Forever) (Nagasaki: Seibo-no-Kishi sha, 1998)

Ozaki, Tōmei, *Shinkō no Deai-tabi* (Encounters with Faith) (Nagasaki: Seibo-no-Kishi sha, 2006)

Ozaki, Tōmei, *Shōwa ni Ikita Shūdōshi Tachi* (The Friars Who Lived Through the Shōwa Era) (Nagasaki: 2019)

Pałasz-Rutkowaska, Ewa, ed., *In Search of Polish Graves in Japan* (Warsaw: Ministry of Culture and National Heritage, 2010)

Pałasz-Rutkowaska, Eva and Romer, Andrzey Tadeusz, translated into Japanese by Shiba, Riko, *Nihon- Pōrando Kankei-shi* (History of Japan–Poland Relations) (Tokyo: Sairyū-sha, 2019)

Pensiek, Sergius, *Koete kita Michi* (The Roads I Crossed) (Nagasaki: Seibo-no-Kishi sha, 1996)

Pensiek, Sergius, *Korube Shinpu sama no Omoide* (Memories of Father Kolbe) (Nagasaki: Seibo-no-Kishi sha, 2016)

POW Research Network Japan: http://www.powresearch.jp/

Ruoff, Kenneth J., *The People's Emperor* (Cambridge, Massachusetts: Harvard University Asia Center, 2002)

Shioura, Shintarō, *Yaketa Rozario* (Burnt Rosary) (Nagasaki: Seibo-no-Kishi sha, 2009)

Shirabe, Raisuke and Yoshizawa, Yasuo, *Ishi no Shōgen – Nagasaki Genbaku Taiken* (Doctors' Testimonies – Experiencing the Nagasaki Atomic Bomb) (Tokyo: University of Tokyo Press, 1982)

Shiraishi, Masaaki, *Sensō to Chōhō Gaikō* (War and Intelligence Diplomacy) (Tokyo: Kadokawa, 2015)

Sono, Ayako, *Kiseki* (Miracle) (Tokyo: Bungei Shunjū-sha, 1977)

Southard, Susan, *Nagasaki: Life After Nuclear War* (New York: Viking Penguin, 2015)

Sueyoshi, Yasaku, *Haha e no Tegami* ([Kolbe's] Letters to His Mother) (Nagasaki: Seibo-no-Kishi sha, 1984)

Suga, Shinobu, *Mata, Sakura no Kuni de* ([See You] Again, in Cherry Blossom Country) (Tokyo: Shōden-sha, 2016)

Sugihara, Sachiko, *Rokusen nin no Inochi no Viza* (Visas for 6,000 Lives) (Tokyo: Taishō Shuppan, 1993)

Sweeney, Charles W. with Antonucci, James A. and Antonucci, Marion K., *War's End: An Eyewitness Account of America's Last Atomic Mission* (New York: Avon Books, 1997)

Tagawa, Kōichi, *Sei Korube Rainichi 75 Shū-nen Kinen-shi* (A Commemorative Book on the Occasion of the 75th Anniversary of St Kolbe's Arrival in Japan) (Tokyo: Order of Friars Minor Conventual, Japan Province, 2005)

Takada, Tomoko, *Atomic Evangelists: An Investigation of the American Atomic Narrative Through News and Magazine Articles, Official Government Statements, Critiques, Essays and Works of Non-Fiction* (Kyushu University, doctoral dissertation, 2020)

Takahashi, Shinji, *Life and Death in the Nuclear Age. Philosophising in Nagasaki* (Tokyo: Hokuju Shuppan, 1994)

Takeda, Kiyoko, *Ten-nō kan no Soukoku* (Conflicting Views of the Emperor) (Tokyo: Iwanami, 1987)

Tibbets, Paul, *Return of the Enola Gay* (Columbus, Ohio: Mid Coast Marketing, 1998)

Treece, Patricia, *A Man for Others* (New York: Harper & Row, 1982)

Umemoto, Hiroshi and Matsumoto, Teruo, *Warushawa Hōki* (The Warsaw Uprising) (Tokyo: Shakai-Hyōron-sha, 1991)

Watanabe, Katsumasa, *Ketsudan – Inochi no Viza* (Decision – Visas for Life) (Tokyo: Taishō Shuppan, 1996)

Watanabe, Katsumasa, *Shinsō – Sugihara Viza* (Truth – Sugihara Visas) (Tokyo: Taishō Shuppan, 2000)

Watanabe, Katsumasa, *Monogatari Pōrando no Rekishi* (A Polish History Story) (Tokyo: Chūō-Kōron Shinsha, 2017)

Williams, Mark and Gessel, Van C., *The Handbook of Japanese Christian Writers* (Tokyo: MHM Ltd., 2023)

Winowska, Maria, *The Death Camp Proved Him Real* (Libertyville, Illinois: Prow Books, 1971)

Wontor-Cichy, Teresa, article in *Biuletyn Towarzystwa Opieki nad Oświęcimiem* (Magazine of the Union of Auschwitz Survivors) (Oświęcim, 2011)

Yamada, Kuniaki, *Pōrando Koji – 'Sakura Saku Kuni' ga Tsunaida 765 Nin no Inochi* (Polish Orphans – 765 Lives Saved by the 'Cherry Blossom Country') (Tokyo: Gendai Shokan, 2011)

Yoshida, Yutaka, *Sengo Kaikaku to Gyaku Kōsu* (Post-war Reforms and the Reactionary Course) (Tokyo: Yoshikawa Kōbun-kan, 2004)

Young, Louise, *Japan's Total Empire: Manchuria and the Culture of Wartime Imperialism* (Los Angeles: University of California Press, 1998)

Zamoyski, Adam, *Poland: A History* (London: William Collins, 2015)

Acknowledgements

During the research and writing of *The Martyr and the Red Kimono*, I was immensely fortunate to receive help and advice from a large and diverse group of talented men and women around the world.

The book couldn't have been written without the involvement and encouragement of the two Japanese protagonists – Masatoshi Asari and Tōmei Ozaki – and of people connected to Father Maximilian Kolbe in Japan, Poland and elsewhere. While Kolbe was murdered in Auschwitz almost two decades before I was born, I continually felt his presence via his writings and his well-documented life story.

Both Asari and Ozaki talked with me openly and in depth about their extraordinary lives. Between 2019 and 2023, I travelled from London to Hokkaido, Japan, four times to meet Asari, and we continued our conversations over the phone several times a week. He kindly shared diaries, photos, writings and newspaper clippings with me.

I met Ozaki in person just once, in Nagasaki, before the pandemic. But we talked frequently and at length over the phone. He also provided me with some diaries and photos. Even as his body weakened near the end of his life, his spirit remained strong, and he was always willing to discuss his feelings about his life and that of Father Kolbe. Sadly, Ozaki passed away in April 2021.

At the Niepokalanów friary in Poland, archivist Annamaria Mix showed me invaluable materials about Father Kolbe and supported my cherry-hunting research with passion and patience. Polish Sister Mediatrix, who belongs to Militia Immaculatae and is fluent in Japanese, was unfailingly helpful in responding to my research queries, and she mediated with nuns at the Strachocina convent. There, Sister Klara Machulska, the head nun, and her fellow nuns welcomed me with unconditional kindness. After listening to my stories about the cherry trees from Japan, Sister Klara placed pebbles around the surviving trees for protection. The former Mother Superior of the Nagasaki convent, Sister Kazuko Nishimura, provided me with photos and letters.

At Auschwitz, Teresa Wontor-Cichy, a Father Kolbe specialist, guided me in his footsteps. She also kindly checked the manuscript about Kolbe's days in the concentration camp. Teruo Matsumoto, a Warsaw-based Japanese journalist and expert on Siberian children of Polish descent, showed me around Warsaw and connected me with relatives of former Siberian orphans.

I am also indebted to Magdalena Cooper, a Polish resident in England, who translated some Polish materials into English for me. Konrad Wierzbicki, a resident of Kraków who knew Ozaki well, went out of his way to call friaries and priests to investigate my questions. He also helped explain Polish expressions.

I would like to extend special thanks to several people who read and commented on the entire manuscript. Clare Gummett and Catherine Coldstream, a former Catholic nun and author, corrected some of my wording and gave me insights into the Catholic religion.

Professor Mark Williams, vice president at the International Christian University in Tokyo and an expert on Japan's 'hidden Christians', offered precious suggestions. Hungarian journalist Ilona Móricz, a long-time friend, read each chapter thoroughly and advised on the fraught politics and history of eastern Europe. All these contributions were invaluable, although I alone remain responsible for any errors.

The photos in the book came from various institutions in Japan and Poland. I am especially grateful to the Niepokalanów Archives and to the Nagasaki friary. Annamaria Mix and Father Masatoshi Yamaguchi each provided many images. Uwe Pleban, a family friend and computer expert, kindly colourised several photos taken in the 1930s.

The Martyr and the Red Kimono would not have materialised without the support of my agent, Patrick Walsh, at Pew Literary in London. He approached Clara Farmer, the publishing director of Chatto & Windus, with the book idea. My editor at Chatto, Kaiya

Shang, guided me through the editorial process with care and good humour. Thanks also to the managing editor at Chatto, Graeme Hall, and to copy editor Duncan Heath for their thorough work on the manuscript.

A couple of points about style. I have written Japanese people's names in the Western way, with the surname after the given name, i.e., Masatoshi Asari. In Japan, where the surname comes first, he is known as Asari Masatoshi.

Lviv, the Ukraine city where Kolbe lived as a young student, had several names in the twentieth century because of its occupiers. I have called the city Lviv throughout the narrative. The English translations of many Polish names often differ in research materials and books about Father Kolbe. I have tried to use the most frequently cited names. For quotations from Kolbe's writings, I have usually referred to the Polish-to-English translations of Dr Claude R. Foster and Brother Heronim Wierzla.

My final thanks go to my family. My mother, aged ninety-two, lives in a care home in Japan and has always fully supported my career from afar, as she has done throughout my life. My two sons, Sean and Kenji, together with Sean's wife, Sophie, encouraged me all the way.

Like my previous English-language book, *'Cherry' Ingram: The Englishman Who Saved Japan's Blossoms*, this book is really a joint effort with my English husband, Paul Addison. We travelled together to Japan and Poland, and Paul suggested different angles and perspectives for the narrative. When writing, he polished and edited my English. We shared the journey and completed it together. *The Martyr and the Red Kimono* is dedicated to him.

Notes

1 Cited in *The Born–Einstein Letters: Correspondence Between Albert Einstein and Max and Hedwig Born* (Walker and Co., New York, 1971), p. 205. Max Born, a German physicist, won the 1954 Nobel Prize in Physics. J. Robert Oppenheimer, the physicist who headed the Manhattan Project, received his PhD under Born. Enrico Fermi, the architect of the nuclear age, and Edward Teller, known as the father of the hydrogen bomb, were among his assistants. Born was the grandfather of the singer and actress, Olivia Newton John.

1. The Patriot

1 Details about Kolbe's early life and Poland's history are contained in numerous English, Polish and Japanese books, magazines, journals, diaries and other reference sources listed in the bibliography. Facts, details and anecdotes have been cross-referenced for accuracy.

2 Chopin's heart now resides in a stone pillar inside the Basilica of the Holy Cross church in Warsaw with the inscription: 'For where your treasure is, there your heart will also be.'

3 For more, see Brian Porter, 'Hetmanka and Mother: Representing the Virgin Mary in Modern Poland', in *Contemporary European History*, 14(2), 2005, p. 154.

4 Christianity was officially adopted in Poland in 966 AD and Catholicism had become the dominant religion by the thirteenth century. Yet significant numbers of Jews, Orthodox Ukrainians, Protestants, pagans and Muslim descendants from Central Asia coexisted with the Catholics.

5 Francis of Assisi founded the Franciscan Order, or Order of Friars Minor, in 1209. The order has three branches. The Order of Friars Minor Observant (OFM) strictly observes St Francis' rules. Even more strict is the Order of Friars Minor Capuchin (OFM Cap.). Friars in these orders wear brown habits. The Order of Friars Minor Conventual (OFM Conv.), to which Kolbe

eventually belonged, follows more moderate practices, preferring community life and pastoral services. Their habits are black.

6 It had been the Roman Catholic Church's doctrine since 1854 that God preserved the Virgin Mary from the taint of original sin from the moment she
was conceived. This is what Catholics call the Immaculate Conception.

7 Maria Kolbe revealed the 'two crowns' incident to a Franciscan who visited her
in Kraków during the war to inform her of her son's death at Auschwitz. After
the war, Maria testified during the beatification process: 'I have always known
Father Maximilian was going to die a martyr because of an extraordinary
event in his childhood . . . He was always thinking about it. And whenever
there was an opportunity, he talked to me of his desire for a martyr's death.'
Patricia Treece, *A Man for Others* (Harper & Row, New York, 1982), pp. 1–2. See
also Maria Kolbe's letter to Niepokalanów, 12 October 1941, Niepokalanów
Archives.

8 Maria Winowska, *The Death Camp Proved Him Real* (Prow Books, Libertyville,
Illinois, 1971), p. 16.

2. Doubts and Ambition

1 Letter from Kolbe to his mother in 1919. Father Maximilian Kolbe, *The Writings of Fr. Maximilian Kolbe* (*Pisma o. Maksymiliana M. Kolbego*) (Niepokalanów:
Niepokalanów Publications, 1970), Vol. 1, No. 23, pp. 61–3.

2 In reaching his decision, Kolbe had help from the novice master, Father Dionysius. After Kolbe confessed to Father Dionysius that he had doubts about
continuing on a religious path, the priest told Maximilian to substitute his
vow with an old Marian prayer for the Virgin Mary. Maximilian wrote later
that he recited the prayer daily for years. Masaru Kawashimo, *Kolbe* (Shimizu
Shoin, Tokyo, 1993), pp. 37–8.

3 Tension between the Church and the state had been palpable since the struggle for Italian unification. That had pitted the Pope against Italian nationalists
and led in 1870 to the consolidation of several different states on the peninsula
into a single entity.

4 Francis Kolbe died in January 1945 at Buchenwald-Mittelbau, a sub-camp of
the Buchenwald concentration camp, after being transferred from Auschwitz.
Claude R. Foster, *Mary's Knight: The Mission and Martyrdom of Saint*

Maksymilian Maria Kolbe (West Chester University Press, West Chester, Pennsylvania, 2002), p. 108.

5 Testimony of Bishop Francis Mazzieri. Dokumenty O. M. Kolbe, Testimonies of Brothers, No. 27, pp. 223–6, Niepokalanów Archives.

6 *The Death Camp Proved Him Real*, pp. 52–3.

7 A sharp and logical thinker, the young Kolbe could also be stubborn and at times confrontational and argumentative. Once, while he was walking the streets of Rome in his Franciscan habits, an atheist philosopher challenged him to explain the existence of God. Kolbe immediately began arguing that Aristotle's theory of cause and effect ultimately led back to what the Greek philosopher had called the prime mover, or God. Disarmed, the middle-aged atheist walked away from the debate. *Mary's Knight*, pp. 121–2.

8 In unpublished testimony in 1935, Kolbe wrote that the genesis of the Militia Immaculatae came from the masonic demonstrations in Rome in 1917. 'When they started to distribute vicious tracts against the Holy Father, the idea to establish a company to fight the freemasons and other agents of Lucifer was born,' he wrote. *The Death Camp Proved Him Real*, pp. 40–42.

9 The Catholic Church followed Pope Leo XIII's 1884 Encyclical denouncing freemasonry as 'the great error of this age' and pronouncing Catholicism as 'the only [religion] that is true and cannot be regarded as merely equal to other religions'.

10 A year after Kolbe's arrival in Rome, in 1913, the Italian film director Enrico Guazzoni released one of the world's first blockbuster movies, *Quo Vadis*. A historic portrait of Christian resistance under the Roman Emperor Nero, the film was based on the novel by Kolbe's – and Poland's – favourite author, Henryk Sienkiewicz. The movie was a sell-out on Broadway and lauded by King George V after a showing at the Royal Albert Hall in London.

3. Cranking the Presses

1 Józef Piłsudski had arrived in Warsaw on 10 November, the day before the war officially ended, after sixteen months in jail in Magdeburg, Germany. Germany had arrested Piłsudski for declining to swear a loyalty oath to Emperor Wilhelm II of Germany.

2 In unpublished testimony in 1935 about MI's origins, Kolbe wrote: 'For more than a year after the first meeting, the MI did not progress and so many obstacles arose that the members themselves did not dare to talk about it.' Quoted in *The Death Camp Proved Him Real*, p. 49.

3 Although Poland was independent, it was constantly under attack. In August 1920, during what became known as the 'miracle at the Vistula', Polish forces led by Józef Piłsudski had routed the invading Soviet Red Army in the Battle of Warsaw.

4 On 25 January 1921, Kolbe wrote to a Franciscan brother in Rome: 'Because I'm ill and running a fever, I can't keep up with correspondence. Under instruction from the Provincial, I'm not engaged in matters of the Militia. [But] whenever and wherever I have an opening, I discuss the fallacy of socialism, the irrationality of atheism and the happiness and truth of the Catholic faith.' *The Writings of Fr. Maximilian Kolbe*, Vol. 1, No. 40 A, pp. 193–6.

5 Thérèse of Lisieux, 1873–94, was canonised in 1925 by Pope Pius XI. She is the patron saint of missions and florists.

6 Kolbe also mourned the death earlier that year from tuberculosis of a thirty-one-year-old priest and MI member, Father Venance Katarzyniec. Father Venance had been a mentor to Kolbe during his 1912 vacation. They were kindred spirits from poor Polish families who shared similar ideals and ambitions.

7 Wiesław Theiss and Teruo Matsumoto, *Siberian Children* (Kancelaria Sejmu, Warsaw, 2018), p. 155.

8 Japan had sent more than 70,000 troops to fight the Red Army alongside soldiers from the UK, the US and other countries. After the Western powers withdrew their troops, only Japan remained.

9 Born in Irkutsk in central Siberia, Innocenty Protalinski later moved with his Polish father, Russian mother and two siblings to a remote Siberian port called Nikolaevsk-on-Amur, named after Tsar Nicholas I. Innocenty's father, Alexander, died in January 1920 while fighting for the Red Army partisans. His wife, Dalia, fled with the children to a Siberian river port near the Chinese border, where she met the orphans' committee and begged them to take Innocenty with them. They agreed. 'I was pretty robust,' Innocenty Protalinski told Teruo Matsumoto, a Japanese historian and journalist who has lived in Warsaw for more than fifty years and is an expert on the Siberian orphans. 'You had to be if you wanted to survive in Siberia. I would have died there if I'd been weak because life was brutal.'

10 During the Russo-Japanese War of 1904–05, about 80,000 Russian soldiers –
16,000 of whom were Polish – were shipped to Japan as prisoners of war. The
Japanese treated the Poles with special care, knowing that they'd been forced
to fight for Russia.

11 Kolbe insisted that members of MI wear the 'miraculous medals' as a 'heavenly weapon' against evil and a sign of their total consecration to the Virgin
Mary. The medal was inspired by the Marian apparition to St Catherine
Laboure in Paris in 1830. The Virgin Mary appeared to Laboure as the
Immaculate Conception, standing on a globe with light streaming from her
hands. Kolbe had heard that a French freemason called Alphonse Ratisbonne
had converted to Catholicism while wearing a medal. Before moving to Japan
in 1930, Kolbe made a pilgrimage to the Chapel of the Miraculous Medal in Paris.
For more, see: www.catholicnewsagency.com/news/42022/the-miraculous-
medal-st-maximilian-kolbes-weapon-for-evangelization

12 'I'm in pain. My health isn't good,' Kolbe wrote in his diary in the summer of
1923. 'Sweat drips from my brow. Once again it was necessary to work through
the night.' Kolbe diary entry in *Notatki Pamięt*, Vol. 5, No. 866, p. 218, Niepokalanów Archives. Cited in *Mary's Knight*, p. 248. One friar, Albert Olszakowski,
collapsed and died from overwork in December 1926. *The Death Camp Proved
Him Real*, p. 83.

13 *Mary's Knight*, pp. 255–6.

14 Żebrowski was born on 27 December, but it's unclear what year. Some biog-
raphers, including Kōichi Tagawa, say 1891. Others say 1898.

15 Tōru Matsui, *Zeno Shinu Hima Nai* (Zeno Has No Time to Die) (Shunjū-sha,
Tokyo, 1998), pp. 51–2.

16 Prince Lubecki is one of only three non-Franciscans buried in Niepokalanów's
cemetery. The other two are Dr Jan Stankiewicz, a long-time friary physician,
and Franciszek Gajowniczek, for whom Kolbe sacrificed his life in Auschwitz.

17 *Mary's Knight*, p. 293.

18 Letter from Kolbe in Niepokalanów Archives. *The Writings of Fr. Maximilian
Kolbe*, Vol. 1, No. 167, pp. 490–92.

19 Pope Pius XI consecrated the first Chinese bishops in 1926 and spoke often
about the need for Catholic orders to combat anti-secular movements such as
communism and freemasonry by conducting more missionary work overseas.
Head of the Catholic Church from 1922 to 1939, Pius XI was the first sovereign
of an independent Vatican State, which had been created in February 1929.

4. A Catholic Boy in Northern Korea

1 The Japanese had occupied the remote ice-bound Siberian port of Nikolaevsk-on-Amur in 1918 as part of an international intervention against the Bolsheviks during the Russian civil war. In 1920, a bloody episode called the Nikolaevsk Incident aggravated tensions between the Japanese and the Soviets. In January 1920, partisan fighters linked with the Soviet Red Army surrounded the port, where about 800 Japanese civilians and soldiers were living. One of those partisans was Alexander Protalinski, the father of the Siberian orphan Innocenty Protalinski. After the Japanese unsuccessfully attacked the partisan fighters, the Russians killed most of the Japanese civilians and threw their bodies into an ice hole on the frozen River Amur. Children were simply dumped in the hole next to their mothers, alive. After the Russians razed the port, Japan occupied the north of the politically sensitive Sakhalin Island until 1925. Sakhalin lies east of Nikolaevsk-on-Amur and north of Hokkaido.

2 In Korea, where Catholicism had started to spread in the eighteenth century, 200 years later than in Japan, the Joseon dynasty carried out similar mass persecutions. There, its leaders were concerned that the religion would undermine the Confucian class-based society. At least 10,000 Catholics were beheaded during four major persecutions in the nineteenth century, many of them at Jeoldusan, the 'mountain of decapitation', near the capital, Seoul.

3 The underground network to which Kōichi's ancestors belonged was run by a small group of Christian men. One kept a calendar of important religious dates; another christened believers, and others were responsible for quietly passing on need-to-know information to other members of the network.

4 In 1657, 608 people were arrested, of whom 411 were beheaded, during the so-called *Koori Kuzure* in the Ōmura district in Nagasaki.

5. The Arrival of the Beards

1 19 May 1930, letter from Kolbe. *The Writings of Fr. Maximilian Kolbe*, Vol. 2, No. 226, pp. 70–72.

2 *Zeno Shinu Hima Nai*, pp. 91–2.

3 *The Writings of Fr. Maximilian Kolbe*, Vol. 2, No. 194, pp. 25–6.

4 Ibid., Vol. 2, No. 198, pp. 30–31. St Thérèse of Lisieux should not be confused with St Teresa of Avila, who is sometimes referred to as the patron saint of chess.

5 *Mary's Knight*, p. 337.

6 The first *daimyō* to become Christian was Sumitada Ōmura, who ruled large parts of present-day Nagasaki and Saga prefectures. After converting in 1564, Ōmura demanded that his aides, samurai and everyone else in his domain, including Shinto and Buddhist priests – more than 60,000 people – become Christians. He ordered the destruction of temples and shrines and expelled anyone from his lands who refused to convert. In 1570, Ōmura agreed to open Nagasaki port to Portuguese ships for trade. In an age of almost non-stop civil wars between the daimyō lords and their samurai armies, it was a smart tactic. Ōmura reasoned that his rivals would hesitate to attack anyone who had such close links to the powerful gun-toting Portuguese.

7 Tōmei Ozaki, *Nagasaki no Korube Shinpu* (Father Kolbe in Nagasaki) (Seibo-no-Kishi sha, Nagasaki, 2010), p. 11.

8 Ibid., p. 12.

9 The story of Sugimoto's encounter with Petitjean was greatly dramatised and exaggerated by the French missionary, according to Kentarō Miyazaki, an academic who specialises in the history of hidden Christians. See Kentarō Miyazaki, *Senpuku Kirishitan wa Nani o Shinjite Itanoka* (What Did the Hidden Christians Believe?) (Kadokawa, Tokyo, 2018), pp. 183–4. According to Petitjean, the fifty-three-year-old Sugimoto also asked him, 'Where is the statue of Santa Maria (the Virgin Mary)?', and he led the group to a small bronze statue of Mary carrying the baby Jesus that stood next to the main altar. During their time in hiding, the hidden Christians had reportedly encouraged each other with a saying: 'In seven generations, the Pope will send a priest from Rome who will bring a statue of the Virgin Mary to Japan.' Petitjean's story was probably apocryphal. Miyazaki notes that without priests to guide them or churches to visit, the Christians' beliefs and traditions had morphed during their years underground. For example, many Christians incorporated native Japanese animistic, or Shinto, tenets into their religion, most notably ancestor worship. Even Petitjean, the French priest, wrote that none of the Christians he met knew the true meaning of an 'absolute God' or what Jesus or the Virgin Mary signified. Concerned that Japanese Christians were incorrectly interpreting Christian principles, Petitjean invited the

leaders of several clandestine networks to his home at Ōura Cathedral for re-education lessons. Petitjean also created a secret seminary in the attic of his home where young Christians gathered. Four secret churches were also created within Japanese houses in the Urakami district and Petitjean quietly visited other island communities by boat to offer Mass.

10 *Senpuku Kirishitan wa Nani o Shinjite Itanoka*, pp. 182–3.

11 According to Miyazaki, many hidden Christians resisted giving up their Christian faith and chose to become martyrs because they didn't want to disrespect their families and their ancestors, not because they were committed to a Christian God or to Christ. Ancestor veneration is of utmost importance in Shintoism, particularly the need to continue the family's lineage.

12 *Mary's Knight*, p. 345.

13 *Nagasaki no Korube Shinpu*, p. 24.

14 *Zeno Shinu Hima Nai*, p. 117.

15 Father Umeki, 'Memories of Father Kolbe', in *Seibo-no-Kishi* magazine, May 1995 issue. Quoted in Kōichi Tagawa, *A commemorative book on the occasion of the 75th anniversary of Father Kolbe's arrival in Japan* (Seibo-no-Kishi sha, Nagasaki, 2005).

16 *The Writings of Fr. Maximilian Kolbe*, Vol. 2, No. 240, pp. 92–3.

17 *Mary's Knight*, p. 347.

18 Interview with Takashi Nishida on 11 November 2021.

19 H. Neill McFarland, professor at Perkins School of Theology, Southern Methodist University, Dallas, Texas, *The New Religions of Japan*, nirc.nanzan-u.ac.jp/nfile/3247, pp. 33–6. McFarland visited Ittō-en in December 1956 when Tenkō-san, as Nishida was known, was in his eighties. McFarland noted that Ittō-en's sanctuary had three altars. The central one was dedicated to Ohikari ('Light'). Flanking it were altars representing Buddhism and Christianity.

20 *Hikari* magazine, No. 108, published by Ittō-en.

21 The friendship between Ittō-en and the Polish friars continued after the war. Brother Zeno met Tenkō in a slum in Tokyo in 1955, nearly thirty years after their first meeting in Nagasaki. Zeno visited Ittō-en many times afterwards. Takashi Nishida, Tenkō's grandson, met the Polish Pope, John Paul II, in 1990 in Rome when he attended a world peace conference in Italy. He showed the Pope a framed photo of the statue that Kolbe had given his grandfather and explained their friendship. Tenkō Nishida, according to at least one account, was baptised at the end of his life by a Polish Franciscan priest. Iwona

Merklein, author of *Polish Franciscans in Japan – The Beginnings of the Mission in Nagasaki (1930–1945)*, said Father Janusz Koza (1913–85) baptised Nishida in 1967 when Nishida was ninety-five, about three months before his death. Merklein's account is included in *In Search of Polish Graves in Japan*, published by Poland's Ministry of Culture and National Heritage, Department of Cultural Heritage, Warsaw, 2010. In an interview, Takashi Nishida told the author that the account is 'half true and half untrue'. He said that Father Koza visited Ittō-en in the late autumn of 1967 and performed the rites of baptism. However, at the time, Tenkō was bedridden and was not aware of what was going on around him after suffering two severe strokes. Takashi said Tenkō had not requested the baptism. But during the ceremony, Takashi said, Tenkō grabbed the cross that Koza had handed him and refused to return it. He said that incident might have led Koza to believe that Tenkō had accepted Christianity. Koza had gone to Ittō-en specifically to baptise Tenkō, saying he had been told by Father Kolbe that it needed to be done.

22 *The Writings of Fr. Maximilian Kolbe*, Vol. 2, No. 275, pp. 164–7.
23 Ibid., Vol. 2, No. 299, pp. 227–9.
24 Ibid., Vol. 2, No. 288, pp. 196–7.
25 Ibid., Vol. 2, No. 265, pp. 142–3.
26 Ibid., Vol. 2, No. 281, pp. 182–4.

6. Fashioned by Fire

1 In March and October 1931, members of a secret right-wing society within the army called the Sakura-kai, or Cherry Society, had launched efforts to bring down the government. The officers had chosen the name because *sakura*, or cherry blossoms, were military symbols of nationalism and self-sacrifice at the time.

2 In January 1932, a member of the secret Korean Patriotic Corps, Bong-Chang Lee, tried to assassinate Emperor Hirohito in Tokyo by throwing a hand grenade towards his horse-drawn carriage. No one was hurt in this so-called Sakuradamon Incident, but the thirty-three-year-old Lee was arrested and hanged. Sakuradamon is a gate at the Imperial Palace where the incident happened. Three months after the Sakuradamon Incident, in April 1932, another member of the Korean Patriotic Corps, Bong-Gil Yung, detonated a bomb in

Hongkew Park, Shanghai, on the emperor's birthday. It killed an army general and wounded other Japanese dignitaries. Yung was taken to Japan and shot. By then, it was well established that anyone who tried to harm the Japanese imperial family or to organise anti-Japanese movements would pay the ultimate penalty.

3 The Asaris moved into the large house after Asakichi's elder sister, Sue, moved out. Sue had been married to a businessman who ran a soy sauce brewing company, which went bankrupt. The man left Sue and the house became run down until Asakichi moved in.

4 'Kanzan' wasn't a universally popular tree. Many Japanese thought its blossoms were too showy and preferred the less dramatic petals of the mountain cherries. Collingwood Ingram, the British plant hunter and cherry expert, called 'Kanzan' vulgar and obscene. See Naoko Abe, *'Cherry' Ingram: The Englishman Who Saved Japan's Blossoms* (Vintage Press, London, 2020), pp. 166–8.

5 Japanese historian Shunsuke Tsurumi and some liberal academics prefer the term 'the Fifteen Years' War', arguing that the Second World War began with the Manchurian Incident in 1931 and ended with Japan's surrender in 1945. They argue that the Manchurian Incident was the beginning of Japanese aggression in Asia, which in turn led to the Second Sino-Japanese War, which began in 1937, and the Pacific War. China now calls this period 'the Fourteen Years' War' rather than 'the Eight Years' War', a phrase the Chinese government used previously.

6 While Chie's brothers were fighting in China in the late 1930s, her mother died of appendicitis. Chie blamed her mother's death on the paucity of good doctors in Hokkaido, since many had been sent to the battle fronts to care for soldiers. Fortunately, Asari's uncles both returned to Hokkaido from the war unharmed.

7. The Struggle

1 When the friars started flattening the land for the friary, they found many human and animal bones and old coins in the soil. They also discovered a stone with a cross engraved on it. Kolbe reported to Nagasaki Archbishop Hayasaka that it appeared the land was once a place where the remains of persecuted hidden Christians had been dumped. Hayasaka replied: 'It must

be good land because Catholic blood runs through it.' In the autumn of 1936, a seminary student found a brass cross under the soil near the friary. A local historian said that it was 300 years old and had likely been passed from one generation of hidden Christians to another. The student gave the cross to Father Mirochna, who kept it in the friary. *Nagasaki no Korube Shinpu*, pp. 94–7.

2 After the original monastery was destroyed in a fire in 1903, the Trappist monks built a new one, which opened in 1908. The monks also set up a replica of the Lourdes shrine in a grotto behind the monastery. By 1921, fifty-five monks lived in the monastery – forty-four Japanese and eleven foreigners. At the start of the Second Sino-Japanese War, in 1937, the monastery became a strategic fortified zone, and fourteen Japanese monks were drafted into the military. Four died during the Pacific War. Seven Cistercian communities exist in Japan today. To generate funds these days, the Hokkaido monks sell butter cookies and ice cream to visitors.

3 *Nagasaki no Korube Shinpu*, p. 88. Mirochna would soon play a significant role in the development of the Nagasaki friary. He remained in Japan and died in Nagasaki in 1989, aged 80.

4 Letter to father provincial, 17 August 1931. *The Writings of Fr. Maximilian Kolbe*, Vol. 2, No. 317, pp. 288–92.

5 Fukabori was interviewed by NBC TV Nagasaki for a programme called 'Father Kolbe, his life and death', broadcast 21 February 1981.

6 Letter to father provincial, 5 July 1931. *The Writings of Fr. Maximilian Kolbe*, Vol. 2, No. 307, pp. 252–5.

7 *Mary's Knight*, p. 412.

8 The friars invited thirty-one boys to a Christmas party in 1932, during which Santa Claus made an appearance. One boy, Aijirō Komori, recalled: 'We were so curious about the foreign friars and so excited to go inside the buildings.' Komori later became Catholic, the only known person from the Ōkouchi area to convert. *Nagasaki no Korube Shinpu*, pp. 224–5.

9 'I agree with the Papal Nuncio Joseph Mooney [in Tokyo], when he said that it is essential to have exceptionally competent priests to work with the Japanese, who have a culture of such high standards. They need to understand the language thoroughly.' Correspondence to Father Kornel Czupryk, 11 July 1931, and 5 July 1931, quoted in Masaru Kawashimo, *Kolbe*, p. 137.

10 *Nagasaki Shimbun*, 4–6 May 1932.

11 *Nagasaki no Korube Shinpu*, p. 117.

12 The Buddhist monk told Kolbe that the Japanese believed that a person who passed away a hundred years earlier with a stone in his hand would be reborn with that same stone in his hand. This belief stemmed from a combination of Buddhist beliefs about the cycle of life and an indigenous folklore belief that possessions and thoughts get passed on through ancestors. 'These things are just too difficult for me to believe,' Kolbe wrote, 'although I do share the idea that somebody from above comes to help men during their lives.' 'The writings of St Maximilian Maria Kolbe', in *Rycerz Niepokalanej*, April 1934, p. 244. After he returned to Poland in 1936, Kolbe accurately analysed the Japanese religious situation. Kolbe said that although Buddhism came to Japan from India through China, it adapted itself to the local situation to such an extent that there was no difference between entering a Buddhist *otera* (temple) or a Shinto *omiya* (shrine). He observed that even in a primary school's textbook, Buddhist temples and Shinto shrines were described as existing alongside each other.

13 'The writings of St Maximilian Maria Kolbe', in *Rycerz Niepokalanej*, April 1934, pp. 307–08.

14 The four men who arrived in Japan on 19 May 1932 were Father Konstanty Onoszko and three religious brothers – Bartlomiej Kalucki, Kasjan Tetich and Henryk Borodziej.

15 In Ernakulum, Kolbe met Archbishop Angelus María Pérez Cecilia, a Spanish Carmelite missionary, who invited him to set up a mission in the city. Enthused, Kolbe also dreamed of establishing friaries in the US, Italy and England, though he conceded that 'to maintain uniformity of all Niepokalanóws in the world is a major challenge'. *The Writings of Fr. Maximilian Kolbe*, Vol. 2, No. 384, p. 479. Letter to Father Florian Koziura, the guardian of Niepokalanów, 30 July 1932. *The Writings of Fr. Maximilian Kolbe*, Vol. 2, No. 397, pp. 512–14.

16 *Mary's Knight*, p. 419.

17 'I am going to die soon. I don't have much time,' he wrote in a rare letter written in Japanese *romaji* characters from India to a seminary student in Nagasaki. *The Writings of Fr. Maximilian Kolbe*, 1 July 1932, Vol. 2, No. 394, pp. 499–507.

18 The city known today as Lviv was called Lemberg when Kolbe and Konstanty were students. Its name changed to Lwów in 1919 and later it was also known as Lviv and Lvov.

19 *Nagasaki no Korube Shinpu*, p. 309.

20 *A Man for Others*, pp. 60–61.

21 *The Writings of Fr. Maximilian Kolbe*, 7 October 1932, Vol. 2, No. 405, pp. 537–40. Neurasthenia was often cited as a form of mental disorder associated with nervous breakdowns, anxiety, fatigue and depression. In another letter to Father Kornel, Kolbe wrote: 'Because of his [Konstanty's] attitude and the fact that he is here, I often fear divine punishment. One can't even dream of his cooperation. Because he practises no restraint, I try to keep him segregated from the friars and from our Japanese guests so that he won't infect them with his ideas.' In turn, Konstanty complained to the Franciscan provincial administration in Poland about Kolbe's extremism. *The Writings of Fr. Maximilian Kolbe*, 25 February 1933, Vol. 2, No. 431, pp. 599–603.

22 *Nagasaki no Korube Shinpu*, pp. 239–40.

23 Ibid., pp. 165 and 279.

24 Ibid., p. 248.

25 Ibid., p. 267.

26 Brother Romuald went to Japan in 1931 and stayed the rest of his life in Nagasaki. He died there in 1989 at the age of 78.

27 Ibid., p. 182.

28 Testimony of Father Kornel, quoted in *A Man for Others*, p. 64.

29 Quoted in 'In the Silence of the Night', in *Seibo-no-Kishi* magazine, October 1935, pp. 2–5.

30 Hidden Christians survived for centuries on Hisaga-shima. Many of them visited the French Father Petitjean in 1868 but the new Meiji government persecuted them severely. At least 200 were arrested. After being tortured, they were thrown into a tiny jail, where forty-three died, including young children. Following protests from Petitjean and other foreigners, the remaining Christians were eventually released.

31 Jin Ishitobi, *Kaze no Shisha Zeno* (Zeno, A Messenger of the Wind) (Shizen-shoku Tsūshin-sha, Tokyo, 1998), pp. 65–6.

32 Letter to Father Mirochna on 11 November 1936. *The Writings of Fr. Maximilian Kolbe*, Vol. 4, No. 600, pp. 14–15. After leaving Japan, Kolbe wrote at least four letters between 1936 and 1941 expressing his wish to die there. See his letters on 8 May 1938 (*Writings*, Vol. 4, No. 693, pp. 193–4); 20 August 1938 (Vol. 4, No. 706, pp. 229–31); and 31 January 1941 (Vol. 4, No. 826, pp. 435–6).

33 Kōya Takita, an Ittō-en disciple who lived with the friars in 1930, was baptised as a Catholic in 1938. He had long been trying to understand both Buddhism

and Christianity and said that Kolbe had been 'the mentor of my heart'. Another convert was Hideo Yamaki, an academic and Protestant priest, who visited the friars frequently after their arrival in Japan. Skilled in Italian, Yamaki translated Kolbe's Italian articles into Japanese. He also helped Kolbe negotiate for the land on which the friary was built. For more, see Iwona Merklein's article in *In Search of Polish Graves in Japan* (Polish Ministry of Culture and National Heritage, Department of Cultural Heritage, Warsaw, 2010), p. 107.

34 'Memories of Father Kolbe', part of *A commemorative book on the occasion of the 75th anniversary of Father Kolbe's arrival in Japan*, p. 79.

35 Iwona Merklein recounts some of the Polish friars' encounters with their Buddhist counterparts in *Polish Franciscans in Japan – The Beginnings of the Mission in Nagasaki (1930–1945)*. For example, Father Konstanty and Brother Zeno visited a Buddhist temple one New Year's Day to talk with the monks. A young monk from the temple later paid a return visit to the friary to explain how Buddhists used *juzu* beads when praying to Buddha. On another occasion, three Buddhist monks visited to ask the Poles how Catholics applied the words of Jesus Christ in practice.

8. The Emperor or Jesus

1 Louise Young, *Japan's Total Empire: Manchuria and the Culture of Wartime Imperialism* (University of California Press, Berkeley, 1998), pp. 33, 65, 67, 72–3.

9. Spiritual Resistance

1 *Mary's Knight*, p. 486.

2 Diana Dewar, *Saint of Auschwitz* (Darton, Longman & Todd Ltd., London, 1982), p. 75.

3 Ronald Modras, *The Catholic Church and Antisemitism: Poland, 1933–1939* (Routledge, New York, 1994), pp. 38–41.

4 Ibid., pp. 222–3, 252–3. Among others, Modras cites articles in the *Little Daily* on 28 July and 4 July 1935, 26 January 1936, 24 November 1937 and 16 February and 13 March 1939.

5 *The Writings of Fr. Maximilian Kolbe*, Vol. 3, No. 557, pp. 234–9. In his letter to Wojcik, Kolbe said he hoped the newspaper would 'be above partisan politics', but he added: 'The government should know that in all its equitable legislation *Mały Dziennik* will support it. Poland is our native land. The government of our native land must occupy our attention. I believe the government is aware of the influence which Niepokalanów can command. Let's seek to ally with government forces of goodwill to purify Poland from the influences of Free Masonry.'

6 '*Mały Dziennik* cannot publish articles which represent Prelate Trzeciak's line of thoughts.' *The Writings of Fr. Maximilian Kolbe*, Vol. 4, No. 634, pp. 83–6.

7 *The Catholic Church and Antisemitism: Poland 1933–1939*, p. 398.

8 Details from Father Marian Wojcik, cited in *A Man for Others*, p. 75.

9 *A Man for Others*, pp. 83–4.

10 *Mary's Knight*, pp. 487–8. Three of the twelve divisions focused on the work of the Militia Immaculatae. One dealt with MI matters at Niepokalanów, another with MI within Poland and a third with MI's global mission. The other divisions were printing, finance, editorial, distribution, construction, maintenance, transport, academic, and fire and security.

11 *Mary's Knight*, pp. 511–12. Kolbe spoke on Polish National Radio at 5.50 p.m., 8 December 1937. Among his anecdotes, he told his radio audience about a visit to the self-sufficient Niepokalanów community by two Jewish communists who were collecting scraps of paper. After looking around, one said: 'I am a communist, but real communism is here.' Kolbe continued: 'At Niepokalanów, there is genuine communal life, founded not on hatred and coercion but on mutual love.'

12 *Saint of Auschwitz*, p. 78.

13 On 4 May 1938, after receiving their licences, the brothers, Gustav and January, flew a biplane over the friary.

14 By promising to tear up the hated Versailles Treaty, stamp out the threat of Bolshevism and propel Germany out of depression, the Nazi Party made major electoral gains in the early 1930s. On 30 January 1933, just a month before Franklin Delano Roosevelt was elected 32nd president of the United States, Hitler became the leader of the self-styled Third Reich. In quick succession, the Nazi Party suspended civil rights and banned or dissolved other political parties. Following the death of the German president, Paul von

Hindenburg, in August 1934, Hitler gained full dictatorial power. Attacks on Jews, other religions and anyone else who disagreed with Nazi policies became the norm.

15 *Mary's Knight*, p. 522.

16 Danzig had become a 'free city', run by the League of Nations, in 1920 to serve as a port for Polish trade. Most of its population was German, and German politicians with Nazi allegiances controlled the state senate and the police. Hitler was intent on wresting this land from its current occupiers.

17 *A Man for Others*, p. 90.

18 *Mary's Knight*, p. 524.

19 The Polish Pope, John Paul II, is said to have secretly visited the monastery as a student pilgrim during the Nazi occupation. John Paul II also prayed there on his papal visit to Poland in 1979. He made five more visits after 1979.

20 In Vilnius, now the capital of Lithuania, the friars prayed at the shrine of Our Lady of Ostrabrama (the Gate of Dawn). It was just a ten-minute walk from the Rasos cemetery in which the heart of Józef Piłsudski, the former prime minister, had been buried three years earlier. In the Polish sepulchral tradition, a person's heart and body are often buried separately. Piłsudski's heart lay next to his mother in a crystal urn bearing the image of the Lady of Ostrabrama. During the pilgrimage, Kolbe decided to build a friary in Vilnius, and he returned there in May 1939 to erect a cross on a plot of donated land.

21 At the start of each broadcast, Radio Niepokalanów aired 'Ave Maria', an uplifting hymn to the Virgin Mary that was in sharp contrast to the daily onslaught of negative stories in the newspapers.

22 André Frossard, *Forget Not Love* (Ignatius Press, San Francisco, 1991), p. 143.

23 Prince Lubecki testimony during the Kolbe beatification process.

24 *Mary's Knight*, p. 686.

25 *Mary's Knight*, p. 543. Kolbe first mentioned the vision to a handful of friars in January 1937 and told them to keep it a secret.

26 Ibid., p. 547.

27 Ibid., pp. 549–50.

28 Adam Zamoyski, *Poland: A History* (William Collins, London, 2015), p. 314.

29 In a 1 December 1940 letter to Mugenzai-no-Sono, Kolbe wrote that the building constructed for novices was now a centre for forcibly displaced civilians administered by the Polish Red Cross. He added that the friary was taking

care of Polish prisoners of war who were unable to work because of their injuries. *The Writings of Fr. Maximilian Kolbe*, Vol. 4, No. 804, pp. 403–06.

10. *Kōichi Tagawa's War*

1 Ironically, given their enmity, Japan and the Soviet Union never fought each other during the Second World War and signed a neutrality pact in 1941. It wasn't until 9 August 1945 – the day of the Nagasaki atomic bombing – that the Soviet Union declared war on Japan.

2 Roosevelt strongly opposed the tripartite Axis alliance of Germany, Italy and Japan, signed in September 1940, a year after Germany's invasion of Poland.

3 Interviews with Kōichi Tagawa, 2019–21.

4 Three and a half years later, Shirabe would become renowned in Nagasaki as an atomic bomb survivor who spent years helping radiated patients, and as an expert member of the A-Bomb Survivors Medical Treatment Council. For more on Shirabe and the A-Bomb Survivors Medical Treatment Council, see: www.genken.nagasaki-u.ac.jp/abcenter/shirabe

5 *Zeno Shinu Hima Nai*, pp. 164–5.

6 Father Samuel Rosenbaiger remained in the US until 1952. In all, he worked in Japan fifty-five years, spending his last years as chaplain to Japanese sisters at the Konagai convent built by Father Mirochna northeast of Nagasaki. He died in November 1981, aged 83, and is buried there. For more, see *In Search of Polish Graves in Japan*, published by the Polish Ministry of Culture and National Heritage, Department of Cultural Heritage (Warsaw, 2010), pp. 79–80.

7 *Zeno Shinu Hima Nai*, pp. 166–7.

8 Ibid., p. 169.

9 Ibid., pp. 172–3.

10 Japan's population at the time, including its colonies, was about 100 million. During the initial phase of the war, when Japan was victorious, the military used the slogan *Ichioku hi no tama* (100 million fireballs) or *Ichioku isshin* (100 million, in one spirit) to symbolise the country's vigour. By 1944, these slogans had begun to emphasise the beauty of death.

11 Tōmei Ozaki, *Jūnana-sai no Natsu* (His Seventeenth Summer) (Seibo-no-Kishi sha, Nagasaki, 1996), pp. 55–6.

11. Masatoshi Asari's War

1 'Cherry' Ingram: The Englishman Who Saved Japan's Blossoms, pp. 190–91.

2 Ibid., pp. 204–07.

3 Ibid., p. 284.

4 Ibid., pp. 212–25.

5 Ibid., pp. 218–19.

6 Shōwa: Niman-nichi no Zen-kiroku (Shōwa: The Entire Record of 20,000 Days) (Kōdan-sha, Tokyo, 1989), Vol. 7, p. 84.

7 Hokkaido Shimbun, 15 July 1945.

8 The Americans also bombed other Hokkaido cities, including Muroran, Kushiro and Nemuro. www.airuniversity.af.edu/Portals/10/AUPress/Books/B_0020_SPANGRUD_STRATEGIC_BOMBING_SURVEYS.pdf, p. 86.

12. 'A Rain of Ruin'

1 Charles W. Sweeney with James A. Antonucci and Marion K. Antonucci, War's End: An Eyewitness Account of America's Last Atomic Mission (Avon Books, New York, 1997), p. 185.

2 Ibid., pp. 170, 185.

3 'An atomic bomb . . . is a harnessing of the basic power of the universe,' Truman's statement said. 'The force from which the Sun draws its power has been loosed against those who brought war to the Far East.'

4 'An experiment in the New Mexico desert was startling – to put it mildly,' Truman wrote in his diary on 25 July 1945. 'I have told the Secretary of War, Mr [Henry] Stimson, to use it so that military objectives and soldiers and sailors are the target and not women and children.' www.web.mit.edu/21h.102/www/Primary%20source%20collections/World%20War%20II/Truman,%20Diary.html

5 Kazutoshi Handō, Shōwa-shi (History of Shōwa) (Heibon-sha, Tokyo, 2004), pp. 453–65. After the German surrender in May 1945, the Japanese government secretly started looking for ways to attain peace, using the Soviet Union as an intermediary. Japan's ambassador in Moscow, Naotake Sato, contacted the Soviets. Emperor Hirohito supported this idea and made clear to the Supreme

War Council on 22 June his intention of ending the war as soon as possible. However, no negotiations took place because Stalin had already told Churchill and Truman at the Yalta Conference in February 1945 of his intention to declare war on Japan. The Japanese government ignored the Potsdam Declaration in part because it was waiting for a reply from the Soviet Union about its request to be an intermediary, according to Handō.

6 *War's End*, pp. 186–9. The just war theory was originally proposed by St Augustine of Hippo (354–430 CE).

7 As many as 40,000 US military lived in tents and Quonset huts on Tinian, which was laid out in a Manhattan-style street grid. One area was called 'The Village' after New York's Greenwich Village. The thirty-nine-square-mile island also had its own Central Park. The road along the shore was called Riverside Drive after the north–south thoroughfare in the Upper West Side of Manhattan that runs parallel to the Hudson River.

8 Salantai, also known as Salant, was part of the Polish–Lithuanian Kingdom until 1795. It came under Russian rule when the kingdom was divided up by Russia, Prussia and Austria. Siew's family lived in a small wooden house that used candles for lighting and well water for drinking and cooking. The village had changed little since the fourteenth century, which was exactly how the residents liked it. But not Siew, who read secular books by German and Russian authors such as Goethe, Schiller and Tolstoy, and who yearned to leave.

9 Laurence reportedly purloined 'William' from Shakespeare, 'Leonard' from Leonardo da Vinci and 'Lawrence' from a street he lived on in Massachusetts. He altered the spelling to 'Laurence' in homage to Schiller's romantic poem, 'Rapture – to Laura'.

10 William Laurence, 'Physicists bare discovery of greatest amount of energy liberated thus far', *New York Times*, 24 February 1939.

11 *Holocaust Atlas of Lithuania*. See also Tomoko Takada, 'Atomic Evangelists: An Investigation of the American Atomic Narrative Through News and Magazine Articles, Official Government Statements, Critiques, Essays and Works of Non-Fiction' (Kyushu University, doctoral dissertation, 2020), p. 217.

12 David W. Dunlap, 'Witnessing the A-Bomb, but Forbidden to File', *New York Times*, 7 August 2015.

13 For more on Laurence's arrangement with the *New York Times*, see Beverly Ann Deepe Keever, *News Zero: The New York Times and the Bomb* (Common Courage Press, Monroe, Maine, 2004).

14 In early July 1945, Laurence wrote a letter to his managing editor, Edwin L. James, hinting at the enormity of a story he was covering from a secret destination, according to a *New York Times* story on 31 July 2017 by David W. Dunlap, called 'Breaking the Dawn of the Atomic Age'. 'This story is much bigger than I could imagine – fantastic, bizarre, fascinating and terrifying,' Laurence wrote. 'The world will not be the same after the day of the big event.' Laurence was trying to give the newspaper advance notice to prepare for 'the big event', without explaining what it was, Dunlap's story said.

15 Patty Templeton, 'Plutonium and poetry: Where Trinity and Oppenheimer's reading habits met', 14 July 2021. Oppenheimer called the test site Trinity in homage to a sonnet written by the seventeenth-century poet John Donne that began 'Batter my heart, three-person'd God'. Upon seeing the Trinity detonation, Oppenheimer was said to have recalled the line from the *Bhagavad Gita*, 'Now I am become Death, the destroyer of worlds', according to Templeton.

16 Laurence was the 'great neglected celebrity of the Manhattan Project', according to science writer Mark Wolverton: https://undark.org/2017/08/09/atomic-bill-laurence-manhattan-project/

17 William Laurence writing in the *New York Times* about the 16 July 1945 atomic bomb test, published 25 September 1945.

18 The watching scientists clapped and jumped around with glee, Laurence wrote. 'The dance of the primitive man lasted but a few seconds, during which an evolutionary period of 10,000 years had been telescoped. Primitive man was metamorphosed in those few seconds into modern man.'

19 The Brien McMahon Papers, Georgetown University Library; Booth Family Center for Special Collections.

20 Leonard Cheshire, *The Light of Many Suns: The Meaning of the Bomb* (Methuen, London, 1985), pp. 6–7.

21 Ibid., p. 7.

22 Earlier in July 1945, Cheshire had flown to London to meet his younger brother, Christopher, who had spent four years as a prisoner of war in the Stalag Luft III prison camp. Located in present-day Zagan, Poland, Stalag Luft III was renowned for the 'Great Escape' of Allied prisoners in March 1944.

23 *The Light of Many Suns*, p. 7.

24 Ibid., p. 22.

25 *The Screwtape Letters* left Cheshire convinced of the reality of Satan as the living, personalised spirit of Evil, whose objective was the disorientation and downfall of man. *The Light of Many Suns*, p. 45.

26 *War's End*, p. 181.

27 Ibid., p. 202.

28 Ibid., pp. 204–05.

29 Ibid., pp. 210–11.

30 Ibid., p. 216.

31 Ibid., pp. 217–19. Sweeney wrote that the bomb was released at 11:01 a.m.

32 Laurence's story, datelined 9 August, wasn't published until 8 September 1945. The story was headlined: 'Atomic bombing of Nagasaki told by flight member'. Laurence was referred to as '*a science writer for The New York Times and a special consultant to the Manhattan Engineer District, the War Department's special service that developed the atomic bomb*'.

33 For more, see Richard Tanter, 'Voice and Silence in the First Nuclear War: Wilfred Burchett and Hiroshima', in *The Asia-Pacific Journal*, Vol. 3, Issue 8, 3 August 2005.

34 *New York Times*, 8 September 1945.

35 *The Light of Many Suns*, p. 58.

36 *War's End*, p. 229.

37 Robert O. Harder, *The Three Musketeers of the Army Air Forces. From Hitler's Fortress to Hiroshima and Nagasaki* (Naval Institute Press, Annapolis, Maryland, 2015), p. 160.

38 Barry Scott Zellen, 'Hansai or the Cleansing Fire: How the Interplay of Fog, Friction and Faith Resulted in the Unintended Atomic Annihilation of Nagasaki's Christian Community', in *Wild Blue Yonder* magazine, 29 September 2020.

13. Torment

1 The contents of this chapter come from Ozaki's wartime diaries and extended interviews with the author from 2019 to 2021.

2 The leaders of the Japanese government and military received a translation of President Truman's statement about the dropping of an atomic bomb on the

morning of 7 August. They also confirmed the news by sending a doctor to Hiroshima. However, the general public was told via newspapers only that the Hiroshima bomb was 'a new bomb'. Japanese newspapers started reporting that the bomb was an atomic device from 11 August onwards. Newspapers were often difficult to find in the chaos following the war's end and the papers sometimes had to restrict circulation. Dr Tatsuichiro Akizuki, who survived the attack in Nagasaki, testified that he and other doctors at the Nagasaki Medical University did not know the blast was caused by an atomic bomb until they read a flyer dropped by an American plane on or around 13 August. Tatsuichiro Akizuki, *A Memoir of the Nagasaki Atomic Bomb* (Nihon Book Ace, Tokyo, 2010), pp. 113–14. Dr Raisuke Shirabe, who conducted Kōichi Tagawa's spinal tuberculosis operation in 1941, said he was only sure that it was an atomic bomb after he was briefed in detail by US military doctors in Nagasaki in September 1945. Raisuke Shirabe, *Experiencing the Nagasaki Atomic Bomb* (Tokyo University Press, Tokyo, 1982), pp. 32–3.

3 The ten Polish men who had been interned at a hot springs resort in nearby Kumamoto prefecture included Father Donat Gościński, Father Janus Koza, Brother Maciej Janiec, Brother Kasjan Tetich, Brother Eligiusz Zaremba and Brother Romuald Mroziński.

14. MacArthur and the Emperor

1 *Shōwa: Niman-nichi no Zen-kiroku*, Vol. 7, p. 146.
2 John Dower, *Embracing Defeat: Japan in the Aftermath of World War II* (London: Penguin, 1999), p. 44. US special presidential envoy Edwin Locke Jr reported to President Truman in mid-October 1945 after meeting with MacArthur and his aides that 'the American officers now in Tokyo are amazed by the fact that resistance continued as long as it did'. So great was the economic disarray, that in the opinion of some Americans the atomic bombs 'while seized upon by the Japanese as an excuse for getting out of the war, actually speeded surrender by only a few days'.
3 *Embracing Defeat*, p. 93.
4 Among other reforms, MacArthur also released imprisoned wartime dissidents who were mainly communists, allowed workers to form labour unions and introduced gender equality. Boys and girls who had been educated

separately before the war, now sat together. Women, including Chie, were allowed to vote for the first time.

5 *Embracing Defeat*, p. 299.

6 Ibid., p. 24.

7 Kiyoko Takeda, *Ten-nō kan no Soukoku* (Conflicting Views of the Emperor) (Iwanami, Tokyo, 1987), p. 276.

8 *Embracing Defeat*, p. 299.

9 Ibid., pp. 330–32.

15. Silence

1 *Kaze no Shisha Zeno*, pp. 81–3. Father Mirochna and the Japanese students were in the process of moving books and materials to the compound's air-raid shelter in case of a raid. Brother Zeno was alone in his work shed trying to repair a stone mill. At 11.02 a.m., Zeno saw an incredibly bright and sharp light and said he fell unconscious for a short while. As the buildings shook, the seminary students crawled under the desks in the library. They later ran to the air-raid shelter.

2 One man who had recently returned to Nagasaki after being discharged from military service was a Trappist monk called Kaemon Noguchi. In October 1945, while visiting the ruins of Nagasaki Cathedral, he found amid the rubble the blackened head of a wooden statue of the Virgin Mary. The six-foot statue had been imported from Italy when the cathedral was built and had been placed at the centre of the altar. Only the head survived the atomic blast, though its eyes were hollow, and parts of the face and hair were burnt. Father Noguchi took the head to his monastery in Hokkaido, where it remained in his room until 1975, the thirtieth anniversary of the bombing. He then returned it to Nagasaki. The statue, known as 'the Radiated Virgin Mary', is in a chapel at the cathedral.

3 In the aftermath of the bombing, Nagasaki's meteorological observatories were barely functioning. That meant residents were unprepared for the 140-mile-per-hour gusts of wind generated by Typhoon Ida, known in Japan as the Makurazaki Typhoon. Hiroshima was also badly affected by the storm.

4 The term *hibakusha* for the atomic bomb survivors didn't become widely used until the late 1950s, largely as a legal definition for the purpose of allocating national medical relief to sufferers, according to Chad Diehl. For more, see

Chad R. Diehl, *Resurrecting Nagasaki: Reconstruction and the Formation of Atomic Narratives* (Cornell University Press, Ithaca, New York, 2018), p. 3.

5 A sixteen-person British mission that visited Nagasaki in November 1945 reported that the scale of the disaster had brought life and industry to a standstill and had prompted a panic flight of the population. For more, see *The Effects of the Atomic Bombs at Hiroshima and Nagasaki*, Report of the British Mission to Japan (His Majesty's Stationery Office, London, 1946), pp. 3–4.

6 Tatsuichirō Akizuki, *Nagasaki Genbaku-ki* (Nagasaki Atomic Bomb Record) (Heiwa Bunko, Tokyo, 2010), pp. 154–7. Akizuki's book was originally published in 1966 by Kōbun-dō.

7 Paul Glynn, *A Song for Nagasaki: The Story of Takashi Nagai: Scientist, Convert, and Survivor of the Atomic Bomb* (Ignatius Press, San Francisco, 2009), pp. 172–3. In the immediate aftermath of the bomb, Nagai spent two days looking after bomb victims in the ruins of the hospital before returning home to find his wife.

8 Takashi Nagai, 'The Miracle of Lourdes', in *Seibo-no-Kishi* magazine, December 1946.

9 *A Song for Nagasaki*, p. 187.

10 Nagai's speech was published in *Nagasaki no Kane* (The Bells of Nagasaki) (Hibiya Shuppan-sha, Tokyo, 1949).

11 Nagai also spoke about the significance of 15 August, which was the day of the Japanese surrender and also the day of the great feast of the Assumption of the Virgin Mary, to whom Urakami Cathedral was dedicated. He wondered whether this convergence of events was coincidental or whether this was also God's providence.

12 Gwyn McClelland, *Dangerous Memory in Nagasaki* (Routledge, London, 2020), p. 36.

13 *Embracing Defeat*, p. 414.

14 Shinji Takahashi, *Life and Death in the Nuclear Age. Philosophising in Nagasaki* (Hokuju Shuppan, Tokyo, 1994). Takahashi, a sociology professor at Nagasaki University, coined the phrase 'Urakami Hansai Setsu', which is often referred to as Nagai's 'Urakami holocaust theory'. See also Anthony Richard Haynes, 'Nagai Takashi on Divine Providence and Christian Self-Surrender: Towards a New Understanding of Hansai', in *The Handbook of Japanese Christian Writers*, edited by Mark Williams and Van C. Gessel (MHM Ltd., Tokyo, 2023).

15 *A Song for Nagasaki*, pp. 257–8.

16 *Nagasaki no Kane*, p. 157.

17 Ibid., p. 158.

18 Some critics said that the GHQ only allowed *The Bells of Nagasaki* to be published because Nagai's theory of God's Providence gave the US an excuse to justify the bombing. The GHQ also allowed a book of Nagai's essays, called *Leaving My Children Behind*, to be published. It also became a bestseller. The book carried his message for his children to live as Christians and to strive for world peace. Nagai also wrote a medical report in October 1945 about how radiation affected survivors. He presented it to the Nagasaki Medical University. It was most likely censored by the GHQ and was lost until 1970, when a local TV reporter discovered it. For more, see John Dower's *Embracing Defeat*, p. 415.

19 *A Song for Nagasaki*, foreword by Shūsaku Endo.

20 Nagai's residence in Nagasaki, Nyoko-dō, was originally built by the doctor's supporters. It has been preserved and is open to the public. *Nyoko-dō* means 'a house where you love yourself'.

21 Nagai's original paintings are exhibited in the Nagai Takashi Memorial Museum in Nagasaki.

22 Translation by the author. The original words in Japanese were: *Hansai no honō no naka ni utai tsutsu, shira yuri otome moe ni keru kamo*. In a message that accompanied the song, Nagai explained that Hansai was a festival during the Old Testament period, when lambs were burnt at an altar as a sacrifice to God. The song is still sung every August during the school's memorial service for the dead.

23 Takashi Nagai, *Itoshi-go yo* (My Precious Children) (San Paulo, Tokyo, 2014), pp. 207–09. Reprint of the 1949 original. Nagai is well remembered in postwar Japan as a strong advocate for preserving the Constitution, adopted in 1947, which declared that Japan would give up arms for ever.

24 In 2008, sixty years after being planted, only twenty or so trees were alive. Tomoji Kobata, former director of the Nagasaki Nyoko-no-Kai Society, who had known Nagai as a boy, arranged for grafts to be taken from three healthy trees. Hundreds of these second-generation trees were subsequently planted in Nagasaki and Unnan City in Shimane prefecture, where Nagai had grown up. www.asahi.com/hibakusha/english/shimen/nagasakinote/note90-03e.html

16. The Reading

1 *Jūnana-sai no Natsu*, p. 74. Brother Kasjan Tetich, 1902–88, had arrived in Japan in May 1932 at the same time as Father Konstanty.

2 Kōichi's other uncle, Ikuichi, who ran the butcher's shop in Unggi with Fuji-nosuke, remained in Korea after the war, with his wife and stepdaughter.

17. 'The Truth'

1 Kōichi Tagawa wrote two books about Kolbe's life, and numerous articles. This chapter is based on his writings as well as other biographies of Kolbe, the testimony and depositions given during Kolbe's beatification process, and the author's interviews and research.

2 Brother Juventyn Młodożeniec, in testimony and depositions given during Kolbe's beatification process. Cited in *A Man for Others*, pp. 93–4. According to Brother Juventyn, Kolbe said that suffering was the third stage of life, following two other stages – preparation for activity and activity itself.

3 *Mary's Knight*, p. 555.

4 Ibid., p. 554.

5 Prince Drucki-Lubecki, testimony during Kolbe's beatification process. *A Man for Others*, p. 95. Marian Wojcik, the editor-in-chief of *Mały Dziennik*, the *Little Daily* newspaper, crossed the border to Romania with Prince Lubecki, the benefactor of the friary. *Saint of Auschwitz*, p. 128.

6 The brother who shaved Kolbe's beard secretly kept strands of it in a jar. The jar eventually ended up in the archives in Niepokalanów after the war. Another jar contains Kolbe's hair from a haircut in December 1940.

7 Brother Juventyn Młodożeniec, in testimony and depositions given during Kolbe's beatification process. Cited in *A Man for Others*, p. 94.

8 *Mary's Knight*, pp. 558–61.

9 Ibid., pp. 564–5.

10 Brother Juventyn Młodożeniec and Brother Jerome Wierzba, in testimony and depositions given during Kolbe's beatification process. Cited in *A Man for Others*, pp. 101–02.

11 Ibid., p. 104.

12 When the friars visited Schildberg, local people willingly donated food to them. Many told the priests that they subscribed to Niepokalanów publications and were members of Militia Immaculatae. Mulzer allowed the priests to conduct services at the school and was regarded as a rare compassionate German. He told Kolbe that he had not wanted to be the commandant of an internment camp but that he had been drafted from a reserve unit at the start of the war and been sent there. Mulzer was later transferred to the Wehrmacht's chaplain duties. *Mary's Knight*, pp. 579–84.

13 Claude Foster, author of *Mary's Knight*, speculated that Hans Mulzer may have asked someone in Berlin on behalf of the Franciscans to release them. A brother at Niepokalanów told Foster that the mayor of Teresin had written a petition to the German authorities saying that he guaranteed that the Franciscans wouldn't be a threat to order in occupied Poland. *Mary's Knight*, p. 583.

14 *Mary's Knight*, p. 586.

15 Ibid., pp. 586–7.

16 Ibid., p. 592.

17 *The Writings of Fr. Maximilian Kolbe*, Vol. 4, No. 763, pp. 328–9.

18 Kolbe's first request, to the German occupational district governor's office, went nowhere. So Kolbe approached the newly created Board of Public Education and Propaganda in the General Government. The board in turn referred the application to the office of the Governor General in Kraków, which approved the request before the Gestapo intervened, according to Brother Cyprian Grodski's testimony during Kolbe's beatification process. Cited in *A Man for Others*, p. 141.

19 *Mary's Knight*, p. 691.

20 Ibid., p. 601.

21 Kolbe letter to the brothers exiled from Niepokalanów, dated 21 May 1940. *The Writings of Fr. Maximilian Kolbe*, Vol. 4, No. 774, pp. 343–8.

22 A third group of about 2,000 displaced civilians arrived at the friary later in the year. These included injured Polish prisoners of war, who were cared for by the Polish Red Cross.

23 Masaru Kawashimo, *Kolbe*, p. 184. Kolbe, the officer told him, could be regarded as having German ancestry. It is possible that Kolbe's ancestors were German settlers who had moved into the Kingdom of Bavaria, according to Claude Foster, author of *Mary's Knight*. The family's original name may have

become Germanised at some point during the rule of the Holy Roman Empire of the German nation.

24 Brother Juventyn Młodożeniec, in testimony and depositions given during Kolbe's beatification process. Cited in *A Man for Others*, p. 143.

25 Father Donat Gościński arrived in Nagasaki in 1938 and died there in 1976, aged sixty-five.

26 *The Writings of Fr. Maximilian Kolbe*, Vol. 4, No. 821, pp. 428–9.

27 Letter to Brother Henryk Borodziej, 31 January 1941. *The Writings of Fr. Maximilian Kolbe*, Vol. 4, No. 826, pp. 435–43.

18. The Final Days: Six Months in Hell

1 Father Pius Bartosik died at Auschwitz on 13 December 1941. Father Antonin Bajewski died at Auschwitz on 8 May 1941. Father Justin Nazim and Father Urban Cieslak were transferred to Dachau concentration camp on 3 May 1941. They both survived and went to Japan as missionaries after the war. Cieslak died in Japan in November 1960, aged fifty-six. Nazim lived in Illinois from 1946 to 1952, Japan from 1952 to 1966, and died in the US in December 1966, aged sixty-three.

2 *The Writings of Fr. Maximilian Kolbe*, Vol. 4, No. 838, p. 660.

3 *Mary's Knight*, p. 661.

4 Teresa Wontor-Cichy, article in *Biuletyn Towarzystwa Opieki nad Oświęcimiem* (Magazine of the Union of Auschwitz Survivors) (Oświęcim, 2011).

5 To pass the censors, letters from Auschwitz needed to be upbeat and avoid any criticism of the camp. *The Writings of Fr. Maximilian Kolbe*, Vol. 4, No. 839, p. 459.

6 *A Man for Others*, p. 180.

7 After thirty-one months in Auschwitz, Pilecki escaped from the camp. He later fought in the Warsaw Uprising. He was executed by Poland's communist government in 1948. Dr Diem became a general practitioner in Warsaw after the war. He died in 1986. Pilecki's network was called the Military Organisation Union (Związek Organizacji Wojskowej or ZOW). Another resistance organisation, the Union of Armed Struggle (Związek Walki Zbrojnej or ZWZ) also existed in Auschwitz from February 1941. For more, see 'Polish Military Resistance Movement at Auschwitz', by Auschwitz-Birkenau

State Museum, at: artsandculture.google.com/story/polish-military-resistance-
movement-at-auschwitz-auschwitz-birkenau-state-museum/dQUhQpyPGgo
A8A?hl=en-GB. See also: Jack Fairweather, *The Volunteer: The True Story of
the Resistance Hero Who Infiltrated Auschwitz* (W. H. Allen & Co., London,
2019).

8 Joseph Stemler, testimony during Kolbe's beatification process. *A Man for
Others*, p. 188.

9 Ladislaus Lewkowicz, testimony during Kolbe's beatification process. *A Man
for Others*, pp. 210–11.

10 Based on an account by Auschwitz researcher Teresa Wontor-Cichy.

11 Henry Sienkiewicz, a young prisoner who slept next to Kolbe when he first
arrived at the camp, testified that Kolbe once handed him a quarter of his
daily bread ration, saying: 'You must take it, you are going to do hard labour
and you're hungry.' *A Man for Others*, pp. 189–92.

12 Mieczysław Kościelniak, testimony during Kolbe's beatification process. *A
Man for Others*, pp. 200–02.

13 After the war, Kościelniak made more than 100 paintings of Kolbe. He
donated many of these to Niepokalanów, where they are exhibited in the
Kolbe museum. The paintings include Kolbe listening to a prisoner's confession, giving a clandestine talk to prisoners in a circle, and stepping out from
the rows of standing prisoners to offer his life so that another man could live.

14 *A Man for Others*, pp. 199–200. Patricia Treece interviewed Sigmund Gorson in
1982. Gorson died in 1994 in the US state of Delaware, where he worked as a
radio and TV producer. See also: Richard Cowden, *A Man Who Knew Maximilian Kolbe*: www.poles.org/db/G_names/Gorson_S/Kolbe1.pdf

15 www.timesofisrael.com/champion-of-auschwitz-new-book-tells-story-of-
boxer-who-brought-hope/. See also *The Volunteer*, pp. 139–41.

16 *Saint of Auschwitz*, p. 109.

17 Several details about this event – the prisoner's name, the actual date, the
number of prisoners in Kolbe's block – are hazy. *Mary's Knight* by Claude
Foster names the prisoner as Zygmunt Pilawski, as do numerous websites
and other books. Researchers at Auschwitz have concluded that there is not
enough evidence to name the prisoner definitively, as there were other escapes
around that time. Because some prisoners were released and others died, it's
impossible to know exactly how many prisoners lived in Block 14 at any one
time.

18 Details of the escape and its aftermath differ in many books, magazines and websites, depending on the recollections of those present. This account stems mostly from testimony given during Kolbe's beatification process, some of which is recounted in *A Man for Others*, pp. 218–33 See also: https://sites. google.com/site/testimonianzedifede/santi-e-beati-del-900/san-massimiliano-kolbe/auschwitz

19 Interview with Japanese journalist Teruo Matsumoto, an expert on the Siberian orphans, September 2020.

20 Innocenty Protalinski told Matsumoto that he had been so frightened while standing in line that he didn't know Kolbe had volunteered to take Gajowniczek's place until after the war. He said he was simply relieved not to have been chosen. In November 1944, Protalinski was transferred to a concentration camp in southern Germany. He died in January 2000, aged ninety-two.

One of the most influential of the 765 Polish orphans who had been rescued from Siberia by the Japanese in the 1920s was Jerzy Strzalkowski. In 1928, seventeen-year-old Strzalkowski founded an association called the Far East Youth Union as a way for the orphans to maintain contact. Every spring, the Japanese embassy in Warsaw hosted a cherry blossom evening for the group and for influential Poles. Strzalkowski also set up an orphanage in Warsaw close to the embassy.

The union's close ties with the embassy continued after Germany's invasion. Commanded by Strzalkowski, the union became known as Insurgent Special Forces Jerzyki and grew into a militant anti-Nazi resistance force. While the core members were Siberian orphans in their late twenties and thirties, Special Forces Jerzyki also attracted other young Polish fighters and boasted as many as 15,000 members at its peak.

When the Gestapo raided Strzalkowski's orphanage, a Japanese diplomat would rush to the complex and tell the Germans that the facility was under Japanese protection. During Gestapo searches, the orphans sang songs in Japanese, taught them by Strzalkowski, to prove their links to Tokyo.

During the Warsaw Uprising in August 1944, about 600 members of Special Forces Jerzyki died, including Strzalkowski's fiancée, Karol, who had also been a Siberian orphan. Strzalkowski remained single until his death in 1991, according to Matsumoto. 'The orphans were united by their shared experience in childhood and their pride in being the descendants of Poles who had stood up against their Russian oppressors,' Matsumoto told me.

21 https://militia-immaculatae.asia/english/info896.php. See also: *A Man for Others*, pp. 226–7; *Mary's Knight*, pp. 674–6; *Saint of Auschwitz*, p. 113. See also: https://christianhistoryinstitute.org/magazine/article/offering-himself-for-a-stranger. Detailed accounts of Kolbe at Auschwitz were printed in *Seibo no Kishi* magazine in January, February, April and May 1947.

22 Some testimonies say Bock's injection was given directly to Kolbe's heart muscle and not to his arm, according to Teresa Wontor-Cichy.

19. The Awakening

1 'Veteran Who Caught Japan's Tōjō Finally Breaks His Silence', Associated Press, 11 September 2010; 'John Wilpers Dies at 93; Captured Tōjō', *New York Times*, 4 March 2013.

2 China and Japan have long disputed how many people died in the Nanjing Massacre. China says that between 300,000 and 400,000 people were killed. In Japan, some say the number of deaths was between 100,000 and 200,000. Others say as few as 10,000.

3 Madoka Futamura, 'Japanese Societal Attitudes Towards the Tokyo Trial: A Contemporary Perspective', in *Asia-Pacific Journal*, Vol. 9, Issue 29, No. 5, 19 July 2011: https://apjjf.org/2011/9/29/Madoka-Futamura/3569/article.html. See also *Embracing Defeat*, pp. 452–3, 510–11. See also Arnold C. Brackman, *The Other Nuremberg: The Untold Story of the Tokyo War Crimes Trials* (Fontana Paperbacks, London, 1990), pp. 122–5.

4 The general mood of repentance about the war was reflected in a bestselling fictional book that Asari read in the late 1940s. It was called *The Burmese Harp* (*Biruma no Tategoto*), written by Michio Takeyama, a German literature scholar who had translated books by Goethe and Nietzsche. First serialised in 1947 in a magazine for children, Takeyama's book was about a Japanese soldier who had fought in Burma near the end of the war. After witnessing many atrocities, the soldier had chosen to become a Buddhist monk and to remain in Burma. There, he spent his life collecting the bones of his dead colleagues and consoling their souls. A talented singer, the soldier strolled through the jungle in an orange monk's robe, accompanying his voice with his hand-held harp. In the book, he wrote a letter to surviving soldiers explaining the reasons for his actions: 'Many innocent people became

meaningless victims . . . Our country started a war and lost, and it is now suffering. That is because we had futile desires. We were conceited and forgot what is the most important thing as humans . . .' Takeyama's goal was to inspire Japanese youth with hope for the future while emphasising the traditional Buddhist ideals of altruism and compassion. His and others' reflections about the horrors and sorrows of war helped turn many Japanese into pacifists.

5 After the war, some communists became national 'heroes' when they were released from prison. For example, when Sanzō Nosaka, the leader of pre-war Japanese communists, returned to Japan in January 1946 from exile in China, thousands of people gathered in central Tokyo to welcome him. He was elected as an MP in the first post-war general elections in 1946.

6 Andrea Davis, 'Bridging the Pacific Gap: Hollywood in post-WW II Japan', W&M News Archive, 10 August 2011: https://www.wm.edu/news/stories/2011/kitamurabom.php

7 Professor Ukita and other faculty members would occasionally join these heady debates on the trains. They encouraged the students to remain in Hokkaido, believing that Japan had been drawn into totalitarianism in part because local governments hadn't been powerful enough to counter the central government.

20. No Time to Die

1 Details of Zeno's activities are based on interviews with people who knew him well, including Kōichi Tagawa and Zeno's biographer, Jin Ishitobi. Other details come from three Japanese-language books: Tōru Matsui, *Zeno Shinu Hima Nai* (Zeno Has No Time to Die); Jin Ishitobi, *Kaze no Shisha Zeno* (Zeno: A Messenger of the Wind); and Takashi Nagai, *Kono Ko-o Nokoshite* (Leaving These Children Behind).

2 Quoted in *Zeno-san*, a Japanese TV documentary, 2022.

3 Edward J. Flanagan, *Child Welfare Report (Japan and Korea)*, published 9 July 1947.

4 *Zeno Shinu Hima Nai*, p. 201.

5 Japanese Health Ministry's statistics, cited in *Kaze no Shisha Zeno*, p. 188.

6 Iwona Merklein, *Brat Zeno Żebrowski. Polski Misjonarz w Japońskich Mediach* (Wydawnictwo Trio, series: Oblicza Japonii, Warsaw, 2006).

7 Seibo-no-Kishi-en still exists. Today, the nuns look after children who cannot be cared for at home. Interview with Sister Kazuko Nishimura, the former head of the convent, on 15 August 2022.

8 *Nagasaki no Korube Shinpu*, p. 25.

9 The Gospel of John 15:13, New King James version of the Bible.

10 Clark Parker, 'Satoko Kitahara, Maria of Ants Town', published in The Tokyo Files, 23 August 2016: https://thetokyofiles.com/2016/08/23/satoko-kitahara-maria-of-ants-town/

11 Paul Glynn, *The Smile of a Ragpicker: The Life of Satoko Kitahara* (Marist Fathers Books, Hunters Hill, NSW, 1992; Google Books).

12 Harry Allagree, 'The Mary of Ant Village', in The Good Heart blog, 23 January 2013: http://thegoodheart.blogspot.com/2013/01/the-mary-of-ant-village.html

21. The Children's Cherries

1 South Sakhalin was the northernmost outpost of Japan's empire until August 1945, when the Soviet Union invaded it. The Russians expelled some Japanese inhabitants to Hokkaido and sent others to Siberian labour camps.

2 Sugawara's mentor was Professor Kingo Miyabe (1860–1951), who attended Harvard University in the 1880s and wrote *Flora of the Kurile Islands* in 1890 and *Plants in Sakhalin* in 1915. Miyabe had graduated from Sapporo Agricultural College, later Hokkaido University, which had been established in 1876 by William Smith Clark of Massachusetts. Sugawara also admired Tomitaro Makino (1862–1957), a University of Tokyo professor known as the father of Japanese systematic botany.

3 Miyoshi wrote the book on the taxonomy of more than 100 cherry cultivars in German because he had studied botany at Leipzig University.

4 The ousting of the aristocrats had the unexpected consequence of connecting Matsumae with Kyoto's imperial family. Three Matsumae daimyō lords married women from the imperial household, and they brought their favourite cherry trees to their new home.

5 Asari's first teaching job was at Kiyobe Elementary School on the fringes of Matsumae where most adults were poor fishers or farmers. A lot of families couldn't afford to pay for occasional school trips or to provide their children

with packed lunches. Asari made rice balls for the poorest pupils every morning before school and secretly paid their fees for school trips. In 1954, the government started providing school lunches for pupils. The school closed several years ago because of depopulation.

6 Between 1942 and 1951, when it was renamed, the school was known as Motomachi Girls' High School. Its emblem is a white lily, representing the Virgin Mary.

7 For more, see Tomitomo Nagata, *Ezo Kirishitan* (Ezo's Christians) (Kōdansha, Tokyo, 1972).

8 Hokkaido's 'gold rush' coincided with the shōgun's persecution of Christians. At the time, Japan was one of the world's largest gold producers. The Tokugawa shogunate used gold mined on the island of Sado in the Sea of Japan, and elsewhere, to consolidate its power throughout Japan and to buy manufactured goods via traders in China. After gold was discovered in Matsumae, the daimyō gave gold to the shōgun in exchange for the right to set up mining operations there. In turn, the daimyō leased tracts of land along the rivers of the Daisengen region to gold speculators from Japan. The Christian families lived in wooden huts in the mountain's forests, which were covered in snow for as long as six months each year. They extracted minute gold particles from the alluvial sands in the rivers using rectangular wooden pans called *yuri-ita*. The hidden Christians were visited several times between 1618 and 1622 by two Jesuit priests – Jerome de Angelis from Sicily and Diego de Carvalho from Portugal. De Angelis was burned at the stake in 1623. De Carvalho was drowned in a pit filled with icy water in 1624. On penalty of death, other hidden Christians were forced to verify at Buddhist temples that they had given up their faith.

9 One rehired politician was Class A war criminal Nobusuke Kishi, who became prime minister in 1957. He was the maternal grandfather of Shinzo Abe, the premier from 2006 to 2007 and again from 2012 to 2020. Abe was assassinated in 2022.

10 The US–Japan Security Treaty was revised in 1960 under Prime Minister Nobusuke Kishi and made de facto permanent. The revision, which outlined mutual defence obligations, was contentious in Japan and led to waves of protests. In Hokkaido, Asari again actively participated in demonstrations organised by the Teachers' Union in Hakodate.

11 At meetings of the Botanical Society of Japan, Asari said, researchers 'often asked stupid questions such as "Do you have cherry trees in Hokkaido?" This really infuriated me, and I vowed that someday I would make them realise that Hokkaido has more beautiful sakura than anywhere else in the world.'

12 The 'Naden' cultivar was created from a 300-year-old tree in Kozen-ji temple in Matsumae known as 'Kechimyaku-zakura'. Its creator was Kanesuke Kamakura, a high-ranking town official who had hoped to revitalise the town by planting cherry trees. Kamakura propagated the old Kechimyaku-zakura tree by grafting scions onto the trunks of other trees. He named the cultivar 'Naden' and planted them throughout Matsumae, where they still thrive. It took weeks for the schoolchildren to gather the seeds because a 'Naden' tree produces only a handful of non-edible fruits. Using a thirteen-foot bamboo stick with a pair of scissors attached to the tip, the pupils obtained four or five fruits at the top of the tree and extracted seeds from them. They sowed these in fishermen's boxes at the school.

13 In the 1920s, Collingwood 'Cherry' Ingram, from Benenden, Kent, became the first person in the world to hybridise ornamental cherries. For more, see 'Cherry' Ingram: The Englishman Who Saved Japan's Blossoms, pp. 156–61.

14 Asari and his pupils called one cultivar 'Genkotsu-zakura', meaning the fist cherry, after Asari playfully brandished his fist at some misbehaving children one day. They named another hybrid 'Hana-guruma', meaning flower-bedecked car.

22. A Friar's Secret Love

1 The accounts in this chapter are based on extensive interviews with the author and on Tōmei Ozaki's writings. These include Shinkō no Deai-tabi, An Encountering Journey of Faith (Seibo-no-Kishi sha, Nagasaki, 2006) and articles in several magazines.

2 Japanese hold ceremonies for deceased family members according to the Buddhist calendar. These are held in years one, two, six, twelve and thirty-two after a person's death. Thirty-two years is a special year for ceremonies. Since Mitsue's family were Buddhists, Ozaki decided to hold the ceremony in the thirty-second year.

23. Peace Offerings

1 Descriptions of the Koreans' working conditions are based on interviews with Asari and the report *Kokutetsu Matsumae-sen husetsu kōji no keika to roudou no jittai* (The process and the reality of the construction of the Matsumae railway) by the Matsumae History and Education Circle, Hakodate, July 1972. Asari was one of the researchers for a local-history project about Matsumae Town sponsored by Hokkaido prefecture.

2 The extension of the wartime railway was never completed, but a line connecting Matsumae and Hakodate was finished in 1953. The cherry tunnel stretched from Oyobe station to Matsumae station and included the Ōshima-zakura, 'Naden', 'Kanzan', 'Beni-yutaka' and 'Hanagasa' varieties. The line was abandoned in 1988 but about fifty trees still blossom there.

3 The conditions endured by the Korean labourers became an acute political issue between the two countries in the 1990s. Some Korean labourers who returned to Korea after the war, or who remained in Japan, began researching the matter. Japanese researchers, including Asari, followed later. Japan and South Korea resumed diplomatic relations in 1965 and signed a treaty in which Japan pledged $800 million in 'economic aid' to Korea. The Japanese government regarded this as compensation for the sufferings of the Koreans. The issue remains thorny. This century, former labourers have sued more than seventy Japanese firms who employed them during the war. In October 2018, the Korean Supreme Court ordered Nippon Steel Corporation to pay reparations to four former labourers. A month later, it ordered Mitsubishi Heavy Industries to pay reparations. The Japanese firms appealed against the decisions and the firms' assets in Korea were frozen. The two countries continue to seek diplomatic solutions to the impasse.

4 Asari published his findings about the Chinese railway workers in an official 'History of Matsumae' booklet in 1985. Although most documents about the labourers had been destroyed at the end of the war, Asari found some hidden in boxes in local authorities' offices. They included registration forms that recorded the labourers' identity.

5 For more on Hakodate prisoners of war, see the POW Research Network Japan at www.powresearch.jp. For more on Asari's research and gifts of cherries to the UK, see *'Cherry' Ingram: The Englishman Who Saved Japan's Blossoms*, pp. 284–92.

6 Peter V. Russo, 'A Model Japanese', *The Argus* (Melbourne, Victoria), 15 October 1948. The camp's first director, Colonel Toshio Hatakeyama was sentenced to twelve years' imprisonment at the International Military Tribunal for the Far East at Yokohama in 1948 for the mistreatment of Hakodate prisoners under his command from December 1942 to March 1944.

7 In a letter to Asari on 17 February 1982, Jefferson said he planned to travel officially in Japan between 10 March and 17 June 1982 looking for 'superior ornamental cherry trees for introduction into the US. I would like to collect this material from both native and cultivated trees and shrubs growing in areas of climatic diversity with special emphasis on seed and budwood from disease-resistant plants.'

8 Asari's brothers and his schoolchildren also collected seeds from hardy cherries such as Kasumi-zakura, Miyama-zakura and Ōyama-zakura. Jefferson retired from the US Department of Agriculture in 1987 but lectured in Japan until 1998. He died in November 2020, aged 97. The author interviewed him in January 2015.

   I am indebted to Stefan Lura, head of Plant Records at the US National Arboretum in Washington, for his research on the outcome of Jefferson's visits to Hokkaido in 1982, 1983 and 1986. According to Lura, 'Pink Flair' and 'Spring Wonder' are both sold as cultivars of *Prunus sargentii*. The 'Pink Flair' seedling was probably originally sent to the J. Frank Schmidt & Son Co. nursery in Boring, Oregon, but it was trialled for its cold-hardiness at North Dakota State University. 'Spring Wonder', also known as 'Hokkaido Normandale', was introduced by Bailey Nurseries of St Paul, Minnesota. Jefferson visited the Japanese garden at Normandale Community College in Bloomington, Minnesota, in 1984 and sent fifty seedlings from Hokkaido seeds there. Before this, plant experts did not believe that flowering cherries could grow there or in North Dakota. In 2012 and 2016, the National Arboretum sent some propagules of cherries from the 1982–83 expedition to North Dakota State University and to Chicago Botanic Garden, mainly *Prunus nipponica* var. *kurilensis*. Recipients of cherries from Jefferson's 1986 Japan expedition, mostly *Prunus sargentii* and natural hybrids of it with either *Prunus nipponica* or *P. nipponica* var. *kurilensis*, included the US Botanic Garden, Longwood Gardens, Chicago Botanic Garden, the Minnesota Landscape Arboretum, Morris Arboretum, Missouri Botanical Garden and several more nurseries. Matsumae cherries are still quite rare in the US, according to Lura. The

National Arboretum received its first grafted plants of 'Matsumae-benihigoromo' and 'Matsumae-oshio' from quarantine in March 1992, nine years after Jefferson collected them with Asari in January 1983. The arboretum received Asari's 'Ran Ran' cultivar from quarantine in 2000, but it later died.

9 Takuboku wrote a diary in 1909 in Romaji – Roman script used to transliterate Japanese characters – so that his wife wouldn't understand his writing. One entry said: 'What will become of me? A useless key that does not fit! That's me. Wherever I go, I can't find the keyhole that fits me!'

10 Takuboku was only eighteen when he wrote eight columns for the *Iwate Nippo* newspaper, a daily in Iwate prefecture. He died in 1912 of tuberculosis, aged twenty-six.

24. The Bunker

1 Chad R. Diehl, an American historian, questioned why Nagai's theory gained so much attention in the late 1940s compared to other atomic narratives on Nagasaki. Diehl said Nagai's story of sacrifice led to a failure to include and recognise other Nagasaki residents who died in the bombing. Japanese critics such as Kan Yamada and Shinji Takahashi said that because Nagai's narrative regarded the bombing of Nagasaki as God's Providence, America's responsibility for using the bombs was nullified. See Diehl, *Resurrecting Nagasaki: Reconstruction and the Formation of Atomic Narratives*. See also Takada, 'Atomic Evangelists: An Investigation of the American Atomic Narrative Through News and Magazine Articles, Official Government Statements, Critiques, Essays and Works of Non-Fiction'.

2 'Auschwitz Friar Beatified by Pope', *New York Times*, 18 October 1971, p. 7: https://www.nytimes.com/1971/10/18/archives/auschwitz-friar-beatified-by-pope-vatican-honors-kolbe-who-gave.html

3 Homily of Pope Paul VI at the beatification of Father Kolbe, Vatican City, 17 October 1971: https://www.piercedhearts.org/heart_church/paul_vi/oct_17_71_beat_max_kolbe.htm

4 After the beatification ceremonies in Vatican City in 1971, Wojtyła had conducted a Mass at Auschwitz for more than 100,000 people in a cold, drizzling rain. *A Man for Others*, p. 238. Kolbe was beatified just thirty years after his death, an unusually short time. In his case, Pope Paul VI gave an exemption

from the Code of Canon Law that required that any beatification process begin only after fifty years had passed from their death.

5 During their centuries of persecution, the hidden Christians had encouraged each other by saying that after seven generations of suffering, a Western Christian would come by ship and rescue them. The Pope, they said, was that man.

6 The Hiroshima Peace Memorial, or Genbaku Dome, became a UNESCO World Heritage site in 1996 as a 'symbol of human wishes for peace'.

7 Tōmei Ozaki, *Haru Itsumademo* (Spring Forever) (Nagasaki: Seibo-no-Kishi sha, 1998), p. 142.

8 Today, Ōura Cathedral is a designated national treasure and a UNESCO World Heritage site. A statue of the Virgin Mary stands adjacent to the cathedral's main altar, symbolising the discovery of the hidden Christians. Urakami Cathedral was rebuilt in 1959 after being destroyed by the atomic bombing. Since 1962, Urakami Cathedral has been the central cathedral of the Nagasaki archdiocese.

9 Ishitobi, *Kaze no Shisha Zeno*, pp. 6–7.

10 Henry Kamm, 'The Saint of Auschwitz is Canonized by Pope', *New York Times*, 11 October 1982.

11 John Kifner, 'Solidarity Chiefs Urge Resistance to Union Ban', *New York Times*, 11 October 1982.

12 Henry Kamm, 'Saint Charged With Bigotry; Clerics Say No', *New York Times*, 19 November 1982, section A, p. 5. The *New York Times* quoted the Reverend Błażej Kruszyłowicz, president of the Church Committee for the Canonisation of Father Kolbe, as saying that he hoped statements by Kolbe which hinted at antisemitism would be placed in the context of what he called the substantial Jewish presence in the pre-war Polish economy. He said many Poles perceived this as a social problem. To call Father Kolbe's views antisemitic would be unjust, he said.

13 Daniel Schlafly and Warren Green, 'Kolbe & Anti-Semitism', *New York Review of Books*, 14 April 1983. See also: 'Scholars Reject Charge St Maximilian Was Anti-Semitic', Jewish Telegraphic Agency, 3 January 1983. See also: Ronald Modras, 'The Interwar Polish Catholic Press on the Jewish Question', *The Annals of the American Academy of Political and Social Science*, No. 548, November 1996, p. 182. See also: Modras, *The Catholic Church and Antisemitism: Poland, 1933–1939*.

14 The International Holocaust Remembrance Alliance (IHRA) in 2016 adopted the following definition of antisemitism: 'Antisemitism is a certain perception of Jews, which may be expressed as hatred toward Jews. Rhetorical and physical manifestations of antisemitism are directed toward Jewish or non-Jewish individuals and/or their property, toward Jewish community institutions and religious facilities.'

15 Kamm, 'The Saint of Auschwitz is Canonized by Pope'.

16 *Haru Itsumademo*, p. 142.

17 Tōmei Ozaki, *Migawari no Ai* (Love as Sacrifice) (Seibo-no-Kishi sha, Nagasaki, 1994), p. 49.

25. Encountering Kolbe

1 The book was *Nagasaki no Korube Shinpu, Father Kolbe in Nagasaki, a Story of the Knights of Immaculata* (Seibo-no-Kishi sha, Nagasaki, 1983).

2 Ten of the twenty trees were Chishima-zakura. He also sent five Ōyama-zakura (Sargent cherry), three Ōshima-zakura, one 'Ezonishiki' and one Shidare-zakura cherry tree.

3 Asari made a solution of water and slaked lime, a white alkaline substance, and poured it over the soil where the cherries were growing.

4 To protect the trees from snow and frost, Asari buried them diagonally at a 20- to 30-degree angle with the tips showing on the ground and the roots at a depth of 40 centimetres.

5 Asari decided to send three species of wild cherries: forty Chishima-zakura, eight Miyama-zakura and several Ōyama-zakura. He chose six different Matsumae cherry varieties, all his creations, such as 'Beni-yutaka' and 'Hanagasa'. He also chose nineteen diverse varieties from all over Japan, such as 'Fugenzo' and 'Ichiyō', and others which had historical significance. These included 'Nara-no-yaezakura', reputed to be the oldest cultivated cherry in Japan, and 'Beni-shidare', an offspring of one of the oldest living weeping cherries. Asari sent dogwood trees because he had read that they were symbolic to Christians. Some said dogwood was the wood used to build the cross on which Jesus was crucified, although no such trees grew in Israel. Others said the dogwood's abundant blossoms were a reminder of the resurrection of Christ.

6 In 1988, in recognition of his cherry tree creations, research and initiatives, Asari was awarded the Hokkaido Philanthropy Award for 'having contributed widely to nature conservation', and the 'Good Deed' Award from the Japan Good Deed Association for his long-term research and preservation of sakura and 'for his devotion to promoting international friendship by donating many cherry trees he grew'. The head of the association was the president of the Japanese Red Cross. Asari also received a certificate from the General Association of Korean Residents for his research into Korean labourers, the construction of a cenotaph, and his long-term activities of sending gifts of cherry and plum trees.

26. The North Korean 'Spy'

1 The fifty-seven cherry trees consisted of fifty Chishima-zakura, four Ōyama-zakura, one Miyama-zakura, one 'Nara-no-yaezakura' and one 'Kanzan' tree.

2 Michael J. Green, *Japan's Reluctant Realism: Foreign Policy Challenges in an Era of Uncertain Power* (Palgrave, New York, 2001), pp. 117–18. See also: Hong Nack Kim, 'Japan's Relations With North Korea', in *Current History*, University of California Press, Vol. 90, No. 555, April 1991.

3 *Asahi Shimbun*, 7 April 1989.

4 North Korea released the Japanese seamen in October, paving the way for normalisation talks between Japan and North Korea that eventually failed. See also: 'Japan's Relations With North Korea', pp. 164–7.

5 The forty cherries consisted of twenty Ōyama-zakura, seventeen Chishima-zakura, one Miyama-zakura, one Shidare-zakura and one Beni-yutaka.

27. 'I Said Nothing'

1 George Zabelka spoke many times about his conversion from blessing the bombs to becoming a fervent anti-nuclear demonstrator: https://www.plough.com/en/topics/justice/nonviolence/blessing-the-bombs

2 Article by Father Charlie McCarthy, *The Catholic Worker*, Vol. LIX, No. 4, 1 June 1992.

3 In his 1985 speech, Zabelka also said that for the previous 1,700 years the Church had been making war respectable and inducing people to believe it was an honourable Christian profession. 'This is a lie,' he said. 'War is now, always has been, and always will be bad, bad news. I was there. I saw real war. Those who have seen real war will bear me out. I assure you, it is not Christ's way. There is no way to conduct real war in conformity with the teachings of Jesus.'

4 Oral history interview with William Downey, 19 January 1987, in: https://www.manhattanprojectvoices.org/oral-histories/william-downeys-interview-part-2

5 On 9 August 1945, the Federal Council of the Churches of Christ in America, a liberal Protestant organisation, sent a telegram to President Truman: 'Many Americans deeply disturbed over the use of atomic bombs against Japanese cities because of their necessarily indiscriminate destructive efforts and because their use sets extremely dangerous precedent for future of mankind.' Truman replied on 11 August: 'Nobody is more disturbed over the use of atomic bombs than I am, but I was greatly disturbed over the unwarranted attack by the Japanese on Pearl Harbor and their murder of our prisoners of war. When you have to deal with a beast, you have to treat him as a beast.' For more, see: https://ww2db.com/doc.php?q=230. Albert Einstein, in a statement in August 1945, said: 'The time has come now, when man must give up war. It is no longer rational to solve international problems by resorting to war. Now that an atomic bomb, such as the bombs exploded at Hiroshima and Nagasaki, can destroy a city, kill all the people in a city, a small city the size of Minneapolis, say, we can see that we must now make use of man's powers of reason in order to settle disputes between nations.'

6 *US Strategic Bombing Survey*, 1946; Truman Library, President's Secretary's file; Atomic bomb: www.trumanlibrary.org

7 Gar Alperovitz and Kai Bird, 'Was Hiroshima Needed to End the War?', *Christian Science Monitor*, 6 August 1992. For more, see Alex Wellerstein, 'The Decision to Use the Bomb: A Consensus View?', in Restricted Data, the Nuclear Secrecy Blog, 8 March 2013: http://blog.nuclearsecrecy.com/2013/03/08/the-decision-to-use-the-bomb-a-consensus-view/. In an article in the *New York Times* on 9 October 1994, titled 'The Curators Cave In', Kai Bird wrote: 'Many well-known scholars – including Barton J. Bernstein, Martin J. Sherwin, Robert Messer, James Hershberg, Gar Alperovitz, Melvyn

P. Leffler and Stanley Goldberg – have noted that there is compelling evidence that diplomatic overtures, coupled with assurances on the post-war status of the emperor and the impending entry of the Soviet Union into the war, probably would have led the Japanese to surrender long before an American invasion could be mounted. Unfortunately, this evidence didn't begin emerging until the 1960s, long after the public had been convinced that dropping the bomb had saved many American lives.' See also Gar Alperovitz and Martin J. Sherwin, 'US leaders knew we didn't have to drop atomic bombs on Japan to win the war. We did it anyway', *Los Angeles Times* op-ed, 5 August 2020. See also Takada, 'Atomic Evangelists: An Investigation of the American Atomic Narrative Through News and Magazine Articles, Official Government Statements, Critiques, Essays and Works of Non-Fiction'.

8 Cheshire, *The Light of Many Suns*, p. 68.

9 Cheshire interview with RAF Centre for Air and Space Power Studies (CASPS) TV, February 1978.

10 *The Light of Many Suns*, p. 68.

11 https://spartacus-educational.com/2WWcheshire.htm

12 Cheshire interview with RAF CASPS TV.

13 Leonard Cheshire, *The Nuclear Dilemma, a Moral Study* (Catholic Information Services, Abbots Langley, Herts, 1983), p. 5.

14 Ibid., p. 11.

15 Cheshire married Sue Ryder, also an avid philanthropist, in 1959 and the couple dedicated themselves to humanitarian work. A member of the Polish section of the Special Operations Executive during the war, Ryder helped coordinate resistance activities. She became Lady Ryder of Warsaw and set up more than thirty care homes and hospitals in Poland after the war. She also brought former concentration camp survivors to England for respite care. These days, the Sue Ryder Foundation is a neurological and bereavement support charity in the UK and has several hundred charity shops throughout Britain.

16 Memory lapses, embellishments, rear-end covering, omissions and inaccuracies, among other issues, pervaded the content, according to military historian Robert O. Harder. For more, see Harder, *The Three Musketeers of the Army Air Forces*, and John T. Correll, 'Near Failure at Nagasaki', *Air & Space Forces* magazine, 1 July 2011: https://www.airandspaceforces.com/article/0711nagasaki/

17 Paul Tibbets, *Return of the Enola Gay* (Mid Coast Marketing, Columbus, Ohio, 1998), pp. 245–51. See also Zellen, 'Hansai or the Cleansing Fire: How the Interplay of Fog, Friction and Faith Resulted in the Unintended Atomic Annihilation of Nagasaki's Christian Community'.

18 Mark Wolverton, ' "I am destiny": Reporting on the Atom Bomb', Historynet, 21 April 2017: https://www.historynet.com/destiny-reporting-atom-bomb. htm

19 Mark Wolverton, ' "Atomic Bill" and the Birth of the Bomb', *Undark* magazine, 9 August 2017: https://undark.org/2017/08/09/atomic-bill-laurence-manhattan-project/

20 Deepe Keever, *News Zero: The New York Times and the Bomb*.

21 William J. Broad, 'The Black Reporter Who Exposed a Lie About the Atom Bomb', *New York Times*, 9 August 2021.

28. The Storyteller

1 Ozaki, *Migawari no Ai*, pp. 92–95.

2 I am grateful to Annamaria Mix of the Niepokalanów Archives for her translation of numerous Polish-language articles and government documents about the friary during the communist era. These include articles by Jarosław Zawadzki on the history of the church 1948–54, and from *Echo Niepokalanów*, an internal bulletin published since the 1930s. They also include documents from the communist-era Ministry of the Interior, the Ministry of Public Administration, the Office for Religious Affairs, and the Office of Press, Publications and Performance Control. The Polish government maintains many documents referring to the friary, Father Kolbe and other friars in its central archives, the State Archives in Warsaw and in the Archive of the Institute of National Remembrance (IPN). The IPN, set up in 1998, investigates Nazi and communist crimes between 1917 and 1990.

3 MI's 'miraculous medals' – tiny devotional medals – were produced in Częstochowa until 1952, after which they were made in Niepokalanów. In 1959, the government banned the friary from producing medals that showed an image of the Virgin Mary, and the metal pressing machines were sealed. Somehow, the friars continued their production. In 1962 a friar was arrested for producing images without permission. During an inspection in 1964, the

investigators found eleven types of medal embossed in Niepokalanów, according to records in the archive.

4 A visit to Niepokalanów on 5 June 1947 by the Catholic Archbishop of Westminster, Cardinal Bernard Griffin, was a major propaganda coup for the communist government. The government's Polska Kronika Filmowa captured the event for its weekly cinema newsreel, showing eight black horses carrying uniformed cavalry preceding a limousine carrying Griffin and Warsaw Bishop Zygmunt Choromanski to the gates of the friary. The totalitarian regime had hoped that Griffin's visit would persuade the public that the government was taking a tolerant approach towards Catholicism and towards Niepokalanów's role as a major publishing house and internationally recognised institution.

5 After the printing presses were confiscated, *Rycerz Niepokalanej* was printed in Warsaw and other cities. To save money and ensure distribution, priests and MI members distributed the magazine by hand, rather than using the postal service. The December 1952 issue couldn't be published because the government's Office of Press, Publications and Performance Control declined to return the issue to its editors.

6 Live Passion Plays began in 1947 and continued during Lent throughout the 1950s, after which the friars performed what were called 'movable handmade figure' Passion Plays.

7 *Migawari no Ai*, pp. 248–53.

8 *Jūnana-sai no Natsu*, p. 179.

9 *Migawari no Ai* included events from Ozaki's first five pilgrimages to Poland, including visits to Zduńska Wola, Kolbe's birthplace; Pabianice, the town where Kolbe grew up; and the bunker at Auschwitz. It also featured three interviews with Gajowniczek.

10 Ozaki made ten pilgrimages to Poland – in 1971, 1982, 1983, 1990, 1993, 1995, 1997, 2002, 2003 and 2004. On his last five pilgrimages, he visited places where Kolbe had lived. They included Lviv, where Kolbe had attended the seminary, now part of Ukraine; Grodno, where Kolbe first started printing the Militia Immaculatae journal, now part of Belarus; and Nieszawa, a village where Kolbe had recuperated from tuberculosis.

11 Nicholas Kristof, 'Through Survivor's Tales, Nagasaki Joins Japan's Timeless Folklore', *New York Times*, 9 August 1995: https://www.nytimes.com/1995/08/09/world/through-survivors-tales-nagasaki-joins-japan-s-timeless-folklore.html

12 Mariko Oi, 'What Japanese History Lessons Leave Out', BBC News, 14 March 2013: https://www.bbc.co.uk/news/magazine-21226068

29. *End of an Era*

1 Ozaki started his blog in 2008 as 'Tōmei Ozaki's room'. From 2011, he called it 'Tōmei Ozaki's diaries'. In his final years, the title became 'Tōmei Ozaki's ninety-one-year-old diaries'. He changed its title every birthday.

2 Blog, 27 March 2017.

3 Ozaki was the second Japanese to be awarded this medal. The first was Dr Kōichi Kuyama, who translated many Polish books into Japanese and introduced Polish movies and theatre to Japan. He received the award in 2017.

4 Ozaki's essay, titled 'The difference between Auschwitz and the atomic bomb', appeared in a booklet called *Memories of Eighteen Days – the Nagasaki Atomic Bomb*, published on 9 August 1999.

30. *The Martyr and the Red Kimono*

1 For more, see: https://notesfrompoland.com/2022/01/03/devastating-decline-in-religious-practice-among-young-poles-says-catholic-primate/, published 3 January 2022.

2 The number of Catholics in Japan fell about four per cent between 2009 and 2021 to 431,100 people, according to Catholic Bishops' Conference of Japan statistics. The data showed that Catholic churches in Japan conducted just 1,824 infant baptisms, 1,699 adult baptisms and 1,007 marriages in 2021. Only fourteen pupils were attending minor seminaries in Japan, all in Nagasaki, and fifty students were attending major seminaries throughout the nation. For more, see: https://www.cbcj.catholic.jp/wp-content/uploads/2022/08/statistics2021.pdf

3 Sister Mediatrix helped Ozaki translate his stories on hidden Christians into Polish. Before Ozaki went to Poland in 1993, he visited Sister Mediatrix at the convent in Konagai and made a tape recording for her family in Poland, which he took to her home.

Epilogue

1 Father Kolbe's name has become ubiquitous in Catholic communities over the past seven decades. Schools, churches and parishes bearing his name can be found across the globe. Among many others, these include Mississauga and Aurora in Ontario, and Vancouver, British Columbia, in Canada; Delano, Minnesota; Houston, Texas; West Lake Village, California; Marmora, New Jersey; and Pocono Pines, Pennsylvania, in the US; Runcorn, Cheshire, and Leeds, Yorkshire, in England; Ottoway, South Australia, Rockingham, Western Australia, and Greenvale, Victoria, in Australia. In 2000, the US National Conference of Catholic Bishops established Marytown, a national shrine to Kolbe, in Libertyville, Illinois. A chapel of St Maximilian Kolbe has also been established at Lourdes in France. Father Kolbe Missions thrive in California; in Bari, Bologna, Conoscio, Santa Giusta, Rome and Verona in Italy; and in Argentina, Brazil, Bolivia, Luxembourg and Poland, among other countries.

Index

Page references in *italics* indicate images.

Kolbe, Julius, 17–24

Kolbe, Maria, 17, 18, 20, 22, 23–4, 27,
216, 351

Kolbe, Maximilian Maria, 3, 10, 11–14,
17–43, 23, 32, 57–71, 201–27, 206
antisemitism, views on, 106, 287–8
Auschwitz, internment in (1941), 2,
3, 12, 13, 197–9, 200, 212–27, 214,
289
beatification (1971), 281, 283–4, 321
biographies, 292, 330
canonisation (1982), 12, 286–8, 291,
321
death (1941), 3, 13, 197–9, 200, 222–7,
244, 259, 281, 292, 333
draconian principles, 80–83, 87, 89
education, 13, 23–4, 25–33
German invasion (1939–40), 201–10
India visit (1932), 86
Maria, naming as (1914), 30
Maximilianus, naming as (1910), 27
Militia Immaculatae, see Militia
Immaculatae
Nagasaki museum, 324–5, 327
Nagasaki period (1930–36), 12, 53,
57–71, 59, 63, 64, 78–94, 92, 292, 333
Niepokalanów friary, see
Niepokalanów
Nishida, relationship with, 69–70
Ozaki and, 197–9, 200, 262, 266,
281–4, 292, 323–5, 332, 333, 350
Pawiak Prison, internment in
(1941), 210, 211–12
Rome period (1912–), 12, 28–33
space travel, interest in, 13, 24,
29–30, 90–91
technology, views on, 327
'Truth, The' (1940), 208–9
tuberculosis, 13, 32, 35, 36, 57, 81, 217,
218
vows (1914), 30, 35

Kolbe cherries, 294–300, 306–9, 320,
336–45, 348–52
Konagai, Kyushu, 243, 261–6, 306, 324,
339, 340, 342
Konoe, Fumimaro, 131–2
Korea
DPRK (1945–), see North Korea
Japanese occupation (1905–45), see
Chōsen
ROK (1945–), 236, 255, 271, 278, 291
Korean Air Flight 858 bombing (1987),
303–4
Korean language, 46
Korean War (1950–53), 236, 255, 256
Kościelniak, Mieczysław, 221
Kosina, Poland, 347
Kosone, Hōjirō, 68
koto, 262
Kozaki, Tomas, 260
Koziura, Florian, 70
Kraków, Poland, 24–9, 35, 38, 39, 89, 92,
106, 110, 113
German occupation (1939–45),
203, 205
Król, Zygmunt, 58, 59, 59, 81
Krott, Heinrich, 217
Kumamoto, Kyushu, 129
Kurile Islands, 250
Kurosaki, Kyushu, 167–8
Kwangtung Army, 47, 98
Kwiecień, Roman, 289, 295, 297, 299,
308, 328, 337, 339, 342
Kyōiku Chokugo, 50
Kyoto, Honshu, 68–9, 252, 257
Kyushu, Japan, 9, 38, 59, 71, 242, 254

labourers, see forced labour
Łambinowice, Poland, 202
Lamsdorf, Poland, 202
Lane, Chris, 274
Lange, Oskar, 297